The Watchdog That Didn't Bark

COLUMBIA JOURNALISM REVIEW BOOKS

COLUMBIA JOURNALISM REVIEW BOOKS

Series Editors: Victor Navasky, Evan Cornog, Mike Hoyt, and the editors of the *Columbia Journalism Review*

For more than fifty years, the *Columbia Journalism Review* has been the gold standard for media criticism, holding the profession to the highest standards and exploring where journalism is headed, for good and for ill.

Columbia Journalism Review Books expands upon this mission, seeking to publish titles that allow for greater depth in exploring key issues confronting journalism, both past and present, and pointing to new ways of thinking about the field's impact and potential.

Drawing on the expertise of the editorial staff at the *Columbia Journalism Review* as well as the Columbia Journalism School, the series of books will seek out innovative voices as well as reclaim important works, traditions, and standards. In doing this, the series will also incorporate new ways of publishing made available by the Web and e-books.

Second Read: Writers Look Back at Classic Works of Reportage, edited by James Marcus and the Staff of the *Columbia Journalism Review*

The Story So Far: What We Know About the Business of Digital Journalism, Bill Grueskin, Ava Seave, and Lucas Graves

The Best Business Writing 2012, edited by Dean Starkman, Martha M. Hamilton, Ryan Chittum, and Felix Salmon

The Art of Making Magazines: On Being an Editor and Other Views from the Industry, edited by Victor S. Navasky and Evan Cornog

The Best Business Writing 2013, edited by Dean Starkman, Martha M. Hamilton, Ryan Chittum, and Felix Salmon

THE WATCHDOG
THAT DIDN'T BARK

The Financial Crisis and the Disappearance
of Investigative Reporting

DEAN STARKMAN

COLUMBIA UNIVERSITY PRESS  NEW YORK

Columbia University Press
Publishers Since 1893
New York   Chichester, West Sussex
cup.columbia.edu
Copyright © 2014 Dean Starkman

Library of Congress Cataloging-in-Publication Data
Starkman, Dean.
    The watchdog that didn't bark : the financial crisis and the disappearance of
investigative reporting / Dean Starkman.
        pages cm — (Columbia journalism review books)
    Includes bibliographical references and index.
    ISBN 978-0-231-15818-3 (cloth : alk. paper) —ISBN 978-0-231-53628-8 (e-book)
    1. Financial crises—United States—Press coverage. 2. Investigative reporting—
United States. I. Title

    HB3722.S792 2014
    070.4′493309730931—dc23   2013023077

Columbia University Press books are printed on permanent and durable
acid-free paper.
This book is printed on paper with recycled content.
Printed in the United States of America

c 10 9 8 7 6 5 4 3 2 1

Jacket design by David High
Jacket photographs by Getty Images

References to websites (URLs) were accurate at the time of writing. Neither
the author nor Columbia University Press is responsible for URLs that may
have expired or changed since the manuscript was prepared.

To the memory of Mark Pittman, the great financial reporter whose untimely death on Thanksgiving, 2009, was an incalculable loss to the public's understanding of the financial crisis.

And to the memory of my father, Stanley Starkman, and to Alex and Julian.

"Wrong hatbox! Wrong hatbox!"
—CLARENCE W. BARRON, a founder of modern financial journalism

CONTENTS

ACKNOWLEDGMENTS

This book is a project of the *Columbia Journalism Review* and would not have been possible without its support. Founded in 1961, *CJR* considers itself a friend and watchdog over the press, and it is in that spirit this book is written. So thanks are owed to its chairman and guiding spirit, Victor Navasky, and to Nicholas Lemann, the outgoing dean of the Columbia Journalism School. I'd also like to express special thanks to Mike Hoyt for encouraging this project and for his friendship, wise counsel, and invaluable editorial support. Ryan Chittum, deputy chief of "The Audit," *CJR*'s business section, which I run, has been a stalwart in upholding its values while emerging as one of the bright stars among media bloggers.

Warm thanks also go to funders of *CJR*, starting with supporters of "The Audit." Our major funder, Kingsford Capital Management, has supported "The Audit" throughout. I'm particularly grateful to Mike Wilkins and his family for their warm hospitality, as well as to his longtime Kingsford partner, Dave Scially. I also thank Peter Lowy for his friendship and support, along with my friend Gary Lutin. I also thank Esther Kaplan and the Nation Institute for their support of my work over the years. I thank *CJR*'s vice chairmen, David Kellogg and Peter Osnos, and its board: Stephen Adler, Neil Barsky, Emily Bell, Nathan S. Collier, Cathleen Collins, Sheila Coronel, Howard W. French, Wade Greene, Joan Konner, Eric Lax, Kenneth Lerer, Steven Lipin, Michael Oreskes, Josh Reibel, Randall Rothenberg, Michael Schudson, Richard Snyder, and Laurel Touby.

Thanks also Brent Cunningham, Liz Barrett, Brendan Fitzgerald, Greg Marx, Michael Murphy, Justin Peters, Curtis Brainard, Cyndi Stivers, Stephanie Sandberg, Dean Pajevic, Tom O'Neill, Cathy Harding, Marietta Bell, Lt. Jose Robledo, Elinore Longordi, Christopher U. Massie, Sang Ngo, Kira Goldenberg, and Dennis Giza.

I also wish to extend warm thanks to Philip Leventhal, my editor at Columbia University Press, for asking to me to do the book in the first place and for his skillful edits and wise counsel in guiding it to completion. Same goes for Michael Haskell for his superb edits, suggestions, and fixes. I also thank James Jordan, the press's outgoing president and director, for his support and wish him well on his next adventure. Warm thanks also to Tom Wallace, my agent, as well as Deirdre Mullane, *CJR*'s agent on its Best Business Writing series.

By a stroke of luck, *CJR* happened to share an office suite at Pulitzer Hall with Professor Richard R. John, who went far beyond normal standards of collegiality and enormously improved *The Watchdog* with his insights and authoritative knowledge of the field. I owe great thanks to the library staff of Columbia University for their tireless help in researching this book, most especially Kathleen Dreyer, head librarian at Thomas J. Watson business library, for cheerfully responding to my endless requests for information and references. Thanks also to Jane Folpe for brilliant edits and big-picture suggestions that did much to help shape this argument; Alyssa Katz for taking time to read and offer wise suggestions on a key chapter; and Michael Massing for a stimulating conversation on the work of the great Ida Tarbell. Warm thanks also to Anya Schiffrin for her friendship, encouragement, and steadfast support.

I thank Mike Hudson, a reporter and an important figure in this book, for getting in touch with me five years ago to show me his Citigroup story, and for his time and cooperation and his friendship.

The Watchdog That Didn't Bark is the culmination of a nearly twenty-five-year reporting career, which was influenced by a remarkable set of mentors, colleagues, and friends. I learned what a writer looks and sounds like from the late Hugh MacLennan, the great Canadian novelist, and an English professor and a mentor at McGill. Penn Kimball, my master's project advisor at the Columbia School of Journalism, taught me invaluable lessons about long-form news writing as well as his main mantra, "Journalism is a *group activity!*" which he repeated often in a slow cadence in case we didn't understand the first time. I learned about the importance of institutional journalism from the inside-out and was lucky to work at small, medium, and large newspapers, all, as it happens, family controlled. I'm grateful to H. Brandt Ayers and his family for their enlightened stewardship of the *Anniston Star*, where I first went to work as a reporter covering rural Alabama and later cops and courts. At Brandy's *Star*, I learned how deep a relationship can form—even if it was sometimes ambivalent—between a community and its newspaper. I learned the critical role accountability reporting plays in a troubled community during my ten years at the *Providence Journal*, where I began covering night cops and ended as chief of its investigative team. Majority owned by the Metcalf family, and under the leadership of the brilliant Michael P. Metcalf, chairman and chief executive of its parent company, the *Projo* was, with the Rhode Island State Police under Colonel Walter E. Stone, one of a few islands of integrity in a state then beset by the twin plagues of organized crime and political corruption. Michael Metcalf's untimely death in 1988, two years after I arrived, was a severe blow to the organization and to American journalism in general. I'd also like to thank two important editors, James V. Wyman and Thomas P. Heslin, whose sound judgment and unflinching courage made possible groundbreaking news investigations that helped to spur innumerable reforms in that troubled state and led us to a Pulitzer Prize. I offer thanks to the paper's then outside counsel, Joseph V. Cavanagh Jr., the very model of a newspaper lawyer who, while fiercely protective of the institution, always asked how to get stories into the paper, not how to keep them out. My time in Providence was profoundly shaped by my friend, the late Ralph Greco, who flew bombing missions over Europe in World War II and returned home to build a successful jewelry-manufacturing supply business. A member of the board of the powerful Rhode Island Public Buildings Authority, he was a key whistleblower in what turned out to be a sweeping *Providence Journal* investigation into corruption in the state's public contracting system. Ralph provided information at great personal and economic cost only because he knew what he was seeing was wrong and he wanted it exposed. For him, it was as simple as that.

Similarly, I will always be grateful for my eight years at the *Wall Street Journal*, from 1996 to 2004. During my time there, I saw and experienced firsthand not just the inner workings of great American businesses and financial institutions but the inner life of a great American news organization. I interviewed CEOs, covered and did intellectual battle with some of the brightest minds in business, law, and finance, and had a chance to cover—for a readership of millions—momentous events, including the troubled reconstruction of the World Trade Center, destroyed in the attacks of September 11, 2001, as well as high-stakes mergers and acquisitions, including some hard-fought takeover battles. I am probably most proud of my financial investigations into the predations of unscrupulous real estate operators against their shareholders, as well as my work on abuses of private-property rights through the process of government expropriation known as eminent domain. My time at the *Journal* was not, however, an unalloyed pleasure. I left at the end of 2004 as the result of many disagreements with supervisors over stories. In the end, though, the experience provided me with a unique and privileged perspective on American institutional journalism at its highest level. I made deep and lasting friendships and thank the dear friends who remain. Given my current job as a critic, it's probably best they go unnamed.

I thank my editor at the *Washington Post*, Martha Hamilton, a close friend and journalist of unerring judgment and tremendous integrity and who single-handedly restored my faith in editors. I'm grateful to the Open Society Foundation (then Open Society Institute) for naming me a Katrina Media Fellow, which allowed me to set up the experimental Insurance Transparency Project, one of the happiest journalism experiences of my life, and to see the workings of the insurance industry in the Gulf of Mexico from the bottom up. It was, I must say, not a pretty sight. The insurance industry remains, for me, one of the great uncovered stories in American business.

John Sullivan is the best reporter I've ever had the pleasure to work with. He was and is a constant source of good ideas, support, and dry, flinty humor that is only mean-spirited if you think about it. I look forward to our next project. Thanks also to great friends Kathryn Kranhold, Lisa Baines, and Katy Dickey.

I thank my mother, Regina Starkman, and my late father, Stanley Starkman, who, on the weekend I was turning in this manuscript, was struck down by a brain hemorrhage and died five days later at the age of eighty-seven. He was keenly interested in this book's progress right up to the very end of his life. I think of him every day. My gratitude to my sister, Ellen Starkman, and brother, Paul Starkman, for their love and support.

Most of all, I thank my wife, Alexandra Kowalski, my true love and inspiration, without whom this book never happens, and our Julian.

The Watchdog That Didn't Bark

Introduction

Access and Accountability

I have made no criticism in this book which is not the shoptalk of reporters and editors. But only rarely do newspapermen take the public into their confidence. They will have to sooner or later. It is not enough for them to struggle against great odds, as many of them are doing, wearing out their souls to do a particular assignment well. The philosophy of the work itself needs to be discussed; the news about the news needs to be told.

—WALTER LIPPMANN, *Liberty and the News,* 1920

The U.S. business press failed to investigate and hold accountable Wall Street banks and major mortgage lenders in the years leading up to the financial crisis of 2008. That's why the crisis came as such a shock to the public and to the press itself.

And that's the news about the news.

The watchdog didn't bark. What happened? How could an entire journalism subculture, understood to be sophisticated and plugged in, miss the central story occurring on its beat? And why was it that some journalists, mostly outside the mainstream, were able to produce work that in fact did reflect the radical changes overtaking the financial system while the vast majority in the mainstream did not?

This book is about journalism watchdogs and what happens when they don't bark. What happens is the public is left in the dark about and powerless against complex problems that overtake important national institutions. In this case, the complex problem was the corruption of the U.S. financial system. The book is intended for the lay reader—not journalists, not finance aficionados—but those whom the historian Richard Hofstadter called the "literate citizen[s]." That would be anyone who wonders why an entirely manmade event like the financial crisis could take the whole world by surprise.

Few need reminders, even today, of the costs of the crisis: 10 million Americans uprooted by foreclosure with even more still threatened, 23 million unemployed or underemployed, whole communities set back a generation, shocking bailouts *for the perpetrators*, political polarization here, and instability abroad. And so on and so forth.

Was the brewing crisis really such a secret? Was it all so complex as to be beyond the capacity of conventional journalism and, through it, the public to understand? Was it all so hidden? In fact, the answer to all those questions is "no." The problem—distorted incentives corrupting the financial industry—was plain, but not to Wall Street executives, traders, rating agencies, analysts, quants, or other financial insiders. It was plain to the outsiders: state regulators, plaintiffs' lawyers, community groups, defrauded mortgage borrowers, and, mostly, to former employees of financial institutions, the whistleblowers, who were, in fact, blowing the whistle. A few reporters actually talked to them, understood the metastasizing problem, and wrote about it. You'll meet a couple of them in this book. Unfortunately, they didn't work for the mainstream business press.

In the aftermath of the Lehman bankruptcy of September 2008, a great fight broke out over the causes of the crisis—a fight that's more or less resolved at this point. While of course it's complicated, Wall Street and the mortgage lenders stand front and center in the dock. Meanwhile, a smaller fight broke out over the business press's role. After all, its central beat—the one over which it claims particular mastery—is the same one that suddenly melted down, to the shock of one and all. For business reporters, the crisis was more than a surprise. There was even something uncanny about it. A generation of professionals had, in effect, grown up with this set of Wall Street firms and had put them on the covers of *Fortune* and *Forbes*, the front page of the *Wall Street Journal* and the *New York Times*, and the rest, scores of times. The firms were so familiar, the press had even given them anthropomorphized personalities over the years: Morgan Stanley, the "white-shoe" WASP firm; Merrill Lynch, the scrappy

Irish Catholic firm, often considered the dumb one; Goldman, the elite Jewish firm; Lehman, the scrappy Jewish firm; Bear Stearns, the naughty one, and so on. Love them or hate them, there they were, blessed by accounting firms, rating agencies, and regulators, gleaming towers of power. Until one day, they weren't.

Critics contended, understandably, that the business press must have been asleep at the wheel. In a March 2009 interview that would go viral, the comedian Jon Stewart confronted the CNBC personality Jim Cramer with the problem.[1] Stewart said, in effect, that business journalism presents itself as providing wall-to-wall, 24/7 coverage of Wall Street but had somehow managed to miss the most important thing ever to happen on that beat—the Big One. "It is a game that you know is going on, but you go on television as a financial network and pretend it isn't happening," is how Stewart framed it. And many understood exactly what he meant.

Top business-news professionals—also understandably, perhaps—have defended their industry's pre-crisis performance. In speeches and interviews, these professionals assert that the press in fact did provide clear warnings and presented examples of pre-crisis stories that told about brewing problems in the lending system before the crash. Some have gone further and asserted that it was the public itself that had failed—failed to respond to the timely information the press had been providing all along. "Anybody who's been paying attention has seen business journalists waving the red flag for several years," wrote Chris Roush, in an article entitled "Unheeded Warnings," which articulated the professionals' view at length.[2] Diana Henriques, a respected *New York Times* business and investigative reporter, defended her profession in a speech in November 2008: "The government, the financial industry and the American consumer—if they had only paid attention—would have gotten ample warning about this crisis from us, years in advance, when there was still time to evacuate and seek shelter from this storm." There were many such pronouncements. Then the press moved on.

It is only fair to point out that, beyond speeches and assertions, the business press did not publish a major story on its own peculiar role in the financial system before the crisis. It *has*, meanwhile, investigated and taken to task, after the fact, virtually every other possible agent in the crisis: Wall Street banks, mortgage lenders, the Federal Reserve, the Securities and Exchange Commission, Fannie Mae, Freddie Mac, the Office of Thrift Supervision, the Office of the Comptroller of the Currency, compensation consultants, and so on. On it own role, the press has been notably silent. This kind of forensic work is entirely appropriate. But what about the watchdog?

In the spring of 2009, the *Columbia Journalism* Review, where I work as an editor, undertook a project with a simple goal: to assess whether the business press, as it contended, did indeed provide the public with fair warning of looming dangers when it could have made a difference. The idea was to perform a fair reading of the record of institutional business reporting before the crash. I created a commonsense list of nine major business news outlets (the *Wall Street Journal*, *Fortune*, *Forbes*, *Businessweek*, the *Financial Times*, Bloomberg, the *New York Times*, the *Los Angeles Times*, and the *Washington Post*) and, with the help of two researchers, used news databases to search for stories that could plausibly be considered warnings about the heart of the problem: abusive mortgage lenders and their funders on Wall Street. We then asked the news outlets to volunteer their best work during this period, and, to their credit, nearly all of them cooperated. (A description of the methodology can be found in chapter 7.)

The result was "Power Problem," published in *CJR* in the spring of 2009. Its conclusion was simple: the business press had done everything but take on the institutions that brought down the financial system. As I'll discuss in later chapters, the record shows that the press published its hardest-hitting investigations of lenders and Wall Street between 2000 and 2003, even if there were only a few of them. Then, for reasons I will attempt to explain, it lapsed into useful but not sufficient consumer- and investor-oriented stories during the critical years of 2004 through 2006. Missing are investigative stories that directly confront powerful institutions about basic business practices while those institutions were still powerful. The watchdog didn't bark.

To read various journalistic accounts of mortgage lending and Wall Street during the bubble is to come away with radically differing representations of the soundness of the U.S. financial system. It all depended on what you were reading. Anyone "paying attention" to the conventional business press could be forgiven for thinking that things were, in the end, basically normal. Yes, there was a housing bubble. Any fair reading of the press of the era makes that clear, even if warnings were mitigated by just-as-loud celebrations of the boom. And yes, the press said there were a lot of terrible mortgage products out there. Those are important consumer and investor issues. But that's all they are. When the gaze turned to financial institutions, the message was entirely different: "all clear." It's not just the puff pieces ("Washington Mutual Is Using a Creative Retail Approach to Turn the Banking World Upside Down"; "Citi's chief hasn't just stepped out of Sandy Weill's shadow—he's stepped out of his own as he strives to make himself into a leader with vision"; and so on) or the language that sometimes lapses into toadying ("Some of its old-world gentility remains: Goldman agreed to talk for this story only reluctantly, wary of looking like a braggart"; "His 6-foot-4 linebacker-esque frame is economically packed into a club chair in his palatial yet understated office");[3] it's that even stories that were ostensibly critical of individual Wall Street firms and mortgage lenders described them in terms of their competition with one another: would their earnings be okay? There was a bubble all right, and the business press was in it.

Trouble was, the system it was covering was going to hell in a hand basket. Institutionalized corruption, fueled by perverse compensation incentives, had taken wing. The subpriming of American finance—the spread of a once-marginal, notorious industry to the heart of the financial system—was well underway. If this had been a big secret, that would be one thing, but if that were true, how was it that *Forbes*, of all magazines, could write a scathing exposé of Household Finance, then a subprime giant, under the headline "Home Wrecker" in 2002, but not follow it up with a similar piece until it was too late?[4] How could the *Wall Street Journal* publish stories like the brilliant "Best Interests: How Big Lenders Sell a Pricier Refinancing to Poor Homeowners . . ." around the same time, on its prestigious Page One, then nothing of the sort later, when the situation got much, much worse.[5] Meanwhile, still in 2003, a reporter named Michael Hudson was writing this:

A seven-month investigation by *Southern Exposure* has uncovered a pattern of predatory practices within Citi's subprime units. *Southern Exposure* interviewed more than 150 people—borrowers, attorneys, activists, current and ex-employees—and reviewed thousands of pages of loan contracts, lawsuits, testimony and company reports. The people and the documents provide strong evidence that Citi's subprime operations are reaping billions in ill-gotten gains by targeting the consumers who can least afford it.[6]

Who is Michael Hudson? And what on earth is *Southern Exposure*? For that matter, why was an urban affairs reporter for an alternative weekly in Pittsburgh, with no financial reporting experience, able to write this (emphasis added):

By its very nature, the mortgage-backed securities market encourages lenders to make as many loans at as high an interest rate as possible. That may seem a prescription for frenzied and irresponsible lending. But federal regulation, strict guidelines by Fannie Mae and Freddie Mac, intense and straightforward competition between banks, and the relative sophistication of bank borrowers have kept things from getting out hand, according to the HUD/Treasury reporter. *Those brakes don't apply as well in the subprime lending market*, where regulation is looser, marketing more freewheeling and customers less savvy.

The date? 2004.[7]

One type of journalism told one kind of story; another presented an entirely different reality. What accounts for these dramatically opposed representations? And why was the conventional business press perfectly capable of performing *both* kinds of journalism when the problems were small but incapable of providing the valuable, powerful kind later, when it counted?

Walter Lippmann, the great twentieth-century journalist and thinker, is as right today as he was in 1920. It's not enough for reporters and editors to struggle against great odds as many of them have been doing. It's time to take the public into our confidence. The news about the news needs to be told. It needs to be told because, in the run-up to the global financial crisis, the professional press let the public down.

It needs to be told, and told now, because the mortgage crisis and its aftermath have coincided with a crisis in the news business. Google and a new vanguard of Internet companies have wreaked havoc on traditional news-media business models, siphoning away a huge chunk of the advertising revenue that had long sustained American journalism. Once-great newsrooms have been devastated, and thousands of former print reporters are out on the street or in PR. Their former colleagues now operate in a harrowing and harried new environment of financial distress and sped-up productivity requirements. Meanwhile, a new digital journalism ecosystem has bloomed with new publications, models, forms, practices, idioms, tools, and institutions—and new people. A whole generation of journalists, many from technological backgrounds, has entered the field, it seems, even since the *Los Angeles Times*'s parent company went bankrupt in 2008. There is conversation and community. There is also chaos and confusion.

Another fierce argument is underway about the future of news— about who will do it, what it will look like, and, indeed, who—or what—is this "public" that journalism is supposed to be speaking to. As in all times of crisis, the consultants, marketers, and opportunists of various stripes—never far from journalism—step forward to proclaim that they know what the future holds. But in fact, no one really knows. The only thing we *can* be sure of in journalism is that everything is in question, everything on the table: business models, forms, roles, practices, values. Will news organizations survive? Can amateur networks help? Is storytelling out of date? Is statistical analysis—known as Big Data—the next breakthrough? That the new digital era has not lived up to its promise is no reason to dismiss it.

So we stand at a moment when established journalism can be fairly said to have failed in a basic function, and, as usual, the future is uncertain. And the present, well, it's a bit of a mess. Is there no hope?

Actually, there is. One form of journalism has proven itself a reliable and effective advocate for the public interest, a true watchdog, and proven itself at least since the great Ida Tarbell in the early twentieth century. This kind of journalism is not a medium, like print or TV. It's not an institution, like the *New York Times* or the *Huffington Post*. It's neither alternative nor mainstream. It's not necessarily professional or amateur. It's neither inherently analogue nor digital. It's a practice.

The practice—the one watchdog the public can count on—has never really had a good name. Sometimes it's called "accountability reporting." Sometimes it's called "investigative reporting." Sometimes it's called "public-service reporting" or "public-interest reporting." Sometimes it's called something else. We'll go with "accountability reporting." Accountability reporting is a journalism term of art—the shoptalk of reporters and editors, as Lippmann would put it. But it's one the public would do well to better understand.

Accountability reporting sounds like something everyone would be for, but that's actually not the case. It only arrived as a mainstream, professionalized practice in the 1960s and has had to fight for its existence within news organizations ever since. Confrontational and accusatory, it provokes the enmity of the rich and powerful as a matter of course. When Theodore Roosevelt dubbed it "muckraking" in 1906, he didn't mean it as a compliment.[8] Risky, stressful, expensive, and difficult, it perennially faces resistance within news organizations and tries the patience of bureaucrats, bean counters, and hacks. News corporatists, such as the late *USA Today* founder Al Neuharth and the mogul Rupert Murdoch, deride public-service reporting—or anything that resembles it—as a form of elitism, an affectation of prize-mongering and self-important reporters, journalists writing for "other journalists," as one Murdoch biographer puts it.[9] Withholding resources for public-interest reporting, as we'll see, is invariably couched as opposition to "long" and "pretentious" stories foisted on the public by "elitist" reporters. But opposing long and ambitious stories is like fully supporting apple pie but opposing flour, butter, sugar, and pie tins. In the end, there is no pie.

In our digital age, impatience with accountability reporting is, if anything, more pronounced. As we'll see, the economics and technological architecture of online news militate against accountability reporting. As a result, digital-news advocates, too, tend to ignore it or dismiss it altogether. "The whole notion of 'long-form' journalism is writer-centered, not public-centered," as Jeff Jarvis, a leading digital-news thinker, tweeted.[10] Yet accountability reporting is a core function of American journalism. It is what makes it distinctive, what makes it powerful when it *is* powerful, independent when it *is* independent. It is the great agenda setter, public-trust builder, and value creator. It explains complex problems to a mass audience and holds the powerful to account. It is the point.

Now, I would suggest, is a good time to consider what journalism the public needs. What actually works? Who are journalism's true forefathers and foremothers? Is there a line of authority in journalism's collective past that can help us to navigate its future? What creates value, both in the material sense and in the sense of what is good and valuable in American journalism?

Accountability reporting comes in many forms—a series of revelations in a newspaper or online, a book, a TV magazine segment—but its most common manifestation has been the long-form newspaper or magazine story, the focus of this book. Call it the Great Story. The form was pioneered by the muckrakers' quasi-literary work in the early twentieth century, with Tarbell's exposé on the Standard Oil monopoly in *McClure's* magazine a brilliant early example. As we'll see, the Great Story has demonstrated its subversive power countless times and has exposed and clarified complex problems for mass audiences across a nearly limitless range of subjects: graft in American cities, modern slave labor in the United States, the human costs of leveraged buyouts, police brutality and corruption, the secret recipients of Wall Street of government bailouts, the crimes and cover-ups of media and political elites, and on and on, year in and year out.[11] The greatest of muckraking editors, Samuel S. McClure, would say to his staff, over and over, almost as a mantra, "The story is the thing!" And he was right.

Accountability reporting can be juxtaposed against "access reporting," another journalistic term. Access reporting, the practice of obtaining inside information from powerful people and institutions, is the long-standing rival of accountability reporting. They are American journalism's two main tendencies, and the tension between the two can be said to define the field. These are competing sets of journalism practices, values, and worldviews that dramatically affect the content of the news the public reads. The access and accountability schools represent radically different understandings of what journalism *is* and whom it should serve. The two practices produce entirely different representations of reality, and this difference proved critical in the run-up to the crash.

Access reporting emphasizes gaining inside information about the actions or intentions of powerful actors before they are widely known. Its stock-in-trade is the scoop, or exclusive. In business news, the prototypical access story is the mergers-and-acquisitions scoop. Accountability reporting, in contrast, seeks to gather information not from but *about* powerful actors. The typical accountability story is the long-form exposé.

I usually keep in mind proxies for the two schools: Gretchen Morgenson, the great investigative reporter and editor for the *New York Times*, and Andrew Ross Sorkin, who runs a thriving unit of the same paper that focuses on inside scoops about business mergers and acquisitions, Dealbook. Morgenson was the first to reveal—in the face of furious opposition from Goldman Sachs, among others—the beneficiaries of the bailout of the American International Group, namely, well, Goldman Sachs and other Wall Street banks. Sorkin's monumental crisis book, *Too Big to Fail*, lionized Wall Street figures for their (failed) efforts to avert a catastrophe their own institutions had caused. That the two leading representatives of the two journalism poles work for the same newspaper only emphasizes the degree to which journalism must balance both tendencies.

One way to think about the difference is that access reporting tells readers what powerful actors *say* while accountability reporting tells readers what they *do*. The differences are so stark that they can be plotted on a graph, and I do so in chapter 5. Access reporting tends to talk to elites; accountability, to dissidents. Access writes about specialized topics for a niche audience. Accountability writes about general topics for a mass audience. Access tends to transmit orthodox views; accountability tends to transmit heterodox views. Access reporting is functional; accountability reporting is moralistic. In business news, access reporting focuses on investor interests; accountability, on the public interest.

Access and accountability, then, are journalism's Jacob and Esau, Gog and Magog, forever in conflict over resources, status, and influence. But it's hardly a fair fight. Access reporting is journalism's dominant strain, its bread and butter. Its stories are, if not easier, certainly quicker to produce and rarely confrontational, making them more compatible with news-productivity needs. Accountability reporting, meanwhile, is forever marginal, a cost center, burdened with stories that are time consuming, stressful, and enemy making. Access reporting is halfway around the world while accountability reporting is still putting on its shoes. But of the two strains, only one speaks to, and for, the broader public.

I come to this debate from a thirty-year career as a journalism practitioner, ten of those as an investigative reporter, ten as a business reporter. I've done both access and accountability reporting and understand the necessity of both. The problem for journalism and the public, however, is that accountability reporting is at once the most vital and, at the same time, the most vulnerable. The difference between the two is the difference between *probing* Citigroup in 2003 and *profiling* it in 2006. Put simply, accountability reporting—the watchdog—got the story that access reporting missed.

This book will trace the development of the watchdog from its roots in muckraking and its struggle to win a place in the mainstream media. In a sense, I hope to write the story of the Great Story. The reasons for this historical approach are threefold: to demonstrate that accountability reporting is indeed a potent weapon on the public's behalf; to show why its absence was so harmful during the mortgage era; and to secure its future in whatever journalism emerges from the digital disruption—because without accountability reporting, journalism has no purpose, no center, no point.

The first goal is especially important in order to rebut what I regard as facile criticisms, from both the political right and left and the digital-news advocates, that tend to dismiss *all* "mainstream media" as either hopelessly biased (as the right contends), uselessly timid (as the left has it), or just generally lame (as new-media enthusiasts believe). All three critiques may have some merit. Much of the old MSM indeed should be left by the wayside. But the practice of accountability reporting is not one of them.

The access-accountability tension has been a key fault line running through professional American journalism since least the time of Ida Tarbell, the great muckraker who is the subject of chapter 1, and Charles Dow, Edward Jones, and Clarence Barron, founders of Dow Jones & Co., publisher of the *Wall Street Journal*, discussed in chapter 2. Indeed, in business journalism, access and accountability reporting began as separate functions performed by separate institutions representing entirely different journalism subcultures. Both styles of journalism purported to cover business and the economy, yet their work contained radically different representations of reality. One strain of business journalism provided information to emerging markets. But muckraking changed the world. It also laid the foundations for journalism's accountability school and its practitioners were, as we'll see, heroes of their day. Despite the many changes in the business-news industry, exactly *what* the muckrakers did and *how* they did it are relevant for us today.

Business news, as we'll see, has roots in an entirely different tradition, an intramarket messaging function. It was born of access reporting, which remains a core function. Early business journalism was actually part of the emerging financial system that it covered. Valuable in its own way, it also left a problematic legacy.

The history of U.S. business news over the twentieth century is the story of expansion, a broadening of its audience and its own ideas about itself. The flowering of business journalism was led by the great *Wall Street Journal* editor and news executive Bernard Kilgore, who brought storytelling, narrative, in-depth reporting, and investigations to financial news and, in doing so, revolutionized both it and American newspapers in general. Building on Henry R. Luce's ambitious business magazine, *Fortune* (founded 1930), Kilgore bestowed on business journalism its most powerful weapon: the Great Story. As a consequence, he was a key figure in the democratization of financial and economic knowledge for the American middle-class. That's chapter 3.

In chapter 4, we'll see how the accountability values of the muckrakers were incorporated into mainstream media, beginning in the 1960s, in the form of the investigative-reporting movement at metropolitan newspapers, and how those values extended to business coverage. Despite the fact that accountability reporting did not always come easily to business news culture, we'll see that the mainstream business press has in the past grappled with, investigated, and held to account corporate and financial miscreants of all stripes, and done so with vigor. In these chapters, we'll meet, among others, the reporter Michael Hudson of the *Roanoke Times* and later of the *Wall Street Journal*, whose work during the 1990s and 2000s exposed the financial system's radicalization for anyone who wanted to know.

But journalism norms change over time. I'll argue that in the 1990s, with the stampede of the middle class into the stock market, business news shifted to accommodate them. The balance of business news tipped away from public-interest reporting and toward insider, investor-oriented concerns, a process coinciding with and influenced by the rise of CNBC (chapter 5). This emphasis on speedy, access-oriented, investor-focused journalism only increased after 2000, when news organizations' own finances were rocked, first by the "Tech Wreck" and the ad recession that followed and later by the toll taken by the rise of the Internet. As we'll see, the Internet, besides wrecking news-industry finances, also presents severe structural barriers to accountability reporting.

As the twenty-first century dawned, business news pulled back from its own sense of mission, moving toward insiderism, granularity, and scoopism. Meanwhile, business and especially Wall Street grew in size and power. Most consequentially, beginning in the early 1990s, Wall Street and the financial sector generally moved into and vastly expanded the rough-and-tumble business of subprime lending and, in doing so, adopted its ethics and norms. Put another way, the down-and-dirty, street-corner values of the subprime/consumer-finance business, unchecked by Bush/Greenspan-era regulation, spread to mainstream banking while parts of the press fought to keep it check (chapter 6).

One of the most notable and frustrating aspects of the precrash journalism story is that mainstream organizations, feeding off regulatory and public activism about predatory lending, did their most impressive, hard-hitting work, as noted, from 2000 through 2003, *before* the mortgage frenzy did its worst damage. What's more, the reporting was effective in helping to police some of the worst actors in the subprime sector. When Big Journalism took on Big Finance, journalism won (chapter 7).

Generally, though, business news, caught in old paradigms, was incapable of grasping this financial radicalization. Some journalists, including Gillian Tett of the *Financial Times*, reported on the derivatives industry and wrote of looming troubles there and potential risks to institutions and the financial system. Hudson and others, meanwhile, saw the increasingly rogue behavior of the mortgage industry from the street level, but their reporting was published mostly in smaller, alternative publications and was not able to break through and inform the journalists who were trying to puzzle through the new world of financial derivatives. Mainstream business publications, focused on corporate executive boardrooms, had no way of knowing of the unseemly process—the perverse incentives, misrepresentations, forgery and fraud, and mortgage "boiler rooms"—that had produced the loans that made up the raw material of subprime derivatives. As a result, reporting on derivatives could only warn of risk and leverage, which *might* fail, not of institutionalized corruption and systemic fraud, which could *only* fail (chapter 8).

At best, business media produced work that only hinted at the radicalization of the financial sector. And when I say that institutional business media "failed to investigate big lenders and their Wall Street backers," this is not an assertion or a guess. The mainstream business press did produce work that was exemplary, risky, and valuable. But it did not directly confront major financial institutions about basic business practices, a failure that was especially glaring during the critical years of 2004 through 2006. And to repeat, this is not a detail. Muckraking reporting about wrongdoing by brand-name institutions—while they were doing wrong—was the missing "facts" that were not "quickly and steadily available," as Walter Lippmann puts it, during the critical years before the blowup.[12] Meanwhile, investor-oriented, insider-focused journalism—the corporate profiles and features on Wall Street houses and big banks—not only missed the story but was part of the problem, and not a small one (chapter 9).

Now what?

As the argument about the future of news rages on, technologically centered ideas have gained the upper hand, coalescing into something I call the "Future of News" (FON) consensus, which has roots in network theory. Some of the ideas are promising and have already been helpful. On the other hand, it has been unnerving to witness how the Internet's strengths—limitless space, a 24/7 publishing schedule, precise quantity and popularity metrics—have meshed with old-fashioned corporate imperatives of sped-up reporter productivity and indifferent journalism quality. High-flown rhetoric of futuristic digitism is deployed, as we'll see, to justify reckless and unnecessary cost cuts in regional newsrooms and to marginalize reporting in the public interest. Digitally driven journalism, both in current theory and practice, actually shares more traits with access reporting than with accountability reporting. Unless rethought, it represents a darkening cloud over the future of news.

But that's chapter 10. Now, it's time to begin at the beginning.

CHAPTER 1

Ida Tarbell, Muckraking, and the Rise of Accountability Reporting

The story is the thing—S. S. MCCLURE

I da M. Tarbell, a writer for *McClure's*, a general-interest monthly, was chatting with her good friend and editor, John S. Phillips, in the magazine's offices near New York's Madison Square Park, trying to decide what she should take on next. Tarbell, then forty-three years old, was already one of the most prominent journalists in America, having written popular multipart historical sketches of Napoleon, Lincoln, and a French revolutionary figure known as Madame Roland, a moderate republican guillotined during the Terror.[1] Thanks in part to her work, the circulation of *McClure's* had jumped to about 400,000, making it one of the most popular, and profitable, publications in the country.[2]

Phillips, a founder of the magazine, was its backbone. Presiding over an office of bohemians and intellectuals, this father of five was as calm and deliberative as the magazine's namesake, Samuel S. McClure, was manic and extravagant. Considered by many to be a genius, McClure was also an impossible boss—forever steaming in from Europe and throwing the office into turmoil with new business plans, story ideas, and editorial changes. Phillips was the counterweight. "Sam had three hundred ideas a minute, but [Phillips] was the only man around the shop who knew which one was not crazy," William Allen White, another famous staffer, observed.[3] Whatever his flaws, McClure had an innate sense of popular taste: "Genius comes once in a generation," Tarbell once wrote an exasperated colleague who was thinking of quitting, "and if you ever get in its vicinity thank the Lord & *stick*. . . . What you're going through now we've all been through steadily ever since I came into the office. If there was nothing in all this but the annoyance and uncertainty & confusion—that is there were not results—then we might rebel, but there are always results—vital ones. The big things which the magazine has done have always come about through these upheavals."[4]

At *McClure's*, there was always, as Tarbell would later put it, much "fingering" of a subject before the magazine decided to launch on a story, and, in this case, there was more than usual.[5] The subject being kicked around was nothing less than the great industrial monopolies, known as "trusts," that had come to dominate the American economy and political life. It was the summer of 1901.

The editors had struggled for weeks to find an approach, considering and rejecting as targets J. P. Morgan's Steel Trust, Henry Havemeyer's Sugar Trust, and Philip Armour's Beef Trust (Armour dodged his probe by dying in January 1901). "Unquestionably, we ought to do something the coming year on the great industrial developments of the country," an exasperated Tarbell wrote to Ray Stannard Baker, a colleague at *McClure's*. "But it seems clear to me that we must . . . find a new plan of attacking it—something that will . . . make clear the great principles by which industrial leaders are combining and controlling these resources. . . . What I am struggling with is a new plan of attack."[6]

In the end, the natural choice was oil. Tarbell had grown up in Pennsylvania's oil country; her father had run a small refinery and a business making oil barrels; her brother worked for one of the few remaining competitors in an industry almost totally dominated by the greatest of all monopolies, the "mother of trusts," John D. Rockefeller's Standard Oil Company. She drew up an outline, and Phillips approved it. But McClure, recovering from exhaustion, was on a doctor-ordered, year-long rest cure in Switzerland. "Go over," Phillips said, "and show the outline to Sam."

"I want to think it over," McClure said after she had pitched the idea in Lausanne. He then announced that they would mull over the story while traveling to Greece, where McClure's family would spend the winter. "We can discuss Standard Oil in Greece as well as here," he said. So they headed south, stopping along the way for tours of Italy's lake district and Milan—then to rest at the famous Salsomaggiore spa, where they took lengthy mud baths and "steam soaks" and contemplated just whom and what they were about to take on. Finally, eager to get started, Tarbell cut the trip short. Approval in hand, she returned to New York to begin reporting on what stands, to this day, as the greatest business story ever written.

Reading the back story to Tarbell's epic *History of the Standard Oil Company*, published as a series in 1902 to 1903 and later in book form in 1904, one can only smile, maybe a bit enviously, at the deliberate pace at which journalism was done back then. But then again, consider the stakes: Standard Oil was one of the most powerful and secretive organizations in the world. Tarbell had never written an investigative story in her life. McClure, for that matter, had never published one.

"Say the word 'muckraker,'" observes the scholar Cecelia Tichi, "and the listener's mind shuts as quickly as it opens. For muckraking suffers from both too much and too little familiarity. The term floats freely in the popular culture, but the texts themselves lack literary prestige, no matter how skilled their practitioners."[7] It's probably fair to say that modern American journalism and journalists, too, have an ambivalent relationship with the muckrakers, the generation of reporters—really only a dozen or two—who emerged right at the turn of the twentieth century, produced monumental and innovative journalism, galvanized middle-class audiences, and then, with the start of World War I, essentially disappeared. Reading some of their work, the language can seem strange, ranging from turgid to wildly overheated. ("The chief schemer in the service of [the] exploiters," is how one muckraker described a U.S. Senate leader).[8] We smile at their high dudgeon; their moralism seems alien to us.

And if journalism today is not entirely sure what to make of the muckrakers, modern *business* journalism, that particular subculture, sees itself as having little to do with these quirky and outsized figures: the manic McClure, the pathbreaking Tarbell, the bohemian Lincoln Steffens, future socialist. U.S. business and financial journalism traces its lineage along an entirely separate path, to an entirely different set of journalists, who saw their mandate through a different lens, wrote from a different perspective, and served a different audience. Business journalism was conceived to serve the interests of shipping and trade and, later, stock and bond markets and manufacturers—an important but ultimately limiting function. Even when early business journalists and the muckrakers were writing about precisely the same subject, they may as well have been describing different worlds.

While giving early business journalism its due, it is also true that, as a journalistic form, it was inadequate as a means for the broader public to understand the great economic issues of its time: industrial consolidation, the formation of an American oligarchy, and its grip on the political system of the United States. As a form of elite communication, business journalism was not intended for, and not particularly useful to, the general public, which, understandably, stayed away in droves. The circulation of the *Wall Street Journal*, for instance, hovered around 10,000 in the early twentieth century while *McClure's* soared to nearly half a million, larger, adjusted for population, than that of the *New York Times* today.

Despite its high-level sources and expertise in matters economic and financial—or perhaps because of them—business journalism's narrow view of its own mandate left an information vacuum that would be filled by an extraordinary band of outsiders: nonexperts, investigators, and generalists, essentially a group of professional storytellers. Muckrakers would produce journalism that not only endures but, more importantly, was far more valuable in its own time than conventional business news both to markets and to the public.

When Tarbell and McClure first discussed the series at the Salsomaggiore baths in Italy, they mapped out a series of stories. But as copies of the first installments flew off newsstands in 1902 and 1903, it quickly expanded to six stories, then twelve, and soon became a national sensation. New installments became news events in themselves, covered, among others, by the fledgling *Wall Street Journal*. The series finally reached nineteen installments, quickly turned into a two-volume book, a best-seller. A cartoon in *Puck* magazine would depict a pantheon of muckrakers with Tarbell as a Joan of Arc figure on horseback. Another contemporary magazine pronounced her "the most popular woman in America."

Tarbell's Standard Oil work, in particular, and her historic collaboration with Sam McClure illustrate what made the muckrakers so valuable to their time and what was missing in ours before the financial crisis. As we try to figure out what works and doesn't work in journalism today, it's worth keeping in a mind a few elements that stand out in the work of Tarbell, her publisher, and the best (though by no means all) of the muckrakers. Their strength was a certain journalistic purity: They had no political axes to grind; they were after the Great Story and were, in fact, master storytellers. They had a journalistic ambition that was sweeping by today's standards. They combined the Victorian era's faith in science—a scrupulous fidelity to true facts—with its unabashed moralism. As moralists, the muckrakers recognized the importance of human agency and didn't shrink from holding power to account—by name. And they crafted what can be called American journalism's only true ideology.

Samuel Sidney McClure (born 1857) was brought to the United States at the age of nine by his mother after his father, an Irish shipyard worker, was killed in a work accident. Raised amid severe privation in rural Indiana, he was passed among several relatives and grew into a high-strung, impulsive boy, running away dozens of times.[9] He worked his way through Knox College, in Galesburg, Illinois, founded by abolitionists and a center for social reformers, where he met John S. Phillips and other friends who would form the core of *McClure's*.[10] At Knox, McClure started an intercollegiate news service and engaged in literary disputes and collegiate oratory. In one debate, he made a declaration about the abolitionists that presaged his own journalistic ambitions: "It was when they believed in what seemed impossible that the abolitionists did the most good, that they created the sentiment that finally did accomplish the impossible."[11]

McClure's early career was bent not toward politics, or even journalism, but toward literary and commercial interests. An early job was at a bicycling magazine, *The Wheelman*, published by Pope Manufacturing Co., the owner of Columbia bicycles, where he was joined by Phillips.[12] The two entrepreneurs left to form a literary syndicate, assembling a stable of writers to write fiction and poetry for sale to magazine editors. When he and Phillips started *McClure's*, in 1893, its interests were not particularly journalistic. He had collected 2,000 unpublished manuscripts, mostly fiction, and figured he could sell the public on a new literary style—realism—while undercutting the likes of *Harper's* and the *Atlantic* on price. *McClure's* in the early years was a general-interest magazine, an eclectic mix of features with no particular interest in politics, let alone investigative reporting. The magazine came out of McClure's crowded head.

It was in search of a full-time writer for his staff that, while traveling in Paris, McClure called upon a young American woman who had attracted some attention in the States with a piece in *Scribner's* called "France Adoré," about an young American in Paris and her French tutor. When McClure burst into Ida Tarbell's flat, he told her he only had ten minutes to spare. He stayed for three hours.

Ida Minerva Tarbell (also born in 1857) came from a highly conventional, middle-class, Midwestern background. Her father, Franklin, settled the family in Titusville, in Pennsylvania's booming oil country, and built a business selling oil barrels to local producers. Tarbell recalls an idyllic childhood of culture, music, science, and religious instruction, cultivated mostly by her mother, Esther, a former schoolteacher.

Like McClure and many other muckrakers (and their readers), Tarbell was a product of evangelical Protestant institutions that preached a socially engaged style of Christianity grounded in scientific principles. The muckrakers saw themselves, as Harold S. Wilson puts it, as "spiritual midwives to a new social order." McClure would write that he saw his magazine "performing a certain mission," with God "in our plans."[13] In a not-untypical musing, Steffens wrote an essay on ethics, carefully categorizing acts as "good," "bad," "right," and "wrong."

Tarbell attended Allegheny College, founded by the United Methodist Church, in Meadville, Pennsylvania. She arrived in 1876 at the age of eighteen, "without ever having dared to look fully into the face of any boy my own age," she would write in her autobiography. She was the only woman in her class. After establishing her place at school, she concluded that no woman could both be a wife and pursue a career outside the home. She decided to live as a writer, a goal she called "the Purpose," always with a capital "P," and pursued with an unusual single-mindedness.[14] Her first journalism job was at the *Chautauquan*, also in Meadville, affiliated with the adult-education movement popular at the time. Her research led her to the piece on Madame Roland, which led her to an interest in France. Not satisfied with the routine of the *Chautauquan*, Tarbell took the daring and unusual step for a woman of her era and moved to Paris to write freelance and study. She was sharing a Latin Quarter flat with other American women when McClure came calling.

None of *McClure's* fabled staff had joined the magazine with investigative reporting in mind.[15] Ray Stannard Baker was an aspiring novelist. Lincoln Steffens studied ethics, art history, and psychology in Europe before landing a job covering politics and crime for the *New York Evening Post*; he discovered corruption in Midwestern cities only after McClure ordered him out of the office and sent him on a tour of the country. Besides its literary offerings, *McClure's* in the late 1890s, was running a series on what McClure described in his autobiography as the "greatest American business achievements."

McClure considered himself a storyteller first, using "the story is the thing," as mantra and exhortation. In 1906, after *McClure's* had become a national sensation (and was on its way to a crackup as its biggest stars would soon decamp to another publication), he wrote: "When Mr. Steffens, Mr. Baker, Miss Tarbell write, they must never be conscious of anything else while writing other than telling an absorbing story: the story is the thing." Phillips, too, reinforced *McClure's* priority on narrative arts, once writing Baker: "I take it you will make your articles compact with incident and fact. Your strong point is in making things alive, human, with stories of individuals." *McClure's* articles were closely edited and read as many as thirty times, sometimes by everyone on the staff. A *McClure's* story imitated the short story, with quickly initiated action and a climax. McClure aimed to make stories as interesting and exciting on their second or third reading as on the first. Like all Victorian literature, the article needed a moral, one presented unconsciously.[16]

Richard Hofstadter places muckraking within the larger tradition of literary realism of the era and notes that the leading authors of the genre—Stephen Crane, Theodore Dreiser, David Graham Phillips, Jack London—had had training in journalistic observation or, at least, had explored the rough side of life. What the novelists, journalists, and social scientists of the period shared was a passion for getting the "inside story."[17] The reliance on storytelling to explain complex subjects to a mass audience would be adopted by mainstream business news only much later with the foundational journalism figure Bernard Kilgore.

But by 1901, the matter of trusts was almost unavoidable. It dominated the political discussion and was the subject of almost daily newspaper stories and many books. Standard Oil had been investigated repeatedly for decades, by congressional committees in 1872 and 1876 and by New York, Pennsylvania, and Ohio legislators in 1879, among others. In 1892, an Ohio judge ordered the trust dismantled, prompting the company to move its headquarters from Cleveland to New Jersey.[18] In the spring of 1901, the reformer Jane Addams's group, the Chicago Civic Federation, held a "Trust Convention" attended by 500 delegates, including William Jennings Bryan, who called for national legislation against the trusts.[19] The new president, Theodore Roosevelt, was also gunning for the great industrialists; as a New York state legislator he had once dubbed them "the wealthy criminal class."[20]

In the *Age of Reform*, Hofstadter argued famously that the popularity of muckraking among middle-class Americans was a response to bewildering societal shifts that had transformed a mostly rural and small-town country into an industrialized, urban giant. Where individuals had once gotten their news firsthand and participated personally in the affairs that shaped their economic and personal lives, they now saw all around the rise of big business, big labor, and political machines, "clotting" society into what Hofstadter calls the "big aggregates." A central theme of Progressivism, the political movement muckraking helped to fuel, was a revolt of the unorganized against the "consequences of organization." Progressivism was a middle-class movement, made up of clerks, lawyers, ministers, teachers, and other professionals deprived of status and power by a new breed of capitalist arrivistes, as well as union and political bosses. This group of the isolated and disempowered was well educated, genteel in outlook, religious, and, Hofstadter writes, "almost completely devoid of economic organization."[21]

Many, of course, have noted the parallels between Tarbell's time and our own. Then, as now, the country had been undergoing bewildering systemic shifts. Individuals felt isolated, disempowered, and, importantly, believed they lacked adequate information to understand what was happening around them. And when they did find out, the middle class recoiled at the shocking corruption of government at all levels as policy and regulation were bent to serve private interests at the expense of the public interest.

For *McClure's* middle-class audience, it was an open question whether democratic institutions were any longer responsive to the public interest. The investigations of the Pujo Committee (1912) would later confirm what the public had already sensed: industrial America comprised a staggering concentration of wealth and power. One interlocking network of J. P. Morgan interests was found to control aggregate assets of $22 billion, three times the assessed value of all real and personal property in New England.[22] When the new Roosevelt administration sued in 1902 for the dissolution of Northern Securities, a gigantic railroad forged by a spectacular and damaging merger battle between Morgan and competing interests, the symbolic value of the suit was even greater than its substance: "The government's suit encouraged everyone to feel at last that the President of the United States was really bigger and more powerful than Morgan and the Morgan interests, that the country was governed from Washington and not from Wall Street," as Hofstadter puts it.[23]

For *McClure's*, Rockefeller posed a monumental reporting challenge. His empire was gigantic, controlling 90 percent of the nation's oil supply, derricks, refineries, pipelines, and even retail stores. He vied with Andrew Carnegie for the title of world's richest man and had built the greatest industrial corporation on earth.[24] Yet for all that, he remained the most elusive of figures. For decades, independent producers and refiners charged that Rockefeller operated secret cartels with other oil giants, created an espionage network to steal trade secrets, and, critically, cut secret deals with railroads to gain unfair advantage on shipping rates and to block competitors' access to markets. Spurred by local oil interests, state legislatures in Ohio, Pennsylvania, New York, and elsewhere had pursued the company, as did congressional committees and even grand juries. Rockefeller, while formally retired, was still deeply involved in his company and the object of intense public fascination. As the twentieth century dawned, he had inspired more prose than any other private citizen in America, with books about him tumbling out at the rate of nearly one per year.[25]

But through it all, "the Standard" had proved impervious to scrutiny, and Rockefeller remained the most enigmatic of robber barons. His company was deliberately labyrinthine, true to its popular nickname, "the Octopus." He made a point of separating himself from his underlings' most disreputable tactics and carefully controlled his public image, confining his public appearances mostly to dispensing dimes in front of newsreel cameras. His private letters were written with odd elliptical phrases and euphemisms, as if they might fall into the hands of a prosecutor. Ron Chernow begins his biography, *Titan*, by remarking: "The life of John D. Rockefeller Sr. was marked to an exceptional degree by silence, mystery, and evasion. Even though he presided over the largest business and philanthropic enterprises of his day, he remains an elusive figure."[26]

The muckrakers weren't the first to practice what became known as the "journalism of exposure," but McClure and Tarbell brought qualities that particularly matched the sensibilities of their well-educated, middle-class, Midwestern audience, which, while religious as a matter of course, was also influenced by the new social sciences, particularly sociology, then coming of age. The audience demanded not polemic but facts. Where Joseph Pulitzer or William Randolph Hearst went in for sensationalism and scandal-mongering, McClure wanted to analyze complex issues and explore them with scientific precision.[27]

Tarbell's Standard Oil series is, if nothing else, a monument to dogged fact gathering. Indeed, one of the main attractions of Standard as a subject for Tarbell and McClure was the mass of documentation on the company accumulated over the years by the various probes and lawsuits: government reports, court records, and testimony transcripts, including from Rockefeller himself. Tarbell at first staggered under the mass of material to be collected and read. Her autobiography describes the fact-gathering challenge in detail:

> The documentary sources were by no means all in print. The Standard Oil Trust and its constituent companies had figured in many civil suits, the testimony of which was in manuscript in the files of the courts where the suits were tried.
>
> I had supposed it would be easy to locate the records of the important investigations and cases, but I soon found I had been too trustful.[28]

She hired full-time assistant, John M. Siddall, who had worked for the *Chatutaquan* and impressed Tarbell with his energy. He became a close collaborator, working from Cleveland.

The search for a single, key document, gives a taste of their diligence. A pamphlet called *The Rise and Fall of South Improvement Company*, compiled in 1873, exposed the workings of an early attempt at cartel by railroads and the biggest oil refiners, including Rockefeller. No charge was as damaging to Standard as the accusation that it had formed what is now universally acknowledged as a predatory cartel, and Rockefeller at the time of Tarbell's writing disavowed any significant role in the cartel. Tarbell's sources had insisted this thirty-year-old document would prove Standard had, in fact, risen from the South Improvement Company, but Tarbell had been told that Standard had bought and destroyed every copy. "More than one cynic said, 'you'll never find one—they have all been destroyed,'" she later wrote. Three copies of the document still existed, she learned. She tracked down two, in private collections, but the owners refused access.[29]

Tarbell found one remaining copy in a not-so-secret place: the New York Public Library. The document showed that Rockefeller had in fact bought the charter for the company from an estate in 1871 and asked other founding officers to sign a pledge of secrecy. It also included testimony from a refiner, John Alexander, who was asked by a congressional investigator whether he had sold his company to South Improvement. He replied: "To one of the members, as I suppose, of the South Improvement Company, Mr. Rockefeller; he is a director in that company; it was sold in the name of the Standard Oil Company, of Cleveland, but the arrangement was, as I understand it, that they were to put it into the South Improvement Company."[30]

Tarbell's extensive interviewing started with old neighbors in Titusville, who were at first fearful and suspicious and included surprisingly well-placed sources, including Henry H. Rogers, a top Standard executive and a member of Rockefeller's inner circle. She was introduced to him, as it happens, through the celebrity author Samuel Clemens—Mark Twain—who had received financial support from Rogers and was friendly with McClure.[31] Tarbell met Rogers frequently and secretly at the company's headquarters at 26 Broadway, in New York. They spoke off the record, with Rogers confirming or denying Tarbell's findings.

Tarbell's reporting was so thorough that one could even argue that she overdid it. She tracked down old ledgers from Rockefeller's childhood containing religious instruction and found the first public record to mention him: the 1858 Cleveland city directory recorded his first job at age nineteen: "Rockefeller, John D., bookkeeper. h 35 Cedar." Sitting amid heaps of paper beneath framed photographs of McClure and Phillips, she reported for a year before her first piece ran.[32] And it was only a reporting coup that spurred McClure to press for the series to begin, in November 1902.

When President Theodore Roosevelt, the muckrakers' erstwhile ally, coined the new term in a 1906 speech comparing journalists to "The Man with the Muck-Rake," a character in *Pilgrim's Progress*, he in a single stroke identified a new form of journalism and began its marginalization. In referring to John Bunyan's Christian allegory, which was widely read at the time, Roosevelt attacked the new breed of journalists on their own terms and on what they regarded as their strength—their moralism and religiosity: "The man who could look no way but downward, with a muckrake in this hands; who was offered a celestial crown for his muckrake, but who would neither look up nor regard the crown he was offered, but continued to rake to himself the filth of the floor."[33]

Tichi calls Roosevelt's speech a "baleful presidential baptism" for the new journalism and so it was.[34] The speech provoked a national debate about a wildly popular new form of journalism that had been attracting new entrants that were not as scrupulous as *McClure's* and were tilting into excess. In the ensuing hubbub, a furious Steffens called on the president and, to his face, remarked acidly: "Well, you have put an end to all these journalistic investigations that have made you." Roosevelt sought to reassure the Steffens that he didn't mean *him*.[35] Steffens was not appeased. Calling the term "a name of odium," he would throw it back at Roosevelt in lectures around the country. Baker, too, was furious. Phillips never forgave the president.[36] And Tarbell, for her part, would tartly retort: "Roosevelt had of course misread his Bunyan."[37] She once argued with Roosevelt at the While House, telling him that *McClure's* writers "were concerned only with facts, not with stirring up a revolt." Roosevelt replied: "I don't object to facts. But you and Baker are not *practical!*"[38]

The association with filth and negativity has, to this day, tainted journalism's most potent weapon, the investigative narrative, which, at its best, set new standards for ambition, diligence, and storytelling. To be sure, muckraking also has itself to blame for its mixed reputation. The commercial success of *McClure's* and others brought out of the woodwork hacks, hustlers, and careerists—those hardy journalism perennials—and opportunists like William Randolph Hearst, who bought *Cosmopolitan* magazine in 1905 and helped usher in a period of excess. As Tarbell would later write: "The public is not as stupid as it sometimes seems. The truth of the matter is that the muckraking school was stupid. It had lost the passion for facts in a passion for subscriptions."[39]

Roosevelt's coinage would stick, but he was wrong in one important respect. The original muckrakers didn't search through muck to find stories. Rather, they searched for great stories—and found them in the actual corruption that had overrun political and corporate institutions. One could just as easily argue that the muck-rakers didn't look up or down, just around. Nothing was less pre-meditated, for instance, than *McClure's* January 1903 issue, considered the inauguration (and perhaps the high-water mark) of the muckraking era. In one remarkable edition, it contained the third installment of Tarbell's "History" series, Steffens's "Shame of Minneapolis," and a piece by Baker, "The Right to Work," all classics of the form.

Steffens's piece excoriated the administration of Albert Alonzo "Doc" Ames, the notoriously corrupt turn-of-the-century Minneapolis mayor, who opened the city to grafters and gamblers and was an all-around cad, even to his own wife and children. Steffens interviewed politicians, cops, crooks, editors, and reformers. With an ironic tone that overlay outrage, Steffens described the kleptocracy that Minneapolis had become under its political machine (as he later would later do for St. Louis, Pittsburgh, and other cities). Opium dens, houses of prostitution, and slot machines were set up across the city, all monitored and shaken down by Ames's men. The installment was part of a series, published as *Shame of the Cities* in 1904, that exposed urban corruption as a systemic problem nationally.

Baker's piece described union violence and terror against non-union workers in Pennsylvania and the degree to which strikes tore apart communities. Baker profiled a defiant English-born engineer who refused to join a union and went to work armed with a pistol, only to have a chunk of coal dropped on his head by unionists who had laid in wait for him on top of a railroad car then beat him and left him for dead. Baker tracked down the engineer's mother, who disavowed her son: "He deserved all he got," Baker quotes the mother. "He wasn't raised a scab." Baker adds a final wrenching detail. The mother admits to him that she had called the hospital where her son lay to see if he was alive or dead. "But I didn't give my name," she told Baker. "So he didn't know about it."

What's notable about all three pieces is that *McClure's* hadn't planned to veer into investigative reporting. McClure himself realized only at the last minute that the issue represented something new. Reading the articles before publication, he took a fresh look at what he and his writers had found and saw the common theme:

a general disrespect for law on the part of capitalists, workingmen, and politicians. A common theme of American life—lawlessness—had emerged without planning or agenda. McClure hurriedly wrote an editorial to drive home the point. It stands as a muckraker's manifesto: "We did not plan it so," he wrote. "It is a coincidence that the January *McClure's* is such an arraignment of American character as should make everyone of us stop and think. . . . Capitalists, workingmen, politicians, citizens—all breaking the law or letting it be broken. Who is left to uphold it?" In an appeal to what was then a developing idea of a public interest, he answered his own question: "There is no one left. None but all of us.[40]"

Thus, a good-faith journalistic search for Great Stories—untainted by political agenda—turned up exposés of systemic corruption, and riveting ones at that. And an eclectic literary magazine became the center of a powerful new journalistic form.

The *McClure's* editorial, even with its soaring Victorian prose, resonates today, and it certainly did then. It expressed the helplessness and despair of *McClure's* middle-class readers, who saw economic and political events slipping not just beyond their control but beyond their understanding. American elites, meanwhile, weren't simply failing to live up to their responsibilities; they were the problem.

The reporting coup that triggered the series came when a teenaged clerk working in a Standard office came across documents with the name of his Sunday school teacher, who happened to be an independent oil refiner. The documents, on railroad stationery, were the refiner's shipping records, taken from a local railroad office. They provided the first solid evidence that Standard, as Tarbell suspected, operated a network of company spies to bribe competitors' employees for shipping and pricing information and other trade secrets. The boy turned the documents over to the refiner, who, knowing of Tarbell's reputation, turned them over to her. A thrilled McClure hurriedly published an announcement in the magazine of the coming exposé, promising, "The story of the conflict of two great commercial principles of the day—competition and combination . . . told without partisan passion and entirely from documents."[41]

"The History of the Standard Oil Company" would provide enthralled readers with a monthly torrent of damning facts about

Rockefeller, Standard Oil, and the extralegal means it had used to gain a monopoly over the emerging nation's oil industry. It included court testimony, official company documents, statistics, and charts presented in Tarbell's dry, sober writing style that made the facts all the more convincing. The series included, for instance, the testimony of the bookkeeper of a competitor who told investigators that "Standard men" had tried to bribe him to steal secrets from his employer and send them to an anonymous post-office box. It quotes letters from retailers to their independent suppliers complaining that "Standard men" had ordered them to stop selling competitors' oil or face a price war from neighboring stores. ("They have put their oil . . . next door and offer it as six cents a gallon, at retail," one retailer wrote his supplier, an independent refiner. "Shall we turn tail or show them fight?") Tarbell provided evidence that members of Congress had ties to Standard (e.g., "J.N. Camden of West Virginia, head of the Camden Consolidated Oil Company, now one of the constituent companies of the Standard Oil Trust") and had used their official power to impede regulators' efforts to police shipping rates. Readers weren't just presented with facts; they were bombarded with them. There were excerpts of hearing testimony, court opinions, trust agreements, corporate ledgers, articles of incorporation, railroad contracts, indictments, and graphs showing oil-price fluctuations as far back as the mid-1860s. The *McClure's* series included a string of photographs of Rockefeller and other top Standard executives that look, as one biographer puts it, like "mug shots."[42]

The 400,000 copies of the January 1903 edition of *McClure's* sold out quickly. The spike contributed to a sharp rise in circulation before the magazine's foray into muckraking. The Tarbell series is credited with sparking the antitrust suit, filed two years later, that ended with the landmark 1911 Supreme Court decision to break up the Standard trust. But its significance goes far beyond that. Hofstadter argues that muckrakers' popularity grew from their ability "not merely to name the malpractices in American business and politics, but to name the *malpractitioners* and their specific misdeeds and to proclaim the fact to the entire country" (emphasis in original). Hofstadter puts his finger on a key point: Thanks to the muckrakers, he says, "It now became possible for any literate citizen to know what barkeepers, district attorneys, ward heelers, prostitutes, police court magistrates, reporters and corporation lawyers had always come to know in the course of their business."[43]

The new journalism offered readers a hope, at least, of understanding the tectonic shifts reshaping society beneath their feet, and to learn the identities of the institutions and actors involved and their methods. Muckrakers targeted specific institutions and the individuals who ran them. The McClure editorial contains the seeds of what might be called the muckraker's only real "ideology," if that's the right word. I call it an ideology of anticorruption; McClure might call it "anti-lawlessness."

Corruption is a strong word, so strong it can seem off-putting. Still, as the financial crisis teaches, it's real enough and has a corrosive logic all its own. Inherently unfair, it rewards the worst actors and punishes the best. An oil refiner who might have had the prescience to establish a factory in a strategic location will always lose to the competitor with the clout to force the railroad into offering favorable rates for the cheater and higher rates for the competitor. (Just as, during the mortgage era, lenders with high underwriting standards lost out as the system rewarded those who sold loans under any circumstances.) Corruption coddles incompetence, discourages achievement, and wrecks markets. Ultimately, it undermines the legitimacy of any system that tolerates it.

While Tarbell and other muckrakers might see its roots in individuals' moral failings, they were also savvy enough to realize that, generally speaking, corruption occurs when individual and corporate economic incentives are out of alignment with the laws, rules, or other norms that define fair play. As Tarbell put it in (with some heat) in insisting that Standard had engaged in behavior that was far below even the rough-and-tumble business norms of the day: "Everybody did *not* do it. In the nature of the offense, everybody *could* not do it. The strong wrested from the railroads the privilege of preying upon the weak, and the railroads never dared to give the privilege save under the promise of secrecy."[44]

The ideology of anticorruption or anti-lawlessness of *McClure's* group and other muckrakers was purely journalistic in motive. It was about exposing wrongdoing for its own sake, without partisan agenda. It held whether the offender was government or business or labor or anyone else. It's a foundational idea that endures for American journalism today. In a speech in 1974, when a new era of muckraking was beginning to take hold, *Washington Post* publisher Katharine Graham made a distinction between two kinds of investigative reporting: The more widely understood type exposed "hidden illegalities and public official malfeasance." The second, she said, "zeroes in on systems and institutions in the public or private realm, to find out how they really work, who exercises power, who benefits, and who gets hurt."[45]

Tarbell and her colleagues at *McClure's* understood the importance of taking on big, broad systemic questions. The Tarbell series offered not incremental snapshots of the previous day's news but a sweeping overview that helped readers come to grips in concrete terms with what they had only sensed—things *had* changed; trusts *had* become enormously powerful and were tilting the political and economic playing field—and explained exactly *how*. It is also not surprising that the well-educated readers of *McClure's* appreciated the story told through a (colossal) compilation of facts, coherently arranged and offered without much rhetorical adornment. Tarbell correctly identified the threat Standard posed not just to competitors and consumers but to the larger economy by tracing how Standard's founders leveraged their gains to move into other industries. This was the big picture.

Tarbell and McClure believed that the rise of trusts, and Standard Oil as the greatest of them, could be understood only in context and that incremental news reporting, even stories that documented isolated instances of wrongdoing, wouldn't do. That's why Tarbell began her narrative in 1872, with Standard Oil's genesis as an illegal cartel, and why she labored to document so thoroughly the secret system of rebates and "drawbacks" from railroads that allowed Standard to undercut its rivals. "Cutting to Kill," an installment in the summer of 1903, was a landmark because it showed the systematic nature of Standard's espionage network, that it wasn't the work of rogues here and there, as Rockefeller maintained, but tightly organized and the result of corporate policy.

Ninety years later, the historian Ron Chernow would gain access to a trove of Rockefeller's personal papers for his authoritative 1998 biography, *Titan*. Among them, he found confirmation not just of the espionage network but also of what Tarbell had begun to demonstrate but that the titan had long denied: his personal involvement in blatant wrongdoing, even according to the standards of the time.

To hold Tarbell as an exemplar is not to say that she or her monumental "History" was without flaws. While historians have generally vindicated her findings, they have included important caveats. The flaws of her series can be said to fall into two categories: flat-out mistakes and errors of emphasis. The most serious reporting mistake, cited by both Allan Nevins, a Rockefeller defender writing in the 1950s, and the more balanced Chernow, was her resurrection of the tale of so-called Widow Backus, Mrs. Fred M. Backus, whose tearjerking tale had already been told (also in error) by Henry Demarest Lloyd in his *Wealth Against Commonwealth*, a polemical, proto-muckraking work written in 1894. Mrs. Backus's late husband had once worked for Rockefeller and taught Sunday school at his church before starting his own small refinery. He died and left the refinery to his wife, who would later claim Rockefeller robbed her blind when buying the works in the late 1870s. Rockefeller wryly observed of the story, "If it were true it would represent a shocking instance of cruelty in crushing a defenseless woman." Tarbell's version uncritically accepts Mrs. Backus's side. As it turns out, the widow received a fair or even generous price for what was in fact an outmoded refinery and died rather wealthy, having wisely invested the proceeds of the sale in Cleveland real estate.

A second, serious error of judgment came after the series in a two-part "character study" published at McClure's urging in 1905. Abandoning fact-based reporting and sober language, Tarbell employed instead sheer invective and descriptions that were vengeful and mean. Tarbell described Rockefeller as the embodiment of evil, a "living mummy," hideous and diseased, leprous and reptilian. "It is this puffiness, this unclean flesh, which repels, as the thin slit of his mouth terrifies," she wrote, in one example of the unfortunate prose.[46] The result was counterproductive on every level.

Tarbell is also faulted, justly, for idealizing the independent producers and refiners that lost out to Rockefeller, a group that included her own father and brother. Nevins and Chernow say she was wrong to blame Rockefeller for initiating the illegal cartel in 1872. It was the railroads' idea, even if he went along with it and then drove it to its logical conclusion. Other legitimate complaints fault misplaced emphasis. Historians argue, for instance, that Tarbell placed too much blame on Rockefeller personally and not enough on other actors in a sprawling enterprise. Finally, Tarbell is faulted for what is seen as her excessive moralism and inability to place Rockefeller's rise in the context of structural changes overtaking the oil business and the American economy.

All fair enough.

Tarbell's work, it should be clear, was not a history but a work of journalism, written while Rockefeller was still alive (he would live until 1937) and, if retired, still active (a telegraph stood ready in the company's headquarters to receive his orders from Cleveland). The company was at the peak of its powers, one of the most feared institutions on the face of the earth. And while Standard Oil never retaliated or even responded during the series, its silence, which today seems self-defeating, could then be seen as ominous. Tarbell, of course, had no way of knowing the outcome when she was writing it.

Tarbell (like Roosevelt, for that matter) never condemned Standard for its size, only for lawless acts. And while she can be faulted for recycling the problematic "Widow Backus" story, she had no problem flatly exonerating company executives of involvement in the explosion of a competing refinery in Buffalo, for which Rogers and other Standard officials had been indicted (the case seems to have had little merit). She also had no trouble acknowledging the genuine achievements of Rockefeller and his cohorts and devoted an article to "The Legitimate Greatness of the Standard Oil Company." "There was not a lazy bone in the organization, not an incompetent hand, nor a stupid head," she wrote.[47]

It wasn't that Standard was big or even that it played rough. It was that it cheated. It broke the law. It was the fact that it could have succeeded *without* resorting to unethical acts that so exasperated Tarbell. As she says in her memoir, "I never had an animus against their size and wealth, never objected to their corporate form. I was willing that they should combine and grow as big and rich as they could, but only by legitimate means. But they had never played fair, and that ruined their greatness for me."[48]

In the end, the last laugh was Rockefeller's. In 1911 in Tarrytown, New York, while playing golf with Father J. P. Lennon, a message arrived with word of the Supreme Court decision breaking up his company. Rockefeller hardly blinked. "Father Lennon," Rockefeller asked blandly, "have you some money?" No, the priest answered, why? "Buy Standard Oil," Rockefeller cracked.[49] And in fact, shares of the new companies created from the breakup would later soar, turning Rockefeller from a mere millionaire into nearly a billionaire.

But Tarbell's legacy is secure. She and other muckrakers (not uniformly, but at their best) brought to their era and handed down to ours their journalistic and commercial motivations and a fidelity to fact gathering, accuracy, and storytelling—journalistic qualities still familiar to us today. They also brought unusual journalistic ambition; a willingness to step away from the incremental news of the moment to examine systemic changes; and a willingness to expose malpractitioners as well as malpractices, to challenge official accounts of powerful institutions, and do it while those institutions were still powerful. If in her "character sketch" of Rockefeller Tarbell was crude and unfair, that is to be regretted. But no one could accuse her of avoiding the main actor at the main institution involved in the main economic problem of the day.

Tarbell retired to a farm in Bridgeport, Connecticut, ambivalent about her masterpiece. She had come to doubt the practical effects of her personal victory and the degree to which it had helped curb abuses of economic power. On the other hand, she understood she had done something special. In the 1930s, then in her seventies, she was lunching at the National Arts Club in New York with a young history professor and his wife. The professor asked about her Standard Oil epic: "If you could rewrite your book today, what would you change?" With a flash of her eyes, Tarbell emphatically set down her knife. "Not one word, young man," she answered steadily. "Not one word."[50]

CHAPTER 2

Access and Messenger Boys

The Roots of Business News and the Birth of the Wall Street Journal

In a chance encounter near Wall Street around the turn of the twentieth century, Edward Jones, a founding partner of Dow Jones & Co. and a well-known financial journalist in New York, bumped into William Rockefeller, the brother of the oil titan John D. Rockefeller and a high-ranking Standard Oil executive in his own right. The men, who were friendly, got to talking. According to Lloyd Wendt's 1982 book *The* Wall Street Journal, a history of the paper, the exchange went something like this:

> Rockefeller: "Edward, would it mean anything to you to get a little advance Standard Oil news?"
> Beaming, Jones replied: "Kind sir, would you dare say that again?"
> "Here's something I jotted down for you, if you care to use it," Rockefeller said, handing him a note. "Only, please, keep your authority confidential!"[1]

The news was that Standard was issuing new stock and increasing its dividend. Standard's stock soared on the news. And Jones had another scoop.[2]

The image of one of the patriarchs of American financial journalism jumping at the chance for a scrap of news from a top Standard executive isn't altogether a flattering one, particularly when compared with muckraker Ida Tarbell, who didn't rely on favors from the company and received none. In the minds of some, this is the very image of the financial journalist—the flatterer, the scribe of the powerful. It's a view expressed, for instance, in Stieg Larsson's wildly popular novel *The Girl with the Dragon Tattoo* by the main character, Mikael Blomkvist, an investigative reporter for an alternative paper who holds a dim view of his colleagues in the mainstream financial press:

> His contempt for his fellow financial journalists was based on something that in his opinion was as plain as morality. . . . The job of the financial journalist was to examine the sharks who created interest crises and speculated away the savings of small investors, to scrutinize company boards with the same merciless zeal with which political reporters pursue the tiniest steps out of line of ministers and members of parliament. He could not for the life of him understand why so many influential financial reporters treated mediocre financial whelps like rock stars.[3]

While irresistible, the image of the journalist flapping around a titan's brother on a street corner, hoping for a scrap of news, is hardly a full representation of business reporting. Indeed, Wendt also chronicles a second incident in which Jones approaches the beef mogul, Philip Armour:

"Your friends are saying I misquoted you," Jones begins angrily.

"What's that?" a surprised Armour replies.

"Your friends say I misquoted you," Jones icily repeats, "and that you repudiate me."

"What's a little fuss," Armour says, attempting to defuse the situation.

"And just what do you say?" Jones insists.

"I say that Dow Jones is nobody's goat," Armour says.

Whatever that means, clearly Armour is backpedaling. The mogul tries to mollify the angry reporter, promising not to dispute any more quotes: "Shake. And if you shoot out another bulletin saying I say just what you said I said, say that I meant it . . . Jones, I like you—it's great to meet a Man! [*sic*]."[4]

The scene presents a different image of Jones, certainly, and a no-less-accurate representation of a financial journalist than the fawning encounter with Rockefeller's brother. In comparing the work of Tarbell and the journalism of the muckrakers to early financial reporters, it's not my intent to disparage the latter or, for that matter, to glorify the former. There is no need to choose sides between muckraking and market reporting. For now, it's enough to see the utility of both while differentiating between the two. But the differences are crucial in understanding why business news could cover something in granular detail and yet be scooped by others on the greatest story on its beat.

Both scenes show the roots of business journalism in access reporting. Whether the story is positive or negative, whether it curries favor with the source or the opposite, the reporting is "top-down," entirely reliant on powerful players for the information on which the story is based. It is investor oriented, market serving, incremental, and self-referential. It is communication between and among elites, without reference to broader public interests.

The market for financial information is as old as markets themselves. Indeed, as the historian Wayne Parsons notes, business news, as the underpinning of the pricing system, is a precondition for capitalism itself.[5] Until the seventeenth century, the flow of pricing and other financial information passed through private networks, like those controlled by the Medicis. The first business-news entrepreneur is believed to be Joseph Fugger, a German financier and a member of one the seventeenth century's great commercial families, who sold market information to clients as a sideline. As capitalism grew, so did business news, propelled in the eighteenth century by public curiosity—or mania—about early public stock companies, including Britain's notorious South Sea Company. Granted a monopoly to trade in South America, the company's stock soared on the prospect and crashed on the reality that Britain didn't control South America. Indeed, the economist Robert J. Shiller pointedly notes that the history of financial bubbles coincides with the advent of financial media, and it's difficult to imagine the former without the latter.[6]

In Europe, the commercial press actually predated the political press, taking root in London, Amsterdam, Hamburg, and other centers of commerce and trade. Because its content was deemed uncontroversial, it was subject to less censorship than political news. The earliest business press in London circulated shipping news and pricing information. In 1734, Edward Lloyd began publishing *Lloyd's List*, a source of shipping and pricing news for underwriters of shipping insurance who met at his Lloyd's Coffee House, an important news hub in the City of London. The paper, which also provided stock and commodities prices, continues to this day. By the end of the eighteenth century, the market for commercial information was established and had spread to the American colonies.[7] As Parsons and others have noted, the first newspapers in America were essentially commercial papers. They were aimed at merchant classes eager for news about commerce, shipping, and trade and eager to advertise their own products. One function of an early news cooperative, the New York Associated Press (not to be confused with the Associated Press, which survives), for instance, was to meet ships entering New York harbor and relay information about their freight via fast boats.

The value of the early commercial press wasn't so much its specific stories. Rather, it functioned as the circulatory system of the market and provided the very language of capitalism—markets, trade, individualism, and profit. Its value was its role in creating and disseminating what Parsons calls "the capitalist culture."[8] The early financial press served as a voice for the rising merchant, commercial, and industrial class that read it. *The Economist* was founded in 1843 by the Scottish businessman and banker James Wilson to argue for the repeal of the Corn Laws, a system of import tariffs. Under Walter Bagehot, its iconic editor from 1861 to 1877, it advanced the cause of laissez-faire economics and enshrined market-based ideas as a widely shared form of public discourse about economic life. Along the way, *The Economist* helped establish a new professionalism and intellectualism in business and economic reporting and an ideology of sorts that underpins business news to this day.

Early business news was almost by definition a form of elite, as opposed to mass, communication, a press geared to a small band of market participants.[9] The merchant class was the main audience for one of the most influential early business papers, the *Journal of Commerce*, founded in 1827 by Samuel Morse, the telegraph inventor, and a partner, Arthur Tappan, who later helped to form the Associated Press (also an important early purveyor of business news).

William Buck Dana modeled New York's first business weekly, *Commercial and Financial Chronicle*, on *The Economist* and used it to advocate for laissez-faire economic policy, the gold standard, and labor-capital comity. The *Chronicle* (founded 1865) would become an authoritative source on the growing transportation and communication sectors, and later on banking, government, and railroad bonds and other securities. It was the most influential business publication of the late nineteenth and early twentieth centuries, much more so, for instance, than the fledging *Wall Street Journal* (founded 1889). It compiled so many business statistics that the U.S. government would rely heavily on it for its own statistical compendium, *Historical Statistics of the United States.*[10] A Yale graduate and member of the Skull and Bones secret society, Dana was never confused about his target audience: the *Chronicle*'s circulation included the nation's top industrialists and financiers and peaked at around 17,000.

The mid-nineteenth-century rise of financial markets in the United States—driven mostly by railroads—created a need for a new kind of business news: financial news. It also created a new set of problems for journalism, problems that have not been solved to this day. As Peter Thompson has pointed out, the financial world is almost entirely symbolic.[11] The key "facts" of financial news—value, money, securities—are human constructs. That is, they "exist" only because of a general agreement that they do. A police reporter covering a fire can state with some confidence that the fire broke out at, say, 4:23 in the morning at the corner of Elm and Main, but a financial reporter walking down Wall Street has a much more difficult task in making the public understand the world he covers. The symbolic nature of financial news makes it vulnerable to manipulation in ways that other types of news—politics, government, arts, sports—are not. And, of course, as the history of panics has shown, manipulation of symbols can have catastrophic consequences on the lives of people who have no direct involvement in, or perhaps even awareness of, this symbolic world.

Among other things, the symbolic nature of finance heightens the need for journalistic specialization. The ability to read financial statements, for instance, is considered a must in business journalism (though such expertise is actually rarer than one might suspect). The symbolic nature of finance—along with its obvious importance to social stability—means business news requires more accountability reporting than other areas. As we've seen, even the multiple layers of official oversight—internal auditing departments, board audit committees, external auditing firms, rating agencies, regulators—have all proven inadequate individually and in combination. The last line of defense is journalism.

Yet the need for specialization also creates a dangerous insularity. Business journalists can, and usually do, spend their entire careers in the subculture, one with its own idioms, norms, and values. Sealed off by its expertise from the rest of journalism, business journalism operates in a bubble. Much as with the Washington press corps, intellectual capture becomes an occupational hazard. Unspoken assumptions about what is and isn't a story narrow, as does the circle of acceptable sources.

Finally, the symbolic nature of finance makes for a kind of relativism not found in other journalism spheres since much of business journalism boils down to an argument about value: How much is something worth, in dollar terms, now and in the future? How much pay for a CEO is too much? Four times an average workers' pay? Or 40? Or 400? How much is a mortgage-backed security worth? How much in points and fees should a subprime borrower pay? And given the rough-and-tumble nature of markets (and life), how much blame should be assigned—and to whom—when values collapse? Is it the seller's fault for selling? Or the buyer's for buying? Or should we just throw up our hands and say both? Or maybe no one is to blame: that's just the way it goes. This last view is accepted as a matter of course in some business and financial circles, which see the "madness of crowds" as the driving phenomenon behind bubbles and panics.

In *Railroaded*, a history of the rise of transcontinental railroads, Richard White argues that it was not capital per se but credit that drove the wild railway boom that, in turn, dominated the American economic scene of the second half of the nineteenth century. The very word "corporation" was in the nineteenth century virtually synonymous with railroads, which dwarfed textile mills and other existing industries and required vast organizations and even vaster amounts of capital. This overwhelmingly took the form of debt—railroad bonds. After the American Civil War, the bond market expanded dramatically, with the total face value of railroad bonds spiking from $416 million in 1867 to $2.23 billion just seven years later.[12]

The railroad business was both the broadband and Internet of its day: a sector of seemingly limitless potential, able to attract huge amounts of capital from the sophisticated and unsophisticated for projects both worthy and dubious. It was a sector populated by as many scam artists and confidence men as visionaries and builders. As White notes, "The ultimate buyers of most railroad bonds lived at a distance from the railroad that they invested in, and they had no independent knowledge of the seller or the veracity of his claims. An investor encountered a virtual world of financial statements, prospectuses, newspaper accounts, and market values that at once stood in for and was inseparable from the actual railroads of a developing nation." And while the need for trust has always been a constant in commerce, the new virtual world was, then as now, temptingly easy to manipulate. White says: "Numbers and words that were supposed to stand in for things could be changed and still maintain their influence; news could be altered or withheld; reports could claim assets that didn't exist and deny trouble that did exist. Altering the numbers and changing the words of this virtual world could prompt actions in the parallel universe where people paid money for bonds." And unlike other long-standing financial instruments, like promissory notes, bonds were replicated thousands of times with no other prior relationship between seller and buyer. The ascendance of the railroad bond—and finance capitalism—brought with it a parallel rise in the opportunities for fraud and manipulation.[13]

Enter journalism. A single newspaper article could have a huge impact on bond issues. Reporting—or not reporting—on an investor lawsuit, for instance, could make or ruin the value of securities. Understandably, railroad moguls obsessed over news coverage. As one furious railroad baron wrote to another in 1885: "I seriously wish that some legislative measure could be passed, which could make the shooting of reporters wholly justifiable on sight, punishable by a fine not exceeding $10 dollars."[14] The Associated Press held particular power since it aggregated and sent out over the Western Union stories gleaned from local newspapers, greatly amplifying their impact. It had particular discretion over smaller news items, such as events affecting railroad bonds.

Not surprisingly, railroads actively sought, by one means or another, to bend coverage to their interests, and all too often they succeeded. The press of the day was neither necessarily disinterested in the events it reported on or particularly clean. Moguls bought some newspapers outright or cultivated publishers with free passes, printing contracts, and advertising, often at above going rates. Sometimes they recruited newspapermen as agents and lobbyists or lent them money. Press ethics of the day weren't too different from business ethics generally. White quotes an 1881 memo in which a newspaperman, who also sidelined as a railroad lobbyist, carefully lays out various newspapers' attitudes toward the mogul's railroad, based on whether they had thrown in with bears or bulls: the New York Times was hostile, the memo said, but largely because bears were using it to drive down the stock; the Indicator and the Graphic were friendly but only because they were tools of bulls; The Stockholder was waiting until its owner, Jay Gould, decided where his interests lay; The Financial Chronicle was frankly open to be bribed by either side; The World was hostile but only because its owner, Joseph Pulitzer, was in a bitter feud with the owner of the Star, William Dorsheimer, who was friendly. And so it went.[15]

This Wild West of financial information created a need for a new kind of journalism that could sort through the complexities of this symbolic world and bring some sort of integrity to the role of distributing it among market participants. While much of the journalism on early finance capitalism was beholden to the interests that controlled the sector, some early business journalists stood apart. One was Henry Varnum Poor. Poor was born into a striving Maine farm family that would produce a number of success stories, including his brother, John, who became a minor railroad magnate in the state and owned a railroad trade journal. H. V. graduated from Bowdoin in 1835 and went to work for his brother. He went on to edit *The American Railroad Journal* and important compendia, including the *History of Railroads and Canals of the United States*, an annually updated guide to railroad finances and operations. Poor fashioned himself into a knowledgeable, sober, but nonetheless fierce advocate for railroad investors, one of the earliest business writers to assume such a role. He angered railway magnates and managers by warning against overinvestment and overcapacity and tried to use information as a tool to mitigate the industry's debilitating boom and bust cycles, which, he argued, would drive away capital in the long term. In 1852, as the industry expanded wildly, he announced in an editorial that his *Journal* would adopt an "altered tone" and would become less an advocate for the railroad industry, more a analytic journal, an advocate for, if anyone, bondholders: "It is now our duty, as it is equally for the interests of railroads and the public, to point out the dangers to which we are exposed from an excessive investment in these works, to expose merely speculative schemes, which are encouraged by the ease with which money is had for anything like a railroad."[16]

Poor pioneered the art of securities analysis and set a standard for integrity and care that future Wall Street analysts would not always be able to meet. His biographer, Alfred D. Chandler Jr. (a great-grandson of Poor and noted historian), described how Poor deftly critiqued a $1 million bond offering of a southern Illinois line seeking to expand. The company claimed it had already raised another $1.4 million for the project, but Poor pointed out that part of the sum was to be raised from municipal bonds that hadn't yet been voted on and that the offering documents refused to say how much of their own money the project's backers had put in. The offering statement included no engineering report, Poor noted, and the projected cost of the line, $17,000 a mile, was far too low. For these and other reasons, Poor wrote, "the proposed loan would not only be unsafe, but its negotiation would establish a precedent to the most injurious results." Considering that he operated decades before the Securities and Exchange Commission, the value of his reporting becomes all the greater.[17]

Poor is not normally thought of as a journalism pioneer. His granular approach wasn't intended for a broader audience and was ill equipped to deal with the broader questions posed by the rising power of the railroads and their tightening grip on the chokepoints of the American economy and, for that matter, the political system. But he represented a not-small step forward in cleaning up and professionalizing the world of financial information.

Poor died a respected editor in Brookline, Massachusetts, in 1905, and the firm he started with his son, H. V. and H. W. Poor Co., had the securities-ratings business to itself until the turn of the twentieth century, when rivals, including the Standard Statistics Bureau, would arrive. The two firms merged in 1941 to form the predecessor to Standard & Poor's Ratings Services, which would, of course, became a pivotal actor in the financial crisis of the early twenty-first century, an "essential cog in the wheel of financial destruction," in the words of the Financial Crisis Inquiry Commission of 2011.[18] One reason for the firm's failure to maintain its integrity can be found in a change in the company's business model. To avoid the conflicts that plagued his newspaper competitors, Poor relied on subscriptions from investors for his income and never charged the bond issuers—precisely the fateful step taken by his successors.

Railroad bonds and the rise of finance capital inexorably pulled the attention of business news to New York City, which by the late nineteenth century was an important global financial center, driven by the New York Stock Exchange in Lower Manhattan. Around it sprang up a new sort of news organization created with the express purpose of ferrying information among the exchange, corporations, and their investors. Many newsrooms appeared; few survived. A special place in business-news history must be given to Dow Jones &

Co., if only because, unlike so many rival financial news services, it survived. But why it did so and later thrived would have little to do with its founders or the type of journalism they produced.

It started behind a soda fountain. Charles Dow, a dour man, bearded like an Old Testament prophet, had grown up on a New England farm and went to work in his youth at newspapers, including the *Providence Journal*, eventually finding his way to New York and a job at a news agency called Kiernan, one of several clustered around the Exchange. An intense and ambitious man, he worked, a colleague would recall, "noiselessly."[19] In his late twenties, Dow pitched his boss on the idea of a daily newspaper, in addition to the short wire reports the service produced. Kiernan wasn't interested but did allow Dow to hire an old friend from the Providence paper, Edward Jones. Sporting a flowing red mustache, well-cut suits, and hand-made boots, Eddie Jones was as garrulous as Dow was taciturn. Jones brought with him a reputation as a heavy drinker and some-thing of a quarreler. But he had incredible contacts among Kier-nan's customers—traders, bankers, and investors—having accu-mulated many of them in the swank bar of the Windsor Hotel on Fifth Avenue and Forty-Sixth Street, sometimes called "All-Night Wall Street."

Dow and Jones began plotting a rival service that would deliver market news to subscribers via messenger boys, a crude but quick and inexpensive medium. The two news entrepreneurs took into their confidence one Charles M. Bergstresser, who contributed capital as well a special stylus he had invented that could make more than two dozen impressions at a time. This offered a huge competitive advantage in a business where minutes, even sec-onds, counted.[20] In November 1882, Dow and Jones opened their new company in a two-story building at 15 Wall Street, behind Henry Danielson's soda-water establishment. Bergstresser's name, deemed too cumbersome, was left off. The operation was modest, a basement room with no paint on the walls or carpet on the floor and a single bare electric lightbulb. Dow had a space walled off by bare pine boards. Jones had a desk at the back of the room. Bergstresser, who walked Wall and Broad Streets looking for news, didn't have a desk.

The New York business-news market, which Dow Jones was part of was highly competitive during this period. Adolph S. Ochs, who had bought the *New York Times* in 1896, quickly expanded the quality and scope of the paper's business coverage as a means of reaching a new, affluent audience.[21] He demanded consistent coverage of financial market reports and real-estate transactions, among other activities that publications previously had considered too boring to warrant an article. According to one of the histories of the paper, Ochs's managing editor, Henry Loewenthal, "injected new life into his Wall Street reporters, goading them to greater output."[22] Carr Van Anda, who took over as managing editor in 1904, also spearheaded finance coverage during his tenure. "While general news reporters at the *Times* and other newspapers assumed that Ochs' drive for business news would make the *Times* duller and less appealing, to their astonishment, Ochs was able to bring in thousands of 'new, substantial readers and a brisk flow of advertising.' "[23]

Of course, business news was in no way limited to New York, and financial-news organs sprang up around the world to chronicle fast-growing stock and bond markets. Paul Julius Reuter, who had won some fame as a distributor of radical pamphlets in Berlin during the Revolution of 1848, developed a prototype news service in 1849 using electric telegraphy and carrier pigeons. In 1851, he installed his eponymous news service at the London Royal Exchange, serving banks, brokerage houses, and other businesses. The *Financial Times*, known first as the *London Financial Guide*, was launched in 1888, styling itself the "Friend to the Honest Financier and Respectable Broker."[24] It began to publish on salmon-pink paper a few years later to distinguish itself from a rival, which it later bought.

Then, as now, corporate news was the lifeblood of the financial-news business, and then, as now, a premium was placed on scoops about earnings, dividends, mergers, and other market-moving events. Competition for information was fierce. Reporters waited outside, or short-posted, corporate board meetings for hours and, if no phone was available, would run to a window to signal a colleague in the street through some prearranged system. One wave of a handkerchief would mean, "no extra dividend"; four might mean, "merger off."[25] Getting beaten by fifteen seconds was considered a sound defeat; a full minute was a firing offense.

Lloyd Wendt describes a scene at the fledgling Dow Jones in which a young man arrived at the modest offices for his first day as a copy boy. A relaxed and affable Jones is explaining the job until a messenger bursts in. "Earnings! Earnings!" he shouts. Jones's feet hit the floor with a crash. Berating the cowering boy, who was slow, Jones believes, Jones snatches his notes and, splitting the work up with another writer, begins to scribble furiously using Bergstresser's special stylus on a pad of twenty-four (later thirty-five) thin sheets. In a matter of minutes, a hundred copies are fired off and the messenger boys dispatched. Deadline passed, Jones put his feet back on the desk and continues to explain the ropes.[26]

Dow Jones's early work hammered raw corporate information into short bursts of prose. For the general public, it might as well have been written in code. This series of items is from September 5, 1883:

> 12.05 P.M. "Hatch & Foote have announced their suspension."
> 12.35 P.M. "The rumor that Peters, Wetmore & Schenck were in any trouble are [*sic*] absolutely false."
> 1:05 P.M. "The House of Cook endangered by Northern Pacific."
> 2:05 P.M. "Hatch & Foote have announced their reinstatement."[27]

Dow Jones was the first Wall Street news service to acquire a printing press and the first to cover London via an arrangement with the *Times* of London to telegraph market summaries. Dow Jones also was the first to cover Boston via a similar arrangement with the Boston News Service, owned by Clarence W. Barron. In 1884 Dow created the first list of stocks and compiled their prices into an "average" that would become the iconic Dow Jones Industrial Average.

Bergstresser, the "third tenor," as it were, of the early Dow Jones, convinced his partners to invest in the printing press and collect the bulletins they produced into a daily summary, to be called the *Wall Street Journal*. The first issue appeared on July 8, 1889. The press allowed the paper to be distributed by three-fifteen each afternoon, fifteen minutes after the close of the NYSE and about an hour before competitors. In 1897, Bergstresser, again, introduced a broad-tape ticker that allowed the transmission of text as well as numbers and symbols, an improvement over the prevailing version. By the 1899, the company was thriving. Customers were paying a hefty thirty dollars a month for the ticker; the newspaper's circulation hit 11,000; and ads crowded the front page.[28]

The early Dow Jones produced valuable journalism, albeit within the narrow context of its self-perceived mission. In 1884, for instance, the wire helped to calm a market panic following the failure of a New York Stock Exchange member firm, Grant and Ward. The fact that the firm's partners included Ulysses S. Grant, the former president, made big news of what was an otherwise inconsequential failure, but Dow Jones issued a series of reassuring remarks from major financial figures, including the railroad mogul Jay Gould, who said, "I think we have seen the worst of it [the panic]."[29]

On another panicky day, Dow Jones tried to calm markets by issuing a steady stream of reassuring statements from bank owners. At 11 a.m.: "The president of the Fourth National Bank says that the street talk about his bank is nonsense"; at 11:50 a.m. the Gallatin National Bank has $1,100,000 in cash in its vaults, the best answer to "any rumors"; at 1:45 p.m.:

> Donnel, Lawson & Simpson failed. The Phoenix Bank has $135 for every $100 liabilities. The largest depositors know this and are not disturbing deposits.[30]

The value—and limitations—of the early *Wall Street Journal* style of reporting were on display during the famous Panic of 1901, involving J. P. Morgan and the Northern Securities Company. Dow Jones reporters smoked out the reason for a gyrating stock price, reported on backroom maneuvering and stock manipulations, and challenged official accounts of what had happened. Then, in columns and editorials, the *Journal* excused the manipulation, displaying the dependence of access reporting on its powerful sources and the intellectual capture that did, and still does, occur.

In the spring of 1901, Morgan and a railroad partner, James J. Hill, began quietly buying control of the Chicago, Burlington, & Quincy, known as Burlington, through the parent of the Northern Pacific railroad. The goal was to control Burlington's vital Chicago line and to create a coveted cross-country link. Meanwhile, though, rival moguls Jacob Schiff and E. H. Harriman, shut out of the deal, began secretly buying shares of Northern Pacific, hoping to out-flank Morgan and Hill and gain control of the Chicago line. Complicating matters for the Morgan-Hill alliance, Morgan was touring with a mistress in France and couldn't be reached. The *Journal* sniffed out the reason behind a sudden jump in Northern Pacific shares and ran a story under the headline: "Combinations Make Combinations": "Headway has been made in the project toward an alliance between Northern Pacific and Burlington. Should this alliance be consummated . . . there would be nominally a Hill-Morgan transcontinental route."[31]

In a May 6 editorial, the *Journal* predicted (incorrectly) that the maneuvering for control would lead to a grand alliance. But it was generally right about the implications of various schemes. As it turned out, the battle turned into an all-out takeover fight that triggered a panic. When Morgan was finally reached in France, he ordered his brokers onto the floor of the New York Stock Exchange in a huge buying push that caused chaos in the market. Short sellers found they couldn't buy enough shares to replace the ones they had borrowed, even at $1,000 each, wreaking havoc on *their* lenders. Wall Street firms called in other stock-market loans, and the market headed for a crash. For a while, a good part of Wall Street was technically insolvent. Thousands of small shareholders were wiped out. The two sides combined to form Northern Securities.

The *Journal*, which had explained the maneuvers in detail, had brought transparency to an otherwise bewildering market panic. Yet, ultimately, it went out of its way to excuse the participants. In a column on May 13, the *Journal* wrote: "The Northern Pacific corner was unintentional and was regretted by those who were the most influential in bringing it about."[32]

The *Journal*'s formula, a pastiche of market-moving news, government and corporate information, and financial commentary, attracted a small but well-heeled readership. Financial success, though, sparked internal dissension. Jones, in charge of ad sales, was constantly at odds with Dow, who ran the editorial operation, over how much page-one space to devote to ads. Jones also clashed with Bergstresser, who wanted to invest in new equipment. Dow also disapproved of Jones's gambling, drinking, and coziness with his millionaire sources. According to an account in Francis Dealy's *The Power and the Money*, one of several histories of the *Journal* and its parent, Dow later complained that Jones "just wanted short term gains, and to hell with the reader." Dow added: "Jones, who was volatile to begin with, became irrational when Bergstresser suggested we buy another printing press. And when I suggested we should stop coddling advertisers, Jones stormed out of the office."[33] Bergstresser eventually moved to Paris and became an absentee owner.

Ultimately, Jones sold his interests and took at job at a brokerage house (and, as it happens, helped Morgan during the Northern Securities buying push). In 1902, in failing health, Dow sold the company to Clarence Barron of Boston, who used money inherited by his wife, Jessie Waldron, a widow who ran a boarding house where Barron lived.[34] Waldron's descendants would remain principal owners of the company for the next 105 years. Dow died months after the sale, his death marked by a black-bordered tribute in the paper authored by his former partner, Jones.

Charles Dow was a journalist of integrity and a respected financial analyst. Edward Jones got plenty of scoops and helped put the fledgling news organization on the map. It is doubtful, though, that either they or their company would be remembered today but for decisions made long after their deaths, decisions that greatly expanded the idea of business news and its mission and would, ultimately, propel the financial news organization to greatness.

Dow Jones was only one of many competitors in financial news during the early 1900s, but it is representative of the genre. It was a form of elite communications, targeted to a narrow segment of society, the 1 percent, in today's parlance. Its circulation hovered around 10,000. It had no aspirations for a mass audience and no particular ambivalence about its utilitarian function. It was less as an outsider than as intermediary among market participants. "Speed, accuracy, and efficiency were wanted, not imagination, literacy, or a grasp of economic subtleties," says one of its historians.[35] Its stock-in-trade was gaining access to insiders and then being first to tell the market what they were doing. The company was engaged in a constant balancing act between the interests of its readers and those of its powerful sources, who, it must be said, were often also its advertisers. Often in the early days, as we have seen, it tilted toward protecting and excusing the powerful.

It should be said that the *Wall Street Journal* in its early years was not reflexively pro-capital or pro-mogul in its coverage or its editorials. When John Mitchell, president of the United Mine Workers, led 140,000 miners on strike against the anthracite industry in 1902, the *Journal*'s editorials showed understanding for the strikers' position and called for arbitration. Indeed, the editorials, by Charles Dow, were so balanced that he was paid a visit one afternoon by three union officials who asked him to have the paper "undertake the preparation of statistics for the side of the miners." Thomas Woodlock, an influential early editor who was there recalled. "Naturally, this could not be done."[36]

Woodlock wrote an editorial strongly supporting Theodore Roosevelt, after the 1904 election, in his campaign against the trusts: "It was manly steadfastness of principle that yesterday won for Theodore Roosevelt such popular endorsement as was never before given by a free people. Against such a frank, fearless, honest personality, capital and combination [the railroad combination] beat as vainly as break the waves on the rock-ribbed shores."[37] The paper was by no means always hostile, for that matter, to Ida Tarbell's series on Standard Oil. Indeed, it treated Tarbell's revelations as news events in their own right and routinely ran lengthy excerpts in its own pages. On November 28, 1903, it ran part of Tarbell's "Cutting to Kill" article from that summer under the headline: "System of Organized Espionage/Secrecy of the Standard Oil Company." On March 4, 1904, it wrote a defense of Tarbell in a comment under the headline: "Will Not Let Him Alone": "We have no sympathy with the indiscriminant denunciations of Mr. Rockefeller. But we do think there is good reason why the world refuses to let him alone. We believe absolutely in the principle of publicity to be applied to such corporations as the Standard Oil."[38]

In fact, it can be hard to tell the difference between the views in some *Journal* editorials of these early days and the positions of leading Progressives. In an October 3, 1907, editorial, it inveighed against the growing power of trusts: "The trusts and combinations have grown so colossal as to overshadow the power of single states. Many of them became practically the masters of states, and the people found themselves virtually powerless in their hands. There was only one way possible to deal with this condition and that was by involving the power of the Federal Government." And a few days later, the paper warned Wall Street to mend its ways: "The Wall Street man looks out upon the country and sees many suspicious, indignant and angry faces turned toward him. Each successive disclosure of financial wrongdoing increases the popular lack of confidence in Wall Street methods and Wall Street securities."[39]

But editorial positions are one thing; reporting is another. And sometimes early business reporting failed woefully, even on its own terms, channeling the interests of moguls, papering over crises, and leaving investors and depositors in the dark. An unpublished paper by Bonnie Kavoussi makes a convincing case that *Journal* coverage of the catastrophic Panic of 1907, for instance, was timid and lackluster, certainly in comparison with the rival *Times*.[40]

The panic began after a failed attempt to buy up and control the shares of a giant company wiped out two prominent financiers. Word of the failed scheme triggered a run on the Knickerbocker Trust Company, whose president had been involved with the failed copper speculators. A consortium of banks, known as the New York Clearing House, attempted to contain the panic, forcing out the Knickerbocker's president on October 21. But when one of the clearinghouse's main members refused to clear the Knickerbocker's checks later that day, the panic began in earnest. The *Wall Street Journal*, however, ran a story that failed to mention either the resignation or the clearing bank's refusal to extend credit. The story said: "The New York Clearing House has the banking situation so well in hand that no doubt is entertained of its ability to all that is necessary."[41] The same day that a headline in the *Journal* declared, "Actions of the Bankers Clearing House Restores Confidence," crowds of depositors, who clearly got their news elsewhere, flocked outside the Knickerbocker's midtown headquarters. After doling out $8 million in deposits, the bank shut its doors two and a half hours before end of business hours. The panic was on.[42]

Meanwhile, Ochs's *New York Times*, with a revived business desk, went deeper into the causes of the panic. The paper named names and attempted to cover the human angle of the crisis, including a sympathetic portrayal of Charles T. Barney, the Knickerbocker's disgraced president, who, a month after panic, shot himself in the abdomen with a .32-caliber revolver. By contrast, the *Journal* shied away from naming actors in the entirely man-made panic, which tipped the country into a recession and was deemed so calamitous that it led to the creation of the Federal Reserve System in 1913. "If one read only the *Journal*, it may appear as though the panic simply happened—entering the economy like a thunderstorm that no one could predict or control. By not assigning agency or describing personality, the *Journal* did not need to blame any particular bank or individuals for the downturn," Kavoussi says.[43]

When push came to shove, the *Journal* abandoned its high-minded editorial positions and ran interference for Morgan. But even the superior business coverage of the *Times* didn't explain the larger issues behind the panic: the concentration of capital and the means by which a few individuals had, over many years, come to hold such sway over the economy and, with it, the political system. Its coverage could only react to events, not explore their roots. So tethered to the cascading series of crises, "business news" didn't perceive it in its mission to step back from the frenzy to understand their causes.

What's more, early coverage was overwhelmingly reliant on information gleaned from institutions and other authorities. Gaining access to insiders, especially to J. P. Morgan, who was understood to be Wall Street's lender of last report, was paramount. At the height of the 1907 crisis, a *Times* reporter stood outside Morgan's apartment until two a.m. (the *Journal* wasn't there) to report on the meeting where Morgan and other financiers decided the Knickerbocker's fate and that of Barney, its chief. As it happens, the *Times* coverage was decidedly favorable to Morgan. Without attribution, it provided a rationale for his decision not to save the Knickerbocker ("Mr. Morgan did not care to assume the responsibilities of previous poor management") and reminded readers that Morgan's financial support during a previous panic, in 1893, "was perhaps the most potent factor in supplying the measure of confidence which averted widespread disaster." In general, Kavoussi finds, the *Times* depicted Morgan, "as both a savvy businessman and a force for the common good."[44]

Even if the *Times* had managed to maintain more critical distance (Ochs's financial and social ties to Wall Street would have made that difficult), it was less the substance of the coverage than the journalistic gestalt—incremental, reactive, dependent on insiders, tethered to the pronouncements of institutions—that relegated the early business press to a passive role in the face of the momentous events sweeping the economy and financial system. The work of describing the roots of the systemic changes and, yes, identifying malefactors would, for a few more decades, be left to others, such as Ida Tarbell and the muckrakers.

Frenzied Finance, a (not particularly temperate) account of the formation of the Amalgamated Copper Company by the businessman and author Thomas W. Lawson (also a problematic figure), sought to explain the "System" that funneled wealth from common people to financiers. "Through its workings during the last twenty years there has grown up in this country a set of colossal corporations in which unmeasured success and continued immunity from punishment have bred an insolent disregard of law, of common morality, and of public and private right, together with a grim determination to hold on to, at all hazards, the great possessions they have gulped or captured."[45] But where muckraking was ambitious, business reporting during the same time was quotidian. Where muckraking set agendas, business reporting was reactive. Where muckraking explored the roots of systemic change, business reporting accepted such change as a given or sought to explain it after the fact. Where business writing provided information for investment decisions, muckraking informed public policy and political life. Where business writing was for elites, muckraking was for everyone.

Clarence Barron has been called the father of modern financial journalism. If so, he is a problematic foundational figure. While Barron raised the intellectual caliber of financial journalism, his greatest journalistic scoops came from jotting down the words of the rich and powerful rather than examining how they had gotten so powerful in the first place. The son of a Boston teamster and his wife, Barron was educated at the city's elite primary schools. He worked at a Boston paper, the *Evening Transcript*, established himself as an expert on the city's finances, and started the paper's financial section. He started the Boston News Bureau in 1887, based on the idea that business people needed news updated several times a day.[46] Like Dow Jones, launched five years earlier, the bureau delivered news via handbills carried by messenger boys. He organized a cooperation agreement with Dow Jones in New York then, as noted, bought out Charles Dow and his partners in 1902 after marrying a wealthy widow, Jessie Waldron, who ran the rooming house where he lived.

Barron is certainly one of the more flamboyant figures in business-news history. A big, round man, he weighed well over 300 pounds, sported a full white beard, and favored commodore outfits complete with brass buttons and sailor cap—"jolly Kris Kringle in the flesh," as an admiring biographical sketch put it.[47] Despite his bulk, he was constantly on the move, traveling to interview and visit with dignitaries, barking out commands, dreaming up story assignments. He dashed off as many as a hundred memos a day to the two or three male secretaries who trailed his every step, even following him to the toilet and the bathtub (which he required to be drawn at precisely 104 degrees). He dictated notes while bobbing in the ocean, his secretaries trailing him in small boats. On train trips, one of the secretaries was designated to carry a hatbox containing a bedpan that had been specially made to accommodate Barron's tremendous girth. Once, in Europe, he urgently called, "Bring the hatbox. Bring the hatbox!"

When a flustered secretary presented a box, it contained a silk top hat. "Wrong hatbox! Wrong hatbox!" Barron shouted.[48]

Barron was, it is fair to say, a tyrannical boss who kept his mostly young staff of reporters on a short leash. One didn't work "with" Barron, an employee would write, only "for" him. Barron's admiring biographers put it this way: "It was part of his policy, as a boss, to 'ride' his men until they were broken to suit him."[49] During the first ten years after the sale, the *Wall Street Journal* was effectively run by a series of editors appointed by his wife. But when Barron took full control of the paper upon being named president in 1912, he made his presence felt by barging into the newsroom in New York and launching into a tirade, recounted by a contemporary biographer: "He strode into the room, kicking over wastebaskets and whacking his cane on a desk to attract attention. He berated them all for their sins and mistakes and told them he intended to straighten them out, at once. They would obey him or they could get out."[50]

Such scenes would be repeated often. The top-down editorial style of the early Dow Jones was a stark contrast with the collaborative if quirky style of *McClure's*. McClure assembled a staff of professional stars and let them run the magazine while he took his cures in Europe; Barron's avowed style was to "break a colt so that he could be trained." A young, inexperienced staff can be controlled and is less of a threat to elites than journalists who are powerful in their own right, as Barron and generations of news managers after him, up to and including Rupert Murdoch, have recognized.

Barron, who ran Dow Jones from 1912 to his death in 1928, was, it must be said, a tireless reporter and gifted writer in his own right. The paper had one star, and he was it. He had a knack for laying out complex subjects in simple language and emphasized those qualities to his staff. In a memo, he put forth "seven points to better reporting and writing," containing strictures that most news organizations follow to this day: "Be intrepid," "no ego," "keep it simple," "be lucid," "Get it right," "tell a story," and "the lead is everything" are among them.[51] Despite his high social and professional standing, he never stopped referring to himself as a reporter. Barron is credited with raising the intellectual level of financial journalism, writing some of the early *Journal*'s most highly regarded stories. When the Federal Reserve Act was passed in 1913, he wrote a lucid and fair-minded series on the reasons for its passage and how it would work. A series on the Mexican oil business was a far-sighted look at the importance of stable oil supplies for the American economy. In 1918, he wrote series on "War Finance" and "Peace Finance" that laid out American prospects for the postwar economy.[52] He wrote frequent columns on Wall Street and inveighed against the dangers of inflation. In 1921, he started *Barron's*, the investment guide published to this day. Unusual among business news editors, Barron pushed his staff to scrutinize financial records, now routine in financial journalism (less today perhaps than it should be). He gave testimony to Massachusetts regulators about a slush fund operated by the New Haven Railroad he investigated. Barron is also credited with exposing Charles Ponzi, the notorious swindler, after the *Boston Post* sought his expertise in 1920.[53]

But it's a mistake to idealize Barron or his legacy. Barron saw his paper not as a reporter about capitalism but as a defender of both the capitalist system and individual capitalists and financiers. As the public grew warier of an unbridled financial system after the 1907 Panic, Barron in columns and editorials would steer the paper toward more conventionally conservative views than those of the editors who had immediately succeeded Dow and argue against increased financial regulation ("Rather than continue the system exactly as is, there are those who would have the government intervene and control Wall Street, as if it were more illegal gamble than legitimate risk," he would write).[54]

Barron's trademark, his métier, was access reporting. He used personal connections and flattering prose to win the trust of the powerful. The stenographic skills that he had learned as a child came in handy to accurately jot down their words. Presidents Roosevelt, Taft, and Wilson all counted him among their trusted advisers.[55] His notes would fill two volumes, *They Told Barron* and *More They Told Barron*, posthumous collections of interviews with the likes of Kaiser Wilhelm and Nicholas II.

Barron enjoyed ready access to the likes of Charles Mitchell, the head of National City, Citigroup's predecessor, later notorious for his role in the Great Crash, and other banking titans. "Breakfast at 8 a.m. with Albert H. Wiggin, president of Chase Bank, in my hotel parlor," is how one of his typical notes starts, or, "Motored to the Gulf Stream Golf Club and spent an hour with [another prominent banker]." "Dropped in for a twenty-minute chat with [John P.] Morgan [son of the iconic financier], who said: 'Politicians don't want to help business in this country, and the people don't want them to help business. . . . Who did more than Theodore Roosevelt to smash business?'" is a not untypical item, dated December 6, 1917, that goes on in a similar vein for several paragraphs. As Barron's biographers observed, "Nobody understood more clearly than Mr. Barron the vital service which banks and bankers render to modern civilization. He praised them whenever he could do so."[56]

Barron's wide circle of powerful friends eventually led him to become entangled in the Teapot Dome Scandal, the Watergate of its day. Barron led what amounted to a crusade in the pages of the *Journal* on behalf of the oilman Edward Doheny, who in 1924 was revealed to have lent $100,000 (about $1 million in 2011 dollars) to Interior Secretary Albert B. Fall while negotiating for rights to U.S. oil leases. Both men were subsequently indicted on bribery charges. Barron, according to Wendt, conducted some twenty-two interviews with Doheny and published several stories attempting to prove him innocent. Until his death, Barron insisted that Doheny was a public benefactor for bidding on leases no one else wanted. In a 1929 criminal trial, Doheny was in fact acquitted of giving a bribe to Fall. In a separate trial the same year, however, Fall was convicted of taking one from Doheny.[57]

Barron's easy tolerance of corruption among his friends extended to his own newsroom. While he formally forbade reporters from writing about stocks they owned, his famously obedient reporters honored the rule mostly in the breech. Barron himself was notorious for promoting companies of stocks he owned. While salaries were low—a copy clerk would earn fifty dollars a week—and the work unglamorous, reporters' jobs were nonetheless highly sought, for all the wrong reasons:

What drew most young men to the *Journal* was an open secret having nothing whatever to do with the fabled fun of the news business or the romance of the rolling presses. Newspaper-men and radio newscasters were privy to inside information that could practically guarantee profits in the stock market. In addition, they were paid—sometimes handsomely—to work in conjunction with speculative rings and stock syndicates. Easy money was all around.[58]

The consequences of this casual journalistic culture would spill into public view a few years later during special Senate Banking Committee hearings into the cause of the Great Crash. While the Pecora Commission, called so after its chief counsel, was looking chiefly into conduct of New York Stock Exchange member firms, Dow Jones came into the spotlight during a surprise appearance by Fiorello H. LaGuardia, then a congressman from New York. LaGuardia hauled a trunk of documents into the hearing room that showed that financial journalists had received under-the-table payoffs from stock promoters for pushing rigged stocks. LaGuardia produced $284,000 in checks made out to "cash" drawn on the account of a stock promoter with ties to many financial reporters. One Dow Jones reporter, a certain Gomber, had cashed $600 in checks made out to him from the promoter. The *Journal* reported on LaGuardia's testimony in the next day's paper with a single story on page eleven. Gomber quietly resigned.[59]

It should not be surprising to learn that Barron's *Journal* did not distinguish itself with its Wall Street reporting during a period rife with hype, stock-manipulation schemes, and, investigators would later learn, systematic fraud. While the *Journal* did issue periodic warnings against excessive speculation and expressed concern over high stock valuations, editorially, the paper for the most part defended Wall Street against attempts to rein it in. An area of particular concern in Congress and at the Fed was the margin loans that brokerage houses made to retail stock buyers, which by 1928 were running around an extremely high 12 percent. These loans were then packaged and sold to investment trusts, similar to today's mutual funds. The market looked, as one historian would put it, like "nothing so much as a dog chasing its own tail."[60] The *Journal* repeatedly pooh-poohed congressional attempts to restrict brokerage loans, as in this March 1928 editorial:

> People who know nothing about credit, surplus bank funds, collateral, call loans or anything else germane to the question profess to be terrified when the Stock Exchange Loans attain of $4 billion or more. They talk of a "pyramid" of speculation, forgetting that the pyramid is the most stable form of all building with the broadest possible base. . . . Nothing can be so easily manipulated in this country as the speculative position in stocks.[61]

While the *Journal* editorialists' grasp of geometry was sound, their understanding of the financial landscape was far less so, and the paper would publish similar howlers right up to the Great Crash. When it finally came, *Journal* reporters—some fully invested—would be caught as flatfooted as their paper, not to mention the rest of the country. One reporter, who had somehow acquired a horse farm in Connecticut while working at the *Journal*, wandered the offices moaning that he no longer had even lunch money. "For God's sake," someone finally snapped, "from now on you'll have to learn to live off your salary like the rest of us." "Salary!?" the reporter is said to have replied. "Oh my God, I forgot about that!" and he bounded off to payroll for checks he hadn't bothered to collect.[62]

But in the end, Barron's *Wall Street Journal* was mostly constrained by its own conception of its mission. It was, in Scharff's words, "a stock and bond sheet." At best, it was a utilitarian tool that functioned an intermediary among market participants, an information broker. The paper explicitly framed its role as serving investors or, at best, as Barron put it in a 1923 memo, "savers":

> In the *Wall Street Journal*, I have sought to create a service. I have striven for a creation so founded in principles that it can live as a service—live so long as it abides in the laws of that service.
>
> I believe there is no higher service from government, from society, from journalism than the protection and upbuilding of

> the savings of the people. . . . *The Wall Street Journal* must stand
> for the best that is in Wall Street and reflect that which is best in
> United States finance.

The paper's motto at the time was a not particularly ringing "The truth in its proper use."[63]

This narrowly defined role for financial media would restrict its popular appeal. Even at its peak during the Roaring Twenties, the paper's circulation hovered around 50,000, a tenth that of *McClure's* at its peak. More than that, its self-definition restricted its journalistic vision: the paper that was about the market, for the market, and, indeed, of the market did not have the inclination or the ambition to step back from the daily news crush, look at problems systemically, and, if need be, expose powerful malefactors while they were still powerful. The irony of the early financial press is that the journalism closest to and with the most knowledge of growing problems in the financial system was unable or unwilling to bring its skill and credibility to bear on looming dangers. As the financial system hurtled toward its greatest panic, in 1929, the *Journal* and the rest of the financial press would be as surprised as the rest of the country.

As it happens, history records a single meeting between Barron, the leading financial journalist of his day, and Ida Tarbell, the great muckraker, long after the publication of her Standard Oil series. What they discussed at this lunch of journalism titans is not known, but Tarbell, in this account from Wendt, was evidently not impressed. Afterward, she is said to have remarked to friends: "That man is a glutton—for food and money!"[64]

CHAPTER 3

Kilgore's Revolution at the

Wall Street Journal

Rise of the Great Story

I n 1932, the *Wall Street Journal* ran a story, datelined San Francisco, that began like this:

> Five years ago, Oliver Twining rarely was early for work. As the chairman on Pacific Bank & Trust Company, Mr. Twining regularly strolled into his office twenty minutes late. "Rank has its privileges," he would explain.
>
> Today, however, Oliver Twining is rarely late for work.
>
> Now self-employed, he operates 14 hours a per day on the corner of Church and California Streets, shouting "Apples for sale!"
>
> Oliver Twining is just one of many former bankers trying to piece their lives back together in the wake of 9,000 bank failures in the last three years.[1]

The lede is catchy today; in 1932, it was startling.

The author was a twenty-three-year-old reporter named Leslie Bernard Kilgore, a name obscure enough even within financial-journalism circles and virtually unknown outside them. Over a career that flowered in the postwar boom, Kilgore would become one of the most significant journalism figures since the muckrakers, and his belief in readers' hunger for deeper knowledge about complex subjects would transform business journalism and American newspapering more broadly.

Around midcentury, business news transformed itself from its narrow messaging function into a profession capable of explaining complex problems to a mass audience. The main method was the Great Story, the long-form narrative that delved deeply into subjects of journalism's choosing. One editor in particular—the great Kilgore—was responsible for creating what was essentially a story factory, laying the infrastructure of the production of Great Stories for a mass readership. The long-form narrative is an essential building block for accountability reporting, the subject of chapter 4.

To understand the problem before Kilgore came along, let's look at a not-untypical story, chosen more or less at random, from the front page of the *Journal* in 1934. It begins: "Atchison, Topeka and Santa Fe Railway had net income in 1933 after all charges approximating, 3,632,819, or $2.93 a share, on the 1,241,727 preferred shares outstanding, S. T. Bledsoe, President, stated. In 1932, the company had net income of 7,545,007, equal after paying preferred dividends to 55 cents a share to 2427060 shares of common stock."[2] Random facts issued by an institution without context—shades of CNBC. The four-paragraph story doesn't mention why the railroad's earnings were off so much year-over-year, though the Great Depression might have had something to do with it. In fact, without news generated by the Roosevelt administration (e.g., "To Concentrate on Debt Erasure Administration Plans Center First on Farm and Home Mortgages," January 8, 1934), a reader leafing through the front pages of the Depression-era *Journal* would have little idea the country was going through particularly hard times at all. But this was "business news" then: meat-and-potatoes coverage, unambitious, unimaginative, and, in a profound way, blinkered. It purported to cover business, finance, and the economy, but its own strictures would not allow it even to approach the things that mattered—great economic shifts and the causes and effects of the Depression. By abstaining from original reporting—or news that doesn't come from a corporate or institutional source—business-news organizations, for all their apparent activity, rendered themselves deeply passive, powerless to affect the public agenda. Instead, business journalism was, like the rest of the country, carried along with the flow of events. Worse, as Noam Chomsky and others might have it, by confining itself to role of intramarket news service, the business press could fairly be accused of amplifying and reinforcing elite narratives, valid or not. Still worse, voices that might be able to provide helpful information to the public, policy makers, and even to markets are excluded.

It's not that the journalism was "wrong," only that its self-imposed limitations were so severe as to produce an understanding of business and the economy that had little to say to all but a narrow band of people on matters of interest in only the short and medium term. By defining its purview as the most recent announcements of business and financial institutions and the government, business news tied its own hands, rendering impossible the idea of looking independently at the economic movers of its world. Had financial papers, for instance, looked more closely at the margin-lending practices of brokerages houses and the new retail "wire houses" in the late 1920s, the public—and investors, too, for that matter—could have been prepared for the Great Crash to come. Instead, poorly informed Americans stampeded into stocks in unprecedented numbers, roughly doubling in number to about 10 million investors, or about 8 percent of the population, between 1927 and 1930, the worst possible time.[3] As recently as 1917, only 0.5 percent of Americans had owned stocks.[4] In this way, even the *Journal*'s wildly bullish editorialists could be seen as victims of this information vacuum.

But change was coming, and the first great catalyst would not be the *Wall Street Journal*, which, during the 1930s, despite the work of its new and only star, was still stuck in the legacy of Clarence Barron's access journalism. It would take another great twentieth-century journalism figure to lead the way.

In September 1932, an article appeared under the headline, "No One Has Starved," an ironic reference to a callous remark made by President Herbert Hoover earlier that year. The piece was a well-reported, sharply written condemnation of the nation's haphazard approach to mass unemployment relief, which at the time relied on an inadequate and inefficient patchwork of private charities that left legions of people homeless. Overwhelmed local governments responded by essentially deporting vagrants from their borders, which resulted in a vast, wasteful shuffling of the poor from town to town, state to state. As the story explains:

> Dull mornings last winter the sheriff of Miami, Florida, used to fill a truck with homeless men and run up to the county line. Where the sheriff of Fort Lauderdale used to meet them and load them into a second truck and run them up to *his* county line. Where the sheriff of Brevard County would *not* meet them. And whence they would trickle back down the roads to Miami. To repeat.

The piece says a recently passed federal relief law, while inadequate to the overall problem, nonetheless marked a turning point:

> The difference will be made by the Emergency Relief Act. Or rather by the fact that the Emergency Relief Act exists. For the Act itself with its $300,000,000 for direct relief loans to the states is neither an adequate nor an impressive piece of legislation. But the passage of the Act, like the green branch with which young Mr. Ringling used to lay across the forks of the Wisconsin roads for his circus to follow, marks a turning in American political history. And the beginning of a new chapter in American unemployment relief.[5]

The author was Archibald MacLeish, who in the following year would win the first of three Pulitzer Prizes for poetry. The publication was a fledgling business magazine called *Fortune*.

When Henry R. Luce was planning a new magazine about the business world to extend his growing *Time* empire in the late 1920s, he was looking for a new journalistic approach, one that avoided both what he believed was the raucous muckraking of the early part of the century and the puffery and the boosterism of Roaring Twenties business news. A leading business publication of the era was *World's Work*, which had been chronicling American business since the 1870s and which Luce biographer Alan Brinkley sees as a precursor and possible model for *Fortune*.[6] The monthly, which had a circulation of about 100,000 in the 1920s, conducted broad-ranging inquiries into in the social, political, and cultural contexts of business. A single issue in 1929, for instance, includes pieces on the economics of managing the White House; the arcane field of book collecting; and the character of the Harvard business school. It sought talented journalists to make stories broadly interesting to a wide readership. At the same time, though, *World's Work* was an unapologetic cheerleader for business. It expressed unvarnished admiration for "captains of finance and industry" and trumpeted its optimism about the "Greatest of Bull Markets." It was blindsided by the Great Crash, and by 1932 it had been merged into another magazine, which itself later folded.

Fortune was to be different. Its mission was to capture the sheer scale, grandeur, and vitality of business, which Luce called "the dominant institution of modern civilization." "Where is the publication," he asked in a business proposal for his new magazine, "that even attempts to portray Business in all its heroic present day proportions, or that succeeds in conveying a sustained sense of the challenging personalities, significant trends, and high excitements [*sic*] of this vastly stirring Civilization of Business?" The real story, he insisted, wasn't just about the day-to-day doings of industry and financial markets but the deeper, hidden workings of economic life, "the daily activity of millions of men throughout the country and throughout the world." His new magazine, he said, would be the "log-book, the critical history of Twentieth Century industrial civilization."[7]

Luce set as the magazine's mission nothing less than to "assist in the successful development of American Business Enterprise at home and abroad." In another departure, he also insisted his new magazine cover companies at arms-length. "Not always flattering will be these descriptions," the prospectus said (in what Brinkley calls high *Time* style), for *Fortune* is "neither a puffer nor a booster. Both of ships and of men, *Fortune* will attempt to write critically, appraisingly . . . with unbridled curiosity." Luce insisted his magazine would, physically, be the "most beautiful in the world," bound in cardboard and printed on mat paper so heavy that only one printer in the country, Osborne Chromatic Gravure Company, in New Jersey, could handle it.[8] He commissioned the artist Thomas Maitland Cleland to revive an eighteenth-century typeface, Baskerville, for the text, along with other eminent artists and designers—Diego Rivera, Fernand Leger—to create elegant covers that, for aesthetic reasons, would eschew headlines. Stories were to be accompanied by elaborate illustrations and even oil paintings. MacLeish's "No One Has Starved" was illustrated by a charcoal-and-pastel tableau of shantytowns by Reginald Marsh. That issue's cover, a gray etching and engraving of a mass of men called *Breadline*, was later acquired by New York's Whitney Museum of American Art. Luce spared no expense. For a feature later in the 1930s, headlined simply "Power," Luce's editors commissioned six original oil paintings by realist painter Charles Sheeler, who had been sent around the country to depict the spectacle of dams and power plants. Photographers for *Fortune* would include Margaret Bourke-White, who took magisterial photos of industrial landscapes and incisive portraits of business elites, for whom Luce's magazine coined the term "tycoons."

Perhaps the most remarkable thing about *Fortune*'s early days was its stable of journalists: an eclectic group of poets, authors, screenwriters, and novelists, including MacLeish, James Agee, Dwight Macdonald, Wilder Hobson (a jazz expert), James Gould Cozzens, Robert Cantwell, and others. When asked why, Luce pronounced that it was easier to turn poets into business writers than to teach accountants to write.[9]

While his relationship with his writers was famously contentious, even Luce's detractors on the staff would allow, if grudgingly, that he was a fierce advocate for storytelling and had a knack for it. In a collection of reminiscences of former *Fortune* writers, one writer recalls how his editor had ordered big cuts in a lengthy story on the

Chicago political machine, including many details about the operation; Luce sent orders down to restore the details on the ground that "successful ward politics is built out of the strictest attention of district politics to very small things." Pieces routinely ran to thousands of words; one on the industrialization of Texas ran to 14,000.[10] Long-form business writing had found a home. *Fortune* pioneered the corporate profile, which its writers called "corporation stories," long, in-depth analyses and critiques of an organization's inner workings; today these are a business-news staple. And its writers explored the growing "documentary style" of the era, which combined elegiac, sometimes sentimental photographs and text to tell individual stories with the statistical analysis of *Fortune*'s reporting.

In contrast to Clarence Barron's *Wall Street Journal* staff of timorous high-school graduates, *Fortune*'s staff was a cantankerous group of bohemians and intellectuals, mostly leftists. It's true that many of the writers went to work for Luce because jobs at the time were scarce. As Macdonald, later a fierce critic of the magazine, would put it: "Nobody bothered talking about 'selling out' while I was at *Fortune*—you don't talk about rope in the house of the hanged." Luce, for his part, found himself forced to tolerate a magazine that often strayed far to the left of his own philosophy of "corporate liberalism," which saw modern corporations and their managers as agents not just for prosperity but for social comity and well-being. When asked why he, a staunch Republican, employed so many "Reds" on his staff, Luce replied, through clenched teeth, "Goddamn Republicans can't write."[11]

Fortune, to be sure, was probusiness. It sought to foster what Luce saw as the country's emerging meritocratic class and had a "declared mission," as one of its writers would put it, to "celebrate the marvelous accomplishments of American business, the virtues of the free-enterprise system and, the sure prospects of millennial prosperity."[12] The magazine explored the new social aesthetic that the modern industrial world was creating. Brinkley notes that the first issue chose, of all places, the Swift Meatpacking Plant in Chicago to illustrate the beauty and power of technology. Photographs by Bourke-White showed rows of hogbacks in almost abstract form, part of an orderly, mechanical operation devoid of carnage. The accompanying text similarly describes the efficiency, even beauty of the process. The choice of the Swift plant was pointed. The same plant had been the target of Upton Sinclair's grisly muckraking 1906 novel, *The Jungle*. The use of Swift made two points for Luce's new magazine: to demonstrate the advances of modern industry and to separate *Fortune*'s new form of clinical, polished journalism from, as Brinkley puts it, "the censorious, emotive language of *The Jungle*."[13]

But from the start, Luce knew the magazine, to succeed, had to be willing to offend the very businessmen at whom it was aimed. *Fortune* would find out why things worked well or how they could work better. An early story that explored the instability of some of the ships on the prestigious Matson Line prompted demands for a retraction from the shipping company. The magazine refused. When the shipper canceled its advertising contract, Luce responded: "Good! Good! Ought to lose an account every month!"[14]

In its early years, *Fortune* succeeded in pushing the definition of what business news could be, not that this was terribly difficult. Under its first defining managing editor, Russell "Mitch" Davenport, the magazine did notable, hard-hitting work. An investigation of Ivar Krueger, a notorious international swindler and maker of munitions for Europe, helped to spark a congressional probe into the international arms trade. Other work included sharp, fair-minded reporting on the labor movement and the New Deal. And some of its journalism would be difficult to imagine even in today's incarnation of *Fortune*. A 1934 piece on the arms trade, "Arms and the Men," carried this subheadline: "A primer on Europe's armament makers; their mines, their smelters, their banks, their holding companies, their ability to supply everything you need for a war from cannons to the *casus belli*; their axioms, which are (a) prolong war, (b) disturb peace."[15]

As the Depression deepened, *Fortune* began to look beyond business per se to explore the everyday lives of unemployed laborers and farmers. In the early 1930s, the magazine presented, "The Faces of Harlan County" during a miners' strike, chronicling the increasing number of Depression-era homeless travelers. It published a series on the "Life and Circumstances" of individual farmers, workers, and merchants. Suddenly, business news was not about what an institution said yesterday. "Articles such as these . . . demonstrated a broadened understanding of the America nation," writes the historian Michael Augspurger in *An Economy of Abundant Beauty*: Fortune *Magazine and Depression America*, a nuanced look at the magazine's early years.[16]

The magazine's radical tilt was not always popular among *Fortune*'s elite readership. Advertising sales representatives complained to Luce that they were having trouble selling ads for a magazine that seemed, to them, to have an antibusiness bias. After "Arms and the Men," the magazine felt obliged to respond in print to complaints that it was "going leftist" by saying that *Fortune* "doesn't plan to join a crusade" and reaffirmed its dedication to objective, "full," reporting.

Eventually, Luce did rein in his extraordinary staff, and the year 1936 was the turning point. The magazine assigned James Agee and the photographer Walker Evans to chronicle the lives of white sharecropper families in the South. Agee, who had a drinking problem and whose work was often deemed unusable by editors, turned in a massive, idiosyncratic manuscript that *Fortune*'s editors ultimately spiked. Agee would take a long time to find a publisher for the work that was the basis for *Let Us Now Praise Famous Men*, published in 1941 to lukewarm critical attention (to be revived in 1960s as an avant-garde triumph). The breaking point for Luce, though, came with a scathing four-part series on U.S. Steel by Dwight Macdonald, by then a Trotskyist sympathizer. Macdonald's fourth installment approvingly quoted Lenin and depicted the company as "bereft of both the social intelligence of Communism and the dynamic individualistic drive of capitalism." The ensuing battle with "the fawning editorial scalpel of Luce's rewrite men," as Macdonald would later put it, prompted him to walk out of his "plum $10,000 a year job."[17] The story was rewritten, Macdonald wrote, "chiefly because I had made it so completely damning that it was simply unanswerable. It was just too good. I wonder if it is still in the files, or if it was burned sheet by sheet in Luce's ashtray."[18]

One staffer of that era, John K. Jessup, wrote, "Luce knew what he wanted: that *Fortune*, without compromising its role as critic of American business, should explicitly accept and support the private enterprise system."[19] The intellectuals on the staff had difficultly accepting a bias of any kind, and Luce's dictum touched off a wrenching period of arguments and bitter intraoffice memos. Jessup, who sympathized with Luce's view, took the position that "the profit-system is a fact, not a cause." Thereafter, *Fortune* steered a more conventional path, one more recognizable to its modern readers.

But even as it navigated a tamer course, *Fortune* represented a sharp departure from the business news that had preceded it, if for nothing else than its emphasis on original reporting, factual rigor, extensive use of surveys, close attention to narrative and storytelling, and experimentation with graphics, art, and photography. Just as important, it set a new standard in business reporting for maintaining critical distance and editorial independence from the institutions that it covered and their powerful leaders.

Fortune also helped to establish the idea that to be relevant, business reporting needed to look beyond the immediate interests of its elite audience at issues of broader social concern. Indeed, the magazine's current incarnation suffers in comparison to the *Fortune* of Luce for the ambition, imagination, and empathy of its journalism. The magazine pioneered the use of surveys and other quantitative social science methods to strengthen traditional journalism's anecdotal approaches in an effort to capture the flesh-and-blood reality, the deeper truth about the Depression. For a piece headlined, "Unemployment in 1937," the magazine sent field crews into eleven different American communities for eight weeks, and each crew documented the lives of "a hundred or more different marginal families." The piece included a seven-page appendix revealing the statistical results of the study. Its goal was nothing less than to "know something about the *nature* of unemployment."[20] Business news was coming of age.

The journalism problem in the 1930s was the same that the muckrakers had confronted and that journalism confronts today: How to explain complex problems to a mass audience? Then, as now, the complex problem was a rogue financial system and a damaged, then wrecked economy. Other journals had picked up on the idea that business and the economy could be of interest to a wider circle and that new journalistic approaches were needed. McGraw-Hill, a New York book publisher with roots as a publisher of trade and technical journals, launched *Businessweek* (originally with a capital internal

W) in 1929, a year before *Fortune*. The weekly would focus particular attention on the nation's economy, an interest represented by a thermometer that gauged its temperature and appeared on the cover of the magazine from the 1930s to 1961. *Businessweek* mimicked *Fortune*'s coverage of subjects in distinct departments—production, marketing, labor, finance, management, etc.—and included a "Washington Outlook" to accompany a "Business Outlook" feature. The magazine, which saw itself appealing to a small-town, Middle American business class, became one of the first publications to routinely cover the regulatory and policy issues affecting business. The idea, McGraw-Hill's president said at the launch, was to write an opinionated form of business journalism while demonstrating that "it is possible to write sanely and intelligently of business without being pompous or ponderous."[21] The last bit was a dig at *Forbes*, the ever-quirky business periodical, which had been published since 1917 and in the 1920s was enjoying a boomlet.

Founded by B. C. "Bertie" Forbes, one of ten children of a village tailor in the Scottish Highlands, the magazine is credited with bringing enterprise reporting to business journalism, prying loose market-moving scoops from investment-banking sources, and bringing a human element by focusing on people and personalities.[22] Forbes started his magazine using money borrowed from rich industrialists, many of whom had been profiled in a book he had written, *Men Who Are Making America*, an uncritical look at the likes of Henry Clay Frick and Jacob Schiff. And for decades afterward, *Forbes* was dogged by suspicions that it cozied up to the powerful, particularly powerful advertisers. Stewart Pinkerton, a former managing editor who wrote a history of the magazine in 2011, relays an incident in which Bertie Forbes submitted an article to Thomas Wilson, the head of a Chicago meatpacking company, for prepublication review. "I have gone over the article and made only one or two slight changes," Wilson wrote. "I am sure you will agree with me on them. Otherwise, the article is fine." And when Bertie Forbes visited the automaker Dodge, Forest Akers, its president asked if he might want a new car. Forbes later wrote a relative, "I said, 'I wouldn't have the nerve to ask for one.' But there is one now on order for me—their best four-door sedan, which should be delivered shortly."[23]

Forbes did include sharp attack pieces, then an innovation, in its editorial mix. The first issue included a piece by Bertie Forbes headlined "High-Placed Misfits," about George Jay Gould, the financier's son, whom Forbes described as incompetent, "the Nicholas Romanoff of American Finance." But the attack piece served mainly as a counterpoint to a broader *Forbes* formula: investment advice, stock market data and forecasts, inspirational stories, advice on how to succeed, lists of notable executives, and adoring profiles. The magazine traded on Bertie Forbes's extensive contacts among industrialists for interviews and included articles, under the heading "What Business Leaders Say," written by the executives themselves. Another feature explained "How Forbes Gets Big Men to Talk." One such piece recounted how Bertie Forbes managed, through extensive research and persistence, to get an interview with the aging John D. Rockefeller. The titan enjoyed the interview so much that he invited Forbes to golf at his country club, where, Forbes later wrote, "he made good on his strategy to lick me." For decades, Forbes would remain, Pinkerton says, a "not much more than a second-tier stock tip sheet . . . type-heavy, gray, and often quite boring to read." But that, generally speaking, was business news, and for all of the journalistic innovations of *Forbes* and *Businessweek*, and even the achievements of *Fortune*, a broader revolution was needed.[24]

The *Wall Street Journal* had made some advances since the Barron days under its editor Kenneth C. "Casey" Hogate, who brought needed critical distance to the paper's Wall Street coverage. Even so, it confined itself to meat-and-potatoes economics and corporate news that was all but impenetrable to those who didn't follow the daily grind. The *Journal*'s narrow, granular, unimaginative journalism was written in a style that dared readers to read it. Page One was haphazardly laid out, marked by randomness in the story choices and lots of ads (for financial services firms, mostly) that took up half-columns on both sides of the page. The paper tracked the economy: "Steel Year-End Let Down Mild" (January 8, 1934), "Real Advance in 1935 Business Seen in Capital" (January 2, 1935), and so on. But the coverage was marked by its narrowness of scope—news that had happened the day before, government statistics and goings-on, and statements from corporations or their executives.

Worse, this journalism wasn't even working financially for the *Journal*'s parent, Dow Jones. After peaking at 50,000 subscribers in 1929, the *Journal*'s circulation slumped through the 1930s, with profits nudging zero toward the end of the decade. Once the paper even missed payroll, and by the end of the decade it was on the brink of extinction.

In biographies and memoirs, Leslie Bernard Kilgore is presented as genial, smart, and unflappable, a straight-talking Midwesterner out of a Frank Capra movie. An iconic photograph shows him sleeves rolled up, tie undone, staring up from a manual typewriter. He rode the train from Princeton each day marking up the day's paper. For fun on weekends, he might swap the engine of the family Ford. Unlike many news executives today, Kilgore spent hours chatting with secretaries, printers, ad salesmen—even reporters. Indeed, his trips to visit news bureaus invariably ended at some late hour in a bar with a gang around Kilgore banging away on a piano and belting out popular songs. His laconic, affable demeanor was betrayed, colleagues said, only during moments of high tension when he would be overcome by a pronounced and mysterious tic. The tic was a clue that beneath his pleasant demeanor was a determined news executive with a radical vision of what a newspaper could be and the coolness to see it through.

Like Tarbell, Kilgore was a child of a middle-class, Midwestern, Protestant home, raised in South Bend, Indiana, by a life insurance agent and a homemaker. His childhood was as idyllic as a Norman Rockwell painting. A good student, he was also a fun-loving kid who liked to build things. Kilgore's pragmatism is rooted in his upbringing. The biographer Richard Tofel, who gained access to Kilgore's personal letters, found among them much homespun and commonsensical advice from his dad. Once when Kilgore was away at college at DePauw and his car, a Model T nicknamed "Pandora," broke down, his father wired back a lecture on personal finance: "DON'T SPEND YOUR MONEY TILL YOU GET IT AND THEN DON'T SPEND IT AT ALL."[25]

Kilgore went to DePauw University, a Methodist institution, and went to work at the college paper. He covered a speech by Casey Hogate, another DePauw graduate who had returned to his alma mater. Kilgore asked good questions and wrote a fluid account, and Hogate eventually offered him a job.

When Kilgore arrived at the paper in 1929, he was only twenty years old, but, just by dint of having a college degree, he was already way ahead of the young and overworked *Journal* staff. A gifted writer and a workhorse, he soon established himself as a star on a paper that had had no stars. He was allowed to experiment with new forms, and started what might be seen as a pre-Internet blog, "Dear George," a loose, conversational column consisting of fictional letters by a correspondent called "C.W.," who wrote to explain the Great Depression to a friend, "George," in a winning, sometimes goofy style (no one knows where "George" or "C.W." came from). A typical entry starts:

> Dear George,
>   You will recall that I told you foreign currency rates—i.e. the value of one currency in terms of another—were determined, within certain limits, by supply and demand for foreign funds.

Kilgore also created the bloggy "Washington Wire," a series of short, pithy dispatches of insider news from the capital that would run on Page One for fifty years. To gauge the mood of the electorate in 1938, he once stood on a corner in Erie, Pennsylvania, and interviewed more than one hundred passersby.[26] Well-sourced among the powerful, he was also constantly on the road talking to businesspeople and workers. He spent weeks in central New York for a probing series on the National Recovery Administration. It started this way:

> The Blue Eagle graces the doors and windows of practically every establishment in the capital city of New York. A parade that required between two and three hours to pass the reviewing stand took place on the half holiday set aside by the Governor to do honor to the NRA and its noble bird. The local NRA chairman described it as a "corker."[27]

The series, which expressed the doubts of small businesspeople that the NRA was working, drew the ire of its powerful chief, Gen. Hugh Johnson, a member of President Roosevelt's "Brain Trust," who denounced it in an address to a Washington convention of the American Federation of Labor:

> There are enemies of the NRA. Yesterday, I heard that a prominent Wall Street journal was going to conduct a survey of small employers for the purpose of demonstrating that the President's Re-employment Agreement was a failure. I know something of Wall Street. I used to work there. It has been much maligned and also properly criticized. But the idea of a Wall Street journal going out to demonstrate through the little fellow the fallacy of a great social regeneration is one of the grimmest, ghastliest pieces of humor of all the queer flotsam of our daily work.[28]

If Johnson denounced Kilgore, Johnson's boss, Roosevelt, praised him publicly after a piece in 1934 explaining the difference between the government's raising money by selling bonds or merely issuing currency. At a news conference around the president's desk the day the story was published, Roosevelt told the gathering:

> There's an article this morning in this morning's Wall Street Journal by Bernard Kilgore that really anybody who writes about finances and bonuses and currency issues and so forth ought to read, because it is pretty good. I don't agree with the story all the way through but it is a good story. It is an analytical story on an exceedingly difficult subject—on the question of issuing currency to meet Government obligations. I think that Kilgore could have gone just a bit further than he did.[29]

Kilgore would use other public compliments from Roosevelt to gain an interview. One 1935 background interview scheduled for a "couple minutes" lasted more than an hour.

While he enjoyed personal success, Kilgore knew his paper was going under. By the end of 1940, the *Journal* was adrift journalistically and financially. Circulation was stuck in the low 30,000s, and the doldrums could no longer be blamed on the American economy, which had begun to pick up steam from the government's war preparations. Editorially, the paper was the worst of all worlds. As a general business paper, the *Journal* lacked the focus that can make some trade publications indispensable. Meanwhile, for a general reader looking for insight into how the economy really worked, how decisions were made inside corporations, how government policies affect ordinary people, whether institutions might be causing harm inadvertently or on purpose, or even whether a decision maker was telling the truth or stretching it, the *Wall Street Journal* of Charles Dow, Edward Jones, Clarence Barron, and even Casey Hogate had little to offer. In January 1941, Kilgore, who was then the *Journal*'s youngest Washington Bureau chief in its history, was called to New York for what he thought was a discussion of creating new columns along the lines of "Washington Wire." Instead, Hogate and Grimes surprised him. They asked if we would take over as managing editor of the paper. Kilgore talked it over with his wife, Mary Lou, and said yes. He was thirty-two.[30]

The Kilgore revolution didn't begin in 1941—and, for that matter, not all of it came from Kilgore but from Hogate; Kilgore's key deputies, William H. Grimes and William F. Kerby; and others. But Kilgore sensed what *Journal* readers wanted: a broad spectrum of news, under sharp headlines, gracefully written in jargon-free prose. With no real model to guide him and in the face of resistance within Dow Jones and among advertisers, Kilgore reimagined the newspaper and its potential. The Kilgore revolution emphasized narrative over inverted pyramids, depth over briefs, words before numbers, context over incremental news, original reporting over press releases from institutions, and, above everything else, clarity. He was an enemy of jargon and insiderism and, as a result, one of the most influential editors in American journalism history. He invented the "leder," the long-form (2,000 to 3,000 words) narrative structure that explained the world of business, markets, and corporations to a perpetually growing audience of nonspecialist, curious readers. The leder was geared to Richard Hofstadter's "literate citizen," and—twice a day, five days a week, year after year—it would play a key role in democratizing the knowledge of complex institutions and systems for America's growing middle class.

And while American journalism has seen its share of starry-eyed idealists, Kilgore was not one of them. He was, to his core, a pragmatist. His letters are devoid of high-flown rhetoric about the public interest and are much more likely to include discussion of his salary and other brass tacks. Kilgore, the record is clear, cared about what worked, that is, what would put a floundering business publication on the road to financial viability. If he broadened the paper's vision, it wasn't because it would make the world a better place, though it did. It was because more people would subscribe to the *Wall Street Journal*, which could then demand higher ad prices. When he talked about his editorial strategy, it wasn't in lofty McClurian terms but with his own brand of Midwestern common sense. When asked, for instance, why he wanted to expand the paper's focus beyond the concerns of Wall Street professionals, he said, "Financial people are nice people and all that, but there aren't enough of them to make this paper go."[31]

The postwar media landscape was changing rapidly, particularly with the advent of television. Even back then, there was a sense that newspapers had to adapt to a new environment, one in which the audience already knew the basic facts about the day's events. However, Kilgore believed readers would sit still for breadth, depth, and even length as long as the story was well told. Kilgore's bet, more than anything else, was on journalistic quality. He paid business-news readers the respect of believing that they were interested in more than just business news, and he believed business news was broader than news about what some institution or executive said yesterday.

When he took over the *Wall Street Journal*, he won over traditionalists working on the paper's staff or drove them off. When a copy editor named Greg Greene refused to brighten a headline according to Kilgore's suggestion, Kilgore quietly told him:

"I'm sorry, but you either do as I say or find another job. And I mean now!"

"Okay," said Green, "I'm fired."

"You are," Kilgore replied.[32]

This was said to be the only time Kilgore fired anyone on the spot, but it was enough. The Kilgore revolution was underway.

Hogate conceived but Kilgore perfected the "What's News" feature, which would become commonplace around the industry. In the *Journal*'s case, "What's News" was more than a convenient feature. Flagging concise summaries of stories on Page One while pointing to full stories inside the paper, "What's News" (known internally at the "10-point") had the effect of training readers to navigate the paper. Readers learned that a story leading the 10-point could generally be found in full on A3, which served as a surrogate front page for breaking news, while economic news could be found on A2 (depending on the era), and so on. The key aspect of the innovation is that readers could easily scan a roster of the most important breaking news stories and understand that they didn't need to be on Page One to be important.

This bit of prosaic newspaper architecture would play an important role in the journalism that would follow. It had the effect of clearing Page One for the long-form narrative leders that would become the *Journal*'s hallmark and a high-water mark of American newspaper journalism. Reserving such prominent display for off-the-news features meant that the quality of those features would have to be raised to justify the display. A single column of words running down right-hand column of the paper—naked, but for the occasional stipple portrait or simple graph—provided nowhere to hide for ill-conceived, irrelevant, poorly executed, or otherwise deficient stories. A factual error might as well have been displayed in neon.

The innovation created a virtuous cycle. The more prominent the space, the better the stories needed to be; the better they were, the more prestige attached to the paper, raising the bar ever higher. In time, column six of the Journal's Page One would become arguably the most prestigious real estate in American journalism. The stacked, single-column headlines of the leders became elegant prose poems, literate word games that were another means to draw a casual reader to a story that might otherwise go unread. Kilgore and company jettisoned trade terms where possible, emphasized careful editing and depth reporting, and even brought in an outside lecturer on writing, who impressed the staff by demonstrating that the greatest English prose could be understood by a twelve-year-old and flattered them by declaring the *Journal*'s Page One "the most readable front page in America."[33]

In 1943, he added the A-Hed, the apropos-of-nothing feature that anchored the front page and showed off some of the paper's most sparkling writing. The features were so light they were said to "float off the page," but the reporting behind them was usually arduous and could take days or weeks. Among the early pieces were "The New Poor: Mr. A. Was Too Busy to Live Expensively; Now, He Hasn't the Money" and "Home Grown Hemp—U.S. Revives Industry of Colonial Days to Assure Supply In War."[34] All these changes to Page One were designed to clear space for, highlight, and make more attractive the main thing the paper did: stories.

The reaction to Kilgore's changes was muted at first. Circulation and advertising remained sluggish through the early 1940s, and the changes faced resistance both within the newsroom and among advertisers.[35] Hogate and the Bancroft family, who controlled the *Journal*, backed Kilgore, who displayed outward calm. But after a while, even he grew discouraged. Things got so bad that Kilgore even considered jettisoning the name the *Wall Street Journal* on the ground that it conveyed too narrow a focus. He ordered readership surveys on whether some other name would drive home to readers the paper's new approach. "I am inclined to think that perhaps we have a double problem":

> One angle is the term "Wall Street" in our name, which ties us close to a specific segment of the financial field and may make our future progress unduly dependent on the prevailing view of the stock market. We do, of course, cover the stock market, and I believe that the broader we make our coverage, the better financial newspaper we are. At the same time, the increasing portion of our readership is nonfinancial.[36]

Among the names he kicked around in a 1947 memo to Hogate was "World's Work." He continued: "I had a notion the other night that perhaps 'North American Journal' might be euphonious. . . . Perhaps the name, 'Business Day,' would not be too bad." Fortunately, the elegant (if narrow-sounding) name stayed.[37]

Eventually success came: The *Journal*'s circulation began to edge up from the trough of around 30,000 to 42,393 in 1943, 55,000 by 1945, 129,878 in 1948, and 145,000 in 1949.[38] Coverage expanded further as the paper reported on events such as the Cold War, *Brown vs. Board of Education*, and the launch of *Sputnik*. A turning point came in 1954, when the rising business paper faced a standoff with its biggest advertiser.

"G.M. Blacklisting *Wall St. Journal*," read the *New York Times* headline over a story detailing how the world's largest manufacturer had pulled its ads from Kilgore's paper and cut *Journal* reporters off from any news from GM.[39] Indeed, when the Associated Press, of which the *Journal* was a member, asked the carmaker for its weekly production figures on the *Journal*'s behalf, GM cut off the AP, too. GM's show of muscle had come in response to beat coverage by the *Journal*'s Detroit bureau, which had unveiled the carmaker's strategy to force newspapers around the country to decline ads for new cars submitted by unauthorized car dealers. (The unauthorized dealers were selling at cut-rate prices surplus new cars they had taken off the hands of authorized dealers. GM didn't mind the practice; it just didn't want it advertised.) The story, combined with the *Journal*'s revealing the designs of new 1955 cars while the '54s were still in the showrooms, led to a confrontation between GM CEO Harlan Curtice and Kilgore. GM threatened to sue for theft of its property.

Kilgore stood his ground, albeit in his low-key style. "The Journal is not mad at anybody," he told the *Times*. "I have a General Motors car—and I certainly don't intend to sell it." On July 12, 1954, the *Journal* published an exchange of carefully worded letters between Curtice and Kilgore in which GM denied any attempt to interfere with *Journal* editorial policy. Kilgore was polite but gave away nothing. GM backed down, and the ads resumed. The standoff was a turning point in the newspaper's history, publicly reinforcing the church-state division between editorial and advertising at the paper and affirming the standard for American journalism. It certainly didn't hurt circulation, which passed 295,000 in 1954, 365,000 in 1955, 570,000 in 1958, and 784,000 in 1961. In 1966, circulation crossed a million.[40]

The *Journal*'s rise from obscure and financially shaky trade journal to the world's leading monitor of markets, corporate behavior, and the economy was attributable, of course, to much more than Kilgore, who was diagnosed with colon cancer in 1965 and died two years later at the age of fifty-nine. Nor was it entirely because of the paper's new journalism. The *Journal*'s parent company, Dow Jones, was, until the late 1980s, a dynamic and innovative company. Kilgore had an important mentor in Hogate, supportive owners in that generation of the Bancrofts, and fine lieutenants on both the editorial and business sides, including Robert M. Feemster, one of his era's great ad salesmen, and Joseph J. Ackell, who laid the foundation for the *Journal* to print in plants around the country via satellite. To a large extent, the *Journal* under Kilgore rode the greatest postwar expansion in U.S. history and reaped the benefits of the creation of the new managerial class that was one of its byproducts.

But few would argue that Kilgore's broad editorial vision didn't play a decisive role in the *Journal*'s rise and that Kilgore's *Journal* wasn't decisive in redefining business journalism and journalism itself. The American business press from its inception through the postwar boom years was characterized by rising economic power, confidence, and ambition, and it championed a broadening of journalistic vision that revolutionized the definition of "business news" and altered the relationship between journalism and the institutions it covered.

Kilgore will never be confused with Sam McClure or Ida Tarbell. He was no muckraker, though, as we'll see, the *Journal* and business news generally added investigative reporting to their arsenal. And while he had bedrock values that made momentous decisions like the GM standoff seem easy, he expressed them in pragmatic terms. As a *Journal* editorial put it during the GM affair, "When a newspaper begins to suppress news, whether at the behest of its advertisers or on pleas from special segments of business, it will soon cease to be of any service to its advertisers or to business because it will soon cease to have readers." Integrity was as much a business equation as anything else. So, too, were his journalism ideas. After all, he still liked Wall Street types, but there just weren't enough of them "to make this paper go."

In emphasizing depth, writing, careful editing, and context; by broadening business journalism's field of vision to include social issues, urban affairs, investigations, and foreign policy, as well as business-news staples like earnings, government reports, tips from insiders, and official pronouncements from institutions; by quieting the front page and relaxing the requirement to report only what happened "yesterday"; and by emphasizing the importance of storytelling, Kilgore played a key role in democratizing business news. While the *Journal* remained in some ways a form of elite communication—and its demographically wealthy audience would support the notion—under Kilgore it became more accessible to the curious layperson who didn't need to work on Wall Street or even in business to gain insight into both. The paper's extensive reach became even more evident in 1979 when its circulation hit 1.76 million, passing for the first time that of the *New York Daily News*, then reigning as the largest-circulation paper in the nation. The *Journal* had become America's most popular newspaper.

The Kilgore revolution and its emphasis on storytelling laid the groundwork for great accountability reporting in the leading business-news organization, and they helped transform business news generally. To read business journalism as it came of age in the 1970s and 1980s is to understand why the comings and goings of business executives and Wall Street bankers suddenly became so interesting to millions. Obviously, many *non*journalistic factors, including the bull market on Wall Street that began in 1982, contributed to the burgeoning reader interest in business and finance. But the *journalism* must also be taken into account. And, after Kilgore, business journalism flourished financially and moved to the front rank of American journalism, powerful, sophisticated, and, in some cases, fearless.

Forbes, which had languished in third place among business-news weeklies behind *Fortune* and *Businessweek* until the late 1950s, came into its own after Bertie's death in 1954 and the assumption of leadership by his flamboyant son. Malcolm Forbes became an iconic spokesman for both the magazine and a brash brand of capitalism. He ostentatiously flouted his private plane, *Capitalist Tool*; ever-larger *Highlander* yachts; and his rich art collection, which included a trove of Fabergé eggs, on display in the lobby of the magazine's headquarters, a mansion on Fifth Avenue. Forbes threw lavish parties, rubbed elbows with global elites, and kept the world guessing about his romantic life, conducting, among others, a long-running "are-they-or-aren't-they?" relationship with Elizabeth Taylor. (They weren't; after his death in 1990, a gay and lesbian weekly, *Outweek*, reported Forbes was gay, a conclusion supported by Christopher Winan's biography the same year).[41] Journalistically, however, Forbes's most important and smartest decision was to elevate James W. Michaels as top editor of *Forbes*.

The son of a Buffalo burlesque owner, Michaels had distinguished himself as a wire reporter by being the first to report Gandhi's assassination in 1948. After arriving at the magazine in 1954, he was quickly elevated and given a relatively free hand by the Forbes family. Michaels would define the magazine's role as the "drama critic" for business—who's doing well, who isn't, and why. As part of that function, he would sharpen the magazine's writing (a colleague said he could "edit the Lord's Prayer down to six words and nobody would miss anything") and would elevate its "attack piece." The business investigation would become a Forbes staple.[42]

By the mid-1960s, *Forbes*'s formula for success was in place. "It was no longer the *National Enquirer* of business publications, as some had seen it, running rumors to titillate rich investors," says Winans. It now included intelligent, tight analytical pieces that exposed fundamental realities of a company's business, organization, and management. True, *Forbes* targets were often smaller companies or those uncovered by rivals, but Michaels also took particular pleasure in going after companies that other business publications fawned over.[43] A 1967 piece about the defense conglomerate Litton Industries, a Wall Street darling, exposed weaknesses in its balance sheet and the quality of its earnings, sinking the stock price. A cover story about Avon in 1973, then a high-flying stock, portrayed its business model based on suburban women selling to their neighbors as bogus and exploitative, again sinking the stock. And the writing could be particularly sharp (a piece describing winemaker Ernest Gallo said that beneath his "crusty exterior . . . sits a heart of stone"). *Forbes*'s edgy pieces were always highly numerate, told with brevity and clarity. "Like well-crafted jury summations," says Pinkerton, "they proved, never asserted."[44]

Former *Forbes* staffers fondly recall Michaels's tirades. "This isn't reporting," he scribbled atop one particularly credulous piece. "It's stenography! Why is this person still on staff?????" During a 1992 meeting, he blurted out, "It's time for a really nasty story. Let's really stir up the animals." The result was a scathing piece on the spend-thrift ways of William Agee and wife, Mary Cunningham Agee, who had achieved notoriety for mixing business and romance at Bendix Corp. and who were then involved with construction firm Morrison-Knudsen (she had had no official position but, as the magazine pointed out, occupied an office next to his and ran its charitable foundation). The headline was "The Imperial Agees." The board eventually ousted Agee as CEO.[45]

Obviously, *Forbes*—home of the ultimate celebration of wealth, the *Forbes 400* (started in 1982)—was no *McClure's*. It did not rake muck. It didn't apply its journalistic skepticism to systemic ques-tions. Its mix was dominated by investing advice, run-of-the-mill corporate and business news, and some of the most fawning pro-files in the business press. Indeed, it never fully shook its reputation, earned in Bertie's day, for trimming its editorial content for favored advertisers and, later, friends of Malcolm Forbes. The magazine's "unspoken dialogue" with advertisers—whether ad dollars would buy leniency—"would continue, on a very subtle level" for years. Pinkerton quotes an unnamed former senior writer who says, "There were so many sacred cows you could populate all of India."[46]

Winans identifies a 1979 piece about Peter S. Redfield, then CEO of Intel, a *Forbes* advertiser, and a friend of Malcolm Forbes. The author, Paul Blustein, wrote a scathingly negative assessment of Redfield's abilities, describing his "fast-buck" approach and pen-chant for borrowing. However, when published, the piece appeared as a bland assessment, the tough language stripped out and a banal conclusion appended: "But does a billion-dollar company have to behave differently from a $100 million-dollar company. . . . Keep tuning in for answers." Blustein, now a respected author of econom-ics books, resigned, writing Forbes in a letter: "At one point does a publisher's 'superior insight' become a matter of altering the truth merely to protect the sensibilities of the publisher's friend?"[47]

STARKMAN, DEAN.

WATCHDOG THAT DIDN'T BARK: THE FINANCIAL CRISIS
AND THE DISAPPEARANCE OF INVESTIGATIVE
REPORTING.   Cloth   362 P.
NEW YORK: COLUMBIA UNIVERSITY PRESS, 2014
SER: COLUMBIA JOURNALISM REVIEW BOOKS.

AUTH: CENTRAL EUROPEAN UNIV. HIST. OF BUSINESS
JOURNALISM & COVERAGE OF 2008 FINANCIAL COLLAPSE.
LCCN 2013023077
  ISBN 0231158181   Library PO# AP-SLIPS

                              List   24.95 USD
  9395 NATIONAL UNIVERSITY LIBRAR   Disc   14.0%
  App. Date   3/19/14   SOBM   8214-09 Net   21.46 USD

SUBJ: FINANCIAL CRISES--PRESS COVERAGE--U.S.

CLASS HB3722   DEWEY# 070.44933097 LEVEL GEN-AC

YBP Library Services

STARKMAN, DEAN.

WATCHDOG THAT DIDN'T BARK: THE FINANCIAL CRISIS
AND THE DISAPPEARANCE OF INVESTIGATIVE
REPORTING.   Cloth   362 P.
NEW YORK: COLUMBIA UNIVERSITY PRESS, 2014
SER: COLUMBIA JOURNALISM REVIEW BOOKS.

AUTH: CENTRAL EUROPEAN UNIV. HIST. OF BUSINESS
JOURNALISM & COVERAGE OF 2008 FINANCIAL COLLAPSE.
  LCCN 2013023077
  ISBN 0231158181   Library PO# AP-SLIPS

                              List   24.95 USD
  9395 NATIONAL UNIVERSITY LIBRAR   Disc   14.0%
  App. Date   3/19/14   SOBM   8214-09 Net   21.46 USD

SUBJ: FINANCIAL CRISES--PRESS COVERAGE--U.S.

CLASS HB3722   DEWEY# 070.44933097 LEVEL GEN-AC

But the issue isn't whether Forbes was *always* tough but whether it had that capacity, and, under Michaels, the answer is clearly yes. By the mid-1980s, Forbes was leading in ad pages among business periodicals and was named among the "hottest" magazines by *AdWeek*.[48] It had won Loeb awards—the top business-journalism awards—for hard-hitting financial investigations. In 1985, Allan Sloan, one of the deans of business journalism, won one of his seven Loeb awards for an investigative piece with Howard Rudnitsky on a highflying savings and loan, Financial Corporation of America ("Damn the Torpedoes; Full Speed Ahead"); Richard Stern won for an exposé on a notorious small-stock boiler-room operator, Robert Brennan and First Jersey Securities ("The Golden Boy").

By the 1980s, business journalism was reaching its peak of prestige and prosperity. In 1986, *Businessweek* and *Forbes* jockeyed for the most readers, each with more than 700,000 subscribers, and *Fortune*, which had shifted to a semimonthly schedule in 1979, not far behind. New entrants streamed into the field, and competition among the leaders was fierce. *Businessweek*, which fought a reputation for being the dowdy tribune of Main Street, made a splash with a hard-hitting story in 1986 about Allegheny International, a Pittsburgh appliance maker, sparking shareholder suits against its CEO, Robert J. Buckley, who was forced to resign. Buckley, in turn, sued *Businessweek* for libel. The suit would be settled on terms favorable to the magazine. And in the fall of 1986, the *Los Angeles Times* would run a story under the headline: "*Forbes* Has the Yacht, *Fortune* Has the Prestige, but Spunky *BusinessWeek* is coming on."[49]

Businessweek's bland, meat-and-potatoes style, established by its postwar editor Elliott Bell, continued into the 1970s. One of Bell's successors was quoted as saying that business magazines should be like bankers. "One of the reasons you trust bankers is because they are sober and boring," he said. "If bankers wore Hawaiian shirts and long hair, you wouldn't trust them."[50] *Businessweek* adapted to business's more glamorous times under editor Stephen B. Shepard, appointed in 1984. The magazine ran a cover on the decline of once-dominant American manufacturing companies under the cheeky one-word headline: "Oops!" It ramped up the number of covers featuring CEOs in a bid to humanize business news and it also added an investigative capacity.[51]

However, despite the more aggressive and flashy reporting, most of it remained comfortably within conventional, narrow frames. The same year that it took on Allegheny International, *Businessweek* ran a cover story that chronicled, and marveled at, the rise of bond king Michael Milken, comparing him to J. P. Morgan.[52] Winans reports that *Forbes* had been planning a cover story making the same comparison before scaling back after it was beaten to the punch. Milken was a key figure in the leveraged-buyout boom that was then upending the country's economy and, more to the point, would later become the center of a criminal probe, ending in a guilty plea to six counts of securities fraud and related charges, an explosive scandal that the business press would follow with particular zeal.

The Kilgore revolution was part of and helped pave the way for a wider opening in American business journalism, one that moved away from formulaic writing styles and dependence on government and other institutions for information. A series of academic studies have shown a sharp break in journalism norms in the 1960s.[53] News grew critical of established power; journalists came to present themselves publicly as more aggressive; and news stories grew longer and less centered on government and electoral politics. The scholars Katharine Fink and Michael Schudson describe this great opening as the rise of what they call "contextual journalism." While no standard definition exists, this new form is generally longer, more in-depth, less tied to the daily flow of events and institutional pronouncements, and, as a result, more critical of those institutions.

Fink and Schudson measure the different types of journalism with a content analysis that breaks down news stories on the front pages of three sample papers (the *New York Times*, the *Washington Post*, and the *Milwaukee Journal Sentinel*) into five categories: conventional, investigative, social empathy, contextual, or other. The data show a steep drop in conventional stories and a sharp rise in the contextual: "Although this category is, in quantitative terms, easily the most important change in reporting in the past half century," they write, "it is a form of journalism with no settled name and no hallowed, or even standardized, place in journalism's understanding of its own recent past."[54]

No American newspaper did more to expand the contextual form and raise storytelling to a highly refined craft, if not an art, than the *Wall Street Journal*. Under Norman Pearlstine's tenure as top editor from 1983 to 1992, the *Journal* was a famously fractured, byzantine, and sharp-elbowed newsroom—no place for tender artists. But after Kilgore, getting "leders" on Page One became a career imperative, and the ability to conceive, report, and structure a long-form narrative was highly prized. With reporters clamoring to find a formula and their careers now riding on it, the *Journal* produced an in-house handbook, later published in 1986 as *Storytelling Step by Step: A Guide to Better Feature Writing*, by William E. Blundell, one the paper's star feature writers. The 150-page guide walked reporters through the basics: "shaping ideas," "story dimensions," "organization," "handling key story," and "wordcraft":

> Too many reporters do not see themselves as storytellers but as something else. Some are lawyers, in effect. They believe their job is to convince people of the rightness or the wrongness of things as they have determined it, so their copy has a didactic or shrill tone. Fixated on ideas, they lack humility in their work. They may talk down to the reader or talk at him, but they seldom talk *with* him as the storyteller does.[55]

This fixation on storytelling, fussing over words, detail, narrative, character, and scene, was not about journalism for its own sake. It was a vehicle for democratizing business news, transmitting detailed information about a technical and abstract subject to a mass audience. It's not an easy trick, and excellence doesn't come cheap. But it's more than a coincidence that in this era, the 1960s to 1990s—the era of the Great Story—business news shed its second-class status and joined the front rank of American journalism. It became, one could even say, glamorous.

Many business reporters became brand names and took their place in the pantheon of major American journalists: Joe Nocera and Carol Loomis at *Fortune*, Allan Sloan at *Newsweek* and later *Fortune*, Gretchen Morgenson at *Forbes*, Connie Bruck at *The New Yorker*, and James B. Stewart, Bryan Burrough, and many others at the *Wall Street*

Journal. The "business book" came into its own as a genre and pushed its way onto best-seller lists, mostly to document the excesses of the go-go Wall Street era. Among the best are Bruck's *Predators' Ball* (1988), on the rise of Michael Milken and the junk-bond-fueled leveraged-buyout business; Burrough and John Helyar's *Barbarians at the Gate* (1989), on the bruising takeover battle for RJR Nabisco; and Michael Lewis's *Liar's Poker* (1989), a subversive insider account of Salomon Brothers during its heyday. The thoroughness of the reporting, the clear and compelling writing, and the eye for cogent detail set standards for the field.

Stewart would draw on his *Wall Street Journal* reporting to write *Den of Thieves*, a riveting account of the insider-trading scandals of the 1980s and one of the best-selling business books of all time. Among the most elegant and sophisticated writers in the annals of U.S. business news, Stewart would have a profound effect on the craft. When business-news outlets produce inside-the-boardroom tales of intrigue and maneuvering, when tight-lipped CEOs bark out commands and pound the table, when details of what they had to eat are offered, reporters and editors, consciously or not, echo Stewart's style of the era.

But while Stewart exemplified the style, he didn't have a monopoly on it. Burrough, another *Journal* star, wrote stories that have the capacity to surprise even today. One eye-popping example was a profile of Jeffrey Beck, a banker at Drexel Burnham Lambert, known as the "Mad Dog." Note the narrative technique as the *Journal* allows the tale to spool out slowly, before the surprise at the end of the passage:

> Inside Wall Street's tightly knit takeover community, everyone knows The Mad Dog. At least they think so.
>
> Jeffrey "Mad Dog" Beck of Drexel Burnham Lambert will go down as one of the top merger "rainmakers" of the Roaring Eighties. A well-connected, often outrageous investment banker who played key roles in the decade's two largest leveraged buyouts, Beatrice and RJR Nabisco, Mr. Beck, 43, may be the only banker in history to wolf down a box of dog biscuits to get a chief executive's attention.

Through his career, an outsized part of Mr. Beck's allure has been his rococo background: heir to a billion-dollar Florida fortune, decorated for heroism as a special forces platoon leader in Vietnam, rumored to have worked for the Central Intelligence Agency. No one, friends say, can make fighting in the steaming jungles of Southeast Asia come alive as can Mr. Beck, who has held many a Manhattan dinner party in thrall with his wartime tales. He likes to pull up his left shirtsleeve, point to a scar on his wrist and explain how it was shattered by a bullet from an AK-47 rifle during fighting in the Ia Drang Valley; only a bulky Seiko watch, Mr. Beck says grimly, saved his hand. For calling in napalm strikes on his own patrols and other exploits, he tells rapt listeners, he earned a Silver Star, two Bronze Stars and four Purple Hearts.

Mr. Beck's is a stirring story, good enough, in fact, to have drawn the attention of actor Michael Douglas, who paired the Drexel banker with a screenwriter to assemble a script based on Mr. Beck's life. Mr. Beck has served as the model for one popular novel's protagonist, and his Wall Street career is the centerpiece of a non-fiction book to be published this fall by Random House.

Filmmaker Oliver Stone, himself a Vietnam veteran, befriended and swapped war stories with Mr. Beck during the filming of the movie "Wall Street," on which the banker served as a technical adviser and even took a cameo role. "Jeff was on the killing edge, the front lines, of the takeovers," Mr. Stone says in an interview. "To me, he really *was* the new Wall Street."

The only problem, as a handful of Mr. Beck's acquaintances now know, is that the banker's stories are almost all lies.[56]

This jaw-dropper, a true "holy shit!" revelation, is fully supported in the lengthy account that follows. The scenes in which Beck is confronted with evidence of his lies are almost painful to read, so thoroughly is he exposed as a fantasist.

The *Wall Street Journal* was the global business news leader, dominant in a way difficult to imagine today. But the explosion of business reporting—of Great Stories—was in no way confined to the *Journal*.

A roster of notable work would fill another book, but a 1988 *New York Times* profile of John Gutfreund serves as an example. Gutfreund engineered the rise of Salomon Brothers to a position of dominance in the bond business. He took it public and set off a trend that transformed the Street. The *Times* story, however, examined how Gutfreund's taste for excess and expansion had caused the firm to slip from the top. The wickedly entertaining profile is built on carefully assembled details that neatly capture Wall Street excesses of the 1980s, such as this one about Gutfreund's second wife, Susan, a former flight attendant: "Mrs. Gutfreund is fastidious about all areas of her life. She went to great pains to have a small refrigerator installed in the bathroom of her former apartment in the River House, in New York, because after bathing she likes her perfume to be chilled."[57]

Fortune remained a source of literate storytelling and pungent stories on the business world—if tamer than in the Dwight Macdonald era. Hedley Donovan succeeded Henry Luce as Time Inc.'s editor in chief and, in the late 1970s, shifted *Fortune* to a biweekly schedule to keep closer to the news. The postwar staff included notables such as William H. (Holly) Whyte, author of a *Fortune* series about corporate life that became the best-seller *The Organization Man*, and the labor writer and prominent sociologist Daniel Bell.[58]

Fortune continued the tradition of stories that probed deeply into mismanagement, screw-ups, and manipulation at corporations. Carol J. Loomis, a business press legend still working, at this writing, after more than fifty years at the magazine, has made something of a specialty of calling powerful CEOs on the carpet. Many times she wrote of corporations increasingly bending accounting rules to make earnings appear better than they actually were (e.g., "ITT's Disaster in Hartford" [May 1975], "Behind the Profits Glow at Aetna" [November 1982]). In a memoir article in 2005, Loomis recounts how American Express CEO James Robinson, among other high-powered figures, pressured her to soften her findings, insisting that she didn't understand business or finance. "The problem was that I did understand how American business was being conducted, and I didn't like it," she writes.[59]

The "corporation story" remained a *Fortune* strength. Luce's successors at the magazine turned its sophisticated and withering gaze on mismanagement and screw-ups across the corporate landscape. Stories by Joseph Nocera in 1997 and 1998 revealed chronic managerial problem at the *Wall Street Journal*'s publisher, Dow Jones & Co, including embarrassing details on snafus in the data unit that would prove the company's undoing as well as exclusive interviews with previously silent Bancroft heirs trying to steer the company on a different course.[60] These valuable stories, unfortunately, were not enough to prompt changes that were badly needed.

The flowering of business reporting created a new genre of deeply reported and well-crafted stories about corporate life, the economy, financial markets, and even complex products such as derivatives. It was primarily through this simple yet time-consuming and difficult vehicle that the curious layman could now quickly and easily learn about technical subjects once reserved for insiders and specialists. One of the most important lessons these stories taught is that these subjects, once well explained, weren't so complicated after all.

But even storytelling has its limits; another element is needed. Valuable as it may be, if kept within a narrow frame, even great business-news reporting does not address systemic problems or speak to the public interest. In other words, while most great accountability reporting finds expression as long-form narratives, only a few long-form narratives qualify as great accountability reporting.

A look at Wall Street coverage makes the point. Even the highly accomplished coverage of the insider-trading scandals of the 1980s in the *Wall Street Journal* and elsewhere—considered to be a high-water mark in business journalism—followed government investigations, principally by the Securities and Exchange Commission and the Department of Justice, which were primarily responsible for exposing the ring surrounding arbitrageur Ivan Boesky, including Michael Milken and other prominent Wall Street figures.

And critics within journalism have long faulted the business press for failing to reveal brewing problems in the savings-and-loan industry during the 1980s. In a chapter entitled "Why *The Wall Street Journal* Missed the S&L Scandal," for instance, Francis Dealy makes a convincing case, mainly through an admission by the paper's reporter in charge of savings-and-loan coverage, that infighting, myopia, turf wars, and risk aversion caused the paper to skip a story that had been brewing in the local press for years. Dealy documented an odd case in which a small local paper, a competitor, actually pitched the story to the paper as something that needed to be widely publicized, only to be turned away.[61]

And the overwhelming amount of conventional business-news coverage of Wall Street banks—access reporting, no matter how deeply reported or beautifully written—in no way qualifies as accountability reporting. The difference is clear in major business-press coverage of Wall Street banks. News-archive databases allow a rough categorization of "major" stories featuring Wall Street firms in four major business news publications: the *Wall Street Journal*, *Forbes*, *Fortune*, and *Businessweek*. These archives extend back to 1984. A "major" story appears on Page One of the *Journal* or runs to more than one page in the magazines. A review of the databases reveals that stories fell fairly easily into three categories: profiles, explanatory stories, and accountability stories.

Stories in the first category—the overwhelming majority—explore the inner workings of a Wall Street firm, usually feature the cooperation of the firm and its executives, and deal primarily with its success or failure relative to its competitors. To be sure, many stories were far from puff pieces (though there were plenty that qualify), but if they were tough they were tough only within the narrow context of profit and loss. A *Wall Street Journal* story from September 10, 1980, "Diversified Offering: Merrill Lynch Expands from Stocks to Gamut of Financial Services," is a typical profile. The subheadline, "Chairman Regan Leads Years of Growth in Real Estate, Insurance, and Banking; Critics Resent the Changes," implies some critical rigor, but a few paragraphs make clear the story's purpose, to document a business success:

> Last spring Merrill Lynch & Co. encountered the kind of customer that its chairman, Donald T. Regan, had been dreaming

about for 10 years. And the man wasn't even particularly interested in the stock market.

The dream customer was an employee of American Airlines who was being transferred from New York to Dallas. American hired Merrill Lynch Relocation Management to handle the details of the move. But that was just the beginning. Here is what followed.

—Merrill Lynch Realty Associates brokered the sale of the man's house on Long Island and helped him find the right home in the Dallas area.

—The man obtained a mortgage through a Dallas lending institution whose funds had come in part from two Merrill Lynch mortgage insurers, AMIC Corp. and Family Life Insurance Co.; the man then insured his mortgage payments against his untimely death through a Family Life policy.

—When he decided to cash in on sky-rocketing interest rates, the customer arranged a money market investment with the local office of Merrill Lynch, Pierce, Fenner & Smith, the securities brokerage arm of Merrill Lynch & Co.

These transactions were made possible by a decade of diversification at Merrill Lynch & Co. It is a diversification that has created a supermarket of financial services and has caused Merrill Lynch to explore areas radically different from the company's traditional securities business.

Even making allowances for this type of story, there isn't much tension to speak of. The "critics" cited in the subheadline don't have much to say. The story tries to point to "controversy," but, in the end, it is pretty weak tea:

> The new activity hasn't been without controversy. Critics have voiced concern that brokerage firm diversification might dilute the company's efforts and thus ultimately hamper its ability to raise money for industry. *And competitors, particularly banks, have looked askance* as Merrill Lynch has elbowed its way into precincts formally considered off-limits for securities brokers.
>
> (MY EMPHASIS)

So much for controversy. But, in fact, the story was perfectly legitimate for what it was. There's no reason to think that Merrill Lynch had *not* benefited enormously from a diversification strategy laid down by Ronald Reagan's future Treasury secretary and chief of staff. And Donald Regan indeed *was* an outspoken and prescient Wall Street executive. He had, as the story notes, called for the abolition of the New York Stock Exchange rule that fixed the commission its members charged to perform stock trades. In 1975 it was removed, ushering in a new, more democratic era of stock trading. In this 1980 story Regan is heard challenging the venerated system of trading stocks by hand on exchange floors, calling it "ridiculous." His calls for "computerized" trading would later become a reality (though remnants of the old system can be found to this day). Finally, it should be remembered, the story was written in a more innocent era, before the series of booms and crises that have gripped the Street since deregulation and when the financial sector played a significantly smaller role in the economy and political system.

The profile is a staple of all corporate reporting, and coverage of Wall Street is no exception. Sometimes the stories lean to the flattering side. "Merrill Lynch Takes a Tip from the Grocery Store" (*Businessweek*, July 9, 1984) looked at the same diversification strategy that the *Journal* had examined a couple years earlier. "Cash, Flash, and Dash: Can This Be Merrill?" (*Businessweek*, May 11, 1987) reported that the bank that had been known for its retail brokerage had taken the lead in securities underwriting. And "Merrill Lynch Bulls Ahead" (*Fortune*, February 19, 1996) looks at the firm's string of success in several business areas: "On Wall Street's sloppy playing field, no team has made a more surprising comeback in blocking, tackling, and most important, in scoring than Merrill Lynch. What was once a fumbling squad of beefy, slow-footed dullards has become a lean powerhouse consistently running up big-point totals against hapless opponents."

Not all the major stories were flattering, and whether a given story is positive or negative is not really the point. There are many examples of profiles that reveal problems and challenges facing the corporations: "Merrill Lynch's Big Dilemma" (*Businessweek*, January 16, 1984) discusses the bank's problems in coping with a newly deregulated environment, trouble with an investment in a Hong Kong brokerage, and increased competition outside the securities business. "Merrill Lynch: The Stumbling Herd" (*Fortune*, June 20, 1988) finds reasons for the bank's low returns on stockholder equity and other problems in the post–Donald Regan era. But what's important is the extent to which the business news relied on access reporting and failed to attempt accountability reporting. To be clear, access reporting or, in this case, an investor-oriented approach to business news is neither unexpected nor even a problem. But it does help resolve the "Jon Stewart question": how can so many cover something so closely, with such expertise, yet miss so much?

Explanatory stories, the second most frequent category, typically examine Wall Street firms in the wake of a government crackdown or financial disaster. Not only are they valuable in themselves, often offering insight into exactly what went wrong and why within an institution, explanatory stories feature notably among the greatest, most readable, most riveting stories business journalism has ever produced. But this category of story also fails to qualify as accountability reporting (as we'll see in the next chapter) and necessarily does not warn the public about problematic behavior in key institutions on the business-press beat. Rather, by definition, these are after-the-fact explanations, often written in a tone of rueful omniscience and finger-wagging at what are often described as avoidable mistakes.

Clearly, even great business reporting and sterling long-form narratives are not enough to provide the curious nonspecialist with timely information about systemic problems, corporate lawlessness, and malpractitioners, and do so while they are still powerful. For what was coming in the mortgage era, it would take a far more ambitious type of journalism.

CHAPTER 4

Muckraking Goes Mainstream

Democratizing Financial and Technical Knowledge

I n 1991, Michael W. Hudson, a reporter for the *Roanoke Times*, was interviewing a legal-aid lawyer for a series about poverty in that small Southern city, earnestly asking questions and scribbling copious notes, when the lawyer abruptly stopped the conversation. It's good to write about poverty, the lawyer said, but you're missing the most important thing. Hudson, then in his late twenties, was something of a rising star at the 120,000-circulation daily, having done long investigative series, to some acclaim, on the state's dysfunctional juvenile justice system, abuses in regional adult group homes, and screw-ups at Virginia's child support enforcement agency. He had written of murders, sex offenders in the state prison system, and much other mayhem. He was well sourced among prosecutors at the Commonwealth Attorney's Office. He had grown up in the region and thought he knew more than most about the grimmer aspects of life in western Virginia.

"But the thing about poverty," this legal-aid lawyer said, is that's not just about a lack of money or even a job. It's about how you get *out of poverty.* And basically, as the lawyer explained, there are only three paths: a house, a car, or an education, or a combination of the three. A house allows you to build equity; a car allows you get to work; and, of course, everyone knows an education is important. The trouble is, the lawyer explained, if you're poor, none of these can be bought without credit. And the low end of the financial-services industry was the problem. Pawnbrokers, check-cashing stores, consumer-finance agencies, for-profit trade schools, and the second-mortgage business were all lightly regulated and dominated by hard-money types, many of dubious ethics. So when poor people *tried* to get a leg up, they found themselves with a loan with unmanageably high interest and fees and were pushed further back down, this time with destroyed credit. It happened over and over, the lawyer said. Hudson thought that was too bad. He also thought, "Great story."[1]

The discussion with the poverty lawyer made a deep impression on Hudson, a practitioner of accountability reporting whose career roughly coincided with the apex of the practice in mainstream media. The trajectory of his professional experiences as a reporter illustrates the tradition of investigative reporting, which has deep roots in American journalism but became a mainstream practice only relatively recently. The stories Hudson covered started him down a path that led, over the course of the next fifteen years, into the heart of the financial system that would ultimately collapse.

In 1991, he applied for a fellowship from the Alicia Patterson Foundation, a Washington, D.C., funder of muckraking journalism projects, which allowed him to take year off from the paper and immerses himself in the poverty-lending business, also known as consumer credit or "specialty finance." He would enter a different world, a veritable Disneyland of sharpies and tough guys. The consumer-credit business bore only a passing resemblance to traditional banking, which emphasized underwriting and risk analysis. Consumer credit was closer to street-corner commerce, the domain of hustlers and confidence men. This was where the most desperate meet the least forgiving. He encountered an endless string of borrowers who, one after another, confirmed what the poverty lawyer had told him: lenders had misled them on them their loans, and not just on the details but the basics: interest rates, penalties, and fees. Other complaints centered on "credit insurance," a basically worthless product that lenders said was mandatory—it wasn't—and "prepayment penalties," which forced borrowers to pay big fees to get out of a loan, adding to their debt if they refinanced. One woman didn't even know her loan was a mortgage—that her house was being used as security—until after the vinyl siding was already up. She nearly broke down in tears, she told Hudson, but didn't put up a fight. "Then you couldn't complain, could you?" she said. "You couldn't say: 'Well, take it off.' "[2]

Over the years, Hudson would become a student of the low-end lending business and its unique culture, one based almost entirely on sales. He encountered legendary players with nicknames like "Doc" and "the Mormon," and famous "one-call closers," including Duayne Christensen, a hard-partying former dentist who looted the savings and loan he ran while illegally prescribing narcotics to the comely "consultant" he had hired; he died after slamming his Jaguar into a bridge pylon. Hudson read up on Bill Runnells, president and CEO of a company called Landbank Equity Corp., based in Virginia Beach. An eighth-grade dropout, Runnells was a former Bible salesman, professional gambler, and loan shark who kept his head shaved smooth and wore sunglasses day and night. Upon founding Landbank, he created its mascot, "Miss Cash," who appeared on billboards and in TV ads. "When banks say 'no,' " LandBank's ad said. "Miss Cash says, 'yes.' "

Despite his record and louche appearance, Runnels secured funding from legitimate banks and savings and loans, then took advantage of Virginia's high poverty rates, lax lending laws, and famously accommodating legislature to sweet-talk borrowers into accepting loans at eye-popping rates. Among his innovations: the fifty-point loan, half loan and half fees. When a bill to limit finance-company fees came before Virginia's part-time General Assembly, Runnells hired the state senator who would cast the deciding vote to do his legal work. The senator voted "no." A voucher for $3,000 to the senator was later found among Landbank's papers. It read: "This was one we agreed to pay after he stopped legislation in Richmond." In the end, Runnells ran off with the investors' money, leading authorities on a two-year global manhunt before being captured. He was sentenced to forty years in prison. Before he left, though, he spoke to a reporter. Runnells discussed his lending philosophy, which can still stand as a watchword for the subprime lending industry as a whole: "When you're broke," he said, "you'll borrow money at any price."[3]

Mike Hudson first became interested in newspapers from watching his dad, Grant Hudson, coach the local high school basketball team, the Highland Springs Springers, near Richmond. Mike would carefully read the game stories in the *Richmond News Leader* and the *Richmond Times-Dispatch*, comparing the accounts with each other and with what he had seen. Hudson worked on his school paper, then at Ferrum Junior College, near Roanoke. He worked part-time at a local thrice-weekly, the *Franklin News-Post*, the kind of place where if someone grew a particularly large tomato or killed a big snake, they brought it to the paper. Then Hudson would photograph it and write the caption. He covered his dad's games. When Hudson got his associate's degree from Ferrum, he covered his own graduation, scribbling notes in cap and gown.

He got an internship at the nearby *Roanoke Times* and began to gravitate toward stories that revealed the inequitable aspects of life in Roanoke: social-service programs that didn't work, police brutality, housing discrimination, and consumer scams. He went to finish his full bachelor's degree at Washington and Lee, in Lexington, Virginia, where he took courses taught by Clark R. Mollenhoff, who was all about bucking the establishment. As an investigative reporter for the *Des Moines Register*, Mollenhoff had won the Pulitzer Prize for national reporting in 1958 for an exposé on racketeering and fraud in Jimmy Hoffa's Teamsters union.

Before long, Hudson would find himself challenging the status quo within Washington and Lee journalism circles, clashing with the leadership of the main campus paper, the *Ring-tum Phi*, and in particular with another rising college journalist, Mike Allen. Today, Allen is chief White House correspondent at *Politico*, a Washington-based news organization whose very name expresses its insider-orientation. According to an extensive 2010 *New York Times* profile of Allen, he is now generally described as the "most powerful" and "most important" journalist in Washington, principally because of his morning newsletter/blog, *Playbook*, which the *Times* describes as

> the principal early-morning document for an elite set of political and news-media thrivers and strivers. Playbook is an insider's hodgepodge of predawn news, talking-point previews, scooplets, birthday greetings to people you've never heard of, random sightings ("spotted") around town and inside jokes. It is, in essence, Allen's morning distillation of the Nation's Business in the form of a summer-camp newsletter.[4]

Hudson was a year ahead of Allen and, while he liked him personally and thought he was a powerhouse reporter, didn't like his style of journalism, which he found obsequious, even as it propelled Allen to stardom. With a stringing job at the *Roanoke Times*, where he was angling to work after graduation, Hudson didn't try out for the *Ring-tum Phi*. Instead he became something of a gadfly. Hudson objected in the spring of 1985 when the paper ran a short story on page 4 announcing that the paper's publisher, the University Publications Board, whose voting members are editors and business managers at campus publications, had named Allen and two others as the *Ring-tum Phi*'s "three top editors" and that Allen would have "overall responsibility for the newspaper." Hudson spoke to two other editors and, in a letter to the editor, said the board had, in fact, rejected a proposal to name Allen top editor and instead had voted to give the three editors equal responsibility. Hudson wrote that it was only after Allen, the paper's most productive staffer, "indicated he might not work at the paper" without a "promotion" (from coediting the previous year) that the two other editors agreed to Allen's taking the title of executive editor. The story's wording, Hudson wrote, was "literally true, but misleading if not deceitful."

Hudson went to work at the *Roanoke Times* and was soon plunging into some of the harshest aspects of Roanoke life, doing series after series involving race, class, institutional failure, and public corruption. His multipart series exploring neglect and abuse in state-run group homes for adults started with an interview with a group-home operator, who admitted that he had slapped a retarded resident across the face. "He p——— all over the living room furniture," the operator is quoted explaining.[5]

But then he took up poverty and, following the legal-aid lawyer's advice, began to look at the low-end credit business and subprime mortgages, which in the early 1990s were beginning to take off. Reporting on dozens of stories, he was struck by the ubiquity of the complaints about bait and switch: borrowers said they agreed to one thing but found—too late—they had been delivered another. Patterns consistently emerged. For instance, African American borrowers in Virginia earning up to twice as much as their white counterparts were still twice as likely to be rejected for conventional loans—a state of affairs that would become a hallmark of the mortgage crisis nationwide years later. And deregulation was making things worse. Hudson found lenders in South Carolina that charged usurious rates of up to 100 percent. One three-day series included photos, sidebars, charts, and graphs and ran some 13,000 words. The headline was "Borrowing Trouble."[6]

Hudson spent months buried in loan documents and talking to plaintiffs' lawyers, borrowers, regulators, and lenders. He did his share of breaking news stories. But he was absent from the office for days at a time and was generally given wide discretion by his editors, who trusted him to spend his time wisely and who also understood that sometimes big investigative projects didn't work out at all. The paper was owned by a company then called Landmark Communications, now Landmark Media Enterprises, based in Norfolk and closely held by that city's billionaire Batten family. The company owned a string of daily and weekly newspapers and broadcast TV stations and, for a while, the Weather Channel. The company was extremely profitable. It could afford people like Hudson.[7]

By the early 1990s, the idea of a staff reporter at a midsized regional daily launching a crusading investigation into lending abuse would not have seemed unusual to American newspaper readers, who took their local papers' sometimes outsized ambitions as a matter of course. Buoyed by their status as quasi monopolies in most markets, some regional papers were stretching the possibilities of what newspapers were supposed to do. They spent lavishly on news budgets (if not on individual reporters' salaries), created investigative

teams, flew in writing coaches, installed computer-assisted reporting units, and sent reporters and editors to conferences and retreats
where they would contemplate the fine points of the secret to powerful prose.

But the Roanoke paper's decision to launch a major investigation
into what was then still known as the "second-mortgage" business,
part of the "poverty economy," reflected the reemergence of investigative reporting after the 1960s, a renaissance that brought muckraking back into the mainstream media—business media very much
included. Many of the media's severest critics reject the notion that
conventional newspapers could be an effective check on established
power. In their classic critique, *Manufacturing Consent*, Edward S.
Herman and Noam Chomsky put forward a propaganda model for
U.S. media and propose that a variety of factors—concentrated
media ownership, the advertising model, the PR power of large
institutions—distort news organizations' editorial lens. While the
public interest is occasionally served, it is only within defined, narrow boundaries of acceptable debate: "This is not normally accomplished by crude intervention, but by the selection of right-thinking
personnel and by the editors' and working journalists' internaliza-
tion of priorities and definitions of newsworthiness that conform
to the institution's policy." Further, the authors argue, the fact that
professionals within news organizations may on occasion actually
succeed in publishing reports that challenge dominant views actually helps reinforce the system by providing false assurance that
dissent is allowed: "The beauty of the system, however, is that such
dissent and inconvenient information are kept within bounds and
at the margins, so that while their presence shows that the system is
not monolithic, they are not large enough to interfere unduly with
the domination of the official agenda."[8]

Whatever the validity of the critique (and there's a lot to it), most
reporters, I think, would argue that what happens on the margins
isn't trivial since that is where accountability reporting usually operates. And what Herman and Chomsky don't take into account is that
the margins, over time, move; they expand and contract. Indeed,
the short history of the U.S. business press shows that the boundaries can move a considerable distance and that their expansion has

provided considerable benefits for the chicken workers, day laborers, and slum dwellers who appear in the stories or, at least, for the curious middle-class readers who, for a few moments, were connected to them. Indeed, the expansion of the boundaries made a democratization of business news possible. Where to draw the lines becomes a source of fierce newsroom debate, with some journalists, depending on their own values, defending the boundaries and even seeking to narrow them; others push against them. Looking over recent investigative journalism, it is surprising to see how far the boundaries of what could be covered were stretched in American journalism, business news very much included.

Historians trace what is called the "journalism of exposure" in the U.S. to pre-Revolutionary times. In his *Evolution of American Investigative Journalism*, James L. Aucoin notes that Benjamin Harris's *Publick Occurrences Both Forreign and Domestick* published what can only be called an early exposé, revealing that Britain's allies, the Iroquois, were guilty of torturing French soldiers during the French and Indian War in the late seventeenth century. During the Revolutionary War, Sam Adams's *Journal of Occurrences* fueled revolutionary feeling by publishing lurid tales of British abuses and corruption. Much later, the New York *Sun* probed bribery in the Grant administration after the Civil War, and *Harper's Weekly* (featuring the devastating cartoons of Thomas Nast) and the *New York Times* under George Jones launched crusading investigations in the early 1870s into the corrupt Democratic boss William Tweed and his Tammany Hall political machine. The *Times* exposé got a boost when a disgruntled Tammany operative handed a copy of the ring's secret accounting ledger to a twenty-six-year-old reporter named John Foord. It documented payments to fake contractors for work on nonexistent buildings, and the *Times* published it in full, setting a standard for documentation for news investigations.[9]

Joseph Pulitzer's crusading *St. Louis Post-Dispatch* exposed everything from crooked real estate deals to protected gambling halls and brothels in the city in the 1870s. When Pulitzer moved to New York to take over the *New York World*, he took on William Randolph Hearst in a heated newspaper war in which exposés helped fill the demand for screaming page-one headlines every day. One *World* highlight was the undercover investigation by reporter Nellie Bly (née Elizabeth Cochrane) into conditions at the Blackwell's (now Roosevelt) Island Insane Asylum for Women. It shocked New Yorkers with its first-person account of cruelty and abuse. Jacob Riis, a police reporter for the *New York Tribune*, brought exposure journalism to the city's Lower East Side slums in the *New York Sun* in 1888 and in a series of books, including *How the Other Half Lives* in 1890.[10]

An early and rare exposé of financial manipulation and corruption was written by Charles Francis Adams Jr., who, with this brother, Henry, documented the floridly corrupt battle for control of the Erie Railway between Cornelius Vanderbilt, on one side, and Daniel Drew, Jay Gould, and Jim Fisk, on the other. Risking not just libel suits but physical injury (the Erie people "were not regarded as lambs," he later wrote), Charles Adams took advantage of his social position to gain access to the top players both at the railroad and on Wall Street, including financier "Diamond Jim" Fisk, whom Adams interviewed in his office stronghold at the New York Opera House. In articles first published in *North American Review* and collected in *Chapters of Erie and Other Essays*, Charles Adams laid out the manipulations and backroom dealing on both sides in ironic, flowery language that was echoed decades later in the work of Lincoln Steffens. Here's Adams's description of Drew, the wily treasurer, who had maneuvered his way from cattle driver and tavern owner to a key position of trust at a major railroad: "Shrewd, unscrupulous, and very illiterate—a strange combination of superstition and faithlessness, of daring and timidity—often good-natured and sometimes generous—he ever regarded his fiduciary position of director in a railroad as a means of manipulating its stock."[11] Vanderbilt, then one of the most powerful men in America, came off only slightly better.

A landmark in the expansion of investigative journalism to business news came with Henry Demarest Lloyd's *Wealth Against Commonwealth*, published in 1894, based on an article, "The Story of a Great Monopoly," published earlier in *The Atlantic*. The book, a sort of proto-muckraking, is part exposé and part diatribe against Rockefeller's Standard Oil. Like Tarbell's work, it relied on public records to describe how the concentration of industrial power had distorted markets and bent the government. Unlike Tarbell, Lloyd doesn't predominantly rely on facts to explain lawless behavior underlying the evolution of trusts but instead uses facts to bolster what is essentially a polemic. "Nature is rich; but everywhere, man, the heir to nature, is poor," the book begins, which gives a flavor of the style that follows. The work was groundbreaking in its time and influenced Tarbell, who consulted the aging reformer on his Sakonnet, Rhode Island, estate in 1902. Both could agree on one thing: that Rockefeller was a great man. "They differed only in the degree of greatness they would accord him," Kathleen Brady recounts. "Lloyd placed him among the five greatest of history; something Tarbell averred was a little strong."[12] It is a measure, however, of the difference in their approaches that Lloyd viewed with alarm the very idea that Tarbell would consider speaking to Standard Oil executives, especially Rogers, during her reporting. It was only after he read the first installment that he wrote to her with effusive praise.

The muckraking era was brief, most often dated from 1903 to around the start of World War I. By 1906, Tarbell and other *McClure's* staffers had left the magazine, defecting to the rival *American Magazine* over disagreements with McClure's grandiose business plans, and the magazine itself was sold to creditors in 1911. The causes of muckraking's demise are much-debated among historians; theories range from financial pressure brought by the magazines' lenders to simple changes in public taste and the arrival of a more conformist age in the wake of the First World War. Muckraking's own excesses certainly played a role as its popularity attracted hacks, hustlers, and careerists looking for a sensational exposé. Still, the era was incredibly productive—by one count, 2,000 investigative articles appeared in American magazines in the period—and set new standards for editorial ambition, fidelity to facts, storytelling, and providing a check on power. It remains a high point of journalism's identification with and advancement of the public interest.[13]

Historians differ over the vitality of investigative reporting in the United States after the muckrakers. Roy J. Harris Jr. argues that some investigative reporting survived, particularly at regional papers, buoyed by Joseph Pulitzer's 1911 bequest to Columbia University that created the Pulitzer Prizes, starting in 1917. The 1921 public service award to the *Boston Post* for exposing (with Clarence Barron's help) Charles Ponzi provided a crucial incentive for papers to engage in such work. The 1927 public service Pulitzer, for instance, honored Don Mellett of the *Canton (Ohio) Daily News*, who uncovered the underworld of mobster Jumbo Crowley—and for his efforts was gunned down outside his home.[14]

Aucoin and others see a drop in mainstream investigations after World War I, with some exceptions, such as probes by the *Post-Dispatch*'s Paul Y. Anderson into the oil leases that led to the Teapot Dome scandal and indictments of Interior Department officials. The fall of muckraking reporting was reflected by the great H. L. Mencken, who denounced newspaper crusades in a 1914 column as "gothic" and "melodramatic" efforts aimed solely at boosting circulation. A 1924 *Atlantic* article declared them "passé."[15]

Bruce Shapiro, in *Shaking the Foundations*, a collection of 200 years of American investigative works, argues that journalists continued investigative reporting after the muckrakers, though, importantly, not as much among major newspapers. Notable work was done by magazine reporters—Vera Connolly, who wrote about conditions on Indian reservations in *Good Housekeeping* in 1929; John Bartlow Martin on a mine disaster in *Harper's* in 1948—and book writers, such as Stetson Kennedy, who published his exposé on the Ku Klux Klan, *The Klan Unmasked*, in 1954. The left-liberal press also carried the investigative burden: *PM* in the 1940s, for instance, probed domestic fascism as well as American firms' and executives' ties to Nazi-controlled firms; Fred J. Cook revealed J. Edgar Hoover's ineffectual record against organized crime—"The Big Ones Get Away"—in the *Nation* in 1958; Ralph Nader published early critiques of the auto industry, "The *Safe* Car You Can't Buy," in that magazine in 1959.

In the decades after the muckrakers, certainly, routinized investigations faded from the mainstream arsenal, and journalists who overstepped conventional boundaries were marginalized almost as a matter of course. We only know this because a few, by dint of luck and enormous talent, managed to overcome setbacks to transcend their in-house detractors: Drew Pearson, as a Washington correspondent for the *Baltimore Sun* in the early 1930s, wrote (with Robert S. Allen, his counterpart at the *Christian Science Monitor*) a scathing critique of Washington's compromised political culture, *Washington Merry-Go-Round*, but had to do so anonymously. When its authorship was discovered, Pearson was promptly fired. George Seldes quit the *Chicago Tribune* to a write a critique of the press, *You Can't Print That!*, in 1929 and became one of the century's most important independent journalists. From 1940 to 1950, he published *In Fact*, an investigative newsletter and a predecessor to the legendary *I.F. Stone's Weekly*, which used obscure public documents to expose wrongdoing and tell larger truths. Jack Anderson, who was hired by Pearson and succeeded him in the syndicated column, would occupy something of a netherworld: read by millions but not fully mainstream during the 1970s and 1980s.[16]

The decades after the muckrakers, and certainly the period after World War II, are widely recognized as a time of press complacency and coziness with authority. The groundbreaking journalism that managed to emerge in the postwar era is most often associated with books written by people who weren't primarily journalists: Michael Harrington's *The Other America* (1962); Rachel Carson's *Silent Spring* (1962); or Nader's *Unsafe at Any Speed* (1965). The political, social, and cultural upheavals of the 1960s, of which these books were an early symptom, brought a new sense of skepticism among many Americans. Investigative reporting began to reemerge in the early 1960s, propelled by changing public attitudes and professional mores. As noted in chapter 3, the media scholars Katherine Fink and Michael Schudson report that after this time there was a dramatic increase in "contextual journalism," the longer, more deeply reported, more analytical stories that were less reliant on official sources and less tethered to the daily flow of events.[17] In a sense, contextualized journalism can be seen to have risen on the storytelling foundation laid by the likes of Luce and Kilgore.

Indeed, a reading of investigative reporting of the last half century shows that work as sweeping and ambitious as the muckrakers' would become incorporated and institutionalized in the mainstream of American media editorial culture. What's more, newspapers could now afford it. Already prosperous in the 1950s, the newspaper industry over the next decades would see steady and constant rises in annual advertising, from around $5 billion in 1960 to more than $50 billion 2000 (in inflation-adjusted terms it about doubled over the period). Circulation revenue increased tenfold to $10 billion.[18]

Even as the number of newspapers declined since the 1920s and circulation dropped in absolute terms since the 1950s,[19] great newspaper chains expanded and consolidated into quasi monopolies. Newspaper companies—McClatchy (*Sacramento Bee, Raleigh News and Observer*), Tribune, Times Mirror (*Los Angeles Times, Baltimore Sun*), Advance Publications (the *Plain-Dealer, New Orleans Times-Picayune*)—held a vicelike grip on advertising markets essential to everything from local grocery stores, department stores, and government agencies to millions of regular people trying to sell a used car. They were cash cows. Even locally owned papers—the *Anniston (Alabama) Star*, the *Providence Journal*—were profitable from the 1960s to the end of the 1990s. Margins of 20 percent (about those of Apple and Google today) were expected, and even 30 percent was not out of the ordinary.

Some media companies, such as Knight Ridder (*Philadelphia Inquirer, Miami Herald, Charlotte Observer*), became renowned for reinvesting in newsrooms and turning out exemplary regional papers. Others, like Gannett (*USA Today* and dozens of local papers, including the *Montgomery Advertiser* and the *Rochester Democrat and Chronicle*), were content to squeeze profits and became a watchword for mediocrity. In the end, quality was determined by ownership. But the resources were plentiful, and accountability reporting became one of the beneficiaries. Readers began to expect investigations are part of their Sunday fare. News organizations made room for a new breed of reporter, and establishment journalism made way for what was a new and, in some ways, an antiestablishment form. It was not always an easy fit.

In 1964, the Pulitzer Prizes, administered by the Columbia University Graduate School of Journalism, added a new category, "Local Investigative Specialized Reporting," which was won that year by the

Philadelphia Bulletin for a probe into police collusion in a local numbers racket. Subsequent winners would explore stories as familiar to us today as they would have been to the muckrakers: wrongful murder convictions (*Miami Herald*, 1967); fraud and abuse of power in a local steamfitters union (*St. Louis Globe-Democrat*, 1969); and the exploitation of prisoners for drug experimentation (*Montgomery Advertiser and Alabama Journal*, 1970).

In the late 1960s, Robert W. Greene, a former investigator for the New York City Anti-Crime Committee and U.S. Senate Rackets Committee, and a journalism legend, created one of the first formal newspaper investigative teams at *Newsday*, elevating the form through a series of high-risk, high-impact stories that exposed wrongdoing at the nexus of business and government. Greene's teams twice won the Pulitzer Prize for Public Service, the most prestigious category. The first came in 1970, for exposing land scandals involving politicians passing zoning changes that enhanced values of property they owned. The investigation went so far as to reveal that among those profiting from the deals was a high-level editor at *Newsday*. The second award winner, in 1974, tracked heroin trafficking from poppy fields in Turkey to the streets of Long Island—an indication of news organizations' ambitions during this period.

The high-water mark of American investigative reporting remains Watergate and the *Washington Post*'s landmark probe led by reporters Bob Woodward and Carl Bernstein; their editors, primarily Ben Bradlee; and the paper's publisher, Katharine Graham. It is true that the years have brought new examinations and a more nuanced, less heroic understanding of the Watergate probe, but it continues to stand as a monument to the potential of the news investigation to expose wrongdoing, hold power to account, and trigger political and electoral reforms. The fictionalized film account of the investigation, *All the President's Men*, solidified the story's iconic status even as it took poetic license with critical facts. "Watergate," Michael Schudson writes, "overwhelms modern American journalism."[20] So powerful is the legend surrounding the story, so mythic the image of the press uncovering a real-life criminal conspiracy at the highest levels of government, that the debates still rage over the role of the press in the fall of the Nixon presidency. Indeed, a cottage industry has sprung up to debate what are described as "myths" about the press's role in general and the *Washington Post*'s role in particular. Schudson argues that even to the extent that the "press" advanced the Watergate story, it was by virtue of the *Post* acting alone (and, he argues, anomalously), while the rest of the Washington press corps did little. Others contend that much of the story wasn't "uncovered" by the *Post* but leaked by law enforcement or other investigators. Max Holland argues that W. Mark Felt, the high-ranking FBI official who revealed himself in 2005 to be the whistleblower known as "Deep Throat," was motivated by internal bureaucratic goals.[21]

But without relitigating the disputes, no one seriously argues that journalism, even if *only* the *Post* for a time, was not instrumental breaking and perpetuating the Watergate story at key moments. That the newspaper was part of an exposure dynamic that involved law enforcement and other institutions, that it was propelled by leaks from official investigators, and that other bodies eventually forced Nixon's resignations do not diminish the *Post*'s achievement.

In the wake of Watergate, newspapers around the country installed dedicated investigative reporters and teams: the *Boston Globe, Philadelphia Inquirer, Chicago Tribune, Chicago Sun-Times, Miami Herald, Minneapolis Tribune, Indianapolis Star, St. Louis Post-Dispatch, Atlanta Journal, Cincinnati Enquirer, Daily Oklahoman,* and *Nashville Tennessean,* among many others, not to mention the *New York Times* and the *Wall Street Journal.* The year 1974 was a landmark for investigative reporting. The year after the *Post* was awarded its Pulitzer Prize for Public Service for its Watergate series (for work published in 1972), investigative work won four Pulitzers: Bob Greene's *Newsday* team won for its "Heroin Trail" series, *Chicago Sun-Times* reporters won for stories that reopened a 1966 murder case; a *New York Daily News* reporter won for revealing abuses in New York's Medicaid program; and reporters for the *Providence Journal* and *Washington Star-News* shared the national reporting award for probes finding irregularities in, respectively, President Nixon's tax returns and the financing of his 1972 reelection. *Time* magazine declared 1974 "The Year of the Muckrake."[22] With the formation Greene's team, the mid-1970s saw the start of an era of neo-muckraking, different from the past in that mainstream media, not entrepreneurial magazines, carried the public-service load. Investigations proliferated. No paper was too small to engage in this kind of hard-hitting journalism, and no topic was too big to take on. By 1975, investigative reporters had their own trade group, Investigative Reporters and Editors, based at the University of Missouri's journalism school, complete with conventions and conferences attended by thousands, with vendors' booths hawking everything from database services to hidden cameras.

A galvanizing moment in this neo-muckraking movement came in 1976, when an investigative reporter for the *Arizona Republic*, Don Bolles, was mortally wounded in a Phoenix parking lot by a remote-controlled bomb taped to the bottom of his car. The precise motive for the crime was never fully discovered, but Bolles had done many stories on organized crime, including one that named 200 known mob figures operating in Arizona. His last words in the parking lot were, "They finally got me—Emprise—The Mafia—John Adamson. Find him." The murder sparked a cooperative journalism effort known as the Arizona Project, headed by *Newsday*'s Greene and drawing three dozen reporters and editors from twenty-three newspapers to continue Bolles's work and investigate his death. It produced dozens of stories. Adamson later confessed to planting the bomb and implicated an Arizona contractor in ordering the murder and another man in helping to carry it out. Adamson and the contractor ultimately served long prison terms. "Emprise" was the name of a company Bolles was investigating, and it was later convicted of concealing its ownership of a Las Vegas casino. It was found to have had nothing to do with the murder. Bolles's damaged car, a 1976 Datsun, was later put on display at the Newseum in Washington.[23]

By the end of the 1970s, as newspapers consolidated their status as local quasi monopolies, their willingness to embark on aggressive investigations became a key benchmark of newspaper quality. Investigative highlights from this period include a *Deseret News* series on radioactive fallout of atomic weapons tests (1979); a *Port Arthur (Texas) News* probe of local polluters (1979); a *Bridgewater (New Jersey) Courier-News* investigation of payments by a state school to an attorney (1980); revelations by the *Louisville Courier-Journal* of irregularities in Kentucky's coroner system (1981); an investigation of Alabama's troubled coroner system by the *Anniston Star* (1984);

the revelation by the *News-Sentinel* of Fort Wayne, Indiana, of fifty-two deaths related to a religious sect's teachings against modern medicine; and an exposé by the *San Jose Mercury News* of the overseas investments of Ferdinand Marcos (1985). Even the investigative reporters' own trade group, the IRE, found itself the target of an exposé of sorts in 1977, a Page One *Wall Street Journal* story revealing that the newly formed muckrakers' group had accepted donations from ethically dubious sources: a foundation created by a financier imprisoned for securities fraud and a Chicago lawyer with Mafia clients. IRE responded weakly that it didn't know the identity of the donors.[24]

Business journalism was a full participant in the investigative movement and eventually could rightly claim some of the most potent works in American journalism history. Business news's particular strengths—its sophistication about corporate culture, its grasp of business idioms, its technical expertise in financial and accounting matters—were brought to bear in startling exposés from the 1960s on, including a remarkable *Wall Street Journal* series in 1964 on how a string of favorable regulatory rulings allowed Lady Bird Johnson to turn a $17,000 investment into a multi-million-dollar media empire. What's more, the fact that the exposés were from mainstream *business news* publications gave them added weight and resonance. Unlike, say, an alternative paper or *Rolling Stone*, these publications could not be accused of having a built-in animus toward business or of pandering to a readership of one political orientation or another.

In 1983, to take one example of hundreds, George Getschow, writing in the *Wall Street Journal*, explored the work camps run by day-labor employment agencies in the Southwest and the labor conditions that amounted to slavery, with workers charged almost as much for room, board, and work tools as they earned in salaries.[25] A story the next day described a camp in Louisiana that plied workers with alcohol and sedatives—and charged for them whether the workers wanted them or not—before sending them off to offshore oil rigs. On entering the camp, they were required to sign over power of attorney. One man told Getschow he never saw a paycheck for the four months he worked offshore and received only a few dollars of pay after the company sent his wife an alimony check and charged him for whiskey, wine, and sedatives like Elavil and Atarax, dispensed, the *Journal* found, by the camp director, who wasn't a doctor and didn't have a license. The slave-labor-camps series, a finalist for a national reporting Pulitzer in 1984, is reminiscent of the journalism of muckraker (and future socialist) Upton Sinclair in the early twentieth century.

The institutionalization of muckraking was accompanied by painstakingly intricate disputes over investigative theory and practice. In 1962 John Hohenberg, curator of the Pulitzer Prizes, wrote about the previous year's public-service entries and drew distinctions between routine reporting and exposure, or "investigatory," journalism. During the 1970s, some journalists sought to refine the definition to the exposure of corruption, graft, and abuse of power. In a 1972 article for *Quill*, K. Scott Christianson, a reporter for the *Knickerbocker News-Union Star*, in Albany, N.Y., defined it as gathering "important secret information that somebody is determined to keep secret." In 1975, Greene added the requirement that the reporting had to be the journalists' original work, not the findings of a government agency. One writer distinguished between "modern" investigators and early muckrakers by asserting that while the latter distilled and interpreted information that was already known, their modern counterparts engaged in "systematic investigations" or original reporting.[26]

An early handbook, *Investigative Reporting and Editing* (1978), by Paul N. Williams, described investigative reporting as an "intellectual process . . . a business of gathering and sorting ideas and facts, building patterns, analyzing options, and making decisions based on logic rather than emotion—including the decision to say no at any of the several stages."[27]

Journalistic thinkers posited, with more or less a straight face, the "holy shit" theory of investigative reporting—defining it by the reaction among readers that they aimed to provoke. Beginning in the late 1960s there were a variety of efforts to catalogue and standardize investigative reporting methodologies. A team of journalists working for the American Press Institute in Reston, Va.—J. Montgomery Curtis; Ben Reese, a former editor of the *St. Louis Post-Dispatch*; John

Seigenthaler Sr. of the *Nashville Tennessean*; and Clark Mollenhoff, Michael Hudson's mentor, then with the Cowles papers—developed a formal system for investigating government or private institutions that included analyzing of the history of the agency, checking for possible conflicts of interest.[28] A deadly serious 1976 handbook, *Investigative Reporting*, includes chapters such as, "Attracting and Evaluating Sources" and "What to Investigate." At one point it declares, "There is no institution of any standing, anywhere, that wouldn't be improved by a bit of investigation."[29]

After Watergate, social theorists began to discuss—and sought to demonstrate empirically—the social and policy effects of journalism investigations. The terms "agenda setting" and "agenda building" came to reflect the complex dynamic among the press, public opinion, and government and other institutions that created the conditions for reform.[30] In *The Battle for Public Opinion*, a 1983 study on how agenda building had worked during the Watergate investigations, Gladys Engel Lang and Kurt Lang analyzed the "collective process" required for reform.[31]

It is hard to know what Tarbell, McClure, and Steffens would have made of all the theorizing of a practice they did by instinct. (Given their own moralizing bent and devotion to scientific methods, they would probably have approved.) It is true that the literature of investigative reporting comes across as rather earnest and self-important. Textbooks speak of "mobilization models"—complete with flowcharts that purport to describe how news effects are generated. But the theoretical work was part of investigative reporting's struggle for legitimacy within the professional culture. Advocates of investigative journalism sought to make investigations a permanent fixture in newsrooms by bureaucratizing and standardizing them.

It's important to note that they were not always successful. As we'll see, institutionalization carries a price, and it is telling that some of our era's great investigative reporters chose, or were forced, to work outside major news organizations. Seymour Hersh was in and out, mostly out, of mainstream media for most of his career before becoming a regular contributor to *The New Yorker*; Wayne Barrett, a muckraking urban-affairs reporter, worked the bulk of his career at the *Village Voice*; Wiliam Greider, the great economics-affairs writer, left the *Washington Post* for *Rolling Stone*; Lowell Bergman, a long-time network reporter and producer, works across multiple media, including for the public-affairs program *Frontline*. For advocates of institutionalized accountability reporting, it is problematic, to say the least, that so many of the country's best investigative journalists worked outside the mainstream and that to do so they in some ways had to transcend it by becoming brands in themselves.

Even if there remained lines that institutionalized accountability reporting would not cross, it did take root within mainstream media, and its very presence there gave it a power it could not find in alternative outlets. As accountability reporting became more accepted, it was no longer limited to narrow topics, such as chasing crooked politicians or exposing nursing-home abuses. Katharine Graham recognized as much in her 1974 speech that distinguished between two kinds of investigative reporting, one exposing "hidden illegalities and public official malfeasance," another that "zeroes in on systems and institutions in the public or private realm."[32] This more sweeping definition built on the work of the muckrakers—exposing wrongdoing but also explaining such broader topics as the rise of newly powerful institutions and the effects of seemingly arcane public policy on daily life and society.

The work of Donald Barlett and James B. Steele in the *Philadelphia Inquirer* and elsewhere illustrates the expanding ambitions—and achievements—of investigative reporting in the era. In the early part of their career, the two reporters pursued classic exposure journalism: abuses of a Federal Housing Administration mortgage program and waste in federal synthetic-fuels subsidies. In the 1980s, the scope of their work expanded; a 1988 series probed how special interests had distorted the 1986 tax reform.[33]

By the early 1990s, they were taking on the economic system, explaining the effects of a decade's worth of tax, trade, and regulatory policies and how they had changed, for the worse, Americans' economic life. The series, "America: What Went Wrong?," ran in the fall of 1991. The first installment was called: "How the Game Was Rigged Against the Middle Class." It started this way:

Worried that you're falling behind, not living as well as you once did? Or expected to?

That you're going to have to work extra hours, or take a second job, just to stay even with your bills?

That the company you've worked for all these years may dump you for a younger person?

Or that the pension you've been promised may not be there when you retire?

Worried, if you're on the bottom rung of the economic ladder, that you'll never see a middle-class lifestyle?

Or, if you're a single parent or part of a young working family, that you'll never be able to save enough to buy a home?

That you're paying more than your fair share of taxes?

Worried that the people who represent you in Congress are taking care of themselves and their friends at your expense?

You're right.

Keep worrying.

For those people in Washington who write the complex tangle of rules by which the economy operates have, over the last 20 years, rigged the game—by design and default—to favor the privileged, the powerful and the influential. At the expense of everyone else.[34]

Barlett and Steele's language clearly echoes that of Tarbell and the muckrakers a century earlier. If anything, Tarbell is arguably the more measured and even-handed in the presentation of facts. While Barlett and Steele represent the outside edge of the breadth and ambition of mainstream media—their series took up twenty-five newspaper pages—the series they wrote was far from an anomaly. As we've seen, ambition—some would call it pretension—became a hallmark of the journalism of the period. Muckraking, in an evolved form, had been thoroughly absorbed into the mainstream. From the 1960s, at the latest, it was what American newspapers did.

And, according to opinion polls, the public embraced the trend. A Gallup poll in 1981 found that 79 percent of respondents approved of investigative reporting, and 66 percent said they would like to see more of it. Polls in 1986 and 1989 showed continued strong support, despite eroding public confidence in the media in general. A report based on the 1989 survey concluded:

> There is . . . a general consensus among the press, the public, and American leadership that news organizations play an important "watchdog" role, with larger majorities of all groups sampled believing that press coverage of personal and ethical behavior or politicians helps weed out the kind of people who should not be in office.[35]

The *Philadelphia Inquirer*'s "What Went Wrong?" series, for instance, generated 20,000 letters, notes, and telephone calls. After the ninth and final article was published, the *Inquirer* reprinted 15,000 copies of the series to be given away to readers the next day at the newspaper's office in downtown Philadelphia. Early the next morning hundreds of people waiting to get a copy formed a line that wound around the building. The entire supply was quickly exhausted. In the days that followed, similar scenes would occur as the newspaper repeatedly went back to press to satisfy demand.

It's worth pausing to remember that these newly formed journalism teams, as their forebears had, did help to "[raise] the level of public and private conduct," as the muckraking *American* magazine actually claimed in 1907.[36] But for a 1977 *Philadelphia Inquirer* exposé, brutal conditions at a state mental hospital might have gone on indefinitely. Absent a *Charlotte Observer* series in 1980, the public might never have known that some textile mill owners had been concealing both the dangers of cotton dust from their workers and incidences of brown lung disease from state health officials.

Today, investigative reporting is the apple pie of journalism debates; everyone is for it, in theory. A 2008 survey found that "91% of all newsroom executives said they considered investigative or enterprise reporting either 'very essential' or 'somewhat essential' to the quality of their news product."[37] But while all professional news people must pay lip service to accountability reporting in principle, its expense, risk, and difficulty engender perpetual resistance within news bureaucracies. Even during its heyday, accountability reporting faced resistance from those who didn't understand it, felt it beyond the scope of daily newspapers, or simply had a different conception of the news.

Many news executives, as we'll see, profess to support accountability reporting but withhold resources, incentivize scoops and other access reporting, and express hostility to the idea of long-form journalism. Likewise, digital-news theorists acknowledge accountability reporting's value but promote business models that cannot support it. Within newsrooms, investigative reporters have sometimes found themselves stereotyped as overly zealous, blinkered, unreasonable, and agenda-driven; as pack rats and flakes; and, perhaps worst of all, as unrealistic. Sometimes, of course, this is the case. Periodic scandals involving overzealous and flaky reporters offer cautionary examples. The tension is real. Investigative reporting almost by definition requires a certain amount of passion for the subject, determination to overcome resistance from the targets of the probe and risk aversion within news organizations, a single-minded focus over weeks and sometimes months, and, often, emotional identification with victims. The line between focus and obsession is not always clear. One result is that investigative reporters have been subject to marginalization within news organizations, much as the muckrakers have been driven to the margins of journalism's historical memory.

And to be sure, many of investigative reporting's most damaging wounds have been self-inflicted. The bureaucratization of muckraking brought many benefits, including professionalism, standards, and institutional support from increasingly prosperous and powerful news organizations. But it also brought its own set of career and institutional incentives that presented risks for readers. With proliferation came screw-ups, excesses, and embarrassment. One early faux scandal, "Billygate," involved the President Carter's brother, who had an unwisely tried to broker business deals with Muammar Gadhafi's Libya without registering as a foreign agent. A frenzy of stories that purported to extend the story—including a supposed presidential cover-up—amounted to nothing. Another nonscandal of the era involved Carter aide Hamilton Jordon. In 1978 Steve Rubell, owner of the Studio 54 nightclub, tried to deflect authorities from his own troubles by alleging he saw Jordon snort cocaine at his club.

A drug dealer called "Johnny C," facing his own charges, emerged to back up Rubell and repeated the allegations for ABC's 20/20. An exhaustive four-month investigation by a court-appointed special prosecutor, Arthur Christy, found the allegations to be baseless.[38]

And, as Aucoin notes, the turn of the 1980s brought high-profile libel cases that exposed reporting methods to years-long public scrutiny, including *Tavoulareas v. Washington Post*, *Westmoreland v. CBS*, *Wayne Newton v. NBC*, and *Ariel Sharon v. Time*. Individually and collectively, the cases damaged the reputation of investigative reporting and raised questions, some legitimate, about the newfound zeal among news organizations. In fact, the cases presented widely varying degrees of fault in the reporting and writing.

Neo-muckraking also encountered cultural pushback as the public wearied of the pieces' sprawling length, grim subject matter, and formulaic presentation: anecdotal leads, bullet-pointed findings, and often clunky, earnest writing. Some critics complained that investigations were launched with journalism prizes in mind or to advance other institutional or career needs. Eventually, the multipart newspaper series would become the subject of mockery, some of it richly deserved.

Accountability reporting as a practice came under attack from the political right, attacks that continue to this day. The *Wall Street Journal*'s editorial page, for one, had far more sympathy for Tarbell and her early-twentieth-century muckraking than it would for her intellectual heirs eighty years later, referring at one point to "the faux journalists Barlett and Steele." That particular piece ("Schlock Populism: Voters Ignore Gore's Blather," August 24, 2000), accused Barlett and Steele (along with a motley list including Kevin Phillips, Pat Buchanan, and Ralph Nader) of peddling class resentments. The conservative complaint was more fully laid out in a 1998 *Journal* op-ed on journalism prizes by James Bowman, the American editor of London's *Times Literary Supplement*. Bowman mistakenly believed the *Philadelphia Inquirer*'s "America: What Went Wrong?" series had won a Pulitzer (it won many other prizes; the error was corrected), but his overall charge was that Barlett and Steel hid behind a guise of journalistic objectivity to advance a transparently liberal view of the world. "The self-evident absurdity of their conclusion, that the policies of the Reagan-Bush years were about to eliminate the American middle class, did not put off the Pulitzer judges, and the series turned into a book that had some influence on the 1992 election," Bowman wrote.[39] In fact, Barlett and Steele, like Tarbell, got some things wrong. But the facts they gathered to describe the shifting political and economic forces arrayed against the middle class were never in dispute, and, sad to say, their conclusions proved to be all too accurate. In 2012, Barlett and Steele published a new book, *The Betrayal of the American Dream*, documenting the trends they had detected two decades earlier.

In the 1990s, one could argue that the best accountability reporting could be found in business news, now fully established in the front ranks of American journalism. Indeed, as business itself became more empowered during this era of deregulation, business news became even more essential in checking corporate excesses. The former journalism backwater, which had once consigned itself to relaying information to market participants, used its particular expertise in accounting, finance, and corporate law to begin to probe beyond "hidden illegalities," to use Graham's terms, to zero in on systemic problems. The era produced stories that reshaped debates and reformed entire industries. Still, as we'll see, even at its height, business reporting had its limits.

One of the most celebrated muckraking stories about business and the economy was a 1994 series on working conditions in various dead-end jobs, "Nine to Nowhere," by the *Journal*'s Tony Horwitz (December 1, 1994), who wrote one of the more memorable openings:

> Morton, Miss.—They call it "the chain," a swift steel shackle that shuttles dead chickens down a disassembly line of hangers, skinners, gut-pullers and gizzard-cutters. The chain has been rattling at 90 birds a minute for nine hours when the woman working feverishly beside me crumples onto a pile of drumsticks.
>
> "No more," she whimpers.

And business journalism did not shy away from big business. A *Journal* series in 1995 by Alix M. Freedman on the tobacco industry—

then at the height of its power—used internal documents obtained from tobacco companies to devastating effect. It (along with reporting from ABC News and other competitors) helped lay the groundwork for the restructuring of the entire industry via the 1998 "master settlement agreement" with forty-six states.

The business press also turned an investigative gaze on Wall Street. In a 1991 article in *Fortune*, Carol Loomis, an iconic figure in the business press, wrote a devastating exposé of the increasingly troubling practice among brokerages of cold-calling retail customers and browbeating them into problematic investments.[40] The article zeroed in on Merrill Lynch's unsavory tactics, including flat misrepresentation and fraud. The piece is especially significant in hindsight because, as we'll see, the practice of scripted cold-calling spread to the mortgage industry and provided a crucial driver of the explosion in defective mortgages that lay at the center of the global financial crisis. With a couple of exceptions, reporting on such boiler-room tactics would disappear during the lead-up to the crisis.

Loomis also brought great sophistication to bear on a complex subject in cover stories about the dangers of derivatives in 1994 and 1995. One carried a photo of an alligator's mouth and the headline "The Risk That Won't Go Away." The article, while not investigative, is valuable in pointing out dangers already looming that would lead to crisis a decade later:

> Most chillingly, derivatives hold the possibility of systemic risk—the danger that these contracts might directly or indirectly cause some localized or particularized trouble in the financial markets to spread uncontrollably. An imaginable scenario is some deep crisis at a major dealer that would cause it to default on its contracts and be the instigator of a chain reaction bringing down other institutions and sending paroxysms of fear through a financial market that lives on the expectation of prompt payments. Inevitably, that would put deposit-insurance funds, and the taxpayers behind them, at risk.[41]

The business press also took on Wall Street practice of selling investments that would quickly collapse in value. During the Internet bubble, *Fortune* examined the record of companies offered to the public by Merrill Lynch in the mid- to late 1990s. The piece explained the rich incentives for bankers to make IPOs, no matter what the company's prospects (5 to 7 percent of the total deal), as well as for company executives, who became millionaires overnight. The piece explored how the incentives for Merrill and other Wall Street analysts corrupted their research and showed that Merrill's army of retail brokers were forced to peddle shares they knew to be wildly overvalued—and then dissuade retail customers from selling shares before the inevitable fall. The piece tracked down a former Merrill broker who quit in disgust. "'Institutions would bail out right away,' says the [former broker Richard Urbealis]. 'But retail customers would be left holding the bag.'"[42]

Businessweek published a cover story in 1998—the height of the stock-market boom—demonstrating how companies manipulated earnings with ploys such as one-time write-downs of acquisitions (to disguise poor operating results) and "restatements" of earlier rosy earnings reports. The magazine pointed to the corrupt practice among Wall Street analysts of bending research reports to help investment-banking colleagues win business from companies the analysts purported to cover.[43]

Also during the height of the Internet bubble, the *Wall Street Journal*'s Michael Siconolfi exposed the bribery-like practice of "spinning," whereby a Wall Street bank allocates shares of a hot initial public offering to the CEO of an unrelated company in hopes of winning the second company's business. The *Journal* described, for example, how the investment bank Robertson Stephens allocated 100,000 shares of Pixar Animation Studios, representing a $2 million profit, to the CEO of a small tech company, GT Interactive Software Corp., which then hired Robertson Stephens to advise it for $5 million. "It's a bribe, no question about it," the story quoted a rival banker on the record. The story named several banks involved in the practice, including Hambrecht & Quist LLC, then a hot boutique firm, and Morgan Stanley. The story also reported that the practice "may violate" regulatory antibribery rules and that neither the SEC nor self-regulatory agencies had even heard of the practice. The story prompted regulatory investigations, and spinning was later barred.[44]

This laudable investigative work shows what the business press can do when it chooses to. Its writers were able not only to match the bankers' financial sophistication but also to employ it to reveal common industry practices to fall far short of society's "expectations of integrity and fairness." Indeed, the stories showed the industry as a whole fell short even of its own standards for fair dealing in the marketplace. Furthermore, the best of these stories are original and don't piggyback on regulatory or law-enforcement work; they qualify as investigations according to the definitions of Bob Greene and others. The fact that the stories came from mainstream business-news publications—that is to say, from within the financial establishment itself—gives them unmatched credibility and potency.

However, a closer look at even accountability-oriented stories shows their limits. They are confined, for one thing, to investor concerns, not those of the broader public. This is not a fault, just a fact. As a result, business-press coverage of Wall Street stops well short of providing the look at systemic shifts of the sort that Tarbell pioneered, that Katharine Graham defined, and that Barlett and Steele cemented as part of mainstream reporting. Clearly, the 1980s and 1990s saw dramatic shifts in both Wall Street and its culture and in its relationship to the broader society. Wall Street firms were growing larger in an absolute sense, relative to their regulators, and, importantly, relative to the news organizations that covered them.

What's more, as Frank Partnoy and others have documented, the mortgage era of the early 2000s was the culmination of over two decades of increasingly normalized reckless and lawless behavior on Wall Street, punctuated by the savings-and-loans scandal of the late 1980s, the derivatives scandals of the early 1990s—when Wall Street firms were found to have knowingly misled corporate clients such as Gibson Greetings and Procter & Gamble about the riskiness of derivatives—and the Internet bubble of the late 1990s, in which Wall Street "research" was later revealed by Eliot Spitzer to have been fraudulent.[45] Wall Street's culture was shifting. It was going rogue even as, or because, official regulatory scrutiny was weakening. Further, Wall Street misbehavior was no longer confined to the sophisticated players involved but was encroaching on public well-being. The S&L scandal cost federal taxpayers tens of billions. Losses from the Internet bubble affected, to a large and unprecedented degree, retail investors, many of whom had recently entered 401(k)s and the stock market.

On occasion, mainstream business reporting did transcend the normative limits of business journalism and struck at the heart of changing norms in the financial sector. In 1999, for instance, the *New York Times* published an extraordinary series of stories that probed allegations of criminality at Bank of New York, one of nation's oldest and heretofore most reputable banks. Both reporting on and advancing a law-enforcement investigation, the series explored the unexplained movement of billions through accounts at the bank, tracing the source to giant Russian banks tied to larger enterprises controlled by Russian oligarchs. The series, headed by reporter Timothy L. O'Brien, ultimately helped to expose a money-laundering ring inside the bank, naming Bank of New York executives connected to the account, three of whom were indicted later that year. The bank settled federal money-laundering charges a few years later.[46]

A forthright late-1990s investigation into the heart of Wall Street came from *Forbes*, which took aim at the corrupt relationship between a rogue brokerage, A.R. Baron, and a Wall Street icon, Bear Stearns, which acted as its "clearing firm," providing back-office support for smaller brokerages to make sure "buy" and "sell" orders are properly executed and delivered and acting as a guarantor. Baron was later indicted on state racketeering charges and found to have committed the worst kinds of financial abuses, including pumping up worthless shares, using "boiler-room" tactics to browbeat often elderly investors into buying shares of fraudulent companies the brokerage secretly controlled, trading without customer knowledge, taking kickbacks from penny-stock promoters ("touts"), embezzlement from customer accounts, and more. One trader would testify to receiving kickbacks from touts of $120,000 in cash, delivered in a brown paper bag and weighing more than a "medium-sized ham." Baron's testosterone-fueled culture, testimony would later reveal, included wild sex and drug parties among employees and prostitutes at New York nightclubs. Baron would be the model for the firm featured in the 2000 film about a corrupt brokerage, *Boiler Room*, a movie that would later figure in the mortgage crisis.

Using documents from lawsuits and arbitration cases against Baron, *Forbes* showed the remarkable degree to which Bear served as Baron's lifeline and enabler, demonstrating that Bear had known of Baron's checkered past before taking it on as a client and knew of Baron's unauthorized trading from the anguished pleas of Baron's customers, who appealed directly to Bear to reverse them. Bear refused. Further, *Forbes* reported, Bear served as clearing firm for many of the worst operators in penny-stock sector, including Sterling Foster, Rooney Pace, D. Blech, and D.H. Blair, all notorious as predatory operations.

Forbes went even further to show that the corrupt brokerage head, Andrew Bressman, had a personal relationship with Richard Harriton, the Bear clearing chief. Citing confidential sources, *Forbes* said Harriton secretly benefited from trading in a Baron's account and noted that Harriton's son Matthew served as chief financial officer for one the "house stocks" that Baron had manipulated. The *Forbes* story concluded: "The whole situation stinks."[47] The author, Gretchen Morgenson, later moved to the *New York Times*.

Later that year, Baron was indicted by Manhattan district attorney Robert Morgenthau for "enterprise corruption," New York State's version of racketeering. Morgenson, along with Gary Weiss, a reporter for *Businessweek*, used the incredibly damaging testimony in the trials of Baron's executives to tighten the connection between the racket and the Wall Street icon; one indicted trader testified Harriton and Bressman lunched weekly at a country club (an assertion Bear denied on Harriton's behalf). Later that year, Weiss and *Businessweek* explored the ties among Bear, Harriton and his son, and another small brokerage later found to be a criminal enterprise, Sterling Foster, which was indicted on fifteen counts of stock manipulation. In the end, though Baron's executives received lengthy prison terms, Bear Stearns escaped with remarkably light punishment. Bear later agreed to pay $38 million to settle charges brought by Morgenthau and the SEC. Harriton agreed to pay $1 million and was barred from the business.[48]

Whether the Bear/Baron investigation represented a regulatory failure is a question beyond the scope of this inquiry. But it could be said to represent a journalistic missed opportunity. Extraordinary efforts by exceptional reporters laid bare a new and troubling paradigm in the financial sector: the connection between boiler-room operations facing the public and the Wall Street firms that profited from and enabled them. Opportunities for an authoritative look into Wall Street's inner workings don't come along often. The sleaziness of boiler-room brokerages, penny-stock touts, and public-company charlatans was well known, but their relationship to brand-name Wall Street firms, without whom they could not exist, was not.

In *Forbes*'s and *Businessweek*'s reporting we see the beginnings of a shift in the relationship between Wall Street and the American consumer public. Bear continued to clear for Baron even while customers howled about unauthorized trades—until, in fact, the day Baron filed for bankruptcy. Bear's partnerships with public-facing financial-services firms provided it with plausible deniability even as its clients descended into predatory and eventually criminal behavior toward their retail customers, financial amateurs. The clients' boiler-room operations roped in consumers who otherwise would never have heard of Baron or its misbegotten shares had they not picked up the telephone. The reporting revealed that the financial industry was turning away from and taking advantage of the American people. Bear was, in a sense, the point of the spear. It had long played the role of Wall Street's naughty firm, willing to push ethical boundaries. But Wall Street was shifting and growing; its reach into the financial lives of everyday Americans was expanding. In this case, the product was stocks. In a few years, it would be mortgages. But the model is the same.

Still, while *Forbes*'s Baron/Bear probe was exemplary, the business press produced other muckraking works that even today are surprising in their ambition, sweep, and fearlessness. Perhaps the high-water mark of the business investigation into Wall Street came on May 16, 1990, when the *Journal* ran a story that explored the effect of the leveraged buyouts that had dominated financial news of the previous decade and made media stars of Wall Street executives, such as Michael Milken, along with bankers, arbitrageurs, and the buyout specialists themselves: T. Boone Pickens, Sir James Goldsmith, Carl Icahn, Robert M. Bass. The story began this way:

Oakland, Calif.—On the eve of the 1986 leveraged buy-out of Safeway Stores Inc., the board of directors sat down to a last supper. Peter Magowan, the boyish-looking chairman and chief executive of the world's largest supermarket chain, rose to offer a toast to the deal that had fended off a hostile takeover by the corporate raiders Herbert and Robert Haft.

"Through your efforts, a true disaster was averted," the 44-year-old Mr. Magowan told the other directors. By selling the publicly held company to a group headed by buy-out specialists Kohlberg Kravis Roberts & Co. and members of Safeway management, "you have saved literally thousands of jobs in our work force," Mr. Magowan said. "All of us—employees, customers, shareholders—have a great deal to be thankful for."

Nearly four years later, Mr. Magowan and the KKR group can indeed count their blessings. While they borrowed heavily to buy Safeway from the shareholders, last month they sold 10% of the company (but none of their own shares) back to the public—at a price that values their own collective stake at more than $800 million, more than four times their cash investment.

Employees, on the other hand, have considerably less reason to celebrate. Mr. Magowan's toast notwithstanding, 63,000 managers and workers were cut loose from Safeway, through store sales or layoffs. While the majority were re-employed by their new store owners, this was largely at lower wages, and many thousands of Safeway people wound up either unemployed or forced into the part-time work force. A survey of former Safeway employees in Dallas found that nearly 60% still hadn't found full-time employment more than a year after the layoff.

James White, a Safeway trucker for nearly 30 years in Dallas, was among the 60%. In 1988, he marked the one-year anniversary of his last shift at Safeway this way: First he told his wife he loved her, then he locked the bathroom door, loaded his .22-caliber hunting rifle and blew his brains out.[49]

The passage's shocking conclusion, which clearly implicates the engineers of the Safeway buyout in a worker's suicide, is a fair indication of what was to follow: a relentless, trenchant, and impeccably documented exposé. One of the greatest business stories of the post-war era, the 7,700-word story challenges the official account of the buyout promulgated by the company's new owners, a team led by KKR, still one of the country's most powerful and media-savvy financial institutions. The piece's author, Susan C. Faludi, would go on to fame as a feminist author and social theorist. Significantly, the story challenged and debunked the narrative put forward by KKR and the Magowan family team that the buyout had brought needed changes to a stagnating company. In fact, the buyout, which showered benefits on the family and its financiers, did little to help Safeway at all. Faludi's account bristles with facts backed by compelling analysis to show that the traumatic financial maneuver left a company hobbled by debt, shorn of some of its most profitable divisions, and without the human capital to prosper. The facts belie the idea that the company required shaking up on the first place:

> But Safeway was already doing—albeit at a slower pace—many of the things LBO experts advocate. It was remodeling its stores and creating the upscale "superstores" that have now proved such a big success. It was experimenting with employee productivity teams, phasing out money-losing divisions, and thinning its work force with a program that included some lay-offs but generally relied on less painful methods like attrition.
>
> All these changes produced earnings that more than doubled in the first four years of the 1980s, to a record $231 million in 1985. The stock price tripled in three years, and dividends climbed four years in a row.
>
> But all that wasn't enough for takeover-crazed Wall Street, where virtually no company was invulnerable to cash-rich corporate raiders.

The story, called "The Reckoning," shifts from the riches earned by directors, KKR ($60 million in fees), and shareholders from the deal to its consequences for others. The extent to which the story implicates the LBO in worker deaths is startling to read even today.

Faludi even manages to report on the misgivings about the deal of Magowan's own mother, Doris Merrill Magowan, wife of the company's deceased founder (and daughter of a Merrill Lynch founder):

Will anyone get hurt? Mrs. Magowan pressed her son at the time, according to company staff members. Will anyone lose his job?

No Mom, Mr. Magowan promised, according to the staffers' account. No one will get hurt.

"Yes, I was greatly concerned about the people," Mrs. Magowan recalls today, in her mansion overlooking the San Francisco Bay. She declines to comment further.

Mr. Magowan's recollection: "Well, I don't ever remember such a conversation ever occurred. . . . I might have said things like, 'We're going to do the best we can for our employees and I'm hopeful that we are going to be able to keep the vast majority with the new owners.'"

The story's particular brilliance comes from its judicious weighing of the deal's slight economic benefits with its heavy social toll, particularly on workers. Even workers handpicked for interviews by Safeway, Faludi notes, can't find much positive to say. The anecdotes are allowed to pile up until a critical mass is reached in the narrative, and, while the company is given ample opportunity to respond to each one, there is little it can say in its defense. The benefits are debatable; the costs, undeniable.

The story remained controversial even among some reporters who questioned the fairness of linking worker deaths to an economic event like an LBO. Peter Magowan wrote a lengthy letter to the *Journal*'s editors making the same point: "To assert or imply that an economic transaction is the primary cause or factor in a tragic event like a heart attack or suicide is to betray a bias that is so sharp and so deep that it defies reasonable discussion, not to mention demonstrating a total misunderstanding of the human heart." He also made an emphatic economic case for the buyout:

Most important, you never confronted the real question: the costs of change vs. the costs of no change. Never once did you mention the primary reason for most of the changes that took place at Safeway: labor costs that were out of line, the consequences, long and short term, of those costs, and the absolute business necessity in a low-margin, highly competitive industry for parity of labor costs. Safeway had to confront its major business problem—labor costs that were so out of line with its non-union competition that they caused a situation where 66% of the company was either making no money or losing money.[50]

Even Magowan's mother wrote to dispute the quote attributed to her in which she expressed concern for workers and protest that Faludi had showed up at her house "uninvited."

A General Accounting Office study of leveraged buyouts that year would find the company achieved "mixed results" after the LBO. But certainly, for its new owners, Safeway was a financial success over the long term by many measures. Soon after the story ran, the company conducted an initial public offering at $11.25 a share (lowered from earlier projections), but by the time of the GAO report the shares had risen past $20. Peter Magowan in 1992 would announce a $100 million investment in the San Francisco Giants. KKR divested itself fully of Safeway in 1999 at a profit to its investors of some $7 billion. Today, the company is one of the top three supermarket chains by market capitalization. Still, the necessity of the Safeway LBO is far from a foregone conclusion, even viewed strictly from the company's financial perspective. In 1988, as Faludi wrote in a sidebar to the Safeway story, Kroger Co. had faced similar dilemma. When a hostile takeover offer threatened a breakup of the company, Kroger managers resisted both it *and* a leveraged buyout. Instead, the grocer remained public but took on debt, paid its shareholders a large dividend, and gave employees a stake in the company. While Safeway cut its workforce by a third, Kroger trimmed its by only 3 percent. As of 2012, Safeway was the nation's fifth-largest food retailer. Kroger was second.[51]

"Safeway," which won the 1991 Pulitzer Prize for explanatory reporting, is one of the greatest business stories since Tarbell's "History of Standard Oil" and a high-water mark of postwar business journalism. The stories share common traits: They both address, in the broadest terms, an important economic phenomenon that had transformed American economic life and bewildered the public. Indeed, each confronts the most important economic event facing the country. In Tarbell's case, the subject was economic aggregation; in Faludi's, industrial dislocation and creeping financialization. The stories were supremely relevant and challenged official accounts and those in the mainstream business press, which claimed that the phenomenon under scrutiny was, on balance, beneficial to the public and, in any event, inevitable. Both rely on exhaustive reporting, a compilation of facts that ultimately achieves critical mass to powerful effect, along with dry, sober language (underpinned, to be sure, by a palpable sense of fury). Both works confront powerful institutions at the center of the transformation and exhibit ambition and courage. Both reporters approach the subject not as uninformed outsiders but as business cognoscenti, speaking of the subject and to the players on their own terms. One can disagree with their approach and their conclusions, but no one could argue that Tarbell didn't understand the oil business or Faludi, an LBO. Indeed, it is the reporters' fluency with the subjects that allows them to decode them for the rest of us (and they turn out to be not so complicated after all).

What good did they do? As noted, historians disagree whether Tarbell's work really brought much change. Even the significance of the 1911 Supreme Court decision to break up Standard Oil remains in dispute. Ron Chernow writes that reformers of the era believed it, at best, a "partial victory," since the standard it set for antitrust enforcement—that only "unreasonable" trusts should be restrained—allowed many to survive. Chernow argues that what the Supreme Court did formally, the market had already been doing as a practical matter, as Standard faced new competition in oil production from abroad and the U.S. southwest while its dominance even in its traditional strength, refining, had also begun to slip.[52]

If the practical "results" of even Tarbell's work are ambiguous, it's even more difficult to credit Faludi's work with any practical result at all. The 1980s binge in LBOs, whatever their economic benefits or harm, had already ended by the time "Safeway" was published. Certainly, LBOs themselves can't be said to have been discredited, at least for long; they returned, in even larger versions, in the 2000s under a new name, "private equity." But to try draw direct causation between works of journalism and this or that reform is to miss the point. Faludi's work, like Tarbell's, drew acclaim from the broader public and deserves study today because it grappled with tectonic shifts taking place in the economy and investigated—at no small risk to the news organization—the economic actors at the heart of them. It examined social metrics beyond the narrow confines of the investors' perspective. Who, after all, could have been happier with the status quo than a Standard Oil or Safeway shareholder?

What was obvious to insiders—oil dealers, railway clerks, government regulators (and reporters) in Tarbell's era; stock traders, union officials, investment bankers, labor lawyers (and reporters) in Faludi's—was made known to any literate citizen with fifteen cents for a copy of *McClure's* or fifty cents ninety years later for a copy of the *Journal*. These works identified not merely malpractices, but, as Richard Hoftstadter notes, malpractitioners. As we'll see in later chapters, journalism's greatest value isn't necessarily in bringing about reform but in creating the context for it. This journalism of ambition can't by itself avert financial catastrophe, but without it, readers have no chance of understanding when the financial system is tilting against them. And even if *nothing* happens as a result, muckraking business journalism of the Tarbell and Faludi type provides Hofstadter's literate—but isolated and bewildered—citizens with the means to understand the role of powerful institutions in helping to shift the economic landscape.

This is why they were great.

If the business press does not perform agenda-setting investigations every day, it is clearly capable of them. Few industries had the resources, public-relations savvy, legal firepower, and political clout of Big Tobacco, yet the business press (along with the general press) didn't shrink from what by any definition was a high-stakes confrontation. Nor were the factual issues simple but rather profoundly technical, to the point that ABC News found itself entangled in a debilitating defamation suit that ended with the news organization issuing a partial apology. The press investigations of the tobacco industries benefited their shareholders not at all; quite the opposite is the case.

It is a mistake to take this kind of accountability-oriented work for granted or to view it as somehow inevitable. Indeed, it was rare then and rarer today. But for the literate citizen, this kind of work in business reporting is indispensable. There really is no substitute.

By the time the mortgage era arrived after 2000, accountability reporting was a powerful, professional, independent, and, importantly, finally, mainstream tradition in American journalism. Certainly, stories like "Safeway" were exceptional, even for an era of ambitious business journalism. And with the usual cautions about romanticizing earlier eras, it is still surprising to look back at some of the highlights of the period and realize that "Safeway" wasn't such an outlier.

CHAPTER 5

CNBCization

Insiders, Access, and the Return of the Messenger Boy

S teve Lipin didn't fit the profile of a transformative media figure when he took over the mergers and acquisitions (M&A) beat for the *Wall Street Journal* in 1995. His look was studious and his manner remarkably affable and low key, given the stress of his new job. His rise had not been particularly meteoric. He had started in 1985 at the bottom of the business-news food chain, financial newsletters, progressed to *Institutional Investor*, a magazine for pension-fund managers, and then *American Banker*, another trade. In 1991, he followed his boss to the *Wall Street Journal* to cover banking. After four years of solid, unspectacular work, he moved to M&A, a beat that was moribund at the time.

Then the scoops started to come. "Kemper Agrees to Be Acquired by Group Headed by Zurich Insurance for $2 Billion," which ran April 11, 1995, reported that the financial-services firm was ending a tumultuous year in which it had rejected a hostile offer from General Electric and had seen a friendly deal fall apart twice. The story was based on information from "people familiar with the transaction," a form of attribution vague enough to encompass just about anyone involved in the deal—investment bankers, lawyers, company executives, public-relations specialists. The scoops got bigger and more frequent: "First Union Agrees to Buy First Fidelity for $5.5 Billion—Swap Valued at $65 a Share" (June 19, 1995); "Kimberly-Clark to Acquire Scott Paper in Stock Deal Valued at About $6.8 Billion" (July 17, 1995); "Upjohn and Pharmacia Sign $6 Billion Merger" (August 21, 1995). Lipin's scoops ranged across industries: banking, consumer products, pharmaceuticals: "Boeing and McDonnell Douglas Are Holding Merger Negotiations—Commercial, Military Aircraft Powerhouse Could Shake Industry" (November 16, 1995). Week in, week out, Lipin seemed to get just about every industry-transforming blockbuster.

A handful of major scoops over the course of an M&A reporter's career is considered a great success. Lipin had, by my count, at least seventy from 1995 through 2001, and the total value of the mergers he reported on was more than half a trillion dollars. He was published on prominent pages of the *Journal* more than five hundred times in five years, which could be a record. Those who traded on Lipin's information early enough stood to make serious money. The WorldCom bid alone added $8 billion to MCI's value in a single day. Most of the time, the names of the companies in Lipin's scoops had never been linked, let alone reported as combining. The stories often announced talks in progress, amplifying a sense of immediacy: this was news that hadn't even happened yet. They often said the deals "could be announced as early as today."

(A word of disclosure: Lipin was a colleague of mine at the *Journal* and a funder of *CJR*'s business desk, "The Audit," which I ran, in 2009 and 2010, before I began this book. He became a funder of *CJR* and member of its board of overseers after I had begun.)

Inside newsrooms and in the markets, major M&A scoops have an electrifying effect. Mergers represent big capital-allocation decisions affecting thousands of jobs and billions of investor dollars. And while M&A is routine on Wall Street, for most companies it is a one-time roll of the dice because of the amount of money involved. An acquisition taken is a dozen alternatives foregone. Big deals are also benchmarks—important pricing moments that help determine values and, in fact, create new realities. What was unthinkable one day—AOL/Time Warner, for instance—is reality the next. For a news organization, deal scoops create an aura of omniscience, a sense that it is plugged into Wall Street.

But Lipin's never-to-be-equaled run was part of a much larger wave, a transformation of the American economy and, with it, business news. The financial sector rose, the number of M&A deals exploded, and, more important for our purposes, the middle class stampeded into the stock market to an extent never before seen in American history. All eyes, it seemed, turned to the stock market—Wall Street—and business news ballooned with new outlets and reconfigured itself to meet this new interest. The push-me-pull-you struggle between access and accountability was about to lurch again.

Many people over the years have tried to puzzle through the question of why the news looks the way it does. In *The Brass Check,* a 1919 exposé of American newspapers, muckraker Upton Sinclair argued that his fellow journalists were little more than servants of elites, plying their craft to serve the political and financial interests of their employers, newspaper owners. The "brass check" referred to the token purchased by a brothel patron who would then give it to the prostitute of his choice—the journalist, naturally, being the prostitute. The propaganda model of Edward Herman and Noam Chomsky can be seen as a variation of the brass-check theory, with an added caveat that professionals within journalism can occasionally escape the boundaries drawn by owners. But those successes, the theory goes, only serve to disguise the fact the boundaries exist in the first place. Herbert Gans, meanwhile, argues that "the news" is a culture unto itself. Rather than being a compliant supporter of elites, or the "Establishment," journalism culture views nation and society through its own set of values and with its own conception of the good social order. Reflecting a less polarized time, Gans asserted journalism could not be categorized as either conservative or liberal but rather reformist in tendency.[1]

The theories have merit. The trouble with them is that they're static, and news culture isn't. Rather, it changes over time, reflecting public tastes, social trends, the political climate, and internal battles for newsroom primacy. In my view, the dynamism of twentieth-century business journalism and newsroom culture generally is most closely captured by Pierre Bourdieu and his "field theory," which holds that society is made up of a network of semiautonomous fields operating within a larger political field. A field is a network of historical and current relations (a profession such as journalism, for instance). Fields are spaces simultaneously of conflict and competition as agents compete to gain a monopoly over the species of capital that's most effective in the field. Each field has its own regulatory logic and internal principles that govern the game on the field. Importantly, each individual field is marked by polarities: opposing forces within the field that compete for primacy, one over the other.[2]

Society, then, is an ensemble of relatively autonomous spheres of play that can't be collapsed under any overall societal logic, like capitalism, postmodernism, or some larger theoretical model. Altering the distribution and relative weight of the different forms of capital within a field is tantamount to modifying the structure of the field. Therefore, fields have a historical dynamism about them; they have a malleability that avoids the determinism of the classical structures, such as class-based models. Fields change over time.

I argue that within the journalism "field" a primal conflict has been between access and accountability, Edwards Jones vs. Ida Tarbell. But this is hardly a fair fight. Nearly all advantages in journalism rest with access. The stories are generally shorter and quicker to do. Further, the interests of access reporting and its subjects often run in harmony. Powerful leaders are, after all, the sources for much of access reporting's product. The harmonious relationship can lead to a synergy between reporter and source. Aided by access reporting, the source provides additional scoops. As one effective story follows another, access reporting is able to serve a news organization's production needs, which tend to be voracious and unending. Access reporting thus wins support within the news hierarchy.

As access reporting circles the globe, accountability reporting is just putting on its shoes. Accountability reporting requires time, space, expense, risk, and stress. It makes few friends. Often, after one investigation is completed, accountability reporting must start from scratch. More than occasionally, accountability reporting must scrap a project altogether, further stressing a busy news organization.

Bourdieu's theories play out in American newsrooms every day. The post-Kilgore *Journal* provides just one illustration. Ed Cony, the *Journal*'s managing editor from 1965 to 1970, seemed "to disdain routine business stories," according to Edward Scharff, and set up a Page One operation of elite writers and storytellers who had his taste for almost anything else—witchcraft in Manhattan, life in a Scottish monastery, and so on. Indeed, when a new managing editor, Fred Taylor, took over, he felt obliged to issue an edict that the front page of the *Wall Street Journal* had to have at least *one* story about business or economics—every single day! On the other side, a Kilgore successor as CEO of Dow Jones, Warren Phillips, Cony's boss, pushed relentlessly for hard news and scoops—especially after Reuters launched a financial newswire to compete with the Dow Jones ticker in 1966. Once, at a dinner of news executives, Phillips harangued the staff about the Reuters threat until Cony, his patience exhausted, finally said: "Oh, fuck Reuters."[3]

The tug-of-war continued through the 1970s then shifted dramatically back to breaking business news under managing editor Larry O'Donnell, a former Detroit bureau chief. Scharff describes a tour of bureaus in which O'Donnell laid down the law in no uncertain terms in San Francisco:

Speaking in a low, flat monotone, O'Donnell accused them all of letting the newspaper down, of growing lazy, self-indulgent and indifferent toward the *Journal*'s true mission as the leading business newspaper. [The bureau chief] and his men had felt their main job was to produce work that was imaginative and informative, stories that were memorable and entertaining. But O'Donnell charged them with pursuing such stories mainly for personal glorification. All that would have to stop, he insisted. They would have to learn to be more on top of the news; they would have to make the *Journal* more of a *news*paper. There would be emphasis on the nuts and bolts, less on the bizarre and irrelevant. In effect, what O'Donnell was telling them was to lower their own ambitions, precisely as he had done with his staff in Detroit.[4]

Office politics? Sure. But such is how news is defined within the field. A push for more "hard news" may sound like a muscular call to arms, but in many cases it represents a retreat from the hard work and risks of agenda-setting reporting. It may sound like a call for objectivity and fact-based reporting, but the question then arises: whose facts? Chances are, those of an institution that represents a particular set of interests whereas journalism—for all its faults, and when it is working right—represents the public's.

The two tendencies represent different journalism subcultures. They rely on different sources—insiders versus outsiders, authorities versus dissidents, top executives versus fired executives (that is, whistleblowers). They require different skill sets, diplomacy versus confrontation. They even presuppose different worldviews. Access journalism might tend to accept institutions and systems as they are and seek to learn their internal goings-on; accountability journalism tends to question institutions and systems. One can be said to transmit orthodox views; the other, heterodox. Indeed, the differences can be listed:

ACCESS	ACCOUNTABILITY
Fast	Slow
Short	Long
Elite sources	Dissident sources
Orthodox views	Heterodox views
Top-down	Bottom-up
Quantity	Quality
Investor	Public
Niche	Mass
Management friendly	Management unfriendly
Inverted pyramid	Storytelling
Functionalistic	Moralistic

A final trait that defines access reporting is its inevitability. The public never need worry about its fate. There will always be news, and, competitive pressures being what they are, journalism will always chase it. Advocating for more "scoops" and "hard news" is like advocating for the tide to come in.

While it may seem that one is the "bad" kind of journalism and the other the good, that's in no way the case. It is essential to know what people in power are thinking, and it is a nontrivial task to find out. Bob Woodward has been criticized during his post-Watergate career for taking part in "a trade in which the great grant access in return for glory." Christopher Hitchens said of his work: "Access is all. Analysis and criticism are nowhere."[5] Yet most, including Hitchens, acknowledge its value. Neither is access reporting synonymous with flattering or favorable reporting. Indeed, it routinely stings powerful actors as part of its daily business. When *Politico*'s Mike Allen in 2008 asked Republican presidential candidate John McCain how many houses he owned (eight), McCain couldn't immediately remember, and the scoop jarred a presidential campaign. Rather, what marks access reporting is its closed loop of sources, its top-down nature, and its lack of interest in systemic problems. Tethering itself to the neverending flow of news events, access reporting allows powerful institutions to set the public agenda, to define the "news." Most of all, one could say access reporting is defined by its insularity, an insistence on looking at its subject through frames set by the institutions on its beat. In business news, the access frame can be widened to include a focus on investor interests as opposed to the public interest.

Here some nuance is in order. Championing investors—particularly small investors—is a point of pride in business news, as well it might be. Some of its most celebrated stories, as we've seen, fiercely took on management for wasting, manipulating, or otherwise misusing the money entrusted to it by shareholders and did so in the face of fierce resistance from highly paid lawyers and public-relations specialists. Indeed, these stories were technically difficult, took a long time, and involved a high degree of risk to the news organization. Let's move *all* of these shareholder-defense stories, which we can call financial investigations, under the accountability reporting frame. But financial investigations are a tiny fraction of conventional investor-oriented stories that explore a company's prospects in its market.

During the mortgage era and afterward, the insularity of access reporting—its exclusive reliance on elite sources, its echo-chamber qualities—hamstrung business-press coverage of mortgage lenders and Wall Street. Indeed, the sped-up, incremental approach to news-gathering seriously impaired the business press's ability to detect corruption in the mortgage market and aftermarket, but its insider focus was fatal.

But business journalism's normative shift toward access reporting was driven by larger forces: the economy was transforming. Lipin's remarkable run of scoops, for instance, came in part because there were more scoops to get. After the economic doldrums of the late 1980s and early 1990s, M&A activity exploded just as Lipin was arriving on the beat. After dipping to about 2,500 a year in the early 1990s, the number of North American transactions crept up to just under 5,000 in 1994 then soared to about 20,000 a year in 1998 and 1999. Total value of the deals shot from about $1.5 trillion in 1994 to $2.4 trillion in 1998—a record that has not been equaled even during the debt-fueled buying spree led by private-equity firms in the next decade.

More broadly, the rising prominence of the financial sector in the economy was becoming increasingly difficult to miss. Economists began to link widening problems of wage stagnation and income inequality to a new economic configuration that had been explicitly promoted by financial sector interests. Financialization had begun.[6] Wall Street itself was expanding. What had been a group of closely held partnerships operating within a tightly knit, albeit highly competitive community where partners risked their own capital was morphing into a consolidating collection of globalized, publicly traded giants that risked other people's money, took on extravagant levels of debt, and exerted increasing influence on the economy, the culture, and the political system.

And business news would be transformed by the great expansion of stock-market investing into the American middle class, which became increasingly curious about all things Wall Street. In Ida Tarbell's day, only about 1 percent of the American public owned common stocks. The figure rose to 10 percent before the 1929 crash (with most of the increase coming in 1928), fell back again to the low single digits through most of the 1950s, and, through the 1970s, never reached above the mid-teens. Indeed, as late as 1980, only 13 percent of the country owned stocks. But by 1989, the figure had soared to 32 percent, and by 1998, more than half the country, 52 percent owned either stocks or equity mutual funds, either directly in their own accounts or indirectly in retirement and trust accounts.

Driving the change was a postwar expansion of the financial-services industry that transformed—and was transformed by—the American public's changing views of credit, debt, stocks, and Wall Street. In 1994, Joseph Nocera wrote *A Piece of the Action: How the Middle Class Joined the Money Class*, which chronicled the metamorphosis of the industry that created the credit card, money-market accounts, discount brokerages, mutual funds, and the financial-planning business. Nocera argues convincingly that the inflation of the mid- to late 1970s forever changed the public's attitudes toward money and investing. Americans flocked to money-market funds offered by the Reserve Fund (launched 1972), because the prime rate would hit an astonishing 20 percent (in 1980) while a Depression-era banking rule capped bank rates on deposits in the mid-single digits.[7] And if inflation sparked the public's search for yield for defensive reasons, the bull market that began in 1982 fed it for more positive ones. When the bull market began, the Dow stood at 776.92. By 1987, it would triple to 2570. After the crash that year, it would keep rising.

Nocera declared that the American middle class had pushed aside elites to take control of the stock market:

> The financial markets were once the province of the wealthy, and they're not anymore; they belong to all of us. We've finally gotten a piece of the action. If we have to pay attention now, if we have to spend a little time learning about which financial instruments make sense for us and which ones don't, that seems to me an acceptable price to pay. Democracy always comes at some price. Even financial democracy.[8]

He was not alone in noting the cultural shift. Chernow, the Rockefeller biographer, would hail the middle class's march into the markets. "Never before in American history have so many middle-class people enjoyed something at least faintly resembling the 'private banking' available to the rich," he noted. "The culture of investing has become an abiding part of the American scene."[9] This triumphalist view, though, did not take into account a fraying safety net that pushed Americans increasingly into Wall Street's arms for their retirement and other basic needs.

Their sanguine view of the stock market notwithstanding, these commentators might have even underestimated its strength. By the time Nocera published his book, the Dow had recovered from the 1987 crash and had reached 3,500, a gain of more than 40 percent beyond the precrash peaks. Then things *really* took off. The Dow would triple, rising to 11,000 by the end of the 1990s, and the middle-class march into the stock market would become a stampede. In *Bull! A History of the Boom, 1982–1999*, Maggie Mahar demonstrates that the first part of the bull market was driven by institutional investors, and it was only in the 1990s that stock investing truly became a common middle-class practice. From 1981 to 1985, the New York Stock Exchange estimated that the number of individual investors increased by just 6 million, to 36 million. The number of mutual-fund accounts increased fivefold during the 1980s (from 12 million in 1980 to 62 million in 1989 according to the ICI *Fact Book*), but the majority of these funds were not based in equities. From mid-1983 to October 1987, there were only two months when more money flowed into stock funds than bond funds. As late as 1992, the largest share of 401(k) money would still be invested in guaranteed investment contracts, fixed-income instruments offered by insurance companies.[10]

By the end of the 1980s, mutual-fund investors had more money in bond funds ($290 billion) than in stock funds ($240 billion) and twice as much again in money-market funds ($428 billion). In 1993, 401(k) investors began to put more than half their savings into stocks and stock funds.[11] As bond yields fell and stock prices rose, stock funds grew, but even as late as 1994, Americans still allocated more to bond ($527 billion) and money-market funds ($611 billion) than stock funds ($852 billion). By the end of the 1990s, however, the public was heavily invested in the stock market, with $4 trillion in stock funds, compared to $812 billion in bond funds and $1.6 trillion in money markets.[12]

A *Wall Street Journal* story toward the end of the decade captured the changed national mood. The 5,000-word story headlined "The Soaring '90s" included a profile of Shirley Sauerwein, a Redondo Beach social worker who aptly symbolized the middle class's new relationship to the market. After never owning a share, in 1991 she heard about a local company that had signed a deal with Russia, opened a brokerage account, and bought one hundred shares at twelve dollars each.

> Today, that company is MCI Worldcom Inc. Her original $1,200 now is worth $16,000, part of a mid-six-figure portfolio that includes Red Hat Inc., Yahoo! Inc., General Electric Co. and America Online Inc. "I've doubled my money in two years," says Ms. Sauerwein, who is 55 years old. "I'm staggered, aren't you? It's amazing. You can't make that in social work." . . . Ms. Sauerwein's stock-picking has been so successful that she's cut back her social work to weekends and spends weekdays trading full-time from home. "I make a few buys and a few sells each day," she says. Her goal: to make $150,000 in annual trading profits to build a financial cushion that she and her husband can live on in retirement.

Wall Street patter had become part of middle class discourse.

> Along the way, Ms. Sauerwein has developed a few investing philosophies that speak volumes about how deeply ingrained "momentum" investing has become—and how utterly unfashionable it is to focus on "value" stocks. "All these people say 'buy and hold,'" she says. "If a stock continues to decline, there comes a time when you better get off the boat."
> The lesson? "You have to sell your losers. If a stock goes up, it's not because I was a whiz. And if the tape goes against me," she adds, "I won't stick around. I keep my losses to 10%."[13]

One August day in 1995, around the time Lipin assumed the M&A beat at the *Wall Street Journal*, another pivotal moment in the evolution—one could say "revolution"—of business news came when the New York Stock Exchange for the first time in its history allowed a journalist, Maria Bartiromo of CNBC, to report live daily from the exchange floor. A native of Brooklyn's working-class Bay Ridge neighborhood, Bartiromo had worked for Lou Dobbs on CNN's *MoneyLine* when she was hired away by Roger Ailes, a Republican political consultant turned TV executive, who put her on the air.[14] The deal with the NYSE came two years later, when she was twenty-eight, and her presence on the floor was an arresting image. Petite, attractive, and well-coiffed, equipped with clipboard and headset, she stood on the exchange floor surrounded by traders, almost all men, coming and going in their multicolored jackets (representing, savvy viewers would learn, different tasks or different firms). Occasionally brushed and jostled, she stood her ground, coolly rattling off information about the market and companies—analysts' calls, earnings estimates, company news, and the like—looking up from the floor at the camera with an air of steely competence. The combination did not escape New York City's tabloids, which soon captured the public's feeling in a nickname: "Money Honey."

What prestige the exchange assignment conferred on Bartiromo and CNBC, the journalist returned in kind, lending a once obscure and not particularly well liked institution a new air of glamour, vitality, urgency, modernity, and sex appeal. As retail investing increased, so did CNBC's ratings, from fewer than 50,000 viewers in the early days to more than 250,000 by the end of the 1990s. Bartiromo's was the attractive face of the people's capitalism.

CNBC had started as a low-budget entertainment channel in 1980 but was recast as the Consumer News and Business Channel in 1988 when NBC, then owned by General Electric, struck a deal to lease the channel's transponder. The network took off only after it won a successful bidding war against a partnership including Dow Jones (one of several botched business moves that would undermine the *Wall Street Journal*'s publisher, as we'll see) for the longer-established Financial News Network, then in financial turmoil. The price was $157 million, which was seen as low even at the time.

The network's lineup, then and now, consisted of a series of programs centered around the trading hours of the New York Stock Exchange from nine-thirty a.m. to four p.m.: On *Squawk Box* (named after an old fashioned intercom system used by Wall Street firms), three anchors discussed the day's economic news and research reports and interviewed such Wall Street analysts as Goldman's Abby Joseph Cohen and Prudential's Ralph Acampora. The scene then shifted to Bartiromo and *Opening Bell*, where she would rattle off financial news and, significantly for her viewers, advance word of the latest Wall Street stock recommendations that she was able to learn from sources within the firms. At eleven, *The Call* focused on real-time market coverage. *Power Lunch* included interviews with top business executives. In the middle of the afternoon, *Street Signs* focused on trends and world events affecting markets. From three to five p.m. *Closing Bell* wrapped up the day's market movements. After trading, the network would shift to a round-table discussion of stocks (the program now in the slot is *Fast Money*, which focuses on stocks for short-term trades). At six p.m. Jim Cramer, a former hedge-fund manager and founder of TheStreet.com, picked stocks on *Mad Money*.

The network is built around and plays to live television's strength: immediacy. The screen is often a jumble of unconnected information. During trading hours, a "ticker" (a modern version of the machine invented by Edward A. Calahan in 1863 and unveiled in New York City in 1867) streams stock prices and price changes of individuals firms), as well as the Dow, the broader S&P 500, and the spot price for oil. The actual information is a recitation of reports, estimates, predictions, and data from Wall Street firms, hedge funds, economic consultants, government agencies (the Labor Department, the Fed), public companies, and other institutions.

CNBC saw itself as a force for the democratization of finance. Its executives claimed their mission was to provide everyday people the same information available to Wall Street professionals. In *Fortune Tellers*, Howard Kurtz profiles a CNBC executive, Bill Bolster, who articulated the network's idealistic view of its mission. Bolster

> liked to reminisce about his childhood in Waterloo, Iowa, where his father was a businessman who dabbled in the stock market. His dad's only source of stock information was *The Wall Street Journal*, which arrived by mail two days late. It was

hard to understand how his old man didn't get taken to the cleaners. The time lag gave a huge advantage to the people who worked in an eight-block stretch of Manhattan, the sort of advantage that CNBC is helping to eliminate.

No wonder the traders felt threatened by this upstart network.... It was the good old white boys of Wall Street screwing around this shadowy system, which was threatened by the rise of electronic trading and the Internet and the searing spotlight of cable television.[15]

CNBC's success lay to an important degree in its style as much as its substance. It put a human face on reporting that is essentially about dry numbers. In the 1990s *Squawk Box* was anchored by Mark Haines, a rumpled curmudgeon who bantered with and gave nicknames to cohosts and reporters. David Faber, "The Brain," was handsome, articulate, and young. Another anchor, Ron Insana, was bald, bespectacled, and cerebral. Bill Griffeth, the old hand who had originally started at FNN in 1981, was avuncular and steady. Bartiromo, as noted, combined comeliness and outer-borough toughness. Becky Quick projected a financially savvy girl next door. Faber's 2000 marriage to a CNN producer was the subject of much good-natured on-the-air ribbing and banter on *Squawk Box*. Insana's decision in the late 1990s to forgo a toupee he wore on the air created a sensation.[16]

The network had been consciously modeled on ESPN's *Sports Center*.[17] The anchors and reporters provided pre-, post-, and mid-"game" reports, complete with sideline interviews with the players, but the game was the stock market. The public—enough of it—responded with enthusiasm. Anchors found themselves stopped on the street. Celebrities pronounced themselves fans: Regis Philbin, Charles Barkley, Andre Agassi, Saudi prince Alwaleed bin Talal. A Cleveland housewife started the "Hunks of CNBC" chatroom. Joey Ramone wrote a song about Maria Bartiromo.[18]

By the late 1990s, print journalists were trooping to the network's studios in Englewood, New Jersey, to learn the secrets of CNBC's soaring ratings and to pronounce that the network had captured the national zeitgeist. "CNBC is the TV network of our time," said *Fortune* in a piece headlined "I Want My CNBC." "The Revolution Will be Televised (on CNBC)," wrote *Fast Company* in a mostly laudatory 8,000-word article that called the network "the live feed of the new economy." It said: "The 1990s witnessed a dramatic democratization of investing. And CNBC has driven that trend by taking some of the mystery out of the stock market and making it more accessible, by giving to anyone with a remote control access to the kind of information that used to be available only to big firms." But even *Fast Company* couldn't help but notice CNBC's limitations, even as a deliverer of facts. "For one thing, it's more opinion and analysis than news."[19]

The *Fast Company* story was dated May 31, 2000—just in time for the revolution, such as it was, to end. The NASDAQ would soon have its historic crash from more than 5,000 to under 2,000 the following spring.

Alongside CNBC, a squadron of new business publications was launched to meet the growing interest in business and money. CNN launched its own financial news network. AOL opened a mutual-fund center. Great metropolitan dailies ramped up staffing on their business-news desks, once newsroom backwaters. The *Los Angeles Times*, which had twenty to twenty-five business reporters in the early 1980s, had ninety by 2000; the *Washington Post* went from eighteen to eighty-one. The same was true for regional dailies: the *Cleveland Plain Dealer* went from nine to twenty-four or twenty-five; the *Tampa Tribune*, from two to fourteen. TV networks' weekly coverage of the stock markets almost doubled between 1988 and 1999, from 152 to 296. In 1996 alone, twenty-two new personal-finance magazines were launched.[20] The changes to business news were reflected in the names of the new outlets—*SmartMoney* (launched 1992), *The Street* (1996), *Fast Company* (1995), *MarketWatch* (1997)—all promising an insider's perspective and a fixed gaze on markets and the latest business news, no matter how granular.

The total number of business-news stories published each year, according to ProQuest's business-news database, ABI/Inform, jumped from about 168,000 in 1989 to 322,000 a decade later, a rise of 192 percent, and it kept rising, to 461,000 in 2009. Mergers-and-

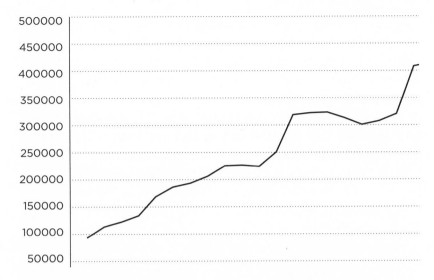

Figure 5.1   The Rise of Business News: Total number of English-language business stories published, 1984–2010
Source: Author research, ABI/Inform Complete.

acquisitions news, once the concern of specialists, also took off, propelled in part by a dramatic rise in M&A itself. The volume of M&A stories grew from about 1,100 to about 4,600, more than 300 percent, from 1989 to 1999, according to ProQuest's tagging system, which provides a rough guide. This rise was even faster than the number of deals themselves, which rose 187 percent, from about 12,800 to 36,800 during the period, according to Thomson Financial. (Both deal stories and deals dropped and then rebounded after the Tech Wreck in 2000, but continued to grow to about 4,900 and 43,000, respectively, in 2009.)[21]

In the tug-of-war over the definition of business news, the 1990s brought a new emphasis on the investor-oriented side. Access reporting was ascendant. A successful run on the M&A beat became a career launching pad for individual reporters, and deal scoops helped to propel entire news organizations. The *Financial Times*

rose to prominence in the U.S. market in the late 1990s, citing its scoops as evidence of its newsgathering prowess.[22] Many of these came from Will Lewis, who became the youngest editor in chief of the *Daily Telegraph* in 2006 at the age of thirty-seven; he went on to a senior position in News Corp.'s News International unit. CNBC rose to even greater prominence, helped to a large degree by the scoop-getting exploits of David "The Brain" Faber, now one of the network's top personalities.

As it was increasing its focus on investor concerns, business news, paradoxically, was narrowing. CNBC-ized news is characterized by two traits: a focus on insider, investor-focused news and speed. And while technology has obviously increased the velocity and volume of business news, the shift represents something less modern: a return to the business press's early-twentieth-century roots as an intramarket information broker, reporting, as in the earlier days, from the inside out.

Actually, the term "revolution," employed by *Fast Company* and others to describe CNBC and the popularization of stock investing, was far more apt than the gushing writers intended. Far from marking a break with the past or ushering in a new era, as the magazine implied, the rush to provide incremental, market-serving news was a revolution in the literal sense—a return to the past, to business news's narrow origins as messenger service between market participants. What Dow, Jones, and Bergstrasser did with a special stylus and a platoon of messenger boys, Lipin, Faber, Andrew Ross Sorkin, and the like do with televisions and graphics.

It's worth pausing here to examine the assumptions that underlie the theory of financial democratization. This paradigm envisions retail investors watching CNBC at home, receiving incremental information about markets or a particular company *at the same time as Wall Street traders*, and, empowered by online brokerage accounts, acting on it immediately. The idea of CNBC putting its viewers on an equal footing with Wall Street traders—let alone high-frequency trading programs—is beyond dubious. It's a myth. In any case, a blow-by-blow stream of incremental stock-market news lends itself not to investment but speculation.

In the Tech Wreck of 2000, the democratization of financial news was revealed as one of a long string of episodes in which the retail investors, the "little guy," turn out to be the "dumb money." As Mahar illustrates, corporate insiders began to sell in earnest well before retail investors, those said to benefit from the CNBC-led information revolution, caught on. From September 1999 through July 2000, insider selling of large blocks of stock (at least $1 million or 100,000 shares) rose to $43.1 billion—twice as much as insiders sold over the same span in 1997 and 1998. The $39 billion in shares sold by insiders in the first six months of 2000 was more than in all of 1999. In the case of Global Crossing, for instance, insiders at the doomed fiber-optic company unloaded more than $1.3 billion from 1999 through November 2001. The company's CEO, Gary Winnick, a former bond salesman under Michael Milken at Drexel, managed to sell shares worth $734 million, netting a personal profit of $714 million, long before the company would descend into bankruptcy in January 2002. The company's 8,000 employees, by contrast, were unable to sell the company's shares in their 401(k) in the period before the bankruptcy; their assets had been frozen. Indeed, most middle- and lower-income Americans who owned stocks in 2001 had only started buying them after 1995. Of households with assets of less than $25,000, 68 percent had made their first equity purchase in 1996 or later, and an alarming 43 percent in 1999 or later.[23]

The granular, insider approach and the focus on incremental news development instead of the larger forces driving events would likewise do CNBC's viewers little good a decade later, on the eve of the mortgage crisis. The network, like the rest of business news, was forced to grope through the crisis with scant knowledge of the true nature of the subprime mortgage market, about which much more in chapters 6, 7, and 8. Its top stock picker and financial commentator, Jim Cramer, host of *Mad Money*, was roundly and justly mocked for declaiming, "Bear Stearns is fine!" in March 2008, two months before the Wall Street firm would crash and be rescued by a buyout subsidized by the Federal Reserve. And while Cramer and CNBC would later argue that he meant only that brokerage accounts—not the common stock—were "fine," in fact, no part of that statement was true. Brokerage accounts, and any other money entrusted to Bear Stearns were in danger at the time. The firm, like the financial system as a whole, was not fine.[24]

And even granting whatever (dubious) benefit granular insider journalism provides to investors, it can be said to be fairly useless to the public at large. It faces the same limitations as its predecessors. It made business journalism ever more dependent on the very institutions it purported to cover. It gave business reporters *less* time to develop stories and made them *less* able—and less inclined—to challenge official versions of events; *less* able to examine systemic shifts that might pose dangers to even investors, let alone the broader society; and less able and less inclined, in the end, to do any kind of original reporting that did not emanate from an institution.

Even without taking into account the increased competition in the market for business news, Robert Shiller points out the undeniable attraction of the stock market as a generator of news to match the immediate needs of news organizations to provide incremental changes, "news," for the perpetual news cycle.[25] The stock market changes not just daily but by the second, perfectly matching the needs of live TV. It also offers drama, big players, and the possibility of fortunes being made or lost at any given moment. And it builds up and tears down prognosticators (Abbey Joseph Cohen, Mary Meeker, Henry Blodget) as the performance of their predictions dictates.

CNBC-ized, insider-oriented journalism—all too conveniently for its advocates within news organizations—had neither the time nor the resources for the arduous, risky, and indispensable investigative reporting of major financial institutions. For instance, Faber in his CNBC biography, claims credit for "breaking" the 2002 story of "massive fraud" at WorldCom, the corrupt telecommunications company. In fact, Faber was the first to report that WorldCom was ready to admit wrongdoing by restating its earnings. He did not through his own reporting unearth fraud at WorldCom. As Mahar points out, WorldCom at the time of his report was trading at sixty-one cents. "That's the difference between being an investigative reporter and getting scoops," Mahar quotes Herb Greenberg, a financial investigative reporter and CNBC commenter.[26] For the general reader, it's the difference between lightning and a lightning bug.

CNBC-ized news stands in opposition to Kilgore's vision, the basis for business journalism's original postwar expansion. Where Kilgore deemphasized what happened "yesterday," deal journalism stressed what happened a few minutes ago. Where Kilgore counseled depth, deal journalism offers speed. Where Kilgore emphasized storytelling—narrative, character, detail—to make the complicated simple, deal journalism offered wire-service writing, the very pyramid style Kilgore abandoned. Kilgore disliked jargon. Deal journalism is marinated in it.

Access journalism is condemned to be forever taken by surprise by events. While it has been widely faulted for hyping the Tech Bubble (a charge, by the way, that Shiller finds overdone),[27] it was completely taken by surprise by the staggering corruption that rocked the corporate world in the early 2000s: Tyco, Adelphia, and World-Com were all brand-name, closely covered companies that collapsed not just in financial failure but as criminal frauds.[28]

Enron was a special case in which accountability reporting did play a role in exposing what would become the era's biggest criminal case. *Fortune*'s Bethany McLean is most often cited as triggering questions about the company's finances with a March 5, 2001, article, "Is Enron Overpriced?," which discussed the company's complexity, mysterious transactions, erratic cash flow, and huge debt. Jonathan Weil, a *Wall Street Journal* reporter, raised questions about Enron and other energy-trading firms even earlier with "Energy Traders Cite Gains, but Some Math Is Missing" (September 20, 2000).

But even Enron, which had been on *Fortune*'s "most innovative" list of firms for six straight years, was not considered a shining moment for the business press. "It's fair to say the press did not do a great job in covering Enron," Steve Shepard, *Businessweek*'s editor in chief, said in 2002. "Enron was really a systemic failure of all the checks and balances we have on corporate governance: integrity of management, board of directors, audit committee of the board, outside accounting firm, Wall Street analysts and ultimately the press. And all of us failed."[29] But coverage of most of the scandals of the time was reduced to after-the-fact explanations, typified by a *Wall Street Journal* series in 2002 that ran under the plaintive headline "What's Wrong?" The series won a Pulitzer—in the "explanatory" category.[30]

The so-called democratization of financial news turned out to be its opposite—news issued by institutions provided to reporters operating within the narrowest of frames. CNBC views business news solely through the frame of stock investors and, at best, reporters might challenge institutions on these terms. Even if they were inclined to stray beyond these boundaries, they lacked the time and support to do so. That's just not what CNBC does. "Democratized news," as proffered, is a welter of reports, presented in an atomized and granular format, that flow from government agencies, public companies, and investment banks. The news is stripped of the depth and context that "literate citizens" need to arm themselves with knowledge of a financial system that was growing ever-larger and playing an ever-more problematic role in their lives as economic actors and taxpayers, as citizens.

CNBC-ized news lends itself to a symbiotic relationship between institution and news organization, a closeness that blurs the line between the two. In October 2000, CNBC's Mark Haines interviewed Enron's chairman, Kenneth Lay, lobbing softball questions, such as, "So you are an old economy company using the new economy to great effect?" and "I imagine that the additional revenue pretty much goes straight to the bottom line. I mean, once you have it set up, there is very little incremental costs, right?" He then interviewed CEO Jeffrey Skilling the following April, asking at the outset: "Enron en route to greater earnings?" But before posing the question to Skilling, he added: "And in fair disclosure terms I will say that I own shares of Enron and have for quite some time, more than a year" (in other words, as Mahar points out, at the time when he interviewed Lay).[31]

In late 2006, Bartiromo herself became the story when the *Wall Street Journal* reported that Citigroup, a central player on any financial reporter's beat, had ousted the head of its wealth-management unit, citing, among other things, his relationship with Bartiromo. The executive, Todd Thomson, had spent more than $5 million from his unit's marketing budget to sponsor a program on the Sundance

Channel hosted, among others, by Bartiromo.[32] Thomson had also arranged for Bartiromo to speak to clients at luncheons in Hong Kong and Shanghai and flew back with her on the corporate jet. CNBC told the *Journal* that Bartiromo received permission for the trip and "payment was arranged."[33]

But beyond the instances where reporters might have straddled ethical lines, CNBC and the financial system it covers often seem so close it's hard tell where one leaves off and the other begins. In 2002, two finance professors at Emory University found an astonishing feedback loop between favorable comments made about individual companies by Bartiromo on her *Midday Call* segment and share prices of those companies: they jumped a tenth of a point within fifteen seconds and six-tenths of a percentage point (not a small number) within a minute.[34] Indeed, the study, by Jeffrey A. Busse and Clifton Greene, found some stocks moving up slightly *before* the CNBC mentions, touching off a flurry of press investigations (which came to nothing).[35]

It is not uncommon for business reporters to follow the path of Edward Jones into the financial-services industry. Lipin, for instance, left the *Wall Street Journal* to run U.S. operations for Brunswick Group, a public-relations firm dealing with financial matters, including mergers and acquisitions. Likewise, few in financial journalism batted an eye when longtime CNBC anchor Ron Insana left in 2006 to start a hedge fund that invested in other hedge funds. The melding of media and market reached a high point in 1999, when CNBC purchased a stake in an electronic stock-trading company, Archipelago. News coverage, such as it was, focused on CNBC's potential conflicts of interest as it would have to cover both Archipelago and a half-dozen electronic trading competitors. Not remarked upon was the fact that its partners in the deal included Goldman Sachs, Merrill Lynch, and other Wall Street players (along with a unit of Reuters, another news organization, which already owned a electronic trading company). CNBC sold its stake a few years later (Archipelago was later bought by the New York Stock Exchange). But the fact that CNBC had become partners with the Wall Street firms it purported to cover was not perceived to be an issue,

A significant percentage of deal scoops are not dug out by industrious reporting but planted with reporters selected beforehand by the buying firm or its representatives. A carefully planned exclusive offers the Wall Street team control over the content and timing of the information. And while news organs beaten on the scoop will want to downplay the deal as much as possible, the importance of the news to its core audience tempers those desires. Hard feelings among competitors are smoothed out—or not—in the days following the scoop. In any event, there is little that competing reporters or news organizations can do about it. If offered a scoop the next time, they can hardly turn it down.

Once, while I was a reporter at the *Wall Street Journal* covering the paper and packaging industries, I received a call from the general counsel of a big industrial company I covered. He had important information for me; could we meet? Sure, I said. When? Now, he answered; he was calling from a payphone downstairs in the lobby of the World Financial Center, where the *Journal* was headquartered. A few minutes later, he strode off the elevator flanked by a PR man and another assistant. Unthinkingly, I offered them seats next to my desk in the newsroom, but the general counsel asked if there was an office where we could speak privately. He wasn't being melodramatic. Behind closed doors, and with the grave tones of a man who was placing his career in my hands, he unveiled his company's plans for an unsolicited, multi-billion-dollar offer to break up an already-announced cross-border merger between two leading competitors. The company was making a bold play. It wanted the attention that only the *Journal* could then provide. The understanding was that in return for the scoop, we would play it big.

My worldwide scoop the next morning led both A3, then the leading page for breaking news, and the "10-point," the stack of top news stories blurbed on Page One. Almost as satisfying, my boss received a note from Lipin and a colleague congratulating us on the scoop but asking, with thinly veiled annoyance, that they be given a heads-up in the future since they could have contributed the expertise of their investment-banking sources. Hah, I thought. This only meant that I had beaten Lipin, the king, and the king was sore about it. It felt glorious.

And, unbelievably, it got better. The next day, the PR sources who had accompanied the executive on his clandestine visit the day before called for a congratulatory postmortem chat and told me in pass-ing that he had been fielding anguished and angry calls from beaten reporters from other news organizations all that morning. They accused him, not incorrectly, of spoon-feeding me the scoop merely because I was at the *Journal* (in "our"—mine and my sources'—defense, I *had* cultivated this particular company for months). Until then, I hadn't believed the euphoria I had been feeling could possibly be heightened, but hearing about my competitors' howls of recrimi-nation made it soar to almost unbearable levels. I didn't known it was possible to feel this good—from a story! I grinned until my face hurt. I laughed and crowed to my pals in the newsroom, waving the paper, pointing out with the mock seriousness that if my story were any higher on the "10-point," *it would be off the page! That's* how high it was! The whole thing felt positively naughty. And unlike a success-ful investigative story, with its grand juries, arrests, and impeach-ments, here all was good. No one was going to jail. No one's life was ruined. The opposite was the case. The buyer got its deal; the seller got paid; the bankers got paid; the *other* bankers got paid; the lawyers got paid; the *other* lawyers got paid; the PR firms got paid, etc., etc. And I got my scoop, clean as a whistle. The anguish and humiliation of my competitors, their fury and noisy protests, their career anxiety rippling over the phone lines—that was just a bonus, the sweet, fluffy center of this marvelous *choux à la crème*. Not long afterward, I was elevated to a better beat.

But access reporting, especially if unbalanced by accountabil-ity reporting, can present a dangerously distorted view of reality. Nowhere is this better illustrated than in what is perhaps the lead-ing post-crisis book: *Too Big to Fail: The Inside Story of How Wall Street and Washington Fought to Save the Financial System—and Themselves,* by Andrew Ross Sorkin. Few business journalism careers have been as meteoric as that of Sorkin, who was assigned to the mergers-and-acquisitions beat of the *New York Times* at the tender age of twenty-two, when the paper was an afterthought in M&A coverage.[36] In 2001, Sorkin developed "DealBook," an innovative idea for a free daily electronic newsletter of major merger news. "DealBook" would attract more than 200,000 subscribers. Before he was thirty-two, he was awarded a column and made an editor of the business section. In 2010 "DealBook" employed more than a dozen reporters and contributors, including some of the most prominent in the business.[37]

One of the top-selling books on the financial crisis, Sorkin's *Too Big to Fail* emerged from remarkable access to key financial leaders, including Henry Paulson, Ben Bernanke, Tim Geithner, Richard Fuld, Lloyd Blankfein, Jamie Dimon, and many others. The scenes are woven deftly together with previously reported and properly attributed material to form a streamlined chronology of the months leading up to Lehman's failure and AIG's rescue, as viewed from the executive suite. Reviews in the financial press were euphoric, and the book won a prestigious Loeb Award for best business book of the year. *Too Big to Fail* was later made into an HBO movie.

So close is the book to its characters, it sometimes records not just what they said but their thoughts as well. Here Sorkin relays Geithner's during an early morning jog.

> This is what it was all about, he thought to himself, the people who rise at dawn to get in to their jobs, all of whom rely to some extent on the financial industry to help power the economy. Never mind the staggering numbers. Never mind the ruthless complexity of structured finance and derivatives, nor the million-dollar bonuses of those who made bad bets. This is what saving the financial industry is really about, he reminded himself, protecting ordinary people with ordinary jobs.[38]

A book so reliant on the information of elites necessarily views the crisis entirely from their perspective and, in fact, casts its characters in mostly heroic terms, with a few exceptions, including Lehman's Fuld, whose fall is depicted as merely tragic. The book steadfastly declines to look beyond the months leading up to the crash, so readers are left without the context to understand that nearly every individual or institution named in the book (Fuld, Bernanke, Geithner, Citigroup, AIG, etc.) played significant roles in causing the crisis in the first place. And the book refrains from explicitly characterizing the motives of its protagonists but does make an exception for Fuld, who is said to be "driven less by greed than by an overpowering desire to preserve the firm he loved."[39] This sense of disconnect, which obscures the larger picture, is clear in a scene at a 2008 dinner for the G7 Summit in Washington, in which Paulson shares his anxieties about leverage with Fuld:

> "I'm worried about a lot of things," Paulson now told Fuld, singling out a new IMF report estimating that mortgage-and real-estate related writedowns could total $945 billion in the next two years. He said he was also anxious about the staggering amount of leverage—the amount of debt to equity—that the investment banks were still using to juice their returns. That only added enormous risk to the system, he complained.[40]

But it was Goldman, with Paulson at the helm, that strenuously lobbied for looser capital requirements in 2004, unleashing the sort of leverage that Paulson is seen fretting about. And it was Paulson's Goldman (as Mark Pittman's reporting for Bloomberg revealed in 2007) that did more than its share to create the defective securities that are seen melting down in *Too Big to Fail*. Sorkin explains none of this. Worse still is the treatment of Fuld and Lehman. The firm's leading role in rise of predatory lending and subprime securitization goes unmentioned, despite, as we'll see, an ample journalistic record, including in Sorkin's own paper. Even Lehman's attempts to manipulate its financial statements—which occurred during the narrow timeline covered by the book and were amply documented— go unmentioned.

    Too Big to Fail is at once a monumental reporting achievement and an upside-down view of the financial crisis in which Wall Street, somehow, is the hero. As such, it exemplifies access reporting and its problems. Perhaps not surprisingly, when *Too Big to Fail*'s publisher held a book party at New York's Monkey Bar in October 2009, many prominent CEOs and financiers named in the book attended, a circumstance for which Sorkin expressed gratitude in a report about the party.

"I must admit," Sorkin wrote us this morning, "I was completely bowled over by the turnout. It was quite incredible to reassemble so many characters from the book in one room, all together. For a book that shows so many of these characters with their warts and all in the midst of the greatest panic of their lives, I am tremendously grateful that they came out to support me."[41]

CHAPTER 6

Subprime Rises in the 1990s

Journalism and Regulation Fight Back

I now realized there was an entire industry, called consumer finance, that basically existed to rip people off.

—STEVE EISMAN, hedge-fund manager, before making a fortune betting
against subprime loans

I n 1991, Peter S. Canellos, an urban-affairs reporter for the *Boston Globe*, started to hear from housing activists about a strange new phenomenon emerging on his beat: swarms of home-improvement salesman were turning up on the front porches of elderly homeowners in Boston's inner city, selling repair work along with a loan to pay for it. The sales pitches tended to be highly scripted and usually deceptive, leaving out basic terms or misrepresenting them altogether. The loans, second mortgages, typically carried high rates, hidden fees, and other onerous terms that were driving residents by the hundreds into foreclosure. This allowed the lender to buy the house from the court for the cost of the loan, usually a fraction of the home's market price. The practice was seen by regulators and activists as a deliberate ploy to profit from foreclosure and was soon given a name: "equity stripping."

The sales pattern was centered on African American neighborhoods where residents had bought their homes decades before—often with the help of a government program—and were thus equity-rich if cash poor. Most of the time, the *Globe* found, the home-owner had never expressed interest in home repair—let alone a loan to pay for it—until a salesman knocked on the door, often repeatedly. Indeed, the salesmen were so persistent that neighbors came up with a name for them, too: "bird dogs." The scams—some criminal, some merely deceitful—were drawing the attention of community activists and plaintiffs' lawyers, and eventually public officials, including Massachusetts attorney general Scott Harshbarger and Boston mayor Ray Flynn.

But Canellos, along with Gary Chafetz, who was working for the *Globe* as a freelancer, also started to notice that one of the most egregious lenders, called Resource Northeast Inc., based in Hingham, Mass., which operated a string of smaller mortgage companies, didn't act alone. Fleet/Norstar Financial Group, later Fleet Financial, a regional powerhouse and one of the fastest-growing banks in the country, provided a line of credit to make the loans and then bought the loans from Resource Northeast, which, while technically an independent company, couldn't operate without Fleet. It was, in fact, a creature of Fleet. "Mortgage Companies Got Credit from Fleet," read the headline on a May 1991 story, one of several drawing on community-group studies and state regulatory investigations that linked Fleet and other regional banks to small mortgage companies making loans in inner cities at rates as high as 24 percent (the prime rate was under 10 percent at the time). Class-action suits alleged borrowers were misled about basic terms of the note. Plaintiffs' lawyers and community activists began to complain that the second-loan business was rife with corruption, that many of the smaller loan companies were nothing more than scam artists that used high-pressure sales tactics, often in cahoots with disreputable home-improvement operations.

Over the spring of 1991, the *Globe* began to unravel the ties binding a reputable brand-name bank with the netherworld of American finance—this peculiar market of "Miss Cash" and termite-spreading exterminator salesmen, of pawnbrokers, check cashers, rent-to-own appliance stores, second mortgages, or "second liens," and the like, all generally known as consumer finance, which would later take on a new name: the subprime mortgage industry.

Hard-money lending—loan sharks, street-corner lenders, pawn brokers, and the like—has been around since biblical times, but its rise
in the U.S. mortgage market is a relatively recent phenomenon. In
the early twentieth century, homeownership was confined mostly to
the well-to-do, and hard-money lending was not a factor in housing.
Early mortgages, when they were available, required a large down
payment, often 40 percent, and full repayment within five years or
so, usually with a balloon payment at the end.[1] The Crash of 1929 sent
housing prices plummeting and dried up credit almost entirely. The
Depression and the New Deal reshaped the mortgage business, laying the groundwork for both the modern prime-mortgage loan, one
of the most successful innovations in modern American finance, as
well as the subprime loan, one of the most disastrous.

The year 1968, pivotal in U.S. history for many reasons, upended
U.S. housing policy as well. In response to a deposit crisis among
banks that was hurting their ability to fund home loans, Congress
vastly changed the game with the Housing and Urban Development
Act of 1968, which transformed Fannie Mae, started in the New Deal
as the Federal National Mortgage Association, from a public-private
hybrid agency that bought government-issued loans into a private,
federally chartered corporation with a new mission: Buying conventional mortgages from the private market and repacking and selling
them to bond investors in the form of mortgage-backed securities.
(Its old job of buying unconventional FHA loans was given to a new
entity, the Government National Mortgage Association, Ginnie
Mae.) Among other things, the move allowed the Johnson administration, then running deficits to fund the Vietnam War, to move
Fannie Mae's giant liabilities off the government's books. A few years
later Congress created the Federal Home Loan Mortgage Corporation, Freddie Mac, to further expand the secondary market. These
"government-sponsored enterprises," or GSEs, quickly ramped
up mortgage buying and bundling of prime (thirty-year, fixed rate)
mortgages. Modern securitization began in earnest, allowing larger
capital markets to directly invest in American homeownership at a
lower cost than the older depository-lending model.[2]

As Bethany McLean and Joseph Nocera and others have explained, in the late 1970s Lew Ranieri and a band of rebellious "fat guys" (so dubbed by Michael Lewis in *Liar's Poker* [1989]) on Salomon Brothers's mortgage desk (as well as other, presumably slender guys at the Bank of America) got involved and helped solve knotty technical and legal problems holding back the mortgage-backed securities (MBS) market, particularly how to handle the borrowers' right to prepay their mortgage, which was problematic for bond buyers who prefer instruments with a guaranteed, fixed term. Ranieri and his colleagues divided the mortgages into tranches (slices) that they ordered and priced in terms of repayment risk. The advances allowed Wall Street to securitize and trade, at first, nonconventional mortgages, such as "jumbo" loans and adjustable-rate mortgages. The innovations allowed Wall Street banks to bypass the GSEs altogether and buy conventional mortgages without a government guarantee then repackage them as mortgage-backed securities that, with certain credit enhancements, could also earn top AAA ratings from Standard & Poor's and other rating agencies.[3] By the early 1990s, so-called private-label securitization conduits became an entrenched and accepted part of the mortgage finance system. By the end of 1996, the residential mortgage market had grown to $773 billion, with $497 billion of that securitized, about $40 billion of that private label.[4]

Meanwhile, a regime of consumer disclosure gradually replaced the New Deal's compulsory interest-rate caps and strict prohibitions of risky products. Congress had passed the Truth in Lending Act (TILA) in 1968 to force lenders to provide borrowers with meaningful information about fees, rates, and other loan components, and the Real Estate Settlement Procedures Act (RESPA) in 1974, which prevented under-the-table arrangements between lenders and title insurers, real estate brokers, and other service providers. In the coming years, the U.S. regulatory regime would give the financial-services industry a much freer hand in the types of products it could sell and the rates and fees it could charge.

A key driver of the deregulatory push was inflation in the 1970s, which Nocera rightly identifies as the fulcrum between financial eras. Inflation wreaked havoc on the New Deal's strict banking-regulatory regime and added force to lenders' long-standing arguments for more flexibility.[5] State legislatures began to repeal or loosen usury laws on their own, and in 1978, the Supreme Court dealt them a severe blow by ruling that credit card companies could charge rates allowed by the states in which their operations were chartered rather than having to abide by local laws prevailing where the products were sold.[6] South Dakota, Delaware, and other states abolished caps altogether, effectively ending usury caps on credit cards as lenders moved operations to industry-friendly states. Congress allowed lenders to set their own interest rates for mortgages in 1980 with the Depository Institutions Deregulation and Monetary Control Act. The Alternative Mortgage Transaction Parity Act two years later allowed lenders to offer a wider range of products, including adjustable-rate mortgages and balloon payments, that shifted risks to borrowers and demanded a greater degree of sophistication. At the same time, lenders' newfound flexibility made full and fair disclosure ever more important. Fatally, DIDA also preempted state laws that explicitly barred such products, removing a critical layer of banking oversight.[7] In 1994, Congress explicitly allowed interstate banking with the Riegle-Neal Interstate Banking and Branching Efficiency Act, creating the conditions for behemoth "too big to fail" banks. The capstone of financial deregulation, of course, was passage of the Gramm-Leach-Bliley Act in 1999, formally repealing the New Deal's Glass-Steagall Act, which had separated commercial and investment banking. The new act ratified the giant Citigroup merger and cleared the way for a seamless mortgage machine, connecting, as we'll see, subprime retail sales forces to Wall Street mortgage-trading desks.

In the prime market, securitization worked. For the American middle class, mortgages became cheaper and more readily available. Banks could move a portion of their loans off their books by selling prime, conforming loans to Fannie Mae and Freddie Mac, which bundled and sold them as securities, and by selling jumbo and nonconforming loans to Wall Street, which packaged them and sold them as well. The value of new mortgages issued went from about $35 billion in 1970 to more than $450 billion in 1990 after real estate recovered from a downturn.[8] And securitization propelled the growth. By 1996, the mortgage market was around $800 billion with nearly $500 billion of that securitized.[9] What's more, for the bulk of middle-class borrowers and for the bond investors who bought stakes in their mortgages, the market was remarkably solid. From the mid-1980s through the mid-1990s, for instance, even during the real estate downturn of that era, delinquency rates hovered in the single digits, while severe delinquencies (more than ninety days past due) were rare, under 1 percent, and foreclosures were even rarer, less than 0.33 percent of total mortgages from 1986 to 1995, according to HUD statistics. The performance of the prime mortgage market and prime MBS from the end of World War II through the 1990s can fairly be called one of the great success stories of American finance.

But what was true of the prime market was never true of subprime. It operated by an entirely different dynamic. As reporters, regulators, plaintiffs' lawyers, and other insiders would later discover, the market was notable for what economists call severe asymmetries of both information and power. Subprime borrowers, by definition, have fewer choices when it comes to credit than their prime counterparts and, as a rule, have not only less money but also less of what sociologists call "cultural capital," the nonfinancial assets—educational, intellectual, or social—that tend to promote social mobility. Studies would bear this out, but no one knew it better than the people who worked in the subprime industry. As Bill Runnells, the creator of "Miss Cash," once said: "When you're broke, you'll borrow money at any price."[10] If the subprime market was not *inherently* corrupt, it was practically so. Corruption can be defined as wrongdoing on the part of an authority or a powerful party involving immoral means. Subprime lending represents a misalignment of interests, knowledge, and power so profound that corruption becomes inevitable. The difference between loan-sharking and subprime lending is necessarily blurred. This observation has been borne out since the beginning of subprime.

It was here that accountability reporting could play a vital role, and in the 1990s, it did. Regulation now became less about prohibition than about disclosure—the idea being that borrowers, if properly informed, could make their own choices. But that was a big "if," particularly given the symbolic nature of finance and financial products. What had been a stable—if unfair—mortgage market became far more volatile. A new dynamic set in as a new generation of sophisticated financial players sought to exploit widening opportunities among a new borrower class defined by its financial vulnerability and its lack of sophistication. Meanwhile, accountability journalism and regulation—both still powerful in their own right—found themselves in the symbiotic relationship of exposure and enforcement, enforcement and exposure. Regulatory investigations and actions created protected documents that reporters could use safe from libel and other legal concerns to expose wrongdoing at the bottom of the financial system. Reporters could on their own initiative use tips, lawsuits, and data from the plaintiffs' bar, community groups, and borrowers to advance original investigations, which regulators could then use to make cases.

It should be noted that early creators of mortgage securitization never contemplated that risky subprime mortgages would ever be a part of the market. The financier Larry Fink, who helped create the security at First Boston in the 1980s, dismissed the idea out of hand in testimony to Congress at the time: "I can't even fathom what kind of quality of mortgage that is, by the way, but if there is such an animal, the marketplace . . . may just price that security out." In other words, investors would demand such a high yield as to make such a deal untenable.[11]

Along with shifting Fannie Mae's mission to buying and packaging prime mortgages, the Johnson administration housing law also created the nation's first formal subprime loan program through private lenders. Tellingly, it ran aground almost immediately after borrowers in the program complained of fraud. As the historian Louis Hyman writes, "In an eerie prefiguring of the 2000s, the subprime lending program soon fell apart as predatory lenders and unscrupulous house flippers defrauded first-time buyers." The government found itself insuring defaulted mortgages on houses that could never be resold. The Nixon administration was forced to freeze the program in 1971.[12]

Congress made another pass at redressing the lingering problem of lending discrimination in 1977 with the Community Reinvestment Act, giving regulators the power to deny merger applications of banks found to have failed to meet the credit needs of low-income groups in their service areas. The law was generally deemed ineffective (notwithstanding its later, mistaken assignment by conservatives as a cause of the mortgage crisis). For decades, inner-city residents, even creditworthy customers, couldn't get mortgage credit at any price.

Regional newspapers, then approaching the apogee of their power, would play a key role in combating the problem known as "redlining," a potent term of disapprobation. In 1988, for instance, the *Atlanta Journal-Constitution* published "The Color of Money," a four-part series that found that whites received five times as many home loans from Atlanta's banks as blacks and that race, not income or home values, "consistently determined lending patterns." One of a number of celebrated press investigations into redlining, the series included devastating side-by-side maps that showed that areas of high African American concentration and low lending were virtually the same. The series, by twenty-seven-year-old reporter Bill Dedman, won the 1989 Pulitzer Prize for investigative reporting. Other papers followed suit. The *Wall Street Journal*, for instance, ran a lengthy Page One story in 1992 based on its own study of Federal Reserve data of 9,300 banks that found that blacks were more than twice as likely to be rejected for home loans as whites and that some black communities remained virtually mortgage-free zones.[13]

Soon, though, a new kind of mortgage lending would begin to fill the void left by redlining. This new practice had its roots in the consumer-finance industry and was expensive, deceptive, and heavily marketed. Indeed, its defining characteristic was that it was, in Wall Street parlance, "sold, not bought." In other words, customers typically don't seek out high-cost financial products, and a high degree of salesmanship was required to move them. In this sense, subprime lending would turn traditional banking on its head. Whereas banking emphasizes underwriting and risk analysis, subprime lending became an exercise in salesmanship. The highest accolade for a mortgage salesman was a single word: "closer."

Activists struggled to find as effective a term as "redlining," which vividly described areas of no credit, to capture this new, toxic brand of lending. To describe it, they believed, would also condemn it, and if it could not be entirely eliminated, it could at least be contained. The failure to find an effective name for this form of lawless lending would seriously hamper the press's attempts to cover it. In a linguistic study of the press and the financial crisis, "How 'Subprime' Killed 'Predatory,'" Elinore Longobardi traces media use of the two expressions and documents how and why the former, industry-sanctioned term for high-cost, high-risk, heavily marketed lending, "subprime," overtook the activist-generated term, "predatory." The latter suffers, while accurate in its way, from being both rhetorically aggressive and, at the same time, vague and ill-defined. This combination of lack of clarity and strong rhetorical punch meant that much of the press—and especially the business press, which already tended to underplay consumer issues—remained uncomfortable with the term, even after years of use, and so ultimately gravitated toward the far more industry-friendly "subprime."[14]

Scholars in the 1990s also struggled to define what was then seen as a rising problem among the poor and the elderly. *Modern Maturity* magazine, for instance, offered this definition: "A loan company is considered predatory . . . when it makes a loan that a borrower can't repay."[15] Allen Fishbein and Harold Bunce, in an article on subprime growth and predatory lending, discussed the problem of definition.

> The term 'predatory lending' is a shorthand term used to encompass a wide range of abuses. Although there is broad public agreement that predatory lending should have no place in the mortgage market, there are differing views about the magnitude of the problem and even how to define practices that make a loan predatory. Although home mortgage lending is regulated by State and Federal authorities, none of the statutes and regulations governing mortgage transactions provides a definition of predatory lending.

Another paper argues:

> In order to address predatory lending adequately, there needs to be a differentiation between what constitutes abusive lending, predatory lending, and mortgage fraud. Descriptions of predatory lending are plentiful, but a precise definition that would inform regulators and consumer advocates is non-existent.[16]

A big problem with the term—one that hampered media coverage—is that it seeks in a single phrase to define a range of interpersonal interactions, from offering (false) assurances that the buyer can refinance before rates go up, misrepresenting basic terms, failing to include escrow costs in payment schedules, colluding with appraisers, changing terms at closing, forging signatures, and more. In short, these are very human situations that involve would-be borrowers eager to obtain a loan, either for a new home or, much more often in the case of subprime, to pay off other debts; a loan sales force incentivized to make as many loans as possible as quickly as possible on, as we'll see, the most onerous terms possible; appraisers incentivized to provide estimates that would support the loan; and telemarketers provided scripts that downplay risks, interest rates, and fees and focus instead on initial monthly payments. It's not surprising, then, that activists struggled to find a single term. It's a long conversation. As Longobardi observes,

> The importance of the term predatory lending is its injection of a much-needed ethical dimension into the public argument. [But] the press, especially the business press, is often uncomfortable with such judgments. That the phrase predatory lending not only raises ethical issues but invites multiple definitions means that, except in the hands of a skilled reporter with a lot of time and inches on hand, its complexity threatens to render it imprecise to a fault. Which is to say that, frequently, any reader looking to move beyond the definition of predatory lending as "bad" lending will run into confusion.[17]

Opponents of lending regulation used the vagueness of "predatory lending" to defeat attempts to police it. In response to forceful warnings from a major 2000 joint HUD and Treasury Department report on the problem, Senator Phil Gramm, then head of the Senate Committee on Banking, Housing, and Urban Affairs, directed staff to report to him on "what the regulators refer to as 'predatory lending,' and what they see as the extent of the problem." The five-page staff report, prepared in only a couple of months and released in August 2000, concludes,

"Predatory lending," not defined by regulators, seems to encompass an ever-changing and broad assortment of terms and conditions associated with a variety of financial transactions. It is difficult to understand how the regulators or Congress can formulate proposals to combat predatory lending when there is no clear understanding as to what it is. A definition of the practice is sin[e] qua non for any progress toward a remedy.

In the absence of a definition, not only might we miss the target, but we may hit the wrong target.[18]

"Subprime," by contrast, has the advantage of precision. It can be measured by a borrower's credit score, down payment, collateral-to-loan value, income-to-debt levels, and other metrics. And for the lending industry, it has another advantage: it shifts the gaze entirely from lender to borrower.

The subprime lending industry initially preferred the even more neutral term "non-prime," to describe itself, according to the Center for Responsible Lending's Martin Eakes, but for investors in the lenders, "subprime" is more exact. Initially, even borrower advocates embraced the term "subprime" and encouraged the distinction from "predatory." Advocates hoped that the relatively new industry would live up to its perennial promises of reform and provide low-income borrowers a fair chance at credit and so didn't want to stigmatize all such lending, which, by its nature, is costlier in order to offset the higher risk. The industry, along with public officials, also encouraged the distinction between "predatory" and "subprime" to convey their belief that problems in the subprime industry were not widespread but rather just a matter of a few bad apples. Eventually, however, from the advocates' point of view—and in fact—such fine distinctions would be overwhelmed by the realities of the market. For all intents and purposes, one became a synonym for the other.

The sharp jump in what I, for the sake of simplicity, will call subprime lending was driven by economic distress of the early-1990s recession. A major HUD/Justice Department report in 2000 specifically traces its rise to borrowers consolidating rising credit-card debt into mortgages, a practice encouraged by the 1986 tax reform law that had left mortgage interest the only consumer debt allowed as a tax deduction.[19] Meanwhile, new money was flooding into the industry as Wall Street refined ways to securitize subprime debt—ironically, with the government's help. The Resolution Trust Corporation, created to clean up the S&L debacle, found itself saddled with motley collection of assets—office buildings, malls, vacant lots—that brought in lease payments but didn't conform to the standards of the main securitizers of the day, Fannie Mae and Freddie Mac. The RTC, in an effective move, allowed Wall Street to find new creative ways to obtain AA or AAA ratings for their securities without the GSEs by adding what became known as "credit enhancements." These could include extra collateral, insurance from third parties, and (later) a senior/subordinated structure where the cash flows from underlying mortgages went to "senior" holders first, minimizing their risk. The agencies rated some of the instruments AAA, allowing conservative investors, like pension funds, to buy them.[20] The infrastructure of a subprime boom was falling into place.

As with the first subprime program of the late 1960s—and in volumes not seen in the prime market—consumer horror stories began to pile up almost concurrently with the subprime boomlet of the early 1990s. Plaintiffs' lawyers and community activists complained that big banks, often acting through unethical mortgage brokers, used deceptive tactics to engage in equity stripping. Among the pioneers on the national scale was Fleet.

With roots dating to early American history, Fleet, which started as the Providence Bank and later became the Industrial Trust, was one among a handful of staid, Yankee-dominated institutions that long dominated Rhode Island economic and social life.[21] After changing its name to the market-tested Fleet Financial Group, the bank in 1982 hired a hard-charging and decidedly gruff CEO, J. Terrence Murray, who almost immediately took advantage of loosening banking laws to acquire smaller banks around the region. (Among his key aides was a lawyer, Brian Moynihan, now CEO of Fleet's mega-bank successor, Bank of America.)[22] Within three years, Fleet was operating in thirty-three states, and Murray had acquired a reputation as a master of creating efficiencies, albeit a ruthless one. Fleet managed to diversify its revenue sources to the point that it weathered the catastrophic real estate crash that followed the S&L debacle in the late 1980s far better than many of its competitors. As the 1990s dawned, Fleet and Murray were Wall Street darlings.

One of the bank's crown jewels, as far as Wall Street was concerned, was its Fleet Finance unit, which specialized in high-interest, high-risk retail lending. In 1990, when banking generally was in a slump and Fleet as a whole posted a loss for the year, Fleet Finance rang up healthy profits of $60 million. A key part of its business was serving an important secondary market for smaller operators around the country who made loans to borrowers with impaired credit and other sub-optimal customers. Fully 60 percent of the loans on the unit's books in 1990, 40,000 loans, had been purchased from smaller operators. Fleet itself was not shy about its reliance on the second-mortgage business. "This is a huge business for us," a bank spokesman, Robert W. Lougee Jr., said of the Fleet Finance unit in 1991. "We have a large appetite for purchasing loans." Indeed, it was Fleet Finance's performance that would enable its parent to buy the assets of the failed Bank of New England in 1991, an acquisition that would make it the region's largest bank and launch it on the national stage. It would soon control 30 percent of deposits in the region and, at the time, it seemed unstoppable.[23]

But American newspapers were powerful then, too. The *Globe*, in particular, owned by a public company but managed by descendants of the prominent Taylor family since the nineteenth century, held enormous sway in New England and Providence. It was considered one of the nation's top papers and one of a handful of preeminent regional standouts. Its hundreds of reporters and photographers roamed the world and had already won a dozen Pulitzer Prizes for work as varied as photographing famine in Ethiopia, analyzing foreign policy in the nuclear age, and a widely praised examination of local racism that included criticism of the paper itself. The paper's Spotlight Team, created during the investigative renaissance of the 1970s, had won Pulitzers for unearthing corruption in Somerville and gross mismanagement of the city's transit authority. Soon the region's most powerful newspaper would be going toe-to-toe with the region's most powerful bank.

Led by Canellos, then twenty-nine years old and assigned to the metro desk, the *Globe* performed a classic newspaper investigation.

It started small, drawing on the work of housing activists and plaintiffs' lawyers who were using the merger-blocking provisions of the Community Reinvestment Act (then taken more seriously than it is today) to call attention to Fleet's connection to the unethical lending practices of smaller mortgage brokers and lenders in Boston's minority neighborhoods and suburbs. As it unfolded in the spring and summer of 1991, the probe expanded further to encompass other brand-name players tied to the poverty industry. As one headline put it, "Mainstream Banks Have Ties to Above-Market Deals" (May 9). The *Globe*'s gaze expanded even further to regions outside Boston, first Atlanta then Chicago, New York, Phoenix, and elsewhere. On June 9, Canellos printed a 2,700-word story that zeroed in on Fleet's practices in Atlanta. The story described the frenzied behavior of loan salesman who fanned out through African American neighborhoods looking to sell home repairs and the loans needed to make them: "Margaret Wright Gay, a resident of northeast Atlanta, maintains that she never wanted any repairs on her house—especially not at the inflated price being offered by the contracting company whose representatives, she said, woke her up for a week running about a year ago by banging on her door early in the morning."

The series, which ran throughout the summer of 1991, reported that the bank was using string of disreputable mortgage brokers, known to plaintiffs' lawyers as "the seven dwarves," to knock on the doors of inner-city homeowners around Atlanta, selling second mortgages to homeowners who were often low-income but sitting on tens of thousands of dollars in equity. The "dwarves" would then resell the loans to Fleet, insulating the bank from the raft of consumer-fraud claims that, in fact, quickly arose.

Fleet hung tough. The June 9 *Globe* story quoted a spokesman saying, "We think the whole issue is totally bogus." But before long, the Federal Reserve, state and local regulators, and state and federal law enforcement officials were investigating Fleet's lending practices. At the same time, the bank was fending off class-action suits, including one certified by a Georgia court under tough state usury laws, that covered 20,000 borrowers and exposed the bank to damages up to $1 billion. The law could have required Fleet to refund all interest and to forgo all future interest on fraudulently sold loans.

The story spread to other news outlets, including the *Boston Herald*, the *Globe*'s rival, which, to its credit, didn't downplay the story but tried to advance it. The *Atlanta Journal-Constitution* dealt another blow to Fleet's wounded reputation with an exposé called "The Loan Trap" (November 11, 1992). Reporter Jill Vejnoska told the story of a sixty-two-year-old suburban grandmother, Lillie Mae Starr, a packer for a local tea company earning $300 a week, who was fighting foreclosure after taking out a $5,000 loan to repair her windows. It turns out the loan included almost much in fees as in principal, and carried a 23 percent interest rate. She couldn't afford the payments the day the loan closed and, after various refinancings, owed $63,000. "All Lillie Mae Star wanted was a chance to stay warm," the 3,300-word story began.

Michael W. Hudson came across the *Globe* series while researching his poverty project for the *Roanoke Times*. In those pre-Internet days, he had asked a news librarian to search clip files and online databases and noticed a wire story with reference to the "Boston second-mortgage scandal." He called the National Consumer Law Center, a nonprofit antipoverty advocacy group in Washington, which sent back a stack of clips, most of them from the *Globe* about Fleet. Seeing the nascent subprime business as a national story, Hudson pitched freelance pieces about it to national liberal magazines. His "Stealing Home" (*Washington Monthly*, June 1992) told the story of Roland Henry, an eighty-four-year-old Los Angeles man with a sixth-grade education who had made his living selling tamales on street corners. Confined to a wheelchair and nearly blind, he took out home-equity loans to buy carpet, then was talked into a high-interest consolidation loan by a man later charged with thirty-two felony counts of fraud. Using the telephone and the U.S. mail, Hudson tracked down court records from a widening network of regulators, lawyers, and advocates from around the country to show that the anecdotes were part of national pattern. Soon after the story was published, Hudson got a call from a producer at *60 Minutes* who had seen the *Washington Monthly* piece and wanted to work on a segment to be reported by Morley Safer. In November 1992, *60 Minutes*, which had long used regional papers' investigative work for story ideas, aired a piece examining Fleet Financial's practices in a working-class neighborhood in Atlanta. This was a scathing piece that maximized the power of television: authoritative voiceovers, deft cuts, and devastating on-camera admissions. The piece interviewed not just borrowers, but such actors as an unlicensed broker, a bird dog ("I'm not a salaried person. I just—I—I get up there every day and go out and find business"), and the owner of a "dwarf," the small lender that sold loans to Fleet, who breezily admitted he was just a proxy for the bank.

> SAFER: (Voiceover) Total control over a company like Georgia Mortgage, for example. Marc Siegel, the owner, says Fleet told him precisely how to run his business. And what percentage of his loans went to Fleet?
> MR. MARC SIEGEL (Owner, Georgia Mortgage): One hundred percent.
> SAFER: Purely and simply 100 percent.
> MR. SIEGEL: One hundred percent, probably from—from the—toward the end of 1984 until maybe 1989 or '90, I'm not sure which.[24]

Among those quoted in the story is Roy Barnes, a successful plaintiffs' lawyer and state legislator, who, as it happens, also had made millions starting a small-town bank in nearby Cobb County.[25] Barnes had started his career as a conservative, voting in favor of removing interest-rate caps on loan, but later had come to regret the vote. He pointed to Fleet's obvious role as funder and beneficiary of abusive loans: "This is so egregious, so wrong, that everybody tries to create this barrier and say, 'My hands are not dirty.' Well, you can't be in this business and you can't look at these loans and say that Fleet's not responsible. They had to know what was going on. They had the profits, they had the pre-approval, they had the connections and they knew that the yields were great."

Fleet issued angry denials, including that it had any control over the "seven dwarves." Still, the *60 Minutes* story triggered an uproar. A *Globe* story said dozens of people called Atlanta's legal-aid office saying they had experienced flimflams similar to those described in the piece. Fleet fielded more than a hundred calls. Rep. Joseph P. Kennedy II, a member of the powerful House Banking Committee, soon issued a call for hearings.

But by that point, Fleet was already in full retreat. Shortly before the *60 Minutes* piece aired, the bank, which had already settled fraud charges in Massachusetts, had announced a $38 million "restitution" program for Georgia residents at a ceremony with Atlanta mayor Maynard Jackson. The bank claimed it would revamp its subprime unit and cease doing business with the "dwarves." Its rhetoric—even its spokesman—had changed. Fleet's CEO, Murray, "wants to do the right thing," a new bank spokesman said. "The commitment is real. We want to get this issue behind us."[26]

The press did not act on its own to expose Fleet's wrongdoing. It was part of a dynamic that, as in many cases, included plaintiffs' lawyers, state and local regulators, and political figures, including the mayors of Boston and Atlanta. A key figure then (and a decade later during the mortgage era) was William J. Brennan Jr., an Atlanta legal-aid lawyer who served as an information clearinghouse and source for journalists. Stories from the *Globe*, the *Journal-Constitution*, and *60 Minutes* were part of a virtuous dynamic of reform—a three-way reverberation among press, regulators, and the public that contributes to collective understanding and creates the context for collective action.

The early 1990s offered an entirely different regulatory environment from the one that existed a decade later, when the radical antiregulatory ideology of the Bush administration and the Greenspan Federal Reserve effectively shut down mortgage-lender regulation at the federal level, creating a fertile environment for fraud. In the early 1990s, by contrast, regulators were more empowered and more stringent. At the time of the Fleet series, special government task forces probing the savings-and-loan crisis were in the process of referring 1,100 cases to prosecutors, resulting in more than 800 bank officials going to jail. The Securities and Exchange Commission had aggressively policed insider-trading scandals involving Michael Milken and Ivan Boesky. Manhattan U.S. attorney Rudolph Giuliani rang up a string of Wall Street criminal cases, including a criminal settlement with Milken's firm Drexel Burnham Lambert and, indeed, was justly criticized for excessive prosecutorial zeal. Robert M. Morgen-thau, the iconic Manhattan district attorney, was widely feared on Wall Street.

While state-level regulators and prosecutors, including New York's Eliot Spitzer, continued aggressive regulation of mortgage lending in the 2000s, the impact of a compromised federal regula-tory system profoundly affected not just mortgage lending but jour-nalism's coverage of it. Reporters rely on regulators for stories, and regulators rely on reporters for cases. Each provides support and public affirmation for the work of the other while educating the pub-lic and creating a context for further reform. The nexus between uncompromised regulation and effective investigative journalism cannot be overstated. That said, regulatory retreat only increases the responsibilities of the press to represent the true state of the finan-cial system.

By February 1993, Congress had taken up the issue, and Fleet bank-ers were called to testify before the House Banking Committee. They were abject in their contrition. The next year, Congress passed and President Clinton signed the Home Ownership and Equity Protec-tion Act (HOEPA), authored by Kennedy and targeting "predatory lending." The law barred some egregious loan terms (e.g., many pre-payment penalties) altogether and required additional disclosure for loans deemed "high-cost," meaning those with first-mortgage rates of more than eight points over current Treasury yields or fees exceeding eight percentage points of the principal. The law gave the Federal Reserve increased powers to police lawless lending. How-ever, in retrospect, the law is not considered a success because "very few consumers benefit from the law's subprime provisions," accord-ing to the 2000 HUD-Treasury task force, mainly because the rate and fee thresholds were set too high; most subprime lenders evaded the law by setting these just below the limits.[27]

But for purposes of examining the financial crisis and the financial press, the history of this now-forgotten law is significant for several reasons. First, in light of what was to come a decade later, it's impor-tant to remember that HOEPA was first and foremost a law about *dis-closure*. Indeed, it was an amendment to the 1968 Truth in Lending Law. Its most onerous provisions, from the banking community's point of view, were those that required the lender to disclose clearly and in a timely manner such basic information as the interest rate, monthly payments, and whether and how these would change under the terms of the contract. In other words, HOEPA was designed to give amateur borrowers a chance to understand what they were sign-ing, and it was this provision that the mortgage industry fought so vigorously. By lowering interest rates just below the threshold that triggered the law, lenders demonstrated that they were *willing to forgo yield in order to avoid clear disclosure.*

Second, as bad as it already was in the early 1990s, the subprime industry was still a threat only to borrowers desperate enough to need it. At a few billions loaned a year, it was a speck compared to what it was to become in the just the next few years, never mind the era of extreme corporate lawlessness that would overtake the mort-gage industry during the 2000s. Before 1994 subprime lending was a negligible portion of the overall mortgage market with a nominal amount securitized. By 1994, however, the subprime total had risen to $35 billion, about 4.5 percent of the overall mortgage market, about a third of which was securitized. By 1998, it was up again by half, to $150 billion, more than half securitized, and would remain more than 10 percent of the mortgage market through the decade.[28]

Third, HOEPA represented a press victory, albeit an incremen-tal one. Investigative reporting by mainstream news organizations, then at the height of their power, had exposed rampant abuses and brought them to the public's attention. The truly crooked operators were policed, and a major financial institution was brought to heel. Broadly speaking, when Big Journalism took on Big Finance, journal-ism won, and won handily.

Fourth, journalism in the early 1990s showed that it was quite capable, without much specialized knowledge, of tracing, explain-ing, and ultimately policing not only retail lenders involved in loan fraud and misrepresentation but also their links to mainstream finance. In this case, Fleet represented both the funding source and the aftermarket for lawless loans, the same basic model that would be in place—on a vastly larger scale—ten years later during the mortgage era. Instead of dwarves, the reckless and unethical lend-ers would become Countrywide, Ameriquest, IndyMac, Washington

Mutual, New Century, and Citigroup. Instead of Fleet, the aftermarket would be made up of Merrill Lynch, Bear Stearns, Lehman Brothers, Goldman Sachs, Citigroup (again), and a small handful of others. The names changed, but the model remained the same. It's true that the aftermarket would become considerably more complex in the later era and that the lawless loans would be put to far more dangerous use in the global financial system. But that's all the more reason to understand the nature of the lawless loans in the first place.

For Hudson, researching the same topic in Roanoke, the *Globe* series was a revelation. He saw the frauds and scams at the low end of American finance as morally reprehensible and a journalism opportunity. He started to report and would eventually trace the subprime industry's roots to the savings-and-loan industry, whose collapse had done little to deter former executives who slid easily into the consumer-finance business. Ground zero for the subprime business was, like the S&L business, Orange County, California, whose libertarian culture and suspicion of government regulation provided a welcoming environment for less-than-scrupulous financiers.

Hudson delved deep into the consumer-finance sales culture and got to know the salespeople, mostly men, who, it turns out, formed a veritable brotherhood, with its own language, mores, and pantheon of heroes. Hudson heard stories of legendary "closers"—experts in the arts of suasion, reputed to be able to convince customers to sign almost any loan, no matter how onerous. He learned the tricks of burrowing into the psyches of the anxious janitors, nurse's aides, and restaurant workers who had the bad luck to wander into these salesmen's offices or were unable to put down the phone when cold-called at home. He read their literature, books with titles like *Creative Visualization* and *Persuasion* ("a very dangerous book as far as the information in it," one loan salesman explained to Hudson). One famous sales script written by First Alliance Mortgage, one of the industry's most notorious, was called "The Track" and was legendary for its ability to lead the salesman to a customer's vulnerabilities. Sales reps called it "Finding the Pain."[29]

He learned that top salesmen knew that the best times to close loans were either late at night, between eight p.m. and midnight, when borrowers were bleary-eyed, or during their harried thirty-minute lunch break. Hudson learned colorful terms, such as the one for pressuring panicky borrowers caught in a refinancing spiral: "nut-squeezing." Among time-tested nut-squeezers: showing up at a debtor's house with a couple guys from the office a couple days before Christmas, threatening to pack the tree and drive the family to spend the holiday in hotel.[30]

He picked up the subprime industry maxims, true insights into popular culture. As one salesman told him, "Eighty percent of Americans are two paychecks away from subprime," Another said, "If you don't find the true pain, you won't make the loan."[31] He came to understand that the subprime lending culture had nothing do with traditional banking values, like underwriting and risk analysis. It was a sales culture and all about one thing: closing. And it was hard-partying and louche. One sales manager handed out crystal meth to keep his staff alert; another made the low producers keep a plastic pile of dog shit on their desk until they boosted sales; a third, to make sure his staff wasn't going easy on borrowers, planted electronic eavesdropping devices in their offices ("We would listen in, such as the telephone company and various other large organizations do, you know," he would testify). Another subprime owner took a more positive approach and gave top producers time inside a "money machine," a small room into which a tornado of cash was blown; loan officers kept whatever they could grab.[32]

The insight Hudson was gaining was that the subprime business was not an ordinary market—not, as Wall Street financial modelers would later assume, a somewhat "riskier" version of the well-established prime mortgage market. Subprime was where the least sophisticated met the most ruthless. Subprimers were more ruthless because their risks *were*, in fact, greater. Everyone, in fact, *did* have a sob story. Default rates *were* higher in subprime, as a matter of course. (Comedian Jon Stewart captured the subprime dilemma with this quip during a bit in 2008: "Absolutely, and if you're going to give money to people who have a tough time paying it back, charge them more. It makes total sense.") By the same token, subprime products were, *by definition*, inferior. Rates were higher. Fees were higher. No one asked for a subprime product. These did *not* sell themselves. The only reason anyone would accept a subprime loan was because either they had no alternative or they didn't know any better. During the 1990s, the numbers of both types of customers were growing, but it was in the second category where subprime lending melded with predatory lending to the point of being indistinguishable. Subprime is the definition of what economists might call an asymmetrical transaction, where one side had the money, the leverage, and, most important, the information. It was in this netherworld of misrepresentation and misunderstanding, feints, fakes, winks, nods, forgeries, buried "good-faith estimates," nondisclosure, semidisclosure, sort-of disclosure, insincere reassurances, and bald-faced lies that the true essence of subprime salesmanship could be found. This was where the art happened.

And Hudson began to notice something important about all these smalltime outfits. They weren't all smalltime. For instance, an outfit called Associates First Capital, based in Irving, Texas, was also working with appliance and furniture dealers to bring in clients. Hudson found that Associates had run afoul of regulators and borrowers around the country. Borrowers complained they had been tricked into loans, with some claiming their names had been forged on loan documents. Most of the suits were settled. In Arizona, Associates agreed to pay $3 million to 8,000 customers after the state attorney general alleged the lender had forced borrowers to buy credit insurance as a condition of their loans. The more he looked, the more he learned that Associates was actually one of the worst actors in a tough business. Associates, it turned out, was a unit of Ford Motor Co.

Founded in 1918 to finance loans for Ford Model Ts, the independent finance company got into mortgage lending soon afterward and in 1968 was sold to the conglomerate Gulf & Western (later Paramount Communications, now part of Viacom) and finally sold to Ford itself in 1989. When Hudson began his story in the early 1990s, it had more than 1,600 retail offices around the world and $20 billion in assets. It was immensely profitable and had just finished its twentieth consecutive year of earnings growth.

In his reporting, Hudson came across evidence that the lawlessness was out of control. An Alabama jury hit Associates with a $34 million verdict, including punitive damages, for forging borrowers' names, then foreclosing on their homes. (A judge ordered a retrial, ruling that he shouldn't have allowed a plaintiff's lawyer to describe Associates as a "company without conscience." The company later settled.) It paid another, undisclosed sum to settle forgery allegations in Seattle. The company settled cases around the country after having been discovered to have slipped costly credit insurance into deals without telling borrowers or after telling them it was mandatory.[33]

It was on this story that Hudson learned the value of a particular kind of source: the whistleblower. Invariably former employees, these were people who challenged the lawless culture of their employers and typically were pushed out or fired. These outcasts were never perfect as sources—often they were bringing suits against their former employer (that's how Hudson found many of them)—but they provided eyewitness testimony from within the bureaucracy, testimony that was usually included in court filings, which provides journalists with a measure of legal protection. Hudson would become a master of tracking down and cajoling whistleblowers. He mined court records for employment cases and tracked down the plaintiffs at home. In many cases, he found through word-of-mouth remorseful former employees who hadn't sued the company and convinced them to talk. Since the subprime business was centered in Southern California, and Hudson lived on the East Coast, he could catch them at home after hours, allowing him to extend his reporting day until almost midnight.

In this case, he found an unimpeachable source in the person of Philip White, a Gulf War veteran who had come home to Alabama in 1991 and taken a job as an Associates loan officer. Within months, he told Hudson, he felt misgivings about what his bosses told him to do. One hard-and-fast rule at the company, for instance, was to never tell the whole truth, unless it becomes absolutely unavoidable. "'If you don't have to tell them, and they don't ask, don't tell them. Just get 'em to initial it. They can read—most of them anyway,'" White told Hudson he knew personally of twenty to twenty-five instances in which customers' signatures had been forged on truth-in-lending disclosure forms mandated by the 1968 federal law. As the months dragged on and customer after customer called to express shock that their payments were much higher than they had been told they'd be,

White finally quit. The pressure to produce, he told Hudson, forced ordinary people to do things they would never normally do. "Some of the people there are very nice. [But] they're put under such pressure to produce to profits that everybody knows what's going on. . . . The people are good but they do things they don't want to do."[34]

Within a few years, Associates would go on to earn one of the most notorious reputations in the subprime industry. The *Wall Street Journal* would describe how an illiterate quarry worker who owed $1,250 for—of all things—*meat* discovered that his consumer loan had been sold to Associates, which convinced him to refinance ten times in four years until he owed $45,000, more than half of it in fees, with payments that took more than 70 percent of his income. He had signed each note with an "X."[35] Associates' abuses—it employed a "designated forger," ABC's *Prime Time Live* would confirm on April 23, 1997—were so extreme that it would be credited with spurring the North Carolina legislature into passing its pioneering anti-predatory-lending law, in 1999. Indeed, Hudson found that the tin men and other flimflam artists almost always worked in partnership with finance companies, which, in turn, were invariably owned by brand-name corporations, CitiBank, Chemical Bank, BankAmerica, NationsBank, and others.

In mid-1996, Hudson edited *Merchants of Misery: How Corporate America Profits from Poverty* and wrote four of the ten chapters, including a long one documenting forgery and fraud accusations against Associates called "Signing Their Lives Away." Other chapters looked at payday lenders, rent-to-own operators, pawnshops, check cashers, home-repair scammers, trade-school scams, and so on. The introduction, by Hudson, expressed astonishment that such low-rent operators as Associates could be underwritten, or owned outright, by some of the most respected names on the New York Stock Exchange: "More and more, the merchants who profit from the disadvantaged are owned or bankrolled by the big names of Wall Street: Ford, Citibank [now Citigroup], NationsBank, BankAmerica [both now part of Bank of America], American Express, Western Union. . . . Add up all the businesses that bottom-feed on the 'fringe economy' and you'll come up with the market for $200 billion to $300 billion a year." Besieged by bad press, Ford had sold a portion of Associates to the public in an initial public offering in 1996 and spun it off altogether two years later, when Associates was examined by yet another congressional panel on predatory lending, this time the Senate Special Committee on Aging. But despite lawsuits and regulatory action, Associates continued to be immensely profitable. In 1999, it completed its twenty-fifth consecutive year of earnings growth, posting a net income of $1.5 billion on about $100 billion in assets. It operated more than 1,500 retail offices around the country and boasted 800,000 customers. Yet because of its down-market niche and notorious reputation, it remained on the margins of the financial system. But that would soon change.[36]

In his classic article, "The Market for 'Lemons': Quality Uncertainty and the Market Mechanism," published in the *Quarterly Journal of Economics* in 1970, the economist George Akerlof highlighted the power imbalances and market inefficiencies that occur when one party lacks either information about future performance of the agreed-upon transaction or the ability to retaliate for a breach of the agreement. Akerlof's paper cited the market for used cars for its discussion of the problem of how defective products ("lemons") are sold by more-knowledgeable sellers to less-knowledgeable buyers in a lightly regulated market. The result, of course, is that transactions go awry. But more, Akerlof concluded, the dynamic wrecks the market itself by creating a situation in which cheaters prosper, and in fact cheaters alone *can* prosper. Because buyers can't be certain of the quality of the product, prices will reflect their uncertainty. In the cases of used cars, the owners of good cars, unable to command a fair price, will withhold their cars from the market. "The cost of dishonesty, therefore, lies not only in the amount by which the purchaser is cheated; the cost also must include the loss incurred from driving legitimate business out of existence."[37]

William K. Black, a former top federal regulator during the S&L cleanup and an associate law professor at University of Missouri–Kansas City, has coined the idea of "criminogenic environment," conditions that foster a culture of lawlessness. In a 2010 interview, he says bad money drives out the good, also known as a form of Gresham's Law:

Deregulation occurs when one reduces, removes, or blocks rules or laws or authorizes entities to engage in new, unregulated activities. Desupervision occurs when the rules remain in place but they are not enforced or are enforced more ineffectively. De facto decriminalization means that enforcement of the criminal laws becomes uncommon in the relevant industries. These three regulatory concepts are often interrelated. The three "des" can produce intensely criminogenic environments that produce epidemics of accounting control fraud. . . . When firms gain a competitive advantage by committing fraud, "private market discipline" becomes perverse and creates a "Gresham's" dynamic that can cause unethical firms and officials to drive their honest competitors out of the marketplace. . . . The combination drove the crisis in the U.S. and several other nations.[38]

As we'll see, precisely this dynamic was to occur during the era of mortgage lawlessness that took hold, on a vastly greater scale, in the 2000s.

What the regional reporters such as Hudson understood was that informational asymmetries are much more profound in the subprime market than those found among prime borrowers, who themselves are often lost in the stack of paperwork to be signed at closing and the many moving parts of a typical mortgage. Lenders, after all, are the professionals in the transaction, and borrowers, the amateurs.

Ground-level reporters, legal-aid lawyers, politicians, and state and local regulators knew full well that subprime was not a normal market. A few on Wall Street also came to understand as well.

Steve Eisman, a Harvard Law School graduate with an antisocial streak, quit his job as a corporate lawyer in 1991 and went to work as a junior analyst for Oppenheimer Funds, an old-school Wall Street partnership where candor about public companies was still permitted. Eisman acquired a reputation as an odd duck and not given to social niceties. Once, meeting with a executive of a Japanese company, Eisman held up the company's financial disclosure and pronounced it "toilet paper," as recounted in Michael Lewis's *The Big Short*, the celebrated post-crisis book that chronicles the Wall Street subculture—or more exactly, counterculture—that saw subprime lending for what it was. When he started on Wall Street, the first wave of "specialty lenders" was going public, and Eisman was assigned to write a report about one of them, Lomas Financial Corp. Eisman looked at its financial statements, the quality of its loans, and its accounting and quickly came to a conclusion: "I put a sell rating on the thing because it was a piece of shit," Eisman recalls.[39]

Eisman would make specialty finance something of a specialty of his own and at first, like many market observers, had high hopes for the idea of securitized subprime loans, the linking of Wall Street to America's lower middle class. Making global capital pools available to people with less-than-perfect credit would allow them to shift debt from high-interest credit cards to low-interest mortgages, so the argument went. Eisman saw it as a rational response to growing income inequality, which he saw as creating a growing need for subprime products.

But it didn't take Eisman long to detect problems in the model. For one thing, the lenders sold many of their loans to other investors, repackaged as mortgage bonds. In essence, lenders were selling a product but had no interest in its ultimate performance. That was the shadow darkening the good idea. He also noticed that subprime borrowers had astonishingly high default rates, which, in turn, indicated problems with underwriting. Even more alarming for stock investors, Eisman found that the default rates had been covered up by misleading accounting entries and euphemisms, such as "involuntary prepayments." Eisman collected data from Moody's (available, by the way, to financial journalists, as well) and concluded that the companies were basically Ponzi schemes, making loans on onerous terms that were certain to result in default but that allowed the firm to collect more money from investors before they did. Accounting manipulation prolonged the scheme by delaying the inevitable.

In September 1997, Eisman came out with a scathing report that said as much, exposing the entire sector of subprime loan originators and creating, in the words of a colleague, "a shitstorm" in the industry. The originators argued strenuously that his data were wrong. But they held up. As it happens, the early subprime firms were all soon wiped out when the global financial crises—which began in Russia and was caused by the Long Term Capital Management hedge fund—shut down their access to credit, sending most of the sector into bankruptcy. In a sense, Eisman was vindicated, but the mass failure obscured the deeper problems in subprime. The sector's failure was chalked up to the credit crisis and to aggressive accounting, which allowed the lenders to record profits before they were realized. What no one understood, Lewis writes, was "the crappiness of the loans they had made."[40]

The 1998 wipeout of smaller lenders, however, did not impede the rise of subprime overall. That year, in fact, subprime originations increased to $150 billion, up from $125 billion the year before, and under $100 billion in 1996. Subprime in the mid- and late 1990s was now more than 10 percent of the overall mortgage market and, after a dip in the early 2000s, would begin to soar. The market was still dominated by old-line lenders, including Conseco, a former insurer that had diversified and bought Green Tree Financial in 1998; ITT Industries, a successor to the old phone company that had diversified in the 1960 and later entered specialty finance; and Transamerica Financial, which had begun as an offshoot of San Francisco's Bank of America in the 1920s.

The most important player was Household International, parent of Household Finance, which was started in the nineteenth century by a Minneapolis jeweler who made small personal loans, allowing customers to pay off purchases in small increments. By the 1990s, it had become the leading national specialty lender, moving into second liens and in 1998 buying a struggling rival, Beneficial Finance. Soon its lending practices would attract attention of investigative reporters, regulators, and, in New York, Eisman and other contrarian investors.

The subprime industry—because of the extreme informational asymmetries at its heart and the fact that it no longer held its own loans—had shown itself to be essentially lawless almost from the start. As Hudson understood, Eisman would learn, and government investigations would later confirm, the problem was more than the mere fact that mainstream finance was taking over subprime. It was that subprime values were taking over mainstream finance.

Perhaps the signal moment in the era's financial radicalization came in the fall of 2000. That's when Associates First Capital, the ransacker of Roanoke, purveyor of meat loans to the developmentally disabled and illiterate, and probably the most lawless of all subprime players, announced it was selling itself for $31 billion, a rich price, even by today's standards. The buyer was Citigroup.

CHAPTER 7

Muckraking the Banks, 2000–2003

A Last Gasp for Journalism and Regulation

Many predatory lenders have gone through a similar cycle: sudden growth, fueled by the predatory loans themselves and stoked by the quick influx of cash provided by the securitization process, followed in a few years by growing allegations of improprieties, allegations which the lenders furiously deny. These allegations are followed, but often slowly, by investigations conducted by regulatory agencies. Only after several profitable years of predatory lending does the entire structure come crashing down. *The crash typically happens when publicity regarding the lender's methods so frightens the lender's financial backers and loan purchasers that the lender suddenly finds itself without the ability to fund or sell its loans.* At that point, the predatory lender goes out of business, perhaps after declaring bankruptcy, leaving its borrowers to contend with the purchasers of their loans over the validity of those loans.

—KURT EGGERT, "Held Up in Due Course" (2002; emphasis added)

Demonstrators chanting slogans and carrying signs gathered near the canyons of Wall Street to protest a financial system they believed had run off the rails. They accused it of raking in profits at the expense of less sophisticated home borrowers and of aggravating wealth disparities between rich and poor. Speakers included bereft former homeowners who told tales of deception, hucksterism, bait-and-switch tactics, and defective financial instruments that had left them destitute. After some initial hesitation, politicians also got involved. Andrew Cuomo, a prominent New York

Democrat, struck a populist tone. "Someone is financing these companies to begin with; someone is buying these mortgages, and it is Wall Street." Senator Charles Schumer of New York, normally one of Wall Street's closest allies in Congress, was even more explicit: "The bottom feeders of society, these predatory lenders, reach up to the highest economic titans in society, and the two work together, and we have to break that link."

The site of the protest was not Zuccotti Park but the World Financial Center, a few blocks from the headquarters of Merrill Lynch, Lehman Brothers, and Citigroup's Salomon Smith Barney unit (and, for that matter, the *Wall Street Journal*, which didn't cover the protest). The protesters were not Occupy Wall Street, still a decade in the future, but borrowers and activists complaining of fraudulent lending practices in the subprime mortgage industry. It was the spring of 2000.

Among the notable aspects of this demonstration—apart from its target—was what had triggered it. According to a lengthy analysis in *Investment Dealers Digest*, a public hearing had been organized by federal officials in May to examine a "predatory lending scandal" that had "erupted" two months earlier. The trade periodical worried that the "scandal" had caused liquidity problems in the market for subprime mortgage-backed securities—fewer buyers of MBS and falling prices—and noted that subprime MBS issuance in response had dropped to $60 billion in the previous twelve months, a third of the volume of the previous year and the lowest level in a decade, when the subprime securitization market was just getting started. While it wasn't clear how much the falloff had to do with the "scandal" and subsequent protests, Wall Street bankers were nonetheless walking on eggshells. "Obviously [predatory lending] is a high-focus item," the periodical quoted a Merrill Lynch managing director, Rob Little. "People are very cognizant of it, and they're very cautious in terms of how they address it." In other words, with the help of public pressure, subprime lending—the sector that would be at the epicenter of the mortgage crisis—was being contained. As the headline put it: "The Predatory Lending Fracas: Wall Street Comes Under Scrutiny in the Subprime Market as Liquidity Suffers and Regulation Looms."[1]

As it turns out the "scandal" that had "erupted" a couple of months earlier was not a regulatory crackdown or bankruptcy. It was a newspaper story, an exposé about scandalous practices and the collusion of a large and notoriously lawless lender and one of Wall Street's brand names, Lehman Brothers. "Mortgaged Lives: Profiting from Fine Print with Wall Street's Help" was published March 15, 2000, in the *New York Times*, with a companion piece airing around the same time on ABC's *20/20* news magazine. It explored the intimate relationship of First Alliance Mortgage Company, which had a long and pockmarked history with state regulators, and Lehman, then the fourth-largest U.S. investment bank. The piece was a tour de force of reporting and writing that, to devastating effect, described how the businessman Brian Chisick and his wife, Sarah, had left a trail of defrauded borrowers, lawsuits, and regulatory actions in the two decades it had taken them to build the Irvine, Calif., company into a subprime powerhouse.

Drawing on court records and interviews with former employees, *New York Times* reporter Diana B. Henriques and journalist Lowell Bergman documented how FAMCO had been carefully constructed as a deception machine. The piece reported that the Chisicks had populated its ranks not with bankers but with salesmen from area car dealers. The company implemented a corporate training program, known as "The Track," designed to deflect borrower's concerns about rates and fees and obscure the true cost of a loan until long after the closing. (Among the scripted lines: "May I ignore your concern about the rate and costs if I can show you that these are minor issues in a loan?") And when The Track didn't work, the lenders agents flatly lied, which the *Times* was able to demonstrate by quoting from a recording made by a cautious borrower—a paralegal from St. Paul—of a conversation with a FAMCO loan officer:

> Mrs. Gunderson was still wary enough to double-check her loan with First Alliance, and to tape the call on her telephone answering machine.
>
> Worried about the $13,000 in fees, she sought confirmation that her loan was for about $47,000.

"Right, your amount financed is $46,172," the loan officer, Brian Caffrey, assured her. "That doesn't change."

"Right, right," she continued. "And then the $13,000 goes on top of that? And then interest is charged?"

"No, no, no," he responded.

As the *Times* story said, the true answer was, "Yes, yes, yes."

Through the sheer weight of the reporting—testimony of former employees, regulators from several states, activists, lawyers, the company's own documents—the *Times* demonstrated that a major national player in the still-seamy subprime business placed deception at the center of its business model. But it did more: in the classic mode of investigative work, it followed the money to its source— Wall Street. The story recounts how FAMCO had been brought public in 1996 by a bottom-tier investment bank, Friedman Billings & Ramsey, but moved up in class two years later when Lehman became its main funding source. The story quotes a Lehman spokesman saying that the company was aware of FAMCO's lengthy regulatory record when it began underwriting the firm but felt it could manage the relationship. The *Times* story drew on an important lawsuit mentioned in the story—a class action spearheaded by a San Jose lawyer, Sheila Canavan, that would yield rich discovery materials from Lehman.

Today, the Wall Street–subprime connection is a given. Then, its implications were only beginning to be understood. Indeed, Lehman's relationship with FAMCO was only a few years old. Henriques and Bergman, like Tarbell and her journalistic heirs, were working in real time, with imperfect information, on a story about active, hostile, and powerful institutions. The information was timely, still actionable by regulators, and, more important, still relevant for the literate citizen to grasp important shifts then occurring in the financial sector. Public opinion had a fighting chance to have an impact on the debate. The length, depth, and prominent display in the nation's most important paper helped to shift its terms.

In the wake of the story, political figures and other officials issued statements and made speeches denouncing predatory lending.

Among them was Alan Greenspan, chairman of the Federal Reserve, who, about a week after the *Times* story, denounced predatory lending in a speech to a group of housing activists. "Discrimination is against the interests of business—yet business people too often practice it," Greenspan said. He announced an interagency task force, including the Department of Housing and Urban Development and the Treasury Department, to create a joint policy statement defining specific illegal practices. It was the first time the Fed chairman had spoken on the subject.[2]

Within weeks, the Clinton administration's Office of Thrift Supervision had moved to close a loophole under a 1982 law that allowed mortgage lenders to opt out of tighter state laws in favor of OTS regulations.[3] The same month, four bills were offered in Congress, including the LaFalce-Sarbanes Predatory Lending Consumer Protection Act of 2000, by John J. LaFalce of New York and Paul Sarbanes of Maryland, which would strictly limit points, fees, balloon payments, and credit insurance and require additional disclosure and counseling, and would force lenders to determine whether the borrower had the ability to pay. Soon, more bills would be introduced, or, as a banking trade publication put it: "More Jump on the Predatory Bandwagon."[4] The Treasury Department and HUD organized public hearings on predatory lending around the country, including in New York, the site of the protests and political denunciations by Cuomo, Schumer, and others.

FAMCO and the Chisicks would eventually agree to pay $60 million to settle deceptive-lending allegations brought by private litigants, state regulators, and the Federal Trade Commission. The settlement covered 18,000 borrowers. But by then, FAMCO was long finished; First Alliance filed for Chapter 11 bankruptcy protection and announced it would stop making new loans. The filing came on March 23, eight days after the *Times*-20/20 story.

Did a single news story do all that? Certainly not—and that's the point. The *NYT*/ABC News story on FAMCO and Lehman was part of a wider network of consumer activism and legislative and regulatory action focused on the nexus of subprime and its funding sources on Wall Street. It's not my purpose here to measure the effect of journalism in containing the brewing financial crisis, only to suggest that journalism, when performed right, has one.

When the *Columbia Journalism Review* began to review pre-crisis business reporting on Wall Street and mortgage lenders, we had a hunch that something had gone wrong. This conviction stemmed from our belief in journalism. As journalists, we have to believe that what we do is not entirely ineffectual and that it has some effect on the outcome of events. Otherwise, why bother? Given that the system failure here was absolute, whatever journalism did, as a matter of logic, was insufficient. But a second idea was that what passed for the "debate" about business-press performance was not really a matter of opinion at all. Either the work was there, or it wasn't. Facts have a way of obliterating assumptions. Our approach was fairly straightforward.[5] But in the end, we were simply looking for the best investigative work on the big financial institutions that brought down the system. We tried to be as scientific as possible, but the issue isn't complicated. It's about the stories. After all, what else does journalism do? The fact that all but one of the business publications in the survey volunteered their best work is to their credit and gave us confidence that we had a fair picture of what was and wasn't done in mainstream business news during the years 2000–2007.

More on the survey in chapter 9, but I'm going to provide a capsule summary of our findings, which, given the title of this book, should not be surprising: the mainstream business press failed to meet even minimum standards of investigative reporting on financial institutions during the bubble period, let alone its own highest standards from the not-too-distant past. This disappearance of investigative reporting had three causes: the rise of CNBCization and dominance of access reporting (explored in chapter 5), deregulation, and financial distress among media outlets (discussed in this chapter). The data that *CJR* collected provide a paradox that begs for an explanation: it was during the years 2000–2003—the period *before* the true madness that engulfed the lending industry—that the *best* business investigations were done, as exemplified by the *Times* exposé of Lehman and its deep relationship with predatory lending. Bizarrely, it was during 2004–2006—the period of the *worst* excesses, what I call the "Locust Years," when subprime lending totaled $1.7 *trillion*[6]—that we find mainstream accountability reporting virtually dormant. The watchdog, powerful as it was, didn't bark when it was most needed.

The accountability paradox resolves when we see that the great journalism from the early range of dates we examined coincided with what would be the final gasp of robust lender regulation at the federal level. As regulation left the field, journalism did, too. The relationship between uncompromised regulation and accountability reporting is symbiotic; one lives off the product of the other. Regulation provides raw material for stories—indictments, settlements, white papers, and testimony. Journalism investigations provide the basis for a substantial number of law enforcement and regulatory investigations. A 2006 study of 263 cases of accounting fraud brought by the Securities and Exchange Commission found that a third were first reported by news organizations.[7] Investigative reporting also amplifies the effect of regulatory action. The cost of what's known as "headline risk" is usually far greater than any fine. A "perp walk"— the shame of publicly exposed criminal prosecution—is a significant part of the risk for white-collar offenders. In some cases, the process is dynamic: a regulatory action leads to a headline, which leads to a tip, which leads to a new headline, which leads to another action, and so on. Most important, the combination of the two presents the public with representations that are different from the airbrushed reality presented by corporate public relations and, to some extent, access reporting. In the early stages of the mortgage era, journalism and regulation combined to police an industry that was starting to career out of control.

The period from the late 1990s to 2003 was one of extraordinary regulatory activism centered on what was correctly perceived to be a growing problem: predatory lending, principally in urban areas. This activism was concentrated at the state and local levels but included the Federal Trade Commission, which brought important fraud cases against Citigroup and other brand-name lenders. The journalism of the period reflected and was part of this emergent reform dynamic.

Of course, the activism—journalistic and otherwise—came in response to real-world problems. Inner-city neighborhoods experienced spikes in foreclosure rates, many related to lending by old-line subprimers: Associates First Capital, First Alliance, Conseco Finance, Household Finance, Delta Funding, and the like. From the mid-1990s to the early 2000s, foreclosures began to jump in urban areas around the country, rising by half again in Chicago's Cook County; doubling in Detroit's Wayne County, Newark's Essex County, and Pittsburgh's Allegheny County; and tripling in Cleveland's Cuyahoga County. In 2002, the American Mortgage Association reported that 1.5 percent of all mortgages were in foreclosure, a low number today but an alarmingly high rate then. A staggering 7.2 percent of all subprime loans were in foreclosure that year.[8] The word "staggering" may seem strong, but for people who cover real estate, it fits. For years, residential mortgages had been so solid that problems were measured not in foreclosures but in delinquencies (late payments) or at worst defaults (missed payments triggering a declaration by the lender) because foreclosure rates had been so low, invariably a fraction of a percent.

Looking back, it is remarkable to recall the vigor with which politicians, regulators, and—as we'll see—journalists responded to what was considered to be essentially a social crisis, not yet a financial one. An array of studies sought to solve the same problem that journalists like Michael W. Hudson faced: how to move beyond anecdotal horror stories to demonstrate that lawless lending was not just the work of a few bad apples, as the industry maintained, but was, in the words of a 2002 law review article, a "pattern and practice" of lenders industry-wide and a product of corporate policy.[9] The problem was proving the very existence of predatory lending, which, without further explanation, can seem almost a contradiction in terms, matching the benign act of "lending" with a malign descriptor, "predatory." How can the act of lending money be shown to be aggressive? And how to get around the not-insignificant fact that each loan was signed by a borrower acknowledging both understanding and agreement?

Community groups, activists, and public-interest lawyers used various methods to chip away at the problem of proof. A 1996 Freddie Mac study of 15,000 consumer credit histories reportedly found that only 10 to 50 percent of subprime borrowers actually qualified for prime loans, an obvious telltale since no one would *knowingly* choose a more expensive loan.[10] A 1999 Chicago study found that subprime loans led to disproportionate numbers of foreclosures relative to other loans, which hinted that the products were doing more harm than regular loans. A 2001 study of Dayton in Montgomery County, Ohio, interviewed 231 borrowers to conclude that the increased foreclosures there were caused by "predatory practices." A 2002 Urban League study in Louisville, Kentucky, studied court records and found that a third of inner-city foreclosures involved loans with "predatory features." A 2003 study of Monroe County, Pennsylvania, found that foreclosures often involved inflated appraisals, indicating collusion between lender and appraiser (borrowers have nothing to do with appraisals).[11]

Predatory lending was a particular concern of state and local governments, then coping with spiking foreclosure rates and complaints from constituents about fraudulent sales tactics by subprime lenders. In 1999, North Carolina became the first state to pass what its sponsors called an "anti-predatory-lending" law, a so-called mini-HOEPA meant to fill in gaps left by the federal law. North Carolina's law lowered interest-rate thresholds requiring disclosure and banned more bad practices, including "loan flipping," repeated refinancing without benefit to homeowners, and lending based on the value of the house, without regard to whether the loan could be repaid. Between 1999 and 2004, more than twenty states, both red (Georgia, 2002; South Carolina, 2004) and blue (California, 2001; New York, 2003), followed suit with some form of anti-predatory-lending law. "Spring Fever for Predatory Lending Bills," read a headline in *Real Estate Finance*, a trade publication, on April 23, 2001.

The state of Georgia's battle with the combined forces of Wall Street and the Bush Treasury Department perhaps best shows how heated the battle over predatory lending became. Led by Roy Barnes, the former Atlanta trial lawyer who had fought Fleet a decade earlier and went on to win Georgia's gubernatorial election in 1998, the state touched off a ferocious finance industry response in 2002 when it sought to hold Wall Street bundlers and holders of mortgage-backed securities responsible for mortgages that were fraudulently conceived. It passed a landmark anti-predatory-lending law that extended liability for violations to any player in the lending chain, including the Wall Street houses that packaged the loans into securities and pension funds that bought them, and it left potential damages open-ended.

Mortgage and securities industries and Bush administration regulators demanded repeal, and the Office of the Comptroller of the Currency, led by the staunchly pro-bank John Hawke, also weighed in against Georgia's new law, declaring that it would not apply to nationally chartered banks, even for business they did in Georgia. The OCC laid down aggressive new federal rules that would block states from enforcing their anti-predatory-lending laws on national banks generally. State attorneys general, including Iowa's Tom Miller and North Carolina's Roy Cooper, objected, calling the OCC's move an unprecedented intrusion on state authority that would harm their states' consumers.[12] Standard & Poor's dealt a decisive blow when it announced that it would "disallow" loans made under Georgia's new law in securities it rated, making securitization all but impossible. Georgia's lending market began to freeze up. Governor Barnes was defeated in the 2002 elections, swept out by Republican gains and his own controversial fight to minimize the Confederate battle flag on Georgia's state flag. With the financial-services industry lobbying furiously, the Georgia legislature rescinded various provisions the following year.

Even as anti-predatory-lending enforcement shrank at the federal level, legal and policy activism if anything increased during this period at the state level. Eliot Spitzer, New York's attorney general from 1999 to 2006, made lender fraud a major priority of his tenure before becoming involved in higher-profile investigations of Wall Street stock-analyst research and accounting fraud at American International Group. Spitzer conducted a well-publicized probe of notorious inner-city lender Delta Financial Corporation. Spitzer emerged as a major opponent of the Bush-era OCC. Indeed, the OCC, siding with a banking group that includes J.P. Morgan Chase and other big banks, famously went to court to block an attempt by Spitzer to enforce New York anti-predatory-lending laws on nationally chartered banks. The OCC argued that national banks should be exempt from state lending laws. The fight against "preemption," federal regulators' assertion that they may override state predatory-lending laws, spread throughout the country. Eventually, forty-nine states, led by Michigan, sued for the right to examine the books of Wachovia's mortgage unit and fought the OCC and the banking industry all the way to the U.S. Supreme Court. (The administration's legal argument was upheld in the fall of 2007 by liberal justices, led by Ruth Bader Ginsburg, months before Wachovia itself cratered.) The fight was the subject of a 2005 series of editorials in the *Wall Street Journal*, which, abandoning its long-standing deference to state authority, sided with the OCC and the banks.[13]

Finally, it's worth noting that even into the first years of the Bush administration, the Federal Trade Commission kept up a credible show of vigilance over growing problems in mortgage lending. FTC cases against the subprime industry in the early 2000s includes some of the industries most notorious names: Chase Financial Funding (now part of J.P. Morgan Chase), Delta Funding, Fairbanks Capital, First Alliance, Nationwide Mortgage, and many others. The most important FTC case of the period was against Citigroup and its CitiFinancial unit, partly the result of its acquisition of Associates First Capital and the negative journalism coverage that accompanied it. In 2002, Sandy Weill's firm was forced to sign a settlement that included $240 million in fines. The FTC's sweeping case had alleged that Citigroup, a market leader and a household name, had "engaged in systematic and widespread deceptive and abusive lending practices" in its subprime lending operations. The FTC's suit, initially filed against Associates and continued against Citigroup and its CitiFinancial unit, alleged that the bank used "deceptive marketing" to "induce consumers to refinance existing debts into home loans with high interest rates and fees," and to "unknowingly" buy "high-cost credit insurance," a product worthless for most customers. When customers noticed the extra fees for credit insurance, bank employees "used various tactics to discourage them from removing the insurance," the complaint alleged.[14] Notably, the settlement covered not a few customers but *two million* borrowers, emphasizing the fact that the abuses were corporation-wide and systematic, indeed, a function of Citi corporate policy. What is notable about this period of vigilance—both journalistic and otherwise—is that it had no trouble drawing a direct line between the rising tide of shady operators making mortgage loans and their funding source: Wall Street.

During the period from 2000 through 2003—which might be called the "pre-mortgage era"—journalism turned in stories that kept bank abuses of subprime borrowers very much in the public eye. The ominous shift in the lending business was, despite considerable resistance from the financial community, thrust into public view. Indeed, the FTC-Citi case came about only after hard-hitting reporting regarding Associates and its practices shortly after Citigroup's 2000 acquisition of the firm. Soon after the deal's announcement, the *New York Times*, again, published "Along with a Lender, Is Citigroup Buying Trouble?" (October 23, 2000), a 3,258-word story that went to impressive lengths to explain the risks to Citi from its association with the notorious Associates and, importantly, to document the firm's execrable practices.

The story, by Richard A. Oppel Jr. and Patrick McGeehan, quoted damning internal Associates memos, including one entitled "The Roadmap to Continued Record Profits in 1995," which emphasized the importance of selling credit insurance ("insist that the insurance offer is written on every application, NO EXCEPTIONS") and pushed sales staff to refinance "aging" loans, no matter the consequences for the borrower. Also notable is the degree to which the story put Citi on the spot. Significantly, bank officials offered no defense of their new acquisition, arguing only that they would reform it. And Charles O. Prince, then Citi's chief administrative officer, later its CEO and chairman, was brought forward to offer assurances. He vowed he would not allow Associates to drag down Citi's reputation.

More examples of hard-hitting investigative journalism on abuses in the subprime mortgage market can be found across mainstream business journalism. John Hechinger of the *Wall Street Journal* wrote exemplary stories on subprime problems, including one about how brand-name lenders were convincing the poor to refinance zero-percent loans from the government and nonprofit groups with rates that reset to the midteens and higher. The lists of lenders named as taking part in the practice amounts to a roll of dishonor: "Some of the nation's biggest subprime lenders have refinanced zero-interest and low-interest loans from Habitat, including Countrywide, units of Citigroup Inc., Household International Inc., Ameriquest Mortgage Co. and a unit of tax giant H&R Block Inc."[15]

Businessweek published "Predatory Lending: Easy Money" (April 23, 2000). It led with, "Subprime lenders make a killing catering to poorer Americans. Now Wall Street is getting in on the act." The piece is mostly anecdotal (a fifty-one-year-old truck driver is double-talked out of a cheap Veteran's Administration loan and into a ruinous one, courtesy of a Bank of America unit) but does note Wall Street's entrance into subprime securitization.

Forbes unleashed "Home Wrecker," a scathing report on Household International, the old-line consumer-finance concern. The story drips with contempt for the company's lawless practices and, for added "oomph," includes the name of its CEO in the lead line: "William Aldinger says his Household International succeeds at lending to bad credit risks by managing smarter. People suckered into his mortgages cite other reasons: lies and deceit" (September 2, 2002). *Forbes*'s reporter, Bernard Condon, turned to former employees to find a lending environment little different from what Mike Hudson had found. "Household pressed its agents relentlessly for growth, raising targets several times in three years. 'It was a pressure cooker,' says Seth Callen, a former branch manager in Colorado. At times this led to deceptive tactics, former loan agents say."

The common thread of these stories is that they put a spotlight on individual institutions for core business practices that are shown to be creeping toward lawlessness. Names are named. Importantly, the stories explain the creeping shift in the industry from an underwriting culture to a sales culture and the importance of compensation incentives in encouraging the highest volume of sales under the most onerous terms. Finally, the smartest stories among them follow the money to its source—Wall Street. Here is real information presented in a way any layman can understand. Something big is happening in the mortgage business.

The national business media's aliveness to the issue mirrored even stronger work by local and regional papers. The *New York Daily News*, for instance, led a true crusade against Delta Funding Corp., the Long Island–based consumer-finance company that preyed almost exclusively on equity-rich, minority-dominated neighborhoods in Brooklyn and Queens. The paper ran a dozen stories in 1999 and 2000, documenting how Delta's salesmen, like Fleet's proxies a decade earlier, had knocked on doors around the neighborhoods to sell loans with high fees and hidden rates. One story, by Heidi Evans, described how a Delta "loan officer," accompanied by a lawyer and (oddly) his girlfriend, approached a woman recovering from emergency stomach surgery in her hospital bed. "'You don't need to read all the documents, just sign each one at the bottom,'" the man told her, according to her account in the *Daily News*.[16]

This good journalism was accompanied by, and may have contributed to, regulatory crackdowns on a lending system that was increasingly tipping out of control. In 2000, Delta Funding was hit by lawsuits from the FTC, the Department of Justice, and HUD for a laundry list of "abusive lending practices," including "paying kickbacks and unearned fees to brokers to induce them to refer loan applicants to Delta," funding loans for "African American females with higher mortgage broker fees than similarly situated white males," among many other abuses.[17] The federal cases accompanied actions brought by New York's Spitzer.

The largest settlement of the period, announced in December 2002, involved Household International in a suit brought by the attorneys general of all fifty states and led by Iowa's Tom Miller and Washington State's Christine Gregoire, who alleged that the parent of Household Finance had also systematically misrepresented basic loan terms—the true interest rates, for instance—and failed to disclose material information. The settlement totaled $484 million. "We are extremely hopeful that this settlement will signal a new day for protecting low- and moderate-income borrowers and every consumer involved in the All-American dream of home-ownership," Miller said in a statement.

Did the journalism spur the crackdown? Did the crackdown create the journalism? In a sense, it doesn't matter. The relationship between forthright journalism and uncompromised regulation is dynamic and symbiotic and, ultimately, salutary, the stuff of democracy. Each uses the other to do its work and is far weaker in the other's absence. Regulators use investigative stories to identify targets and as information sources. Reporters similarly use regulators as sources, to provide documents that come with legal protections and to push investigations forward with their subpoena power. As we've seen, Tarbell relied to an enormous degree on official documentation, particularly from probes by Congress and the legislatures of Ohio, Pennsylvania, and New York, to support her Standard Oil probe. Likewise, the sensation her work created laid the groundwork for the 1906 lawsuit by Theodore Roosevelt's attorney general, Charles J. Bonaparte, which wound up breaking up the company.

There are other similarities between investigative reporters of the early twenty-first century and their forebears a century earlier. What industrial concentration was to the muckrakers' era, financialization is to ours. Both phenomena were equally baffling to the literate citizen. Both demanded an explanation. Both had been brewing for decades. Both were marked by institutionalized lawlessness perpetrated by increasingly brazen brand-name firms. Both were widely known among legislators, lawyers, clerks, cops, bartenders, and prostitutes—just not the public.

There were differences, of course. In some ways, the mortgage story was more difficult to report and analyze for a broader readership. As we'll see, the aftermarket, where the lawless mortgages were bundled into mortgage-backed securities and collateralized debt obligations and where credit-default swaps were taken out on them, was opaque, difficult to understand, and, crucially, *not* the subject of as much regulatory activity as Standard Oil's monopolization of the oil business or, for that matter, lawless lending among financial giants. Tarbell had the critical advantage of having Teddy Roosevelt in the White House; our generation had George W. Bush. But then, Tarbell was working virtually alone, with only John Siddall in Cleveland for help, for a small, entrepreneurial publication, virtually inventing a journalism form as she went along. She didn't have it easy, either.

In the late 1990s and early 2000s, the press could be seen at least to present a challenge to the growing radicalization of the financial sector. True, given the frantic activity of state legislatures, city councils, state officials, and the FTC, the predatory-lending story was hard to miss. But through work in the *Wall Street Journal, Businessweek, Forbes,* and especially the *New York Times,* nonspecialists had at least a fighting chance to understand how the financial world was shifting under their feet. The journalism wasn't perfect, but it was working.

It is true that stories revealing Wall Street's role as the primary engine of mortgage-industry lawlessness were still few and far between in the early 2000s. It is also true that the regulatory crackdown that accompanied the journalism was grossly inadequate to the looming task. Household's record-setting settlement with state attorneys general, for instance, amounted to only a fraction of the losses, estimated to be in the billions, suffered by hundreds of thousands of customers. It was greeted with derision by borrowers and acknowledged as a compromise by state officials.[18] Indeed, it turns out the company's settlement cleared the way for a sale. The next year, its regulatory problems behind it, Household sold itself, and its giant portfolio of subprime loans, to the British financial conglomerate HSBC Group for a stunning $15.5 billion, netting its CEO, Bill Aldinger, a payout of $100 million.

For Steve Eisman, the short-selling hedge fund manager who plays a major role in Michael Lewis's *The Big Short,* the Household settlement and sale were a turning point and hardened his view of the subprime industry and the wider financial system supporting it as fundamentally corrupt. "It never entered my mind that this could possibly happen," he said. "This wasn't just another company—this was the biggest company by far making subprime loans. And it was engaged in just blatant fraud. They should have taken the CEO and hung him up by his fucking testicles. Instead, they sold the company and the CEO made a hundred million dollars. And I thought, *Whoa! That one didn't end the way it should have.*" "That's when I started to see the social implications," he said. "If you are going to start a regulatory regime from scratch, you'd design it to protect middle- and lower-middle-income people, because the opportunities for them to get ripped off was so high. Instead, what we had was a regime where those were the people who were protected the least."[19]

The FTC-Citigroup settlement was also woefully inadequate both as a deterrent and as compensation for borrowers even as it was hailed by its signatories—and the general business press—as a historic crackdown. While its $240 million penalty seemed high, this covered more than two million customers, working out to a mere $120 each. The figure was dwarfed by Citi's net income, which that year, 2002, would hit more than $15 billion and go up from there. The internal reforms it imposed on Citi proved to be easy enough to evade.

But if, as Herbert J. Gans suggests, the actors in the mortgage drama—banks, regulators, activists—were all engaged in a battle to determine what news entered the symbolic arena, the press's role was critical. The question was whether the public would have a chance to learn, as activists, state regulators, and industry whistle-blowers were arguing, that the financial sector was becoming radicalized, its mores were shifting, and a subprime ethic was seeping into mainstream lending.

As we'll see, regulation at the federal level collapsed at the worst possible moment—just as the news media's own business models began to crater as well. The period could be said to be a perfect storm for watchdog journalism. Regulatory failure and financial problems are, however, offered only as explanation, not an excuse. The retreat into access reporting is journalism's problem, journalism's choice. While investigative reporting disappeared at the national level, it continued doggedly on the local level, at modest publications with small budgets, and at regional papers that had no need for access to Wall Street firms or big banks. Somehow, they managed. What's more, the collapse of regulation was true only at the federal level. Accountability reporting saw the failure of federal bank regulation not as a reason to ignore predatory lending but as one more reason to expose it.

CHAPTER 8

Three Journalism Outsiders Unearth the Looming Mortgage Crisis

In early 2003, a few months after the Citigroup/Associates settlement, Mike Hudson was driving down U.S. 45, a two-lane road in northeast Mississippi, finishing up a twelve-hour drive from Roanoke across Tennessee, Georgia, and Alabama to Brooksville, a predominantly African American town of 1,100 between Tupelo and Meridian. He pulled to a single-story house built on a slab and was greeted by John Brown, who was in trouble on his mortgage.

Forty-four years old, Brown was less than five feet tall and barely came up to Hudson's chest when he greeted him with a smile at the door. Born severely retarded, his mental development had stopped when he was a small child. He is sunny and affable. Unable to speak clearly, he relied on his mother, Catherine, to translate the sounds and hand gestures he uses to communicate. When John Brown wrote his "signature," he printed it slowly in block capital letters, carefully copying the letters that someone had already written out for him below in the space on the loan documents. It had taken several minutes. When he demonstrated his signature for Hudson years later, Brown beamed proudly and uttered something unintelligible but that sounded like it ended with the word "cool." A judge would later describe him as "profoundly retarded and incompetent." His mother, who also suffers from a mild form of retardation, tried to explain why they had chosen to refinance a government-subsidized, low-interest loan and some credit card bills into an exploding subprime mortgage with punitive terms issued by the world's largest bank. They needed money, she said, and had none. "I didn't want my baby to starve and have nothing to eat," Catherine Brown explained.[1]

This chapter looks at how outsiders were able to see what insiders did not. Hudson, of course, came at the problem of a radicalizing finance sector from the perspective of a regional investigative reporter looking at the mortgage business from the bottom up. But, as we'll see, it was also possible within major business-news organizations to perceive profound distortions in the derivatives market—what I think of as the mortgage aftermarket. And here, again, an outsider's perspective made the difference.

Since he had first read about Fleet Financial's "seven dwarves" in Atlanta, Hudson had seen the subprime business balloon from the domain of Bill Runnells and "Miss Cash" to a $310 billion behemoth by 2003, the year he visited the Browns. Subprime had outgrown even large "specialty" or "consumer-finance" operations like GreenTree, Conseco, Associates, FAMCO, and Household International. Big enough in their own right, they were doing well-documented damage in lower-income neighborhoods, particularly inner cities. But now something even more profound was occurring. What was happening on the margins was spreading to the center of the financial system, indeed, to the center of the global economy. At this point, Hudson had a vague idea of what happened to mortgages once they were made. He knew that mainstream megabanks and even Wall Street firms provided financing for the hard-sell types and that they packaged and resold them into bonds known as residential mortgage-backed securities, and that the pioneer of this business had been Salomon Brothers back in the 1970s. But the uses to which these mortgages had been put, the amplifying power of derivatives, was another world to him.

What he *did* know was that what had once been merely immoral was now out of control. It wasn't just that mainstream banking was taking over the subprime business. It was that the subprime values he knew so well were now taking over mainstream banking. Its hard-sales culture had overrun banking's traditional underwriting culture. Risk managers and underwriters were being harassed, suppressed, and forced out of mortgage-lending operations at Countrywide, Citigroup, and Ameriquest and across the industry. Hudson, in turn, hunted them down. And they were talking to him.

In the conventional business press, however, the subprime business's long-standing and well-earned reputation for hard-sell tactics and flimflammery was now starting to slip down the memory hole, helped by clever industry public-relations campaigns. The business press, as we'll see in chapter 9, confined itself to conventional frames, describing subprime as a normal business, like conventional banking only "riskier." The *Wall Street Journal, Forbes, Fortune,* and the *Financial Times*—when they were not publishing profiles of Wall Street leaders such as Citigroup's Chuck Prince and Merrill Lynch's Stan O'Neal, profiles that were generally flattering and in any case stuck in old paradigms—conveyed problems in mortgage lending in terms of unsustainable housing prices, "the bubble," and poor-quality mortgage products. An entire journalism subculture could perceive the problem only through investor or consumer-oriented frames—frames set by the financial-services industry.

Hudson saw it for what it was: a question of misaligned incentives and asymmetrical information—in short, systemic corruption. For reasons he could barely grasp—namely the power of securitization, the fact that predatory loans would not stay on lenders' books—the mortgage-lending system was become radicalized. Sales volume became paramount.

Years later, state and federal investigations into the foreclosure crisis would confirm that leading lenders, including Countrywide, Washington Mutual, IndyMac, New Century, Ameriquest, Wells Fargo, Citigroup—in other words, the heart of the mortgage industry—as a matter of corporate policy and on a mass scale engaged in deceptive marketing that "misrepresented" the basic terms of loans, including what the interest rates were, whether they were fixed or floating, and what fees would attach, and changed loan terms at closing. As a lawsuit against Countrywide filed by the California attorney general in 2008 would later explain: the more onerous the terms of a loan for the borrower, the more global bond investors would pay for it. This fundamental misalignment led to higher pay up and down in the loan supply chain, including the sales force, as loan terms were made more onerous. As the California suit said: "The value on the secondary market of the loans generated by a Countrywide branch was an important factor in determining the branch's profitability and, in turn, branch manager compensation."[2]

Such incentives would logically set the table for the creation of vast call centers—"loan factories," where retail sales staff were trained in "high-pressure" sales tactics, complete with scripts, cold calls, and databases of consumer profiles, to "steer borrowers into riskier loans," as California alleges. An eighty-one-page Illinois complaint, also filed in 2008, similarly described a culture in which traditional banking values were turned on their heads and were aimed overwhelmingly toward "selling" loans, which is the opposite of traditional underwriting.

It was a landscape of stressed "loan officers" hunched in cubicles with headsets, trying to hit their numbers, whatever it took. It was about incentives that tilted entirely toward putting borrowers into the most expensive loans possible. The car salesmen were moving in. For a broker or loan officer, a prime loan might yield a few thousand dollars. A subprime loan might yield four or five times that, sometimes $20,000 or more, for a single loan. This wasn't about "risk" in the traditional sense. Indeed, all the risk in the end was on the borrower side and on the books of far-flung buyers of mortgage-backed securities and collateralized debt obligations (CDOs).

And while Hudson didn't know about the CDO business developing in London and New York, he did understand that the financial system was losing its bearings. The lawlessness on the fringe was heading into the mainstream, and he was going to show it. The key was picking the biggest, most visible, most familiar target.

He got in touch with a small periodical called *Southern Exposure* based in Durham, North Carolina, and pitched a major investigation into how a national bank was moving into subprime, how subprime was taking over the bank, and how it was hurting normal people in the South. For the muckraking magazine, published by the Institute for Southern Studies, a think tank for grassroots organizers and community groups, the story was a natural.

"We'll put it on the cover," said the editor, Gary Ashwill.

"How much space can we have?" Hudson asked.

"How much do we need?" Ashwill replied.[3]

All told, Hudson interviewed more than 150 people: whistleblowers, regulators, borrowers like the Browns, and their lawyers. He found Citigroup accused of all the bait-and-switch scams that mark subprime plus a couple of new wrinkles. One bank officer in Mississippi told him of "closed-folder closings," with documents inside and the check placed tantalizingly on top. "The whole time you have the check on top of the folder," the officer said, a reminder that the cash that would solve a borrower's money troubles (temporarily before making them much worse) was only a signature away.

Hudson chose a lender with a subprime unit that boasted 4.3 million customers and more than 1,600 branches in 48 states. He found a study that calculated that nearly three of every four mortgages originated within the company's lending empire were made by one of its higher-interest subprime affiliates—nearly 180,000 loans out of more than 240,000 mortgages in a single year. The lender was Citigroup. "Citigroup has established itself as perhaps the most powerful player in the subprime market by swallowing competitors and employing its vast capital resources and its name-brand respectability," Hudson wrote.[4]

Hudson's 6,000-word piece, with several sidebars and graphics and photos, represented what can only be called an alternative—albeit true and relevant—history of both the bank and its driving force, Sanford I. Weill, then finishing his transformative and much-documented career. Conventional accounts of the bank had traced its roots to its notorious predecessor company, National City Bank. Founded in postrevolutionary America, the City Bank of New York provided capital for the country's industrial expansion, then recklessly expanded during 1920s under its imperious chief, Charles E. Mitchell, who presided over a boom in margin loans for stock purchases that helped to inflate the era's enormous stock market bubble. National City's actions are seen by historians as a prime cause of the Great Crash and subsequent Depression.[5] The story continues with the rise in the late 1960s of Walter B. Wriston, considered a banking revolutionary, who changed the name to Citibank (part of the renamed holding company Citicorp), set wildly ambitious growth targets of 15 percent annually, and proceeded to meet them via a combination of brilliant innovation (Citibank was a leader in the expansion of credit cards and ATMs) and unforgivable recklessness (the bank suffered catastrophic losses on Latin American loans made in the 1970s and early 1980s). The company suffered another near-death experience in the early 1990s from bad commercial real estate loans. Citi's long history, even in conventional accounts, is bad enough.

Mainstream business reporting on Weill, meanwhile, told a rags-to-riches story, albeit with an undercurrent of recklessness and ruthlessness. Born in the Bensonhurst section of Brooklyn, Weill earned an ROTC scholarship to Cornell, started as a runner on Wall Street, and later built his own brokerage called Shearson Loeb Rhoades. He sold it to American Express, clashed with its leadership, and went into the wilderness in 1985 to restart his career (along with his protégé, Jamie Dimon). There he bought a small finance company and, via series of mergers, bought Travelers Group then, in a coup for the ages, merged with Citicorp in 1998. This is widely seen as forcing the repeal of the Glass-Steagall Act the next year, which ratified the joining of commercial banking and investment banking. Weill expanded Citi and drove it to historic levels of profitability (it was one of the world's the most profitable companies in 2000 with $13 billion in net income) before stepping aside as CEO in 2003 and chairman in 2006.[6] True, even conventional accounts couldn't help but note that Weill's hard-driving style had fostered a culture that created a series of scandals, most notably, its central role in publishing bogus stock research and financing fraud-ridden companies including Enron, WorldCom, and Adelphia Communications.

It is fair to call Hudson's piece humorless and not a lot of fun to read. It rambles some and doesn't work as a profile of Weill, who is so remote as to be almost invisible. It reads, rather, like an indictment. It also fails to grasp the mortgage aftermarket that was fueling the lawlessness at CitiFinancial (originally Associates) and doesn't even mention the repeal of Glass-Steagall, which allowed Citi to make lawless loans in Natchez and resell them as toxic CDOs in Nice.

But its power comes from the weight of the evidence it presents and, I suspect, from the freshness of the perspective. Citigroup, a subprime leader? Who knew? That's why in 2004 Long Island University gave Hudson its Polk Award, one of the most coveted in journalism. And when the crash came in 2008, Citi would become the largest bank recipient of emergency bailout funding: a staggering $45 billion in direct bailout funds and $300 billion in loan guarantees, its problems traceable directly to its subprime loan portfolio and the securities it made from it. Then, of course, discussion of Citigroup's subprime "portfolio" became commonplace. But by then it was too late.

While only vaguely aware of it, Hudson was reporting on the underside of a phenomenon that had been building since the late 1970s: financialization, the rise of the financial sector to a prominent then dominant position in the economy and over the institutions intended to govern it. The share of gross domestic product taken up by finance, insurance, and real estate rose from 15.2 percent in 1979 to 20.4 percent in 2005. Total debt in the economy rose from 140 to 328.6 percent of GDP during the period. The financial sector's portion rose from 9.7 percent to 31.5 percent.

While the financial sector grew, the real economy, average annual growth, sagged in the United States, as in most developed countries. Wages have famously stagnated even as productivity has risen. And with wages stagnant, consumer and mortgage debt rose. Mortgage debt increased by a factor of 24 during the financialization era to $12 trillion by 2005 and from 48.7 percent to 97.5 percent of GDP. Credit-card debt rose from a few billion to nearly a $1 trillion.[7]

From 1973 to 1985, as Simon Johnson has observed, the financial sector never earned more than 16 percent of domestic corporate profits. In 1986, that figure reached 19 percent. In the 1990s, it oscillated between 21 percent and 30 percent. In the 2000s, it reached 41 percent. From 1948 to 1982, average compensation in the financial sector ranged between 99 percent and 108 percent of the average for all domestic private industries. From 1983, it shot upward, reaching 181 percent in 2007.[8]

But numbers tell only part of the story. In the 1980s and into the 1990s, Wall Street was powerful, but so were countervailing forces, particularly financial regulation and white-collar-crime enforcement. Where powerful prosecutors had exercised independent authority, smaller figures, many coming directly from the financial-services industry, would take their place. The arms-length relationship between regulated and regulator changed to a revolving door as Wall Street powerbrokers occupied high-level government positions. Robert Rubin and Henry Paulson moved from Goldman Sachs to take over the Treasury Department. Alan Greenspan stepped down as Fed chairman to consult for Pimco. Regulatory control over the financial system began to give way, with the 1999 repeal of Glass-Steagall only the most visible sign. The tilt toward the financial sector could be subtle—the SEC, at the behest of Wall Street banks, agreed to change the "net-capital rule" to allow investment banks to dramatically increase the amount of debt on their books—or not so subtle: at a 2003 news conference on reducing banking regulation, the head of the Office of Thrift Supervision, James Gilleran, wielded a chainsaw over a stack of rules.

In this financialized and deregulated world, mortgage boiler rooms begin to spring up around the country, and new financial products flooded global debt markets. Among them, a strange amalgam of mortgage-backed securities turned into new securities known as the collateralized debt obligation. What had been a negligible market a few years earlier reached $157 billion by 2004—and then would really take off.

In early 2004, Gillian Tett, an editor for the *Financial Times* in charge of newspaper's influential "Lex" section, was asked by a supervisor to write a memo about what the section should focus on in the coming year. Tett, then in her thirties, was a rising star at the paper; she had prospered in various overseas assignments, wrote a book about Japanese banking, and now was running a section of short, punchy columns of market and corporate analysis considered the paper's crown jewel. Tett dutifully sat down to write what she would later think of as the "official" memo, saying Lex should devote a certain percentage of resources to the retail sector, so much to autos, so much to the stock market, and so on. But then she thought about all that and realized there was a strange and yawning gap between the things business news writes about and the world of finance as it actually was.

Tett had trained in social anthropology at Cambridge's Clare College and read the likes of Bourdieu, whose theories of power dynamics in social life had made him, among other things, a fierce opponent of rational choice theory, a key precept underpinning the financial markets covered by the *FT*. For her dissertation fieldwork, from 1989 through 1991, she studied wedding rituals in Tajikistan, a Muslim enclave then in the Soviet Union, and she wrote on how a small ethnic subculture uses ritual and practice to preserve its identity within a larger, dominant one. While there, she freelanced for, among others, the *FT*, eventually landing a staff job and rising quickly to assignments in London, Brussels, Russia, and Tokyo before being reassigned back to the *FT*'s London headquarters. Around the newsroom, Tett generally kept quiet about her anthropology background, assuming her knowledge of Tajik wedding rituals to be of rather tenuous relevance to financial journalism. As it turns out, she was wrong about that.

Mulling the disconnect between finance as it really was and the journalism that purported to cover it, Tett sketched a "cognitive map," a tool used by scholars to delineate the difference between a social reality and the discourse about it, of the City of London, the U.K. version of Wall Street. She noticed something strange: While most business-news reporting centered on glamour beats, like the stock market and mergers and acquisitions, those were far from the biggest part of the financial system. In terms of sheer dollars, including investment-banking profits, the credit markets dwarfed them by an order of magnitude. These were bonds issued by governments and corporations and others that investment banks had created by pooling together various loans—auto loans, corporate loans, credit card loans, and mortgages—into securities that were then sold to investors, such as pension funds, or traded around the globe and used as collateral for other loans. For one thing, there was this roaring business in a thing known as collateralized debt obligations, or CDOs, and other "derivatives," so called because they were derived from some other security, like bonds backed by mortgages, known as residential mortgage-backed securities. Looking at her map, Tett thought of an iceberg—not in the sense that the financial system was heading for one. She just found it remarkable that only a bit of the financial world—stocks, M&A—was visible in the press and the public discourse while the vast bulk of it lurked below, out of view, and out of the discussion.

At first Tett sensed not danger for financial markets but an opportunity for the newspaper. If other outlets ignored this vast and hidden sector, perhaps the *FT* could stand out by helping its readers profit from it. She wrote a series of memos, which became known as the "iceberg memos," pushing for more coverage of debt markets. This kind of advocacy is not always popular around newspapers, which tend to be set in their ways, and in this case led to Tett's transfer from the Lex job to the Capital Markets team, which was not a promotion. Capital Markets stuff typically appeared in the back of the paper, and its desks were in a remote part of the building that overlooked garbage bins and bike racks. The group was about as far away from the top editor's office "as it was possible to be and still be in the same building," Tett would later say. A colleague seeking to console Tett, who was pregnant with her second child at the time, told her, "Capital Markets is a great place to go and have a baby. Nothing ever happens." Here was Bourdieu's theory of "social silences" played out in a working newsroom.[9]

Tett discovered that the debt business, too, held its own paradoxes. The "fixed-income" or "credit" business, as it was also known, fashioned itself as tantamount to a science. Increasingly populated with math Ph.D.'s, its methodology bristled with mathematical terms and elaborate formulas that purported to predict outcomes under every imaginable economic and financial scenario. Underpinning the mortgage-backed securities business, for instance, was a formula known as the Gaussian copula function, which allowed financiers to perform, in the language of quantitative finance, "stress tests" and "robustness checks" on a portfolio of securities under various scenarios that mirrored events in the real world, including "panic regimes." The paradox, though, was that a superstructure that mimicked the hard sciences—like physics—was being built on a very human activity. As Tett noted, the actual word, "credit," came from the Latin *credere*, "to believe." Beliefs, of course, have little to do with math and are based more on shifting sands of consensus, interpersonal relations, and other intensely human activities. The multi-trillion-dollar market was based on someone's belief in someone else's ability and willingness to do something (in this case, pay their debts). That human behavior, and not scientific law, lay at the debt markets' foundation was, as Tett put it, "a flipping obvious point to anyone with a background in social anthropology" (or anyone else, for that matter), but it "came as a tremendous surprise to most people who work in money."[10]

On taking over Capital Markets, which was then turning out other, mostly desultory work, Tett urged her small reporting staff to get out of the office and study bond dealers "in their natural habitat." In early 2005 Tett traveled to the European Securitization Forum in Nice, France, where the talk was all about CDOs, CDSs (credit-default swaps), and other strange acronyms. Walking around the conference, with its PowerPoint presentations, cocktail parties, and strange idioms, she thought of it as a kind of giant Tajik wedding, where members of a particular type of tribe, isolated from the wider financial system, gathered to speak their common language and restate common values and shared myths. One of the myths, stated over and over, was that the participants were involved in a technological revolution of sorts, innovation so profound it would have as much impact on the financial system as the Internet was having on communications media. This myth held that these innovations would benefit not just bankers but society as a whole, expanding credit while at the same time making the system safer. The idea that banks once kept the loans they made on their own books was thought to be an archaism, the bad old days. This was a new era in which risks were distributed among sophisticated parties to the benefit of all. It all sounded good, but what struck Tett was that amid all the discussions of money, math, and models, it almost never came up at these conferences that the system everyone was working on involved human decisions and contracts made under human circumstances.[11]

Tett returned to London determined to write about this strange, new, exploding market. One of her earlier, longer pieces ran to 2,300 words on April 19, 2005, under the headline "Clouds Sighted Off CDO Asset Pool." The lead anecdote featured a lawyer who had just completed a contract to sell some of these ultracomplex securities and was surprised to learn that the buyer was not a hedge fund or bank but an Australian charity. Tett reported that the CDO market had already reached $120 billion in 2004, about as much as all European corporate bonds issued that year. Did investors really know what they were buying? Another piece, in May, tried to pin down even the size of the market, which was still unclear. By July 2005 she had traced the boom back to the U.S. mortgage market, which was providing the raw material for most of the explosion in derivatives and, by March 2006, she had traced the origins of these new financial "products," as they are known, back to a small cadre of bankers and financial engineers at J.P. Morgan, specifically to an "offsite" brainstorming session in Boca Raton, Florida, in 1994, where the idea for an insurance contract against bond defaults, to become known as "credit-default swaps," was first bruited. She learned that this "Morgan Mafia" had since dispersed to other banks to spread the gospel.[12]

By the end of 2006, Tett's writing, while still mostly appearing in the back of the paper, became more explicit and more urgent. "Time to Decode Derivatives," from September 20, 2006, linked the big demand for "derivatives" (collateralized debt obligations aren't mentioned) to low central bank rates. "Take Care When the Sweet Taste of CDS Starts to Turn Sour," on November 3, warned that some of the technical kinks in the market hadn't been worked out. A piece in December probed the vital role played by rating agencies in assigning top ratings to even the most exotic instruments. By the spring of 2007, when the financial world, including the rest of the business press, first began to awaken to the unfurling financial crisis, Tett was bluntly warning that the CDO threat was far more dangerous than investors and regulators understood.[13]

Tett later said that she all along feared that competitors would discover the story and jump in. Before going on a six-month pregnancy leave, in October 2005, she drew up plans for how to respond if other outlets caught on, but when she returned they still hadn't.

The CDO market became more frenetic, with $271 billion issued in 2005; $520 billion in 2006. But all she saw in the business discourse was the same iceberg: reporting about the stock market and M&A—business press as usual. The press "didn't have the foggiest idea the revolution had happened at all," she marveled.[14]

To be sure, even Tett's work, as singular as it was, reads today as somewhat tentative, given the calamity to come. The stories, understandably, contained the usual caveats and hedges ("In some respects, this startling growth is a potentially positive step for global markets") along with probing questions ("if a shock occurs, will it turn out that investors have not understood the potential dangers?").[15] Some followed blind alleys (one piece worried about the role of hedge funds in the CDO market, which turned out to be a different problem than the one she had anticipated); most stories weren't prominently displayed. The piece linking CDOs to mortgages, for instance, ran at 300 words on page 23. Her 4,000-word profile of the "Morgan mafia" doesn't actually mention the term "credit-default swap," which was still gaining currency, or "collateralized debt obligations," the principal instrument that credit-default swaps would insure. The idea that the U.S. subprime mortgage market had something to do with the Morgan invention was even more remote.

But the fact that these stories appeared at all, particularly in 2005 and 2006, made them remarkable. Other news outlets produced stories on the derivatives markets, some of them quite fine, as we'll see, but no one pursued the beat with such penetrating focus. That's why Tett would earn "Business Journalist of the Year" honors from the British Press Association in 2008 and then "Journalist of the Year" in 2009, as the scale of the crisis became more fully understood. She was promoted to managing editor of U.S. operations at the *Financial Times* in 2010 and won global recognition as one of a handful of professionals, inside and outside of journalism, who called attention to looming dangers. All these accolades were well deserved.

While grateful for the recognition, Tett herself would refer to these prizes as "guilt awards," a tacit admission, as she would say, that, by and large, the business media "had missed one of the biggest stories of the decade." She doesn't exempt the *FT* or herself in the critique, despite her lonely work, and has since devoted considerable thought to trying to understand what happened. "Why had no one covered it? Why was this allowed to happen?" she asked. She thought about Bourdieu's "social silences," the patterns of conformity, ideology, and assumption that delineate what is discussed and what isn't—what is deemed irrelevant or beyond question. It was at this "semiconscious level," she would later observe, that social silences are most insidious, particularly when they serve the interests of a particular group, in this case, financial elites. She would later quote Bourdieu in an article for a finance journal (likely the first Bourdieu citation in such a venue): " 'The most successful ideological effects are those which have no need of words, and ask no more than complicitous silence.' "[16]

She also developed a theory of silos, later of "geeky silos," the idea that small cadres of technical experts, hidden from public view, are pushing the frontiers of their particular disciplines in ways that could in fact be quite dangerous. In her 2010 speech to the American Anthropological Association, Tett warned that society was increasingly vulnerable because of intellectual and structural fragmentation, with geeky silos in industries from oil drilling to nuclear power, yet also increasingly interconnected. Who, she asked, will serve as watchdogs? Who will be the generalists who will act as cultural interpreters, break social silences, ignore the ridicule and impatient sighs of the cognoscenti, connect dots, see the systemic changes, and warn of them? Worse, she said, the growing danger from geeky silos comes at a time when the power and reach of traditional watchdogs, including the press, is being eroded.[17] Here, Tett echoes the thinking of McClure, Steffens, Baker, Tarbell, and other muckrakers, generalists, and investigators whose work looked at issues systemically.

The subprime-CDO story was an example of Bourdrian theory brought to terrifying reality. Here were a few hundred experts on a handful of derivatives desks, secluded from society, from the financial world, and *within their own individual firms* by their arcane language and secretive culture. Yet they had demonstrated the capacity to do grievous harm to the global financial system. These financial engineers had sat at flickering screens, seeing the world much as the prisoners in Plato's cave, not reality but shadows of reality. The most unnerving aspect of the derivatives business was that while it cranked out hundreds of billions of dollars in subprime-mortgage-backed CDOs, almost none of the Wall Street and City of London executives Tett knew had encountered a "real-life subprime borrower in the flesh."[18]

But high finance, at least, doesn't pretend to speak to and for the public. Journalism does. It is notable that Tett, a generalist, new to the derivatives beat, was able to see anomalies that others could not. Indeed, she attributes her success to her status as an outsider and a generalist. This freed her from preconceptions, peer pressure, intellectual capture, and the frames accepted by the people and institutions she was covering. It allowed her to move from silo to silo, examining different parts of the system holistically and, most of all, to think about "social silences," the blank spaces on the map.

Hudson and Tett were two points on a spectrum. Hudson roamed the mortgage market; Tett, the aftermarket. To connect the dots, each would have had to follow the money—up, in Hudson's case, down, in Tett's. Hudson would eventually get there, but before he did, another reporter doing similar work on the subprime business—indeed, a friend of Hudson's—would make the connection between systemic corruption on the ground and its ultimate destination in global debt markets through a remarkable book few have ever heard of.

Richard Lord, a reporter for the *Pittsburgh City Paper*, had read Hudson's *Merchants of Misery* and was struck, as Hudson had been, not so much by the predatory nature of the subprime lending business but by the fact it was going mainstream. In the early 2000s, Lord began to look into foreclosure filings in the Allegheny County Prototnotary's Office, which covers Pittsburgh. He found the numbers had risen sharply between 1995 and 2000, from 1,000 to 2,500, and that driving the spike were subprime mortgages, which had risen from a tenth of the foreclosures to more than a third, about 900. He found anecdotal cases of mortgage abuse that were literally hard to believe: the ninety-two-year-old, blind-in-one-eye, ninety-pound, housebound Albert Blank, whose undoing came when he answered to door to a home-contracting salesman with brokers in tow from the Money

Store. "I signed it," Blank told Lord. "I was a damned fool." Lord wrote a series of stories for *City Paper* then looked outside Pittsburgh and found similarly soaring foreclosure rates in other urban centers: Newark's Essex County, Detroit's Wayne County, Cleveland's Cuyahoga County, Chicago, and elsewhere. "The foreclosure tsunami suggests that the very concept of working class homeownership could be in jeopardy," he wrote.[19]

The result was a peculiar, undeniably muckraking work published in late 2004: *American Nightmare: Predatory Lending and the Foreclosure of the American Dream.* The 230-page book has no index or footnotes and is a pastiche of anecdotes and data that ranges over contractor scams; profiles of Conseco, Household, and Citi-Financial; a chapter on mortgage servicers; and an appendix of advice on how to avoid a subprime loan and what to do if you have one. It opens with an anecdote about the Eselmans from the rust-belt town of Evans City, Pennsylvania, a musician making $10,000 a year and his wife, who ran a failing home-based business advising others how to build a home-based business. They had gotten in too deep with Conseco, a $96,000 loan with $18,000 in fees. The book is remarkable in the matter-of-fact way it traces the chaos of this household's dilemma—and the spike in inner-city foreclosures, generally—directly to the MBS market and its sponsors on Wall Street. In a chart, the book uses Federal Reserve and mortgage-trade publication data to document a tenfold increase in subprime lending from the mid-1990s to 2003, which were the most recent data available, and the parallel rise in subprime securitization (32 percent, or $11 billion, of the $35 billion in subprime loans in 1994 and 61 percent of the $203 billion in subprime loans in 2003).[20] Another chart details the spike in subprime-related foreclosures. Chapter 2, "This Little Loan Went from Main Street to Wall Street," describes the technical advances made in the early 1990s in the secondary market for subprime loans that allowed for their securitization and explains how high rates and other onerous terms, such as prepayment penalties, actually increased the value for Wall Street, incentivizing predatory lending. Lord makes this commonsense observation:

*By its very nature, the mortgage-backed securities market encour-
ages lenders to make as many loans at as high an interest rate as
possible....* That may seem a prescription for frenzied and irresponsible lending. But federal regulation, strict guidelines by
Fannie Mae and Freddie Mac, intense and straightforward competition between banks, and the relative sophistication of bank
borrowers have kept things from getting out hand, according to
the HUD/Treasury reporter. *Those brakes don't apply as well in
the subprime lending market, where regulation is looser, marketing
more freewheeling and customers less savvy.*[21]

The paragraph, as simple as it is, contains great insight. Like Hudson,
and unlike the great bulk of the financial press elite, Lord understood
the subprime market not just from a financial point of view but from
a human one. He understood it as a phenomenon *he had personally
experienced* through traditional news reporting. Lord had walked the
streets, knocked on doors, sat scribbling with notebook in hand as
borrowers poured out their stories, their anxieties, their anger, their
sense of betrayal, as well as the misrepresentations, frauds, flimflams, and tacked-on fees they confronted.

Then, using publicly available Securities and Exchange Commission filings, Lord traced the path of subprime mortgages like that
of the Eselmans. He found a Bloomberg terminal at a University of
Pittsburgh library (in fact, he had had to sneak in posing as a student) where he discovered a list of likely purchasers of the Conseco
residential MBS of that vintage, including Great-West Life & Annu-
ity Insurance and other insurers, foreign and domestic. Investors,
Lord reports, earned between 3.8 percent and 8 percent, depending on the tranche. "I want to know if they have any thoughts about
what they helped to do, and the lives they helped to crumble," Lord
quotes the borrower, Jill Eselman, after reading her the names of
the investors.[22]

Once he understood subprime lending for the racket that it was,
Lord, who had no previous financial-reporting experience, was able,
without much fanfare, to trace the funding to its source, Wall Street.
His book doesn't show awareness of the emerging market in CDOs,

which were made from the residential MBS, the derivatives, or what might be called the *after*-aftermarket. But he understood that this was a big, global business based on loans to families like the Eselmans and the others he met in inner-city Pittsburgh and rural Pennsylvania. He understood that the MBS market had been stable for years but that this was a different kettle of fish. This was, "predatory lending and the foreclosure of the American dream," as his book's title would put it.

Lord's book is not without its quirks or flaws, but it made the important connection between the subprime market and the Wall Street aftermarket that fueled it. Put another way, *because* he understood the true and lawless nature of the subprime market, he recognized the need to trace it to its funding source. And so, with relative ease, he did just that.

Since the crash of September 2008, a great battle has been joined over the narrative of the financial crisis—its causes, costs, meaning, and implications. Major government investigations and mainstream business reporting have found the causes, as might be expected, to be manifold. The debate is ongoing and is marked by sharply divergent points of view, often breaking down along political lines. Still, a general consensus has formed around the idea that global capital imbalances, combined with low interest rates, triggered an asset bubble, most consequentially in the U.S. housing market. Financial deregulation and skewed compensation incentives created a flood of defective mortgages, and the harm these caused, already severe, was profoundly exacerbated by a new generation of credit derivatives created by Wall Street for sale on global debt markets. Included among the derivatives were lightly regulated credit-default swaps, which allowed parties to offer "insurance" even on derivatives they did not own and without reserving for potential losses, which allowed virtually unlimited growth in mortgage-related derivatives unrelated to the size of the mortgage market itself. The government-sponsored enterprises Fannie Mae and Freddie Mac contributed to some extent by lowering standards on the mortgages they were willing to buy but mostly by participating in the aftermarket for the defective mortgage securities produced by Wall Street. This consensus is reflected in the final reports of the two main bipartisan governmental bodies investigating the crisis, the Financial Crisis Inquiry Commission and the Senate's Permanent Subcommittee on Investigations, which produced the Levin-Coburn report.

Beyond the relative importance of these and other elements, conservative arguments place the blame primarily on federal housing policy, centering on Fannie and Freddie (the GSEs) and federal housing agencies, whom they blame for an "intensive effort to reduce mortgage underwriting standards," which in turn eroded standards across the board. A related school of thought, represented by the columnists David Brooks and George Will and some elements of the business commentariat, advances the argument of cultural decline: that public attitudes toward debt over the years became casual to the point of irresponsibility, leading millions of Americans to take out mortgages without taking into account their ability to repay. Why this happened spontaneously and en masse sometime around 2003 is not explained.[23]

While government certainly contributed to the crisis, chiefly by failing to adequately regulate the financial sector, the argument that it drove the subprime market has been rejected by the main official investigations and debunked elsewhere. As many commentators have noted, there are a number of things to be mad at the GSEs about—their use of political clout to ward off oversight, their mid-2000s accounting scandals, their purchases of Wall Street–created subprime securities, their huge losses caused by the sheer size of their portfolio—but data show they never bought subprime mortgages per se. They did buy Alt-A (poorly documented) loans but did so late, most aggressively in 2006, and only after losing market share to the private sector, which had vastly expanded and dominated the subprime/Alt-A market. And even after they lowered standards, the loans the GSEs bought or backed significantly outperformed those in the private sector: Even for a subset of borrowers with similar credit scores—below 660—FCIC data show that GSE mortgages were far less likely to be seriously delinquent than non-GSE securitized mortgages: 6.2 percent versus 28.3 percent as of the end of

2008. As for the Carter-era Community Reinvestment Act—another conservative target—the argument for the centrality of a 1977 law in a mortgage boom three decades later is even more far-fetched, but suffice it to say that the FCIC found that only 6 percent of all "high-cost" (subprime) loans had any connection to the law, which didn't even cover some of the worst actors—non-banks like Ameriquest, Countrywide, and the rest.[24]

While the causes of the financial crisis are obviously complex, no one seriously doubts that U.S. mortgages were at its center. And at the center of the mortgage crisis was subprime, along with its deformed cousin, Alt-A. There is no escaping the mortgages, always the mortgages, and at the beating heart of the crisis: subprime.[25]

In 2004, soon after wining the Polk Award for his Citigroup exposé, Michael Hudson was asked by film producer James Scurlock to redo some of his interviews from "Banking on Misery" in front of a camera for an antidebt documentary that would become *Maxed Out*. Followed by a camera crew, Hudson returned to Aberdeen, Georgia, to talk to John Brown and his mother; visited other borrowers in the outer boroughs of New York City; and then headed to Pittsburgh, where he linked up with Richard Lord, who had just finished *American Nightmare*. One night, after a day's interviewing, the two reporters sat in Lord's basement office, trying to figure out what to do next.

Hudson and Lord were dumbfounded by the rise of the street-corner consumer-finance industry and its move to the center of the U.S. financial system. Hudson was particularly struck by the emergence of Ameriquest, one of the so-called new generation of subprime lenders that promised to clean up an industry that had seen virtually *all* its market leaders—Associates, First Alliance, Conseco, GreenTree, Household—embroiled in scandal or collapse or both. The Orange County, California, lender had done a remarkable job of cleaning up its own image.

Roland Arnall, Ameriquest's founder, was one of the more complex and ruthless figures of the mortgage era. Born in 1939, he was the child of Eastern European Jews who fled to Paris to escape Nazi persecution. Arnall and his family moved to Montreal and, in the late 1950s, to Los Angeles. Arnall started out selling eggs door to door then flowers as a street vendor. Eventually, he found his way into real estate. Associates describe him as a man driven to dominate but with a disarming side as well—"the biggest bastard in the world and the most charming guy in the world, and it would be minutes apart," a former executive said. Describing the outcome of a deal he'd struck with Arnall, a former partner conveyed the ambivalence Arnall could provoke: "He fucked me. But within reason."[26]

Considered the father of modern subprime, Arnall was "obsessed with volume" and believed "volume solved all problems." He pushed his loan officers to meet aggressive sales targets and, whatever the target, was prone to say, "We can do twice that." In 1980 Arnall founded Long Beach Savings & Loan, which later morphed into Long Beach Mortgage, a portion of which he sold off to Washington Mutual (fatefully for that lender, it would turn out), a portion of which he changed into Ameriquest. He pioneered the use of computers to find potential borrowers and to speed the loan-approval process. By 2005, Arnall ranked seventy-third on *Forbes*'s list of the richest Americans with a personal net worth of $3 billion.[27]

Ameriquest had its share of scrapes with regulators, including a $4 million settlement with the Justice Department in 1996 over a suit alleging the lender had gouged older, female, and minority mortgage borrowers. In the late 1990s, the FTC launched a new predatory-lending investigation, and the company attracted the ire of housing activists, including ACORN, which denounced the lender as a collection of "slimy mortgage predators." Ameriquest resolved its standoff with ACORN in 2000 by agreeing to establish a fund, administered by ACORN, for needy borrowers and adhere to a list of "best practices." ACORN, in turn, held up the company as an industry model. As it contemplated a public stock offering and a move into the highly competitive market for prime loans, Ameriquest bolstered its political ties. It donated heavily to various political campaigns, including those of Arnold Schwarzenegger, who as California's governor would oversee Ameriquest's main regulator, and George W. Bush. Arnall would be one of the top ten donors to Bush's 2004 reelection campaign. Ameriquest committed $75 million to have the Texas Rangers ballpark dubbed Ameriquest Field. In 2005, it would sponsor the Super Bowl XXXIX halftime show. It owned two blimps.[28]

But that was PR. Insiders knew Ameriquest to be at the center of the boiler-room culture that was then overtaking the mortgage-lending industry. Even as it became the nation's leading subprime lender, in 2004, Ameriquest became notorious among regulators, housing activists, plaintiffs' lawyers, and borrowers—precisely the sources that Hudson talked to and mainstream news organizations ignored. Customers were filing complaints with the Federal Trade Commission against Ameriquest four and five times more frequently than against Countrywide's and New Century's subprime units, respectively, and both of these lenders were already notorious among insiders. Lawsuits and class actions were popping up around the country, alleging a culture of corruption within the lender. According to the affidavit of one former employee, the lender encouraged employees to "promise certain interest rates and fees, only to change those rates at the time of the closing." By the end of 2004, attorneys general were conducting what would be a fifty-state investigation into abusive lending at Ameriquest.[29]

Like a lot of newspapers around the country, the *Roanoke Times*, where Hudson worked, had lost some of the élan of the 1980s heyday. It had cut back on staff, and, in Hudson's view, its appetite for muckraking had slackened. Hudson wanted to move into other types of reporting and to avoid being associated with a single subject. But that wasn't happening. The sight of the subprime industry, and the likes of Ameriquest, rising from its "Miss Cash" origins to dominate the financial system with Wall Street backing it all was too mind-blowing to leave alone.

In 2004, he put together a pitch on Ameriquest and contacted a friend who knew someone at the *Los Angeles Times*, who put him in touch with Rick Wartzman, the business editor, and John Corrigan, a deputy editor. The paper approved the idea—unusual enough for a major newspaper to agree to a green-light an investigative story from a freelancer—and paired Hudson with E. Scott Reckard, one the *Times*'s most respected reporters. Together, Hudson and Reckard produced a series that peeled the façade from Ameriquest's carefully devised public-relations campaign and, to devastating effect, exposed the lender as a lawless marketing machine.

The series introduced readers to the concept of the boiler room and reported that the nation's largest subprime lender—a brand name, the market leader—had assembled a vast archipelago of call centers staffed by salespeople whose main incentives were to churn out as many loans as possible with the most onerous terms to the borrower. The headline on the story from February 4, 2005, says it all: "Workers Say Lender Ran 'Boiler Rooms.'" As always, former employees provided the key to unlock the story. Hudson and Reckard interviewed more than two dozen former employees from around the country, all of whom confirmed accounts that management-imposed quotas forced them to get loans completed by any means necessary, including fraud, deception, forgery, and phony appraisals. The lead quotes a former loan officer:

> Mark Bomchill says he'd like to forget the year he spent hustling mortgages for Ameriquest Capital Corp. in suburban Minneapolis.
>
> Slugging down Red Bull caffeine drinks, sales agents would work the phones hour after hour, he said, trying to turn cold calls into lucrative "sub-prime" mortgages—high-cost loans made to people with spotty credit. The demands were relentless: One manager prowled the aisles between desks like "a little Hitler," Bomchill said, hounding agents to make more calls and push more loans, bragging that he hired and fired people so fast that one worker would be cleaning out his desk as his replacement came through the door.
>
> "It was like a boiler room," said Bomchill, 37. "You produce, you make a lot of money. Or you move on. There's no real compassion or understanding of the position they're putting their customers in."

Indeed, the concept of a boiler room was brought up by numerous former employees and for a good reason. Employees told Hudson and Reckard that watching the 2000 film *Boiler Room*, starring Ben Affleck and Vin Diesel, was part of their training.

To business reporters of a certain age, boiler rooms are associated with the notorious stock swindlers of the late 1990s, many criminally indicted, including A.R. Baron, Stratton Oakmont, and First Jersey Securities. These firms specialized in promoting penny stocks to unsuspecting investors, many of them elderly, who lost their entire investment when the stocks inevitably crashed. The signature of boiler rooms were "pump and dump" schemes—salesmen (and they were mostly men) working from scripts touting the stocks of companies with plausible sounding names (e.g. Health Professionals Inc.) and plausible-sounding stories (temporary health-care staffing)—and the trappings of legitimacy, stock-ticker symbols, financial statements, and so on. The stocks would rise on the manipulation and crash after the brokerage had taken its profits, ignoring the frantic calls of investors.

Boiler-room telephone operations date to at least the 1980s and got their name because many were originally near the actual boiler rooms of office buildings, a cheaper location that had the added advantage of being hidden from prying eyes. The name stuck because the idea of heat became central to boiler-room culture. A telephone operation was said to run at "full burn" when every phone station was manned by salesmen. It generated "heat" when the sales force was working with urgency, cold-calling vigorously and riffing effectively on the scripted sales pitch. "It's a numbers game," Hudson would later quote a longtime sales person. "Make enough calls, and you sooner or later get the deals."[30]

Boiler-room culture, driven by young men earning tens of thousands of dollars a month, is traditionally associated with high living and louche behavior. A lawsuit filed by a bankruptcy trustee of A.R. Baron alleged that former executives charged on corporate credit cards or were reimbursed for "several million dollars" in expenses for prostitutes, vacations, evenings at strip clubs in which "'tens of thousands of dollars were spent,'" orgies that caused thousands of dollars in damage to New York hotel rooms, wine collections, and $50,000 per-seat season tickets to New York Knicks professional basketball games.[31] In *Born to Steal: When the Mafia Hit Wall Street* (2003) Gary Weiss, a former *Businessweek* reporter and specialist in financial fraud, documents epic parties thrown by boiler-room operators, including an amusing anecdote about one who often ended coke-and-prostitution binges by tearfully watching a videotape of *The Lion King*. ("Benny used to have this thing about watching *The Lion King* after we did coke," Weiss quoted a cohort. "I put in the video, and he's crying watching the fucking *Lion King*.")[32]

Ameriquest was all about "the energy, the impact, the driving, the hustling," the *LA Times* quoted Lisa Taylor, a former Sacramento-based employee, who also told the paper she had witnessed other employees tracing forged signatures by the light of a brightly lit Coke machine in the office. One former employee described being threatened with firing nearly every day. Another described the twelve-hour workdays punctuated by "power hours": nonstop cold-calling sessions to lists of prospects burdened with credit card bills; the goal was to persuade these people to roll their debts into new mortgages on their homes. Anecdotes conveyed the idea of an institution out of control: A Spanish-speaking woman in East Palo Alto, California, was put in a mortgage with payments—$2,494 a month—that exceeded the entire income she earned cleaning houses. The only Spanish-language document she ever received was a foreclosure notice.[33]

In May 2005, another story explored how Ameriquest and other big lenders (including Citigroup) had given hundreds of thousands of dollars in donations to community housing groups, including ACORN, muting their criticism and, in effect, buying respectability. Hudson and Reckard reported that their earlier story, in February, had prompted at least one of the groups, the Greenlining Institute, in Berkley, California, to return $100,000 to Ameriquest.[34]

With the *LA Times* series going well, Hudson stepped back and pulled together a story list with eight items—probably five too many, in retrospect, given a typical newsroom's capacity to deal with any single subject. One tried to get at the special nature of subprime—highlighting the particularities of an industry that, unlike conventional lending, seemed to prone to a cycle of rapid growth ending in either collapse, scandal, or both. Hudson proposed to look to the source of subprime funding: Wall Street. "The role of the securities market in producing the 20-fold increase in subprime mortgages over the past decade is an important story that no other news organization has addressed," Hudson wrote *LA Times* editors. "Ameriquest as we know it wouldn't exist without the mortgage-backed securities market, which funnels tens of billions in ready, fast-turn-around cash into the company. Who are the investors that buy Ameriquest's securities? Have they—or any of the ratings agencies—begun to experience concerns about the quality of Ameriquest's portfolios?"[35] Good questions—but they wouldn't be explored until later.

Even so, the *Times* muckraking series continued to good effect throughout 2005, including another story on Hudson's list, which ran on October 24 and struck even closer to the heart of the lawlessness that by then had overrun the mortgage-lending business. Under the headline "More Homeowners with Good Credit Getting Stuck with Higher-Rate Loans," the story pointed to a study of hundreds of thousands of loans by Freddie Mac showing that more than 20 percent of subprime borrowers actually qualified for prime mortgage loans. Since no one would *voluntarily* agree to a higher-priced mortgage or more onerous terms, the findings pointed toward what might be called the "boiler-room effect": deception, confusion, and fraud. The 2,500-word story included interesting support from IndyMac, at the time a prime lender (later bankrupt and seized). It had examined the books of several subprime lenders it was considering acquiring and made a startling finding: at Ameriquest, as many as 40 percent of borrowers in subprime loans had credit scores that actually qualified them for prime loans. Of course, the presence of good-credit customers in bad-credit loans is not proof of lawless lending. There are good reasons that some borrowers with good credit—the self-employed, for instance—might still be penalized with a subprime loan. But Hudson and Reckard raise the possibility of corruption stemming from subprime's takeover of the lending system.

Whether by skill or chance, Hudson and Reckard were right to focus not just on subprime lending in general but on Ameriquest in particular. By this point Ameriquest and its affiliates had become the subprime market leader, making $83 billion in loans in 2004, more than 15 percent of subprime market that had reached over $530 billion, about 18 percent of all mortgages in the United States.[36] Ameriquest's boiler-room sales tactics and anything-goes "underwriting" forced the rest of the market to play catch-up. Ameriquest was a practical example of Gresham's Law, or bad money driving out the good, and William K. Black's theory of how unregulated markets create criminogenic environments.[37]

It was later discovered that no less a figure than Angelo Mozilo, chairman and CEO of Countrywide Financial, had complained about Arnall and Ameriquest and blamed them for driving down standards across the entire subprime mortgage market. *Chain of Blame*, an early history of the financial crisis published in 2008, describes a telling summit of sorts in the early 2000s (the location and date are not specified) between the two mortgage titans, Arnall, then the rising subprime star, and Mozilo, head of overall mortgage-market leader Countrywide, which, to that point, had trodden carefully in the subprime market. Mozilo wanted to know the secret of Ameriquest's runaway growth. He came away appalled:

"He plays by his own rules," Mozilo told an associate. "He's the guy who started stated-income, the guy who started no-documentation loans. All of his people were on commission." Mozilo learned more details about Arnall's tactics after Countrywide hired a group of former Ameriquest employees in New York. He became so concerned, he said, that he forwarded the information to the state's attorney general, Eliot Spitzer. It may seem ironic that Mozilo, the public face of a lawless mortgage era, would turn to law enforcement to police a competitor. But Mozilo merely recognized that, in an unregulated environment, one bad actor could destroy an entire market. In *All the Devils Are Here*, McLean and Nocera also find evidence that Mozilo saw the problem that Arnall's Ameriquest posed during the early 2000s as it captured an increasing share of the market: "'If you had said, "Nope, I'm not going to do this because it's not prudent," you would have had to tell shareholders, "I'm shutting down the company."' '"Ameriquest,"' Mozilo told a friend, '"changed the game."'"[38]

It should be recognized that for its trouble, the *LA Times* faced relentless resistance from Ameriquest, which was then at the height of its influence and political power. But despite its political clout, aggressive public relations, and leading market share in the subprime industry, Ameriquest would become yet another subprime lender shuttered in the wake of aggressive press and regulatory investigations. Concurrent with (but separate from) the Hudson/Reckard series, Tom Miller of Iowa and Prentiss Cox (then an assistant attorney general) of Minnesota were leading forty-nine state attorneys general in an investigation of systemic fraud and misrepresentation in Ameriquest's lending operation. In early 2006, Ameriquest agreed to pay $325 million in penalties and restitution. The settlement also imposed sweeping reforms on its lending practices, requiring Ameriquest, among other things, to disclose truthfully what a loan's interest rate was. The company also agreed to stop "the practice of encouraging homeowners to falsify" their incomes and to eliminate compensation incentives that paid loan officers for putting customers in loans with the most onerous terms. The company also agreed to provide "accurate, good-faith" property appraisals, instead of fraudulently inflated ones. These changes led to its sale to Citigroup when it could not operate both profitably and honestly.

Through the investigative and accountability-oriented mindset displayed by the *LA Times*, important information had a chance to enter the public discourse. As we'll see, Ameriquest did wreck the market, and its boiler-room ethic spread across the lending industry and would include all the brand names: Citigroup, Countrywide, Wells Fargo, IndyMac, New Century, as well into retail operations owned directly by Wall Street firms themselves, BNC Mortgage (Lehman), First Franklin (Merrill Lynch), Chapel Funding (Deutsche Bank), Encore Credit Corp (Bear Stearns), and so on. Unfortunately, the *LA Times* series was the exception that proved the rule about mainstream media coverage of lending in general and by the business press most especially.

This is not to say that Hudson was alone in detecting the systemic shift in U.S. mortgage lending; some regional papers sounded the alarm that something had changed in the financial culture. The *Atlanta Journal-Constitution*, for instance, published a lengthy series in early 2005 that broadly looked at an array of lending abuses— high-cost used-car, personal, and tax loans—and rising personal bankruptcy and foreclosure rates in the state.[39]

Starting in August 2005, the *Charlotte Observer* zeroed in on the problem of subprime mortgage lending with a massive effort that over two years would alert its readers to deep structural problems in the subprime market. A keystone of the then-prestigious Knight-Ridder chain and one of the South's marquee regional dailies, the

Observer analyzed data on more than 2.2 million loan applications from across the country that had been released that year by the Federal Reserve under the Home Mortgage Disclosure Act of 1975. A 1989 amendment had required lenders to disclose data based on race (in response, partly, to the anti-redlining journalism and activism of the era), and, in 2002, the Fed added loan-pricing data (in response, again, to the journalism and activism of the turn of the decade). The data came from the nation's twenty-five largest lenders, including Wachovia and Bank of America (now combined and bailed out), as well the other large lenders, Countywide, Ameriquest, etc.

The Observer, too, turned up signs of an industry gone rogue: Blacks, regardless of income, were far more likely to wind up in a subprime loan (the series called them "high-rate" loans) than whites. And brokers "often . . . can make more money by increasing the interest rate." And so on. The three-day series, "The Hard Truth in Lending," written by Binyamin Appelbaum, Ted Mellnik, and Rick Rothacker, started with a huge display across the Sunday front page and included all the accoutrements of a classic newspaper investigation—photos, graphics, pie charts, and tables. The series went onto describe the rise of the subprime industry and the patchwork nature of federal lending regulation.[40]

Interestingly, the series reported that the lending industry was bracing for a "deluge" of bad publicity following the formal release of the Home Mortgage Disclosure Act data later that year. The Consumer Bankers Association had already scheduled a conference that fall to deal with what it believed would be negative publicity resulting from the data. The conference title was "Preparing for the Storm." For whatever reason, the "storm" of coverage, in the national business press, at least, didn't materialize. The *Wall Street Journal*'s story on the release of the HMDA data, for instance, ran at 1,000 words on page A2 under the headline: "Blacks Are Much More Likely to Get Subprime Mortgages—Weaker Lender Competition in Some Low-Income Areas Is Cited as Part of Problem."

By early 2006, Michael Hudson was running short of cash. He had discovered that investigative reporting was not the easiest freelance market. While he had covered subprime for more than ten years, he wanted to pursue it. The marginal hard-money business he had covered since the early 1990s had grown and moved to the center of the U.S. mortgage market and financial system. And despite the legions of financial reporters working in New York and the reams of stories about Wall Street firms, nobody was doing the obvious story of how Wall Street was underwriting out-of-control lenders and then reselling their defective loans throughout the world. But, first and foremost, Hudson needed a job.

So once again he put together a story list and at the top included a pitch for a piece about the multi-trillion-dollar market for mortgage-backed securities and how it was founded on loans made to people such as Carolyn Pittman—a sickly widow from Jacksonville, Florida, who accused her lender, Ameriquest, of fraud—and thousands of others who had filed similar complaints in one venue or another. While the dangers to the financial system were less clear, it didn't take a finance degree to know that a securities market built on such sold-not-bought mortgages was unsustainable. His pitch quoted a scholar who said the MBS market was "flying blind" because of the scant data on subprime lending and pointed to risks for the market, including the fact that the loans were filled with exploding rate adjustments and pocked with shoddy documentation, inflated appraisals, and worse. "At a minimum," Hudson wrote in the pitch, "we could do a story that explores whether mortgage-backed securities encourage lenders to make risky or predatory loans. The second, more speculative part of the story—what happens if the housing bubble bursts?—would be harder to pull off. But if we could muster enough evidence and analysis to do so, it would take the story to another level."[41]

One target that seemed particularly ripe was Lehman Brothers. After all, it had been a leader in underwriting subprime since the 1990s and had already accumulated a trail of litigation, including a judgment against it in the case the *New York Times* and ABC News had publicized in 2000, implicating it in the predatory practices of First Alliance Mortgage. After a few more letters, a series of serendipitous contacts, and a few interviews, Hudson's hunt paid off. In May of 2006, he began covering the bond market, including mortgage-backed securities, for the *Wall Street Journal*.

CHAPTER 9

The Watchdog That Didn't Bark

The Disappearance of Accountability Reporting and the Mortgage Frenzy, 2004–2006

The government, the financial industry and the American consumer— if they had only paid attention—would have gotten ample warning about this crisis from us, years in advance, when there was still time to evacuate and seek shelter from this storm.

—DIANA HENRIQUES, *New York Times* business reporter, 2008

But anybody who's been paying attention has seen business journalists waving the red flag for several years.

—CHRIS ROUSH, *American Journalism Review*, 2009

The notion that the business press wasn't paying attention is wrong, and the assertion that we were asleep at the switch is wrong. We were attentive. We were aggressive. We were aware. We wrote abundantly. But it is very hard to get the public's attention for stories warning of complex financial risks in the middle of a roaring, populist bull market.

—MARCUS BRAUCHLI, *Wall Street Journal* national editor and managing editor

The story of the 2008 financial crisis is not only a story of hubris, greed, and regulatory failure, but one of these deeply troubling problems of social silence and technical silos.

—GILLIAN TETT, *Fools Gold*

The demise of the mainstream media, especially newspapers, has been forecast for decades, but the years following the "Tech Wreck" of 2000—the period of the housing bubble—opened a new, defining chapter. The crash of the technology bubble set off a severe ad recession, particularly at Dow Jones, which had made what the business press would call "missteps" that left it more vulnerable than most publishers. Starting in 2000 and running through the entirety of the mortgage bubble and subsequent financial crisis, the media industry began a revolution from which it has not yet emerged but whose first phase included the disintegration of the financial underpinnings of the news business. Driving the revolution was the migration of advertising dollars to new Internet companies—Google, eBay, Craigslist, and, later, Facebook—that relied on models that had nothing to do with covering the news. Newspaper advertising revenues, which had reached a peak of more than $60 billion at the beginning of the period, were cut in half by the end of 2008 and, by 2009, had returned, in real terms, to levels not seen since 1965. Once-great newsrooms were cut down beyond recognition.[1]

The total number of newsroom professionals (journalists) dropped 25 percent between 2000 and 2009, from about 56,000 to 41,000, a conservative count that understates the impact on great metropolitan dailies, particularly the *Washington Post* and the *Los Angeles Times*, both of which saw their staffs of professional journalists cut in half, from 1,200 to 650 at the *LA Times*. The steepest decline in value came around mid-2007, just about the time the credit crisis burst into full view. For instance, the market capitalization of the Journal Register Company, publisher of the *New Haven Register* and hundreds of smaller papers, fell more than 99 percent beginning in 2007—long before, it's worth remembering, the credit crisis made business flameouts commonplace. In newspapering, it was the business model itself that fell apart.[2]

Around the same time, the drip of newsroom cuts became a deluge—in all, newspapers lost 13,000 jobs in 2007—and business news wasn't spared. Chris Roush, director of the Carolina Business News Initiative at the University of North Carolina–Chapel Hill, estimates that the number of print business reporters around the country fell from 12,000 to 9,000 between 2000 and 2009. Business pages of major regional papers were hit especially hard: between 2004 and 2009, the *Washington Post* business staff lost thirty of its top reporters. *The Los Angeles Times* lost at least fifteen in the same period, leaving it with a total of around fifty.[3]

The debilitating effects on the news of such financial losses can be seen in the case of Dow Jones, the once-undisputed global leader in financial news and the parent company of the *Wall Street Journal*. Dow Jones's particular problems can be traced to poor strategic decisions, including the failed 1991 bid for CNBC, which became such a cash-generator that it could have saved the company. Other opportunities came and went. The biggest blow, though, was a $900 million write-down of a Bloomberg-like financial-data unit in the fourth quarter of 1997. In an April 16, 2007, story, "Bloomberg's Money Machine," *Fortune*'s Carol J. Loomis wrote: "In the annals of business, the fall of Dow Jones from its financial-information throne and the rise of Bloomberg must be counted one of the great competitive turnabouts in history." In the "annals of business," one of the "great competitive turnabouts" is not something you want to be on the wrong side of. By the turn of the twenty-first century, the financial-news industry's flagship was reliant almost solely on a single asset, a newspaper, and was vulnerable to any shock. These would come in bunches.

The first was self-inflicted. In the spring of 2000, the *Journal*'s managing editor, Paul Steiger, announced a bureaucratic shuffle that replaced the Page One editor, the great if imperious John Brecher, and moved the position itself under the general news hierarchy. The move effectively ended Page One's autonomy within the hierarchy and made it less able to withstand the pressure to elevate routine daily business news at the expense of more in-depth reporting and careful writing. More and more, instead of taking the long view, Page One stories ignored Kilgore's admonition and began to recount what happened "yesterday."

The early 2000s ad recession lowered revenues across the media industry and, with them, Dow Jones's stock price. The *Journal* had struggled to diversify its advertising base and so was hit especially hard by the loss of technology and financial-services ads that had filled the paper in the preceding years. The attacks of September 11, 2001, drove the staff from its newsroom across from the destroyed

World Trade Center but created an esprit that helped win a Pulitzer Prize and reenergized the paper in the days and weeks that followed. The adrenaline rush, however, ended with the kidnapping and murder of Daniel Pearl in January 2002, which cast a pall over the *Journal*, an inchoate atmosphere of depression and bad feeling that no amount of memorializing and tribute could remedy.

The company was increasingly hampered by its ownership structure. Over the years, the Bancroft heirs had multiplied, and by the mid-1990s they numbered more than thirty, working in a variety of occupations (airline pilot, horse breeder) and scattered about the globe, some with a tenuous emotional connection to the paper and, for that matter, one another. Fatefully for the paper, many family members relied on the company's quarterly dividend for income. A dividend is capital returned to shareholders because the business has no better use for it. Everyone knew that Dow Jones needed to grow to remain independent. And everyone understood, certainly by the mid-1990s, that the newspaper business was in transition and that lots of capital was needed to help with the shift. This became especially true after the big write-down of the data unit. But the company's board kept the dividend at $1 per share, or $83 million a year—money badly needed for improving the news organization. The Bancroft family controlled about 20 million shares and so split about $20 million a year.

In 2002, Dow Jones stunned shareholders by posting a $8 million loss, threatening its credit rating, imperiling dividend payments to the controlling Bancroft family, and putting the independence of the company in doubt. The company responded by laying off more than 1,700 employees, including four rounds of layoffs in the newsroom, and slashing expenses by $179 million.[4] It scrapped its generous pension plan in favor of a standard 401(k) and made cuts so deep in its health insurance plans that war correspondents were reduced to writing open letters to company directors, appealing to their conscience. Contract negotiations with the reporters' union, once pro forma affairs, turned into bitterly contested struggles. Newsroom employees held byline strikes, boycotted the office, and picketed the company's Lower Manhattan headquarters, chanting slogans and marching around a giant inflatable rat. The *Journal*'s sense of élan was fraying.[5]

While Dow Jones distributed its working capital in the form of dividends, more adroit—if less enlightened—media competitors were making savvy acquisitions and investments. Rupert Murdoch's News Corporation bought a string of independent television stations to create the Fox Network in the 1980s, established Fox News on cable in 1996, and later gained dominant positions in satellite TV in the United Kingdom, United States, and other key markets. In 2010, its cable news division produced operating profits of $2.2 billion, twenty times that of all of Dow Jones, indeed twice as much as Dow Jones posted in *revenue*.[6] This is simply to say: when it comes to journalism, ownership matters.

Balkanization at the *Journal* worsened, the atmosphere at the office darkened, and the gap between managers on the ninth floor and reporters on the tenth became a yawning chasm. The culture shifted from one of confidence, swagger, muckraking, and storytelling to keeping one's head down and career survival. In some indefinable way, the power of reporters—not unlike that of rank-and-file employees in other industries—diminished, while that of managers increased. Dissent from reporters all but disappeared. Office politics became byzantine, and productivity demands on the newsroom grew ever more pronounced. Time-consuming investigations were undertaken at the reporter's own risk: If a lead didn't pan out—no matter the reason—your productivity numbers took a hit, putting your career in peril. This wasn't subtle. Management grew more remote. In contrast to Kilgore, who walked the floors every day, an appearance by Steiger on the ninth floor was a rarity; one by CEO Peter Kann, rarer still. The *Journal*'s weakened condition, financially and, in my view, journalistically, cleared the way for Murdoch's News Corporation to buy it with an unsolicited offer in mid-2007, just as subprime credit markets were starting to crack.

But problems at Dow Jones were worse than those in the rest of the business media only by a matter of degree. Shares of *Fortune*'s parent, Time-Warner, plummeted more than 80 percent after the disastrous 2000 merger with AOL, to less than fifty dollars two years later, where they have more or less remained. Shares of the *New York Times*'s parent fell nearly 90 percent, to about six dollars, where they remained. *Forbes*'s privately held parent floundered financially in the 2000s, to the point that the family sold a piece to a private equity firm in 2006. *Businessweek*'s parent, McGraw-Hill, prospered, ironically enough, because of its Standard & Poor unit, paid under a conflicted business model by Wall Street banks to provide AAA ratings to defective securities; the magazine itself floundered, particularly after 2006, and was sold to Bloomberg for a small sum in 2009.[7]

The disintegration of the business media's financial underpinnings could not have come at a worse time. Low morale, lost expertise, and constant cutbacks, especially in investigative reporting—these are not conditions that produce an appetite for confrontation and muckraking, for vision and ambition. Instead, newsrooms retreated into CNBCization: tethered to the news cycle, competing ever more frantically for increasingly smaller scraps of news, cranking up the output requirements of reporters, and further marginalizing muckraking and investigations. The intra-newsroom tug of war between depth and speed tilted toward the latter and would eventually become a rout. Much has been made of the increasingly frenetic pace of news and newsgathering today, a phenomenon I refer to as the "Hamster Wheel."[8]

As it happens, increased productivity requirements for reporters can be traced to the late 1990s, when news organizations responded to the rise of the Internet by producing more at a quicker pace and with the same or decreasing staffs. In the late 1990s, for instance, the *Journal*'s newsroom produced stories at a rate of about 22,000 a year while still doing epic, enlightening work that created value for the shareholders. By 2010, that number had nearly doubled to 41,000. The creep began in 2000 with a spike to 26,000, and story counts rose more or less steadily afterward. This count does not include Web-only material, so the figures are conservative. Meanwhile, the number of journalists producing those stories has shrunk. The International Association of Publishers' Employees Local 1096, which represents a substantial number of newsroom workers, says the number of its covered employees dropped 13 percent, from 323 in 2000 to 281 in 2008.

The debilitating effects of this kind of productivity increase can't be definitively measured—measuring quality is always tricky—but nonetheless can't be overstated. Suffice it to say that it can shrink

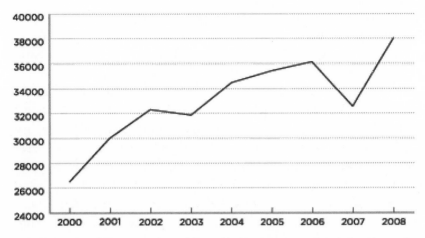

Figure 9.1 Hamster Derby: Number of stories published in the *Wall Street Journal*
Source: Author research, Factiva.

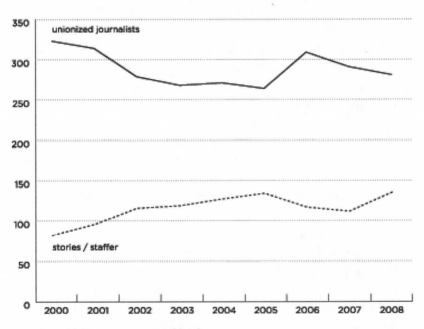

Figure 9.2 Rising newsroom workload
Source: Author research, Factiva.

the horizons of a news organization and the reporters that work within it. The hamster wheel goes hand-in-hand with CNBCization, producing the need for a hurried gathering of incremental scoops. The hamster wheel makes impossible the kind of source cultivation, document studying, stair climbing, and door knocking that created masterpieces like Susan Faludi's "The Reckoning." The wheel is a boon for news managers and bureaucrats because story quantity is easy measured while quality is not. Short, incremental news items rarely entail the kinds of risks and stresses that typically define a news investigation. The hamster wheel is a bane to reporters, who find themselves tethered to their desks, dependent on official sources for stories, and deprived of the time to step back, dig deep, or merely think. Ultimately, this process is also a problem for readers, who are left to sort through a deluge of information, much of it generated from corporate sources, without the benefit of depth or analysis. And of course readers will never know what stories were left by the wayside, which voice wasn't heard, which public service not performed.

In a landmark report on news media trends, the Federal Communications Commission confirmed the trend and slightly bureaucratized the name, calling it "hamsterization":

The broader trend is undeniable: there are fewer full-time newspaper reporters today, and those who remain have less time to conduct interviews and in-depth investigations. In some ways, news production today is more high tech—there is nary a reporter in America who does not know how to tweet, blog, and use a flip video camera—but in other ways it has regressed, with more and more journalists operating like 1930s wire service reporters—or scurrying on what the *Columbia Journalism Review* calls "the hamster wheel" to produce each day's quota of increasingly superficial stories. They can describe the landscape, but they have less time to turn over rocks. They can convey what they see before their eyes—often better and faster than ever—but they have less time to discover the stories lurking in the shadows or to unearth the information that powerful institutions want to conceal.[9]

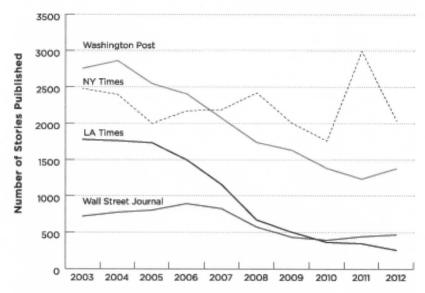

Figure 9.3   Stories of more than 2,000 words
Source: Author research, Factiva.

Across the news business, the number of long-form stories also dramatically declined, coinciding with—if not caused by—a period of
media disruption and journalistic retreat (see figure 9.3).

   This period of disruption and disempowerment in the media business occurred at roughly the same time as the super-empowerment
of the financial sector. In 1996, for example, Morgan Stanley was, as
it is today, an elite Wall Street firm, and Dow Jones was an elite publishing company. Each had a market capitalization (the market's
perceived value of a firm, share price times the number of shares
outstanding) of roughly $5 billion. Morgan was slightly larger, but its
resources were not virtually unlimited, as they would become, and
the enormous cultural prestige of the publisher—a legacy of its journalism—was matched by its balance sheet. Dow Jones had clout.

   A decade later, in 2006, Morgan Stanley's market capitalization had
ballooned more than tenfold, peaking at nearly $70 billion dollars. Its
revenues had increased to $76 billion, riding, like all of Wall Street,
the inflation of the housing bubble and the residential mortgage-
backed securities and collateralized debt obligation factories they
had created. Dow Jones, meanwhile, posted revenues of $1.7 billion

that year, its shares dead in the water and its market capitalization at a mere $3 billion. Its net income was $387 million, a fraction of Morgan Stanley's, but even that low figure was inflated by the sale of cash-producing local newspaper assets. Its income from continuing operations was half that. And its actual cash flow from continuing operations was $35 million. To put that in perspective, Morgan Stanley's CEO, John Mack, commanded a pay package that year of $41 million. Mack's personal earnings rivaled or exceeded, depending on the metric, what of all of Dow Jones was taking in.[10]

As Wall Street rode financialization to a position of unprecedented power, countervailing forces weakened. Most consequentially, the Bush presidency ushered in a deregulatory regime that that not only failed to adequately regulate the mortgage market but actively fought attempts by others to do so, principally state banking commissioners and state attorneys general. Regulation was compromised especially at the Office of the Comptroller of the Currency, which oversees nationally chartered banks such as Citigroup; the Office of Thrift Supervision, which regulated savings-and-loans such as Washington Mutual; the Federal Reserve, which had broad powers over the financial system and specific responsibility for nonbank subprime lenders; the Federal Trade Commission, with jurisdiction over consumer fraud; and the Securities and Exchange Commission, the once-proud watchdog of Wall Street. The Financial Crisis Inquiry Commission report put it simply: "The sentries were not at their posts." What's more, "the financial industry itself played a key role in weakening regulatory constraints on institutions, markets, and products" through more than $3.7 billion in federal lobbying expenses and campaign contributions between 1998 and 2008.[11]

As we've seen from Ida Tarbell's work onward, effective journalism and uncompromised regulation operate independently but together create a dynamic that generates information, public awareness, and, ultimately, reform. Without effective regulation, journalism can have all the resonance of one hand clapping. With the rollback in regulation and the dramatic growth of financial institutions, the financial system changed not just in degree but in kind. Financial news, however, did not. The mortgage era provides a study in the limitations of a narrow, investor-oriented focus that, broadly speaking, privileges access journalism. As crisis loomed, there was no Tarbell, not even a Faludi.

The defensiveness of business-news professionals, as evidenced in this chapter's epigraphs, is understandable. As we'll see, the business press wrote a lot of stories, and a portion of them can be seen as warnings of one sort or another. On the other hand, many of them were the exact opposite of warnings. In any case, it's certainly a mistake—always—to blame readers for inattentiveness. Almost by definition, when the public is caught *this* off-guard about something this big, journalism needs to wonder if there was something, somewhere that it did wrong, something it didn't do. In this case, what wasn't done was accountability reporting. What journalism had done for more than a century, it could not muster when it was needed most. It may indeed be true that "it is very hard to get the public's attention for stories warning of complex financial risks," as Marcus Brauchli, the former *Wall Street Journal* editor, says. But it is less hard, I would suggest, to get the public's attention about stories of institutional or systemic corruption. Those tend to be popular.

Mainstream business coverage of major financial institutions from 2004 through 2006 was trapped in old narratives, trapped in New York, trapped in the Wall Street paradigm, trapped on a spinning hamster wheel of increased productivity requirements, trapped in its comfort zone of risk, strategy, and interfirm competition. It became less mindful of broader societal concerns and ignored sources outside the bubble of investors, analysts, and executives. Jesse Eisinger, a former financial columnist for the *Wall Street Journal* and now a Pulitzer Prize–winning writer for the nonprofit investigative news organization ProPublica, says his old paper, like business journalism generally, clung to outdated formulas. Wall Street coverage tilted toward personality-driven stories, not deconstructing balance sheets or figuring out risks. Stocks were the focus, when the problems were brewing in derivatives. "We were following the old model," he says.[12]

For muckrakers such as Hudson and Lord and short-sellers such as Eisman—attuned to the possibility of systemic corruption—deals such as Citigroup's purchase of Associates and HSBC's of Household Finance were clear landmarks, fraught with meaning and portent.

For business news, these were another set of "risks" among many others. The conceptual difference is important; indeed, it is everything. As Lord described in *American Nightmare* and Eisman demonstrated around the same time with his CDS purchases, it was but a small step on the financial conveyor belt between mass fraud in low-income lending in the mortgage market and the global explosion in securitization of the same debt in the aftermarket. The connection was intimate and, as Lord demonstrated, not especially difficult to understand. And remember: the findings of mass fraud in the early 2000s were not mere allegations but settled cases brought by government authorities. The players involved in the mass frauds were not marginal operators but market leaders. And behind them, Wall Street firms—the world's largest and most prestigious financial institutions—stood as the main market for their defective products, which they repackaged and sold many times over on the aftermarket. In 2004, 2005, and especially 2006, billions then trillions of dollars in debt securities and insurance would be based on these very loans.

If, as a journalist, one believed these loans represented reasonable risks undertaken by two more or less equally sophisticated parties based on reasonably symmetrical information, then one would not necessarily view the debt securities then created with alarm. One might believe it possible, even reasonable, to view subprime mortgage debt as similar in kind to prime mortgage debt, just riskier, but with risks that could be compensated for with extra interest, prepayment clauses, credit enhancements, and other safety measures. Indeed, such a view might not be too different from Wall Street's. The fact that U.S. housing prices had "never" fallen on a nationwide basis (never, that is, since the Great Depression, when they had fallen 30 percent) would even lend plausibility to the idea behind collateralized debt obligations. But if one believed the original mortgages were, in fact, defective products, based—to some substantial degree—on fraud and misrepresentation, on hard-sell tactics and street-corner ethics—that is, if one believed that the subprime industry was as it always had been and will always be—then one's view of the "risks" to the entire global financial system begins to change. A system with fraud at its foundation will, in all likelihood, ultimately fail, and the larger the system, the bigger the failure.

In launching the *Columbia Journalism Review*'s 2009 survey of business news, which I spearheaded, we had a hunch that the professionals were wrong in their assertion they had provided the public with adequate warnings about the transformation of the lending system and its Wall Street roots, and they were. Business news, as our survey demonstrated, failed to hold major lenders and their Wall Street backers to account. As I argued in 2009, it did everything *but* take on the institutions that brought down the financial system.[13]

But these professionals *weren't* wrong that business news produced useful stories, and that's perhaps the source of the disconnect with members of the public—Jon Stewart's audience—who believe, like me, that whatever was done was inadequate. The trouble is, however, that even the best work produced during the years when the subprime sales culture had overrun the financial system was hampered by business news's own narrowing definition of its mission. The run-of-the-mill, conventional business coverage of Wall Street was, because of its investor-centric view, not only myopic but also a contributor to the coming crisis.

The goal of the *CJR* report was to find stories that met past journalism standards for accountability reporting: head-on investigations of powerful institutions that, to use the Schudson and Downie definition, held "business and professional leaders accountable to society's expectations of integrity and fairness."[14] So our survey was a search for the *best* in business reporting during the period and was designed to capture *all* significant warning stories, not just some of them. The survey (for methodology, see note 5 in chapter 7) took three months and involved sorting through many thousands of stories to find those that were relevant and could reasonably be seen as accountability reporting focused on major lenders and their Wall Street backers. Along the way, as noted, we found stories that didn't qualify as accountability reporting but were valuable in other ways. That eight of the nine publications we examined participated by submitting what they believed was their best work bolstered our confidence that we had captured the significant precrisis work.

In the end, what emerges is a fundamental disconnect between the world that Hudson, Lord, and others had been reporting on for more than a decade and the one represented in the mainstream business press. Business news, as sophisticated as it might have been in some ways, revealed itself as surprisingly innocent, even naïve, about the subprime mortgage industry. Major business and financial coverage of subprime lending stayed within established frames, viewing it as an extension of the prime market, only "riskier." Indeed, "risk" is the frame through which business news viewed the mortgage market. But the problem wasn't systemic risk. The problem, as later official investigations amply demonstrated, was systemic corruption.

Some of the best work from 2004 through 2006 is what I call "investor" and "consumer pieces": warning about unsustainably high housing prices and against patently defective new mortgage products then flooding the market. Business-news outlets deserve high marks for early and loud warnings about the housing bubble. [15] Bubble talk appears, surprisingly, as early as the fall of 2001. *Fortune* might well win the prize, if there were one, for bubble-bursting, with "Is the Housing Boom Over?"—4,539 words by Shawn Tully, on September 20, 2004; on October 31, 2005, Tully answered himself with another five-thousand-plus words in "'I'm Tom Barrack and I'm Getting Out,'" about the "world's best" real-estate investor.

Meanwhile, the press was also warning consumers not to agree to a mortgage product containing terms that no well-regulated system would allow (and that have since been banned).[16] Indeed, the *Wall Street Journal* kept after the issue and essentially called these mortgages bad on their face in several articles: "For These Mortgages, Downside Comes Later" (October 5, 2004); "The Prepayment Trap: Lenders Put Penalties on Popular Mortgages" (March 10, 2005); and "Mortgage Lenders Loosen Standards" (July 26, 2005). It should be said these usually ran on page D1, not A1, and so gave the impression of low-priority messages. Even so, there they were, and the defenders of business news have a fair point.

Regulators and lawmakers did have information they could have used had they wanted to. *Businessweek* ran a 4,000-word cover story on September 10, 2006, under the headline: "Nightmare Mortgages" with the subhead: "They promise the American Dream: A home of your own—with ultra-low rates and payments anyone can afford. Now, the trap has sprung." The story relates the dangers of option adjustable-rate mortgages—loans with low teaser rates—and includes several anecdotes about homeowners who had taken them and found themselves in trouble. The story explains accounting rules that allow lenders to book sales on contract signing rather than when the cash comes in, encouraging high loan volume to generate short-term profits, and notes that banks had insulated themselves from risks by selling the lousy loans to Wall Street, which repacked them and sold them to someone else. It mentions that sales brokers are incentivized to "care more about commissions rather than customers" and use "hard-sell" tactics.

But even this laudable story—one of the better mainstream business stories of the period—illustrates the limits of the investor/consumer perspective. The story mentions some prominent lenders in passing as taking part in the practice—Golden West, Washington Mutual—but focuses on none in particular. Instead, the focus is on the dangers of the mortgage itself, not the massive institutions selling them. What the reporting failed to see was that the real danger was not in shoddy consumer products per se but in institutionalized, systemic corruption based on misaligned incentives to put as many of the most vulnerable borrowers into loans under the most onerous terms.

The story recounts four anecdotes of customers who not only bought a bad product but also, in three of the cases, assert that they did not understand the terms of the loan. In other words, the article argues that either the lender misrepresented the terms or, at a minimum, the disclosure was inadequate:

> "They know they're selling crap, and they're doing it in a way that's very deceiving," [Gordon Burger, Sacramento police officer] says. . . .
>
> "We didn't totally understand what was taking place," says Carolyn [Shaw, wife of a retired mechanic with diabetes]. "You have to pay attention. We didn't, and we're really stuck here." . . .
>
> "What reasonable human being would ever knowingly give up a 5.25% fixed-rate for what we're getting now?" says Eric

[Hinz], 36, who works in commercial construction. Refinancing is out because they can't afford the $15,000 or so in [prepay-
ment] fees.

The story calls to account a financial institution for each anecdote.
Each of these declares the problem an anomaly, a consumer-product
problem, not an institutional one. The reporting never rises to make
the distinction that Richard Hofstadter lauded the muckrakers for:
identifying not only malpractices but also *malpractitioners.*

Stories about deficient products are not enough to get the public involved, which requires stories of institutionalized corruption.
There's no way around that particular hard journalistic task. Perhaps the most impressive work during the period were stories that
explored the consequences of the rapidly growing pool of savings
accumulating in global debt markets, which made its way into debt
instruments of all sorts, driving down yields and increasing leverage in the global financial system. In late 2005, for instance, the *Wall
Street Journal* published "Awash in Cash," a five-part series highlighting the dangers of some of these issues.[17] The series explored how the
cash glut led to a rise in asset prices, stocks, commodities, and real
estate. It reported that lower borrowing costs had spurred corporate
mergers globally and fueled corporate stock buybacks and dividend
payments (as corporate profits increased). However, it doesn't mention mortgages in a meaningful way, and when it discusses collateralized debt obligations, it's in the context of those made from corporate debt.

But the very nature of such "system" stories, as I call them—
those that frame issues in terms of "risk" to a particular facet of the
financial system—renders them of limited use because they fail to
take into account the extent to which fraud played a role in under-
mining financial models. The view is top-down when the reporting
needed to be from the bottom up. Without knowing that important
foundations of the financial system—mortgages—were to a large
extent fraudulently conceived, the authors must search among all
the various risks in the financial universe—commodities, corporate
loans used for private equity buyouts, sovereign debt, other asset
classes—to try to find, using numbers alone, which risk is the riskiest.

Second, even if the "riskiest risk" was correctly identified, there's not much for the public to do about it since no individual institution is responsible.

Still, it's not hard to find interesting and useful stories about rising risks in the debt and derivatives markets. Warren Buffett, in Berkshire Hathaway's 2002 annual letter to shareholders, famously proclaimed derivatives to be "financial weapons of mass destruction" after the company had experienced losses in a reinsurance unit. And a reading of business news in the early 2000s shows that the nearly catastrophic losses at Long-Term Capital Management, in 1998, weren't far from business reporters' minds.

The Enron debacle of 2001—which even the *Wall Street Journal* called part of an "upswing" in "corporate corruption" of the era— prompted news organizations to revisit the matter of derivatives and explore the role played by financial deregulation. A *Wall Street Journal* story, for instance, included early accounts of how in the late 1990s Brooksley Born, then chair of the Commodity Futures Trading Commission, had fought Alan Greenspan, Robert Rubin, and other powerful figures over her agency's ability to regulate derivatives— and lost.[18]

In 2005, big hedge fund losses in the derivatives markets related to General Motors debt touched off worries among policy makers and explorations by business journalists into instability in the system. In April, the International Monetary Fund warned in its annual report of a possible meltdown in credit derivatives if investors all tried to "run for the exit at the same time," and even Alan Greenspan, an apostle of derivatives, warned of "unanticipated losses" because "the rapid proliferation of derivatives products inevitably means that some will not have been adequately tested by market stress." *Businessweek* responded by asking, "Will derivatives cause a major blowup in the world's credit markets?"[19] But the limits of this 1,300-word piece are evident. It focuses, understandably, on corporate debt but doesn't mention mortgage debt. And why should it? No one had alleged that corporate debt, in general, or GM's, in particular, was somehow fraudulently conceived. Indeed, fraud would have been far from the minds of reporters engaged with corporate debt, which differs from consumer debt, let alone subprime, in that both parties—issuer and buyer—are professionals and, at least nominally, sophisticated. The balance of information, power, and means between the two parties is much more symmetrical. There may be *expensive* lending in the corporate market, but, by definition, there can be no such thing as *predatory* corporate lending. That's why even the best "system" stories were hamstrung; they viewed subprime mortgage lending as just another form of risk—like GM's corporate bonds—and failed to take into account the possibility of widespread fraud in the system.

The business press began to zero in on the market for mortgage derivatives in the mid-2000s as the market began to balloon. Indeed, even as Steve Eisman and Michael Burry and other characters in *The Big Short*, as well as John Paulson and other hedge-fund managers, were beginning to assemble their positions to short the housing market, business-news organizations were reporting on it. In December 2005, the *Wall Street Journal* ran a 1,000-word story on C-1 discussing hedge funds that were betting against "lower-grade" mortgage-backed securities using something called a "credit-default swap":

> The new market came to life in June, when dealers agreed on a standard contract applying credit-default swaps, already widely used in the corporate-bond market, to the pools of home, auto or credit-card loans known as asset-backed securities. So far, trading has focused mainly on the riskiest part of the market for home-equity securities, which are backed by adjustable-rate loans to folks with shakier credit—a category that has grown in recent years as mortgage lenders have plied high-risk borrowers with easy financing.[20]

One of the most penetrating stories exploring systemic risk came ten months later, on October 30, 2006, when, in a Page One story, the *Wall Street Journal* impressively explained the ties between subprime mortgages and not only mortgage-backed securities but also the market for collateralized debt obligations (CDOs) and credit-default swaps, considered then to be some of the most sophisticated and complex products on the market. The 2,500-word piece by Mark Whitehouse, "As Homeowners Face Strains, Market Bets on Loan

Defaults," explicitly linked the fates of a Los Angeles–based hedge-fund buyer of a synthetic CDO tranche to a subprime borrower living in New York City: "Bryan Whalen and Ike Spirou have never met. But through the world of modern mortgage finance, their fates are inextricably linked."

As the story recounts, Spirou had bought a $300,000 house in Queens, using a $266,000 mortgage from Option One, an H&R Block unit, then refinanced with a $360,000 loan from Long Beach Mortgage, a Washington Mutual unit. Whalen, the hedge-fund manager, had bought credit-default swaps—an insurance contract—against a bond containing Spirou's mortgage: Long Beach Mortgage Loan Trust 2004-2. The party selling the insurance on the bond was Citigroup (in retrospect, unsurprising). Whalen paid only $20,300 a year for a contract that would pay up to $1 million if at least 3.35% of the loans in the bond went bad. The story discusses the potential benefits of spreading risks through credit-default swaps but is clearly a warning that the market's risks were unknown:

> Whatever happens with Mr. Whalen's wager, there's a lot more at stake than his fund's performance or the roof over Mr. Spirou's head. Subprime lending has put as many as two million families into homes over the past decade, helping push the U.S. homeownership rate up to 69% from 65%—a major shift toward an "ownership society" that politicians of all stripes have touted as one of the nation's economic successes. As the bets play out, they will show how much of that success is permanent, and how much a temporary phenomenon fueled by overly aggressive lending.

Sure enough, we learn Spirou can't keep up with the payments and is now in arrears. He admits to living beyond his means and says he only has himself to blame:

> At the time, Mr. Spirou could easily afford the loan. He had seen his monthly income jump to more than $10,000 in the midst of the housing boom. Still, he says, he lived beyond his means, taking friends out to dinner at Ruth's Chris Steak House

and buying new clothes for the brokers who worked under him. He also took on loans to buy two new cars—a Pontiac Grand Prix for himself and a Pontiac Grand Am for his mother.

"I was young, naive," he says. "I had to look like a big shot."

The story ends with Spirou vowing to keep his house and adds, with a touch of irony, that he is "looking into ways to get another loan."

As remarkable as the story is, it also shows the limits of even the best top-down business reporting. Spirou, a mortgage broker earning $10,000 a month at age twenty-three, was unrepresentative of the typical subprime borrower (only one of ten of subprime loans went to first-time home buyers) and was in fact *part of the problem then overrunning the mortgage system.* Using Spirou as the emblematic borrower illustrates how divorced business news had became from the realities of the mortgage system. Put another way, concerned citizens seeking to understand risks in the derivatives market in 2005 and 2006 had no reason to think that predatory lending or fraud might underlie the financial instruments being discussed because the business press did not tell them.

But it was worse than that. While business-news leaders point back to stories that they believe played a watchdog function, it's also necessary to look at other prominent stories, particularly the standard profiles of Wall Street firms and big banks that purported to examine the institutions in depth. These, as we'll see, sent messages that were far from warnings.

A reading of Wall Street profile stories shows them to be so deeply embedded in Wall Street values and expectations that they actually contributed to the atmosphere stoking predatory lending. Coverage of Citigroup and Lehman is perhaps the most notable—and galling—given all that was already known about the two firms when the stories were written. In January 2004, *Businessweek* ran a story on the rising fortunes of Lehman Brothers because, as the story said, it was diversifying away from its roots as a bond-trading house and into investment banking and other services. The lead proclaimed, "Under CEO Fuld, the bond house has become a dealmaking power." The story starts with an anecdote designed to show Fuld's relentless personality:

It was late December, but the holidays were not on the mind of Lehman Brothers Inc. (LEH) Chairman and Chief Executive Richard S. Fuld Jr. In 2003, Lehman had catapulted ahead of a slew of Wall Street rivals to become a serious investment-banking power, and Fuld was not letting up. On his desk, next to a tall Starbucks Mocha Frapuccino, was a list of hundreds of banking clients. He was determined to reach every person by New Year's Day. "When something is on my list," he says, "it will get done."[21]

In hindsight, one can question the relevance of the Lehman-friendly premise. M&A aside, Lehman's profits were and would continue to be concentrated in fixed income; it would relentlessly churn out subprime products—including its own subprime *originations* through retail subsidiaries BNC Mortgage and Aurora Loan Services—after others had backed off and would veer disastrously into commercial real estate and other illiquid bets.[22] But the larger and more common problem is that it addresses Lehman strictly from an investor's perspective and, as a result, betrays a myopic unawareness of the realities of its business. Absent is any awareness of reporting already done by the *New York Times*, and even *Businessweek* itself, on the bank's deep connections to predatory practices at its client FAMCO and predatory lending generally. It was disconnected to the subject Hudson had been writing about for more than a decade, the funding and purchase of subprime loans, and the one Tett was beginning to explore in the aftermarket, the repacking of those loans into opaque derivatives. The word "mortgage" does not appear.

Fair enough. No story can cover everything. But, the *CJR* report shows, the *Businessweek* story was far from an outlier. It is representative of a business-press staple that examines investment banks in terms of their competition with other banks, often via a carefully negotiated profile of the CEO as means of humanizing an otherwise dry topic. In October 2004, the *Wall Street Journal* published a 2,400-word story on Lehman based on a similar premise under the headline "Trading Up: To Crack Wall Street's Top Tier, Lehman Gambles on Going Solo." The leader enlarges on this: "Firm Built on Bonds Expands Without Seeking a Merger; Investment Banking Is Key;

No New Gorilla for Mr. Fuld."[23] The lead paragraphs also illustrate Fuld's drive and ambition, this time in winning an investment-banking deal:

> Last year, data-storage firm EMC Corp. decided to give a big investment-banking assignment to Goldman Sachs Group Inc., bypassing rival Lehman Brothers Holdings Inc. Richard Fuld, Lehman's chief executive, was determined that wouldn't happen again. A few months later, when EMC was looking for bankers on another deal, Mr. Fuld flew to Boston in one of Lehman's private jets to make the pitch in person.
>
> "It was very influential," says EMC Chief Executive Joseph Tucci. That level of attention, unusual for what was a relatively small deal, helped win Lehman the business.

This story, too, is only concerned with Lehman's investment prospects. It doesn't mention the firm's past legal scrapes with predatory lending and, indeed, mentions mortgage-backed securities only in the context of its desire to expand from them into other businesses:

> Lehman's bid to challenge Wall Street's largest firms will soon be tested. Despite its advances, two-thirds of Lehman's 2003 revenue came from bond-related businesses such as trading in mortgage-backed securities and selling corporate debt. That market, which boomed as stocks swooned after the Internet bubble, is now a dicier proposition. Many on Wall Street think a bond-market retreat is likely, although such predictions have yet to materialize. Lehman has continued to make money in the bond market even as rivals stumble.

The issue is not that these stories were wrong about the prospects of the bond market (it may have been "dicier" then, as the story said, but it would boom for the next two years) or even that they focus on less relevant aspects of the firm's business. But the stories were written *about* corporate-suite executives *for* Lehman investors and do not address broader public concerns. In retrospect, we know Lehman investors, too, would have been better served by an examination of broader public concerns. But the narrow, investor-centric lens through which Wall Street firms were examined prevailed and rarely varied, no matter the publication or the firm under review.

In April 2006, *Fortune* ran yet another story lauding Fuld and Lehman: "The Improbable Power Broker: How Dick Fuld Transformed Lehman from Wall Street Also-Ran to Super-Hot Machine":[24]

> Consider this: When Lehman went public in 1994, it had only $75 million in earnings, with a paltry return on equity of 2.2%. Fast-forward to 2005, and the turnaround is breathtaking: Lehman booked $32 billion in revenues, $3.2 billion in profits, and hit 19.4% in return on equity. Over the past decade Lehman's stock is up 29% per annum on average, highest of any major securities firm and 16th best among the FORTUNE 500.

The story aptly notes Lehman's enormous reliance on bonds, which then accounted for nearly half the firm's revenue:

> Fuld's magic has in part been to ignore doomsday predictions that Lehman was too focused on bonds. Instead he chose to exploit that area of strength, building the firm into a fixed-income juggernaut and benefiting mightily from the seismic decline in interest rates over the past decade. Today Lehman derives 48% of its revenue from fixed income.

But that's as far as an investor perspective will take you. The word "mortgage" does not appear.

The business-press view of Wall Street—focused on executive-suite personalities and, more importantly, on a firm's recent and relative financial performance and stock price—dominated coverage by leading business and financial media outlets. It was universal and unshakable. No amount of alarm bells from housing activists, reporting from the alternative press, lawsuits from borrowers and whistleblowers, or regulatory activities by state attorneys general could budge the frames of Wall Street reporting from its investor orientation. The narrowness of the frame is striking. Business-news profiles of Wall Street firms are almost admirable in their resolute unwillingness to look beyond the usual sources and topics.

This is true even for Citigroup, arguably the worst actor during the crisis. This is not to say there wasn't fine conventional business reporting on Citigroup or that the subprime story was the only Citi story worth pursuing. Roger Lowenstein wrote a wonderfully intimate 8,000-word profile for the *New York Times Magazine* in 2000 chronicling Sandy Weill's rise from modest Brooklyn roots, his painful exit from American Express, a stormy relationship with protégé-turned-rival Jamie Dimon, and his unlikely triumph in taking over and vastly expanding Citi, making it for a while the world's most profitable company. *Fortune*'s Loomis and the *Journal*'s Monica Langley did good work on Weill's driven personality and why he is not the world's nicest boss. Much was written, albeit after the fact, about Weill's central role in creating and taking advantage of conflicts of interest that led to a fraudulent stock-research scandal, his relationship to fallen star analyst Jack Grubman, and Citigroup's pivotal role in the crashes of Enron and other scandals.[25]

The *Wall Street Journal* also did interesting work framing the Weill-Dimon rivalry as a battle over the consumer, as opposed to the commercial, market.[26] But the story merely waves at a serious accusation of predatory practices: "The trend has big risks for banks and their customers. The banking behemoths have gained a reputation for ingenuity at generating growth by tinkering with consumer interest rates and tacking on myriad fees." That "tinkering" with rates and "tacking on myriad fees" packs a lot of bad behavior into a very small space, when, in fact, that was the story. That's not good enough. In that sense, it was typical of reporting on Citigroup as a whole.

In October 2006, *Businessweek* ran a story on the megabank that criticized it for its stock-price performance in recent years, noting Citigroup "lags behind" banking rivals Bank of America and JPMorgan Chase and investment banks such as Morgan Stanley or Goldman Sachs in various profit metrics. More acquisitions are urged. The following paragraph illustrates how far the business press discourse had strayed into financial-services industry logic:

By all accounts, Citigroup is still a profit powerhouse. *Earnings surged to $24.6 billion last year, a 37.7% jump since December, 2003. . . .* But almost half of the company's businesses are under pressure to find new sources of growth, and recent investments have yet to pay off. *Moreover, despite $16.8 billion in stock buybacks and $14 billion in dividend payouts in the last 18 months,* the stock has hovered at around $50 a share. Since Prince's appointment in October, 2003, shares are up just 8.6%, vs. 35% for the S&P 500 Financials Index. Bank of America Corp., *with $248 billion in total market value, is quickly closing in on No. 1 Citi, whose stock is worth $252 billion.*[27]

The story is unassailable from a business-journalism perspective, and perhaps that's the problem. From a moral perspective—in hindsight, at least—it's a disaster. The earnings the story describes—put in perspective—were some of the highest ever posted by a publicly traded U.S. company. On top of that, add $16.8 billion and $14 billion in stock buybacks and dividend payments, for total surplus values of more than $55 billion—over and above compensation accrued to Citigroup executives and employees. The *Businessweek* story—it should go without saying—fails to convey the predatory lending machine that Hudson had described three years earlier in *Southern Exposure.* But only in Wall Street's reality-distortion field could $24 billion in profits—by a bank, of all things—be tossed off with such nonchalance.

Likewise, a *Fortune* profile of Citigroup's Charles Prince was published in February 2006, two and a half years into Prince's tenure and three years after Hudson's Citi exposé, near the end of the era of mortgage lawlessness with Citigroup very much in the middle of it. The 4,300-word piece contrasts the low-key, awkward personal style of Prince with that of his hard-charging, charismatic predecessor, Sandy Weill, and describes the challenges Prince faces in controlling the sprawling empire Weill created. It shouldn't be mistaken for a puff piece. It is "tough" but operates only on the ground where Wall Street is comfortable: Citigroup's relative stock performance, which had lagged. As the story puts it:

The pressure to perform—and soon—is almost palpable. During his tenure, Prince has overseen a 40% hike in the dividend and in 2005 alone plowed almost $13 billion into share buybacks. Yet Citi's stock has languished, returning just 10.8%, including dividends, since Prince took the helm, vs. 34% for the S&P 500 and 33% for the S&P 500 financials. When Citi announced its fourth-quarter earnings on Jan. 20, Wall Street was disappointed—for the third consecutive quarter—and the stock dropped almost 5%. Shareholders aren't calling for Prince's head. He is, after all, dealing with less than hospitable economic conditions, including a flattening yield curve and a shriveling mortgage market. Says Citi's biggest investor, Prince Alwaleed bin Talal bin Abdul Aziz al Saud, who owns close to $11 billion of stock: "It's all wonderful and lovely that Chuck Prince has cleaned up Citigroup. But we now need him to execute growth and boost the stock price."[28]

As a matter of perspective, Citi's net income for the previous year, 2005—including the three previous quarters that "disappointed" Wall Street—was, as noted, $24 billion, one of the most profitable years in the history of U.S. public companies. As a comparison, Bank of America earned $16 billion that year, Goldman Sachs earned $5.6 billion, Merrill Lynch, $5 billion, Lehman Brothers, $3.2 billion, Countrywide, $2.5 billion, and Bear Stearns, $1.5 billion, and so on. It is true that these are different businesses of different sizes in different product areas. But this blindness to the magnitude and implications of such profits shows the limits of investor-oriented, CNBCized business reporting.

Finally, a look at Washington Mutual coverage is useful since the savings and loan later underwent one of the most thorough and public forensic examinations after its spectacular 2008 failure. In March 2003, *Fortune* ran a piece examining Washington Mutual's approach to consumer banking and how it was "using a creative retail approach to turn the banking world upside down":

On a blustery afternoon in late February, a thirtysomething woman rushes through the door of a Washington Mutual branch in the heart of midtown Manhattan, stops, and stares. Tucking her hair behind her ears, she surveys the bustling scene. There are no bulletproof-glass partitions visible, no roped-off lines. But what is there is curious enough: In one window display are mannequins, clad in polo shirts, that look as if they belong in a Gap store, and children are playing quietly in a corner. When a smiling "concierge" approaches to greet her, a perplexed look crosses the woman's face. "Um, is this the bank?" she asks.

You can't blame her for being confused. Washington Mutual specializes in turning the accepted banking model upside down. Led by ambitious CEO Kerry Killinger, this Seattle thrift bank has grown from a relative unknown into a $268 billion banking powerhouse in just under a decade.[29]

That November, a *Wall Street Journal* Page One story covered essentially the same ground, also mentioning the "concierge" in the lobby.[30]

When a business-news organization didn't have anything nice to say about a specific bank, it said very little indeed. Examinations of major lenders, like these during the earlier period, were largely either flattering or were not done at all. And when mainstream accounts do fault WaMu, it's for the poor performance of its stock. "What Went Wrong at WaMu," for instance, castigates the bank for failing to hedge the risk of rising interest rates, diversify out of mortgages, and fully integrate acquisitions, but the criticism goes no further. "Take a closer look at the mortgage business, and it's easy to see how profits have evaporated," the story says. "Start with the computer systems."[31] And even this negative story came after CEO Killinger had already publicly apologized to investors for poor financial results released earlier in the year. A story in the *Wall Street Journal* made similar points the next summer and worried about turnover in the executive ranks.[32]

And, as we've seen, those journalistic frames are arbitrary, and they shift over time. However, in the 2000s they fatefully narrowed. Business news had plenty of journalistic capacity to take on the subprime lenders and their Wall Street backers—it had done so just a few years before. Its abandonment of muckraking and public-interest reporting about major banks and Wall Street left it dangerously detached from the realities of the subprime industry and the sweeping changes overtaking the financial system. Indeed, because of its choice of an investor-oriented, access-driven approach, the business press was often a spur to the mortgage frenzy, publishing stories that mocked banks for poor financial performance and goading them forward with unflattering comparisons.

In February 2007, the Money and Investing staff of the *Wall Street Journal* gathered for an unusual newsroom meeting on the ninth floor of the World Financial Center in Lower Manhattan. A crisis was evidently unraveling in the mortgage markets and had been doing so for the past several weeks. "M&I," or the "third front" as it is known internally (it's the third or "C" section of the paper), covers the paper's core financial beats: Wall Street banks, big commercial banks, the New York Stock Exchange and other exchanges, insurers, mutual funds, stocks and bonds as individual beats, and so on. M&I is not for every journalist—some find the pace too demanding or the material too dry—but it is the spiritual heart of the paper. Among the reporters was Mike Hudson, who had been a staffer for about a year.

Housing prices had begun to fall. The previous September, Nouriel Roubini had warned a gathering of the International Monetary Fund that the United States faced a once-in-a-lifetime housing bust, with catastrophic consequences for global credit markets. A wave of subprime lenders, including New Century, were reporting financial problems.[33] The M&I section was about to get hit with what, by all appearances would be a financial storm unlike anything the journalists in the room had seen in their lifetimes. Various reporters were asked to speak. They reeled off potential problem areas and story ideas. Hudson offered a couple of thoughts on abusive lending in the subprime market and how they might affect the MBS markets, but no one paid much attention.[34]

Things didn't go terribly well for Hudson at the *Wall Street Journal*. His career there could fairly be described as unproductive, frantic, and short. During his time at the *Wall Street Journal*, from May

2006 to November 2007, Hudson had story ideas, including a big one linking Lehman Brothers and other Wall Street banks to the subprime industry. But in early 2006, lacking an understanding of the true nature of subprime and of the systemic corruption in U.S. mortgage lending, business-news culture had no frame of reference for understanding Lehman's place in such a system. Hudson, like most new reporters at the paper, was discouraged from something so ambitious so early in his career. Required, not unreasonably, to prove himself, he pitched a number of feature stories, most of which had an investigative cast: predatory lending in student and auto loans and how those might affect securitization pools; how anti-predatory-lending community groups, including ACORN, had been co-opted by the very lenders they were supposed to be monitoring, and so on.

But Hudson's beat wasn't mortgages or fraud but the global debt markets—a vast and complex subject that was essentially new to him. He did his best. He put in long hours boning up on the subject and reporting stories no better or worse than others'.[35] Hudson's job was to become an expert in the bond markets as quickly as possible, to turn out medium-length stories of 1,000 to 1,200 words that would appear on C1 and provide information for investors in credit markets, and to put longer, in-depth pieces on Page One.

Hudson also suffered from what might be called a social-capital deficit. He was unfamiliar with the intricate world of internal alliances and networks, of mannerisms, references, and stylistic cues that can make life in a big national organization as complex and as exquisitely nuanced as an Edith Wharton novel. While the *Journal* newsroom was not exactly a fashion runway, Hudson could look rumpled even in his best suit. Finally, and critically, Hudson did not project the kind of poker-faced cool that prevails at the *Journal* and other big newsrooms. It was fine to care about stories—just not too much. Hudson wore his earnestness on his sleeve. He cared about the stories in and of themselves. He presented evidence with rapid, unblinking force. Some found that jarring.

As it happens, less than a year after his arrival, the beat for which he was responsible and about which he had little knowledge was starting to crack at the seams.[36] Try as Hudson might, his editors sensed he wasn't taking command of the beat and, generally speaking, was not getting it. He didn't get what the paper needed, didn't understand the global debt markets. They began to sense he might not be up for the demanding job. And while it might be reasonably asked why he wasn't switched to another beat—mortgages, for instance, or investigations—the *Journal* had a long-standing, if unspoken, rule against transfers for reporters deemed to be struggling. The paper considered a transfer between bureaus to be a reward and felt that failure should not be rewarded. Reporters, especially new reporters, must make it work on whatever beat they happened to cover with whichever bureau chief they were assigned to.

The policy made the system efficient but also rather airless or, as some would say, suffocating. There was little give, no mediation for rejected stories, no reconsideration for mangled copy, and no appeal for any wrongheaded, reckless, or malignant decision that might have cost a reporter weeks or even months of precious time. For new reporters, without allies, there was no steam valve to release tension that might build up between two journalists who disagreed on stories. Reporters complaining about their bosses were in effect questioning the system, a career-threatening gambit. A senior editor made that point explicitly to Hudson (and to me, for that matter): don't question the system. Whatever the logic, the policy was fairly ironclad. Hudson would rise or fall as a bond reporter.

But if Hudson did not understand the bond beat, the paper didn't get Hudson, either, and it certainly didn't get subprime. His supervisors were not investigators; they were business reporters. Hudson's immediate supervisor, Jon Hilsenrath, now the paper's chief economics correspondent, was an accomplished business reporter. Hilsenrath's supervisor, Nik Deogun, was a mergers-and-acquisitions reporter and an accomplished reporter and editor on other business beats. Hudson, by contrast, was an accomplished muckraker, an investigative specialist. All parties were highly skilled, motivated, professional, and well intentioned. They just didn't connect. One side didn't get the other.

But beyond credentials, it's clear from what it published that the paper as a whole didn't "get" the subprime business; had no grasp of boiler rooms, "Miss Cash," and nut-squeezing; and didn't understand what the mortgage industry had become. That Wall Street was funding systemwide lending abuses—as Hudson knew—was remote from the *Journal*'s understanding. Conventional business reporting did not grasp financial lawlessness on this scale. Hudson didn't get a lot of things. But he got that.

Hilsenrath, the byline on many important pieces on the Federal Reserve for the paper, says he's proud of the work the *Journal* did before and during the crisis, including Hudson's. In an interview, he says Hudson's hiring was part of an expansion of the credit-markets beat precisely because the *Journal* was trying to understand the looming problems there. He says the paper performed exceptionally in staying ahead of the crush of news as the crisis began. "In the early stages of the crisis, we were fully engaged and ahead of the curve on a lot of important stories, especially in 2007," he says. "In 2005 and 2006, we were engaged in trying to figure it out. . . . People were doing very good work and were very, very focused on these issues," he says. "I'm not going to put my head in the sand and pretend we had figured the whole thing out. . . . [But] we were trying very hard to do that stuff, and successful in some cases."[37]

Hudson, for his part, says he felt a like a basketball player playing out of position: a power forward trying to play point guard. Hudson's career at the *Journal* was a study in people talking past one another. He spent many wasted weeks—conducting dozens of interviews— on a feature story that was assigned to him, that would have missed the point of the brewing crisis, and that, in any event, fell through. The Lehman/subprime story, meanwhile, languished.

In early 2007, though, housing prices were already on the decline, subprime operators were already reporting losses or shutting down altogether, and debt markets began to shudder—and the case for Hudson's Wall Street (later Lehman Brothers) subprime story became more apparent and compelling. Getting it into the paper would take months. Sometimes news took precedence. The story was delayed when an editor was forced to take an extended leave. It shifted to another editor, and then it shifted back when the editor returned. Hudson believed some editors understood the story, others just didn't. The editors and Hudson had good-faith disagreements about the writing. Hudson, for instance, wanted to lead with recent allegations of forgery at BNC Mortgage, one of Lehman's wholly owned subprime retail arms. One editor wanted to dispense with anecdotes and write a hard-edged lead with declarative sentences. Another wanted an older anecdote showing that Lehman knew of wrongdoing at its subprime partners as far back as the 1990s (a view that ultimately prevailed). The editors struggled to keep it under 3,000 words, a standard leder length. Hudson wished it was longer.

A big source of delays was, naturally enough, Lehman itself. Its PR people and executives objected vociferously to the premise of the story: that it was directly linked to subprime lending abuses and that the securities it sold on global debt markets were fueling the abuses. Lehman officials even tried to reargue the 2003 federal jury verdict (later upheld on appeal) that found Lehman partly responsible for predatory lending at FAMCO, the case behind Henriques and Bergman's exposé in the *New York Times* seven years earlier.[38] Hudson, though, had an ace in the hole: twenty-five former employees at Lehman's BNC subsidiary who had recently confirmed they had either witnessed or participated in defrauding borrowers.

Under intense pressure, the paper stood firm. Hudson received strong backing from both colleagues and senior editors. The company demanded another meeting, this one on a conference call attended by a half dozen or more PR people and executives who argued that the story was misguided, wrong in its premise, and unfair to the company. The *Journal*'s side included Hudson; Hilsenrath; Michael Siconolfi, the investigations editor; Susanne Craig, who covered Lehman and helped on the story; and Deogun, who led the meeting and, Hudson says, coolly and effectively resisted pressure to drastically revise the story or kill it altogether.

Finally, on June 27, 2007, it ran: "Debt Bomb—Lending a Hand: How Wall Street Stoked the Mortgage Meltdown." Even at 2,600 words, it was classic Hudson:

> Lehman's deep involvement in the business has also made the firm a target of criticism. In more than 15 lawsuits and in interviews, borrowers and former employees have claimed that the investment bank's in-house lending outlets used improper tactics during the recent mortgage boom to put borrowers into loans they couldn't afford. Twenty-five former employees said

in interviews that front-line workers and managers exaggerated borrowers' creditworthiness by falsifying tax forms, pay stubs and other information, or by ignoring inaccurate data submitted by independent mortgage brokers. In some instances, several ex-employees said, brokers or in-house employees altered documents with the help of scissors, tape and Wite-Out.

But one story doesn't make a career. Debt markets were cracking open, and Hudson struggled to get his arms around the beat. Not helping matters was the fact that Rupert Murdoch's News Corp. had announced an unsolicited bid for Dow Jones. The company's century of independence was coming to a close amid a messy, fractious takeover. After a while, all sides decided it was better to part ways. Hudson wanted to write a book and took a job with a borrower-advocacy group, Center for Responsible Lending. After resigning, Hudson stopped by to say goodbye to Deogun, who thanked him for his efforts, wished him luck, and complimented him again on the Lehman "Debt Bomb" story. It was, Deogun remarked, one of the better stories in the paper that year.

By mid-2007, of course, the seeds of the crisis had already been sown—the predatory loans made, the CDOs packaged and sold, the CDS trades done. No story or series of stories could make a difference then. Housing prices were falling; subprime lenders had declared bankruptcy; and debt markets were breaking. Even as the public was blissfully unaware of any serious problems in the financial system— the stock market tanked in the spring but would rebound through October 2007—business publications were summoning all hands on deck to deal with what many sensed would be the story of their lives.

As Hilsenrath points out, the *Wall Street Journal* deserves credit for being early, if not first, to signal that the gigantic global debt markets were on the verge of something resembling a nervous breakdown. Indeed, the unofficial start of the financial crisis could be dated to scoops in June 2007 by Kate Kelly that exposed problems in Bear Stearns–controlled hedge funds that would soon collapse and require rescue by the investment bank itself.[39] The financially savvy understood that while the hedge funds were relatively small, the securities they held—subprime-backed CDOs—were not particularly different from those held at their full face value on the balance sheets of every bank on Wall Street, not to mention pension funds and financial institutions around the world. If lenders didn't trust Bear's securities, why would they trust any of them? Confidence among financial players worldwide began to waver. The system began to resemble Wile E. Coyote at the point of realizing he has just run off a cliff.

From mid-2007 forward, it should be said, mainstream business news played an indispensable role in explaining the depth and implications of the credit crisis and performing the first of the forensic examinations of how it had all happened. The *Journal*'s Serena Ng and Carrick Mollenkamp identified the leading role a Merrill Lynch executive played in creating toxic securities and provided an early exposé of Wall Street banks helping to create CDOs designed to fail in order for hedge-fund clients to bet against them[40]

Bloomberg News, the wire service run by a data provider that was previously considered a journalistic backwater, rose to the forefront of crisis examination, led by the extraordinary Mark Pittman. Big and buff—about six feet four and weighing in the mid-200-pound range—a hard drinker and heavy smoker, this profane and funny reporter had immersed himself in the arcana of the debt market and its "structured products" to the point that he could lecture traders and executives on their ins and outs. A former police reporter and ranch hand, Pittman brought a rare moral empathy to financial reporting and a pure accountability mindset. "I'm going to retire on this story," he once said of the crisis with a weird mix of grim determination and giddy exhilaration. In June 2007, shortly after the Bear revelations, Pittman wrote a story that demonstrated that rating agencies had violated their standards by failing to downgrade clearly devalued mortgage securities, "masking"—that is to say, covering up—the coming crisis. Another exposé documented the role played by Treasury Secretary Henry Paulson in creating toxic securities while he had been head of Goldman Sachs.[41] With Bob Ivry and others, Pittman headed a multipart series at the end of 2007 that was one of the earliest efforts to unravel the crisis. But Pittman may be remembered most as a named plaintiff in Bloomberg's groundbreaking and ultimately successful lawsuit against the Federal Reserve to pry loose information about the Fed's multi-trillion-dollar emergency lending programs to prop up major banks. Tragically, Pittman died of heart-related illnesses in late 2009, leaving a wife and two daughters and a void in the public's knowledge of the financial crisis.

The *New York Times* also distinguished itself with important investigative work once the crisis had hit, notably a story by Gretchen Morgenson less than two weeks after the Lehman bankruptcy of September 15, 2008, that revealed for the first time the true beneficiaries of the American International Group bailout, namely, Goldman Sachs and other Wall Street banks.[42] The story was part of a laudable series, "The Reckoning," a sweeping and hard-hitting examination of the main actors behind the crisis, including Goldman Sachs, Citigroup, Washington Mutual, regulators, housing agencies, and President Bush. But there was much, much more to learn.

The two major government investigations after the crisis—from the Financial Crisis Inquiry Commission and the Levin-Coburn committee—returned findings that essentially confirmed that systemic corruption had taken root across the financial sector. The Levin-Coburn committee (formally, the U.S. Senate's Permanent Subcommittee on Investigations), for instance, included a detailed examination of Washington Mutual that found the bank had engaged, as corporate policy, in "steering" borrowers from conventional mortgages to "higher-risk" (more expensive) loans; used "teaser" rates that led to "payment shock"; ignored its own lending standards; exercised weak oversight over third-party brokers, who supplied at least half of its loans; and, fatally, designed compensation incentives that rewarded loan personnel based on the highest volume of the worst loans. The report noted that subprime loans fetched five times the margin of prime loans in the secondary market, pushing the bank to "sell" as many as possible. As a result, Washington Mutual's lending practices would later be described by its own president, Steve Rotella, as "terrible" and a "mess," with default rates that were "ugly," while internal investigations by the bank's own fraud investigators as early as 2004 would turn up, "extensive fraud" by employees who "willfully" circumvented bank policies. An internal review found fraud of one sort or another on 71 percent of loans sampled and "discrepancies or other issues" in appraisals (which could have nothing do with borrowers' mistakes or fraud) on nearly a third. A second internal sampling turned up "excessive levels of fraud" in 42 percent of the files. Other reviews found evidence of fraud in 58, 62, and 83 percent of loans issued by various offices, the Levin report said.[43]

The report said James Vanasek, WaMu's chief risk officer from 1999 to 2005, made a direct appeal to Kerry Killinger, the chairman and CEO, in 2004, urging him to scale back the high-risk lending practices that were beginning to dominate not only WaMu "but the U.S. mortgage market as a whole." The report quotes Vanasek's testimony: "I went to the Chairman and CEO with a proposal and a very strong personal appeal to publish a full-page ad in the Wall Street Journal disavowing many of the then-current industry underwriting practices."[44] Vanasek was, of course, ignored. He left the company the next year.

The report attributed the rampant fraud to "compensation incentives" that "rewarded loan personnel and mortgage brokers according to the volume of loans they processed rather than the quality of the loans they produced." Policing fraud was difficult, the report said, because loan originators "constantly threatened to quit and to go to Countrywide or elsewhere if the loan applications were not approved."[45]

The Levin autopsy of WaMu, which, it should be remembered, was one of the largest loan originators in the United States, contains telling internal e-mails that echoed what Hudson had learned over the years about subprime sales culture. As part of its "High Risk Lending Strategy," a deliberate and formal program initiated in 2004, the company commissioned focus groups of borrowers and sales personnel seeking to increase sales of a new product, the Option ARM, which *Businessweek* later described as "the riskiest and most complicated home loan product ever created."[46] According to the report, WaMu's own focus groups found that few customers, most of whom sought thirty-year-fixed loans, would ever know to ask for such a product. They had to "sell" it, a process that could take as long as "an hour," greatly inconveniencing already reluctant members of the sales staff, who often "simply felt these loans were 'bad' for customers." Training—and additional compensation—was needed to overcome this feeling, the report said. Later reports would describe a 2004 retreat "at which thousands of WaMu managers chanted the company's tag line, 'The Power of Yes.' "[47] The Levin report and other investigations validated the reporting of muckrakers—Lord, Hudson, Reckard—both in their particulars and in the broader implications about the mortgage-lending market as a whole.

But WaMu was only the lender that happened to be most closely examined. The same incentives applied across the industry, and evidence spilled into view that the subprime ethics had taken hold across a multi-trillion-dollar industry at the heart of the economy and the global financial system. Put simply, as Hudson and Reckard had revealed in the Ameriquest series, the practices once confined to Associates, FAMCO, and their ilk had spread across the U.S. lending market—as no less an authority as Angelo Mozilo himself had feared. Wells Fargo was sued by the Federal Reserve for instituting a compensation system that encouraged its sales force to take advantage of customers. Citigroup's chief underwriter, Richard Bowen, who supervised 200 underwriters and oversaw $90 billion in loans, testified to the FCC that the flaws in mortgage documents, the bank's "defect rate," reached 60 percent. He, too, tried to alert managers but was brushed off. "There was a considerable push to build volumes [sic], to increase market share," he said. "So we joined the other lemmings headed for the cliff."[48]

In 2008, *Businessweek* reported that Wall Street's demand for mortgages became so frenzied that "dozens" of brokers and wholesale buyers confirmed that female wholesale buyers were "expected" to trade sex for them with male retail brokers. GE-owned WMC was later discovered to have hired former strippers and a former porn actress to help entice brokers into selling mortgages "The whole point was to have someone attractive to talk to the brokers," a former WMC executive would confirm. "One of the salespeople did porn before she worked there. When someone told me that, I couldn't believe it. Then I saw the video and I realized it was true."[49]

Bribery between wholesale buyers and retail brokers became common throughout the industry. At BNC, a subprime lender owned by Lehman Brothers, bribes were known as "spiffs." *Businessweek* quotes a former wholesale buyer who said underwriters demanded spiffs of $1,000 for the first ten loans and $2,500 for the next twenty. Failure to pay meant the loan supply chain slowed, drying up commissions. At Washington Mutual's Long Beach unit, a senior lending officer would be convicted on federal charges of receiving cash bribes from brokers of $100,000 to approve fraudulent loans.[50]

But as the Levin-Coburn report makes clear, it was the *legal* incentive to put borrowers in the most-onerous-possible loans—"destructive compensation practices"—that drove the frenzy all along the lending supply chain, from strip mall brokers to lending chiefs like WaMu's Kerry Killinger ("questionable compensation practices did not stop in the loan offices, but went all the way to the top of the company") and onto Wall Street's trading desks. The FCIC makes the same point: "Compensation structures were skewed all along the mortgage securitization chain, from people who originated mortgages to people on Wall Street who packaged them into securities." In 2007, total compensation for the major U.S. banks and securities firms was estimated at $137 billion, according to the FCIC. That led to the headline-making pay packages for CEOs ($34 million for Lehman's Fuld that year, $91 million for Merrill's O'Neal the year before), but also for inflated pay for millions of financial professionals. Bankruptcy documents would reveal, for instance, that no fewer than forty-two Lehman executives were paid at least $10 million in 2007, and, as Ben Walsh, a Reuters finance blogger, would write, "of course, there's nothing special about Lehman, in terms of pay." Down the mortgage chain, twenty-something salespeople with little education or mortgage experience pulled in $250,000 to $350,000 a year while sales managers made $1 million or $2 million, thanks to generous production bonuses and the network of independent mortgage brokers that fed the lender business.[51]

In 2008, an award-winning public-radio documentary, "The Giant Pool of Money," quoted Glen Pizzolorusso, a young sales manager at another lender, WMC Mortgage, who reported earning between

$75,000 to $100,000 a month and described the boiler-room ethic similar to the one Hudson and Reckard had described at Ameriquest:

> PIZZOLORUSSO: What is that movie? *Boiler Room?* That's what it's like. I mean, it's the [coolest] thing ever. Cubicle, cubicle, cubicle for 150,000 square feet. The ceilings were probably 25 or 30 feet high. The elevator had a big graffiti painting. Big open space. And it was awesome. We lived mortgage. That's all we did. This deal, that deal. How we gonna get it funded? What's the problem with this one? That's all everyone's talking about. . . . We looked at loans. These people didn't have a pot to piss in. They can barely make car payments and we're giving them a 300, 400 thousand dollar house.
>
> ANNOUNCER: Glen had five cars, a $1.5 million vacation house in Connecticut, and a penthouse that he rented in Manhattan. And he made all this money making very large loans to very poor people with bad credit.

The former broker's description of life as a high-flying mortgage salesmen also had a familiar ring to students of boiler rooms:

> We would roll up to Marquee [a Manhattan nightclub] at midnight, with a line 500 people deep out front. Walk right up to the door. Give me my table. We're sitting next to Tara Reid and a couple of her friends. Christina Aguilera was doing a—whatever, I'm Christina Aguilera. I'm going to get up and sing. So Christina Aguilera and all her people are there.
>
> Who else was there? Cuba Gooding and that kid from Filthy Rich: Cattle Drive. What was that kid's name? Fabian? We ordered, probably, three or four bottles of Cristal at $1,000 a bottle. They bring it out. They are walking through the crowd. They hold the bottles over their head. There is fire crackers and sparklers. The little cocktail waitresses, so you order four bottles of those, they're walking through the crowd of people. Everybody is like, whoa, who's the cool guys? Well, we were the cool guys. You know what I mean?

They gave me a black card. This little card with my name on it. There's probably like 10 of them in existence. And that meant that I just spent way too much money there.[52]

WMC was a unit of General Electric Co.

And that was just the mortgage market. Big as it was, it was dwarfed by the aftermarket, where defective loans were packaged into mortgage-backed securities, repackaged into collateralized debt obligations, and bet on or against in the form of credit-default swaps. Governmental and journalistic investigations have shown rampant wrongdoing in which the less-canny Wall Street banks—Merrill Lynch, Bear Stearns, Lehman Brothers—merely sold defective securities either knowingly or without regard to their quality to pension funds around the world, keeping what they wouldn't move on their own books or on off-balance-sheet vehicles. Meanwhile, the savvier firms—Goldman, Deutsche Bank, Morgan Stanley (a special case that did not work out well) did the same but also took short positions against the same securities they had sold. Worse, Goldman and Deutsche and others worked with hedge funds to create new CDOs that were doomed to fail, working through malleable CDO managers to hand-pick the worst securities, a maneuver that reaped huge fees for the banks, astronomical profits for the hedge funds, and, unconscionably, created artificial demand for more subprime mortgages, stoking boiler rooms in Ameriquest, CitiFinancial, New Century, Countrywide, and among mortgage brokers in strip-mall America.

In April 2010, ProPublica, in partnership with NPR and *This American Life*, published an investigation that showed how a single giant hedge fund, Magnetar LLC, based in suburban Chicago, beginning in 2005 had driven the creation of at least twenty-eight subprime CDOs made up of mortgage-backed securities valued at more than $30 billion, all while taking out large positions in credit-default swaps against those very derivatives.[53] For a period in late 2006, Magnetar-sponsored CDOs made up more than half the market in that type of particularly risky CDO. Magnetar put up only a small amount to buy the "riskiest" part of the CDO, which made the rest of the deal possible, but the obscure hedge fund stood to gain multiples of its investment when the CDO failed. The word "riskiest" deserves to be placed in quotes because, as ProPublica showed, the deals were designed to fail. Magnetar helped pick the securities that would make up the CDO, overriding supposedly independent CDO "managers" who had a duty to pick securities in good faith that they would perform as advertised. The managers were beholden to Magnetar for business and were often marginal operators. One of the managers, for instance, was a Long Island brokerage firm that specialized in penny stocks. (Among its other ventures was funding a documentary called *American Cannibal*, profiling the aborted launch of a reality TV show in which contestants were stranded on an island and goaded into cannibalism.) Virtually all of Wall Street—Citigroup, Merrill Lynch, JP Morgan Chase—helped Magnetar put these deals together and peddled them to pension funds and other unsuspecting investors. Each new CDO created demand for more mortgage-backed securities, which created more demand for mortgages, which spurred on the boiler rooms that Hudson was exploring for the *LA Times* and elsewhere.

When overall demand for CDOs began to flag in 2006, a parade of investment banks, including Merrill, Citi, Goldman, and others, created new CDOs to buy unsold portions of other CDOs. As ProPublica/NPR put it, "They created fake demand." By 2007, fully 67 percent of the risky portion of the CDOs were bought by other CDOs, which replaced pension funds and others who had begun to balk at the housing market. Indeed, ProPublica found eighty-five instances during 2006 and 2007 in which two CDOs bought pieces of each other. These trades, which involved $107 billion in value, underscore the extent to which the market lacked real buyers, ProPublica said. Often the CDOs that swapped purchases closed within days of each other, making it all the more likely they had been created to provide bogus "markets" for each other. And when creating fake demand proved unwieldy, Wall Street found other sordid means to move soon-to-be-toxic CDOs. At Merrill Lynch, for instance, one unit sold CDOs to another Merrill unit, paying back part of their fees to employees at the buying unit. The payments, known internally as "the subsidy," amounted to nothing more than kickbacks to buyers of securities that would soon be worthless.

It's worth remembering that each CDO deal could net the bank that created it between $5 million and $10 million—about half of which usually ended up as employee bonuses. All incentives, it's worth stressing, pushed for the creation of more deals. To investment bankers, there was no "risk" in turning out CDOs, as business journalists insist on repeating, only fees. The risk was borne by the firm—and only to the extent that it might not unload the defective securities in time. The bankers themselves were compensated in sums that would—and did—set them up for life. It's worth recalling that these perverse incentives—to do deals, no matter the quality or outcome—extended down the entire mortgage chain, from bond traders who bought mortgages in bulk from Ameriquest, Countrywide, Citigroup, and Wells Fargo to their executives, who reaped huge annual bonuses based on the number of mortgages sold, to branch managers paid based on the number of mortgages made, to the brokers themselves, paid a yield-spread premium amounting to thousands of dollars per loan to place borrowers in subprime mortgages. Is it any wonder that by 2006 more than 60 percent of subprime borrowers actually had prime credit?

Looking at the rampant corruption in the derivatives markets represented by the Magnetar trades, one begins to understand why, even as the housing market slowed in 2005 and began to sag in 2006, and as interest rates rose, subprime lending ramped *up* to $625 billion in 2005 and remained at $600 billion in 2006, up from (an already staggering) $310 billion in 2003. The demand for CDOs, "fake" as much of it was, generated spectacular paydays on Wall Street, particularly among hedge-fund managers. (In 2007 alone, Magnetar's Alec Litowitz pulled down $280 million).

This summary of the record just scratches the surface. With federal regulators defanged, Congress compliant, the White House complicit, and a financial sector running amok, who was fighting for the public? The observation Samuel McClure made in 1903 applied a century later: "Miss Tarbell has our capitalists conspiring among themselves, deliberately, shrewdly, upon legal advice, to break the law so far as it restrained them, and to misuse it to restrain others who were in their way; Who is left to uphold it? . . . There is no one; none but all of us."

Why the business press failed to hold financial institutions to account when it mattered most—whether it was because of cultural problems, financial problems, or some other problem—is a valid question. That it failed, especially during 2004 through 2006—is why the public had no meaningful role to play in the workings of a financial system that was doomed to fail. The access view could not see the problems because it was forever looking in the wrong direction—up. The accountability view could see because it looked around. Accountability reporting got the story in 1903. It got the story in 2003. If there's a single journalism lesson from the financial crisis, that's it.

CHAPTER 10

Digitism, Corporatism, and the Future of Journalism

As the Hamster Wheel Turns

I'd love to buy *The New York Times* one day. And the next day shut it down as a public service.

—RUPERT MURDOCH

The whole notion of 'long-form journalism' is writer-centered, not public-centered.

—JEFF JARVIS, journalism academic

In early 2009, a few months after the Lehman crash, Robert Thomson, Rupert Murdoch's pick to lead the *Wall Street Journal*, issued an internal directive headlined "A Matter of Urgency." The memo discussed the need for the paper's hundreds of reporters to step up their production of scoops.

> The scoop has never had more significance to our professional users, for whom a few minutes, or even seconds, are a crucial advantage whose value has increased exponentially. . . . A breaking corporate, economic or political news story is of crucial value to our Newswires subscribers, who are being relentlessly wooed by less worthy competitors. Even a headstart of a few seconds is priceless for a commodities trader or a bond dealer.

The memo announced that "all Journal reporters would be judged, in significant part, by whether they break news" for the *Journal*'s wire service, significantly altering the career incentives for journalists at the most influential business publications in the world.

In assessing the post-crisis world of business news and news in general, the public is confronted with a confusing landscape. In both the subculture of business news and the larger news ecosystem there is plenty of cause for both hope and foreboding. As noted, the business press responded with vigor from mid-2007 onward as, one by one, starting with Bear Stearns in early 2008, the central institutions on its central beat started to crumble. The entire subprime lending industry collapsed as though struck by plague, starting in the spring of 2007 with New Century Financial, a notorious operator. With financial markets gyrating wildly—the stock market plummeted in summer of 2007, recovered in the fall, and dived again in the spring—the financial press was in full alert mode. Soon, the state of Wall Street banks—first Bear Stearns, then Lehman Brothers—became a running emergency as investors saw the huge amount of mortgage-related debt on their balance sheets and waged fierce arguments about their solvency. David Einhorn and Bill Ackman and other hedge-fund managers who had taken "short" positions against the banks and bond insurers argued that Wall Street's accounting practices were seriously flawed, and the balance sheets of financial institutions, grossly misleading. Wall Street, led by Lehman's CEO, Richard Fuld, argued just as fiercely and called for a government crackdown on short-sellers, saying their accusations and dire predictions were intended to destroy confidence and become self-fulfilling prophecies.

True, some CNBCized elements of the press were hampered by a poor grasp of the nature of the subprime market. "Bear Stearns is fine!" CNBC's Jim Cramer famously called out on March 11, 2008. Less than a week later it had been bailed out by the Federal Reserve, its assets sold to JP Morgan Chase.[1] But when Lehman finally collapsed into bankruptcy on September 15, 2008, business news treated it as the monumental calamity that it was, using banner headlines across their front pages of a width normally reserved for declarations of war. "Worst Crisis since '30s, with No End Yet in Sight," read the *Journal* on September 18, 2008.

Business-news organizations continued to turn out quality work investigating and explaining what had happened—exemplified by the reporting by the *New York Times* and Bloomberg discussed in chapter 9 but certainly not confined to that. In this book, I've attempted to highlight a journalism practice—accountability report*ing*, as opposed to individual report*ers*—because it's the practice that counts. Still, a few individuals deserve mention for continuing to probe a story that keeps yielding startling and disturbing revelations long after the majority of the business-news establishment had moved on. These include Gretchen Morgenson and Louise Story for the *Times*, Matthew Goldstein for *Businessweek* and Reuters, Bob Ivry for Bloomberg, Steve Kroft for *60 Minutes*, Lowell Bergman for *Frontline*, and Mike Hudson, who as of this writing is a senior editor with the International Consortium of Investigative Journalists, a philanthropically supported news organization. The McClatchy chain demonstrated, among other things, the tight ties between predatory lenders and Goldman Sachs. The *Miami Herald* exposed how Florida regulators approved thousands of mortgage brokerage licenses for convicted criminals. Special mention should be reserved for Jessie Eisinger and Jake Bernstein of the nonprofit investigative-news organization ProPublica for their groundbreaking "Magnetar" series cited in chapter 9, which exposed shocking lawlessness in the mortgage after-market.[2] The work was awarded the 2011 Pulitzer Prize for National Reporting—the first and probably the only crisis-related work to win a Pulitzer. Matt Taibbi exploded onto the financial scene in July 2009 with his investigative polemic "Inside the Great American Bubble Machine," in *Rolling Stone*, which compared Goldman Sachs to a "giant vampire squid." Michael Lewis wrote a riveting and hilarious look at the short-sellers who understood and profited from a corrupted system in the now-defunct *Condé Nast Portfolio*, later expanded into his book *The Big Short*. This list is hardly exhaustive.

However, even as it is important to acknowledge this invaluable forensic work, it is equally important to acknowledge that it has also been lonely work. It would be gratifying to report that the financial crisis provoked a cultural shift within the profession that covered the financial system, but that is far from the case. Indeed, mainstream business news generally moved on from the greatest business story in several generations with, it is fair to say, stunning complacency and few backward glances to determine exactly where it fit into the system that had so recently collapsed. As Ryan Chittum noted in a comprehensive review of post-crash reporting, the business press in general was guilty of "missing the moment":

> The press has done a decent job in the three years since explaining the . . . easy credit story, but a poor one of investigating the Wall Street–boiler room nexus that implemented what happened in neighborhoods.
>
> This was particularly evident when the press presented homeowners as being just as culpable for the housing bubble and fraud as the financial institutions that aggressively lent to them. Plenty of stories focus on the huge amount of debt piled onto households in the last thirty years. But relatively few of them focus on why households took on so much debt in the first place. The conditions of the crisis were created by the decades-long struggles of the middle and working classes.[3]

The failure was one not of industry but of imagination. The leaders of the business press have shown that they clearly understood they were reporting the greatest financial story of their lives. But only a few understood they were also reporting the greatest financial *scandal*.

Indeed, because of weak reporting even after the crisis on mortgage-industry lawlessness, business news on occasion has been guilty of perpetuating the pernicious myth that irresponsible or unethical borrowers—particularly minority borrowers—drove the system to crisis. CNBC's Rick Santelli's 2009 tirade against "losers' mortgages" helped to trigger the Tea Party movement, based in part on misplaced resentment against homeowners facing foreclosure. But even the mainstream *Businessweek*, now owned by Bloomberg, provoked a storm with its February 25, 2013, issue when, for an otherwise inoffensive story on a new housing boom, its cover depicted caricatures of blacks and Hispanics reminiscent of early-twentieth-century race cartoons, all swimming in cash as it flooded a house.[4] The magazine's editor apologized, but the slip suggested fundamental misunderstandings of the mortgage crisis held by even elite business editors five years after the fact.

Clearly, there is work to do. It is my view that the borrower-lender exchange during the mortgage era remains the least understood, most understudied—and most pressing—area of inquiry left over from the crisis. Again, it must be conceded that accountability reporting after the crisis has been seriously hindered by one the most glaring failures of the post-crisis social and political landscape: the inexplicable absence of a single criminal prosecution to be brought against any major figure either among mortgage lenders or on Wall Street. The Obama administration and its attorney general, Eric Holder, must bear primary responsibility for this law-enforcement failure, which has left a corrosive void in the public's sense of justice about the event and, not trivially, has deprived the public of information about the crisis that could help better understanding. As of this writing, five years after the Lehman crash, two years after the filmmaker Charles Ferguson memorably called attention to the problem at the Oscars, and more a than a year after President Obama, in a State of the Union speech, announced a cross-agency law-enforcement group to prosecute mortgage-era fraud, white-collar law enforcement in the United States remains at a low ebb. Accountability reporting and public understanding suffer as a result. As we're learning, only an indictment has the power to change a narrative. Civil settlements won't do.

But, of course, the business-news landscape has been transformed in the years leading up to and since the crash. While the general news landscape remains in a state of dramatic disruption, the financial health of business-news outlets is more mixed. Major metropolitan dailies, particularly the *Washington Post* and *Los Angeles Times*, have dramatically cut back on business coverage because of financial problems at their parent companies. In 2006, the Forbes family, for the first time, was forced to sell off a stake in *Forbes*'s weakened parent company to outsiders and then sold the magazine's famous Fifth Avenue headquarters. In 2009, *Fortune* trimmed the number of issues it published annually by a fourth, and in early 2013 it was part of a larger list of Time Warner magazine titles slated for sale or spin-off. On the other hand, Bloomberg and Reuters, wire services that had once been business-news backwaters, have considerably strengthened their newsgathering operations, adding long-form features and beefing up investigative capacity. Reuters's 2012 investigations into collusion with competitors at Chesapeake Energy led to the ouster of its chief executive, Aubrey McClendon.[5]

Likewise, the *New York Times*, though battered financially by the Internet, maintains a business desk that more than holds its own against larger competitors and that includes formidable investigative assets. David Kocieniewski's series on tax avoidance at General Electric and elsewhere in 2011 and David Barstow's epic 2012 blockbuster on bribery and cover-ups at Wal-Mart stand as classics of investigative reporting in any era.[6]

On the other hand, the *Wall Street Journal* under Rupert Murdoch is greatly diminished both in its influence and, certainly, in its ability to produce great long-form narratives and investigations on markets, corporate behavior, and the economy. Of course, there are exceptions and always will be across a staff that numbers in the hundreds. The paper's accountability reporting on Internet privacy, for instance, has been unparalleled.[7] But the paper itself explicitly moved away from business and economic coverage—the better, it said, to compete with the *New York Times* on general news—and halved the number of leders it produces to one a day. Sometimes there are none at all. In my opinion, and I'm not alone, the leders by and large lack the depth and certainly the breadth of those of earlier eras. Today's paper, with its Page One festooned with breaking news from one institution or another, has moved toward the narrow investor-centered product of an earlier era. But, as we'll see, the retreat from long-form journalism is not an accident. It's entirely by design and of a piece with Murdoch's long-stated antipathy to it as a form, as well as to the idea of newspapers' role as watchdogs in the public interest.

For what it is worth, the *Journal* routinely won Pulitzer Prizes starting in the Kilgore era and from 1995 to 2007 won at least one in all but two years, including a prestigious public service award for an extraordinary, and extraordinarily difficult, story about the illegal back-dating of options to benefit corporate executives. As of this writing, the paper has gone six years without a prize for the news operation (it won two for editorial writing). Pulitzers obviously aren't the only measure of quality, and prize-mongering is to be deplored. But, if nothing else, they are a measure of effort and ambition, and so the post-Murdoch shutout is indeed telling.

On the positive side of the ledger, a new generation of business and financial websites has helped to—partially—offset losses in the news-gathering apparatus of mainstream outlets. Sites like Calculated Risk, Naked Capitalism, and the Big Picture aggregate important news, offering analysis enhanced by a clear point of view that expresses a sense of moral outrage and frustration largely absent from conventional reporting. Some of these sites rose during the mortgage era and contributed important and groundbreaking analysis that pointed to abuses and dangers in the system. For example, Yves Smith, a pseudonymous blogger at Naked Capitalism, and others at the same site offered early details of Magnetar's activities, information contained in Smith's 2010 crisis book, *ECONned: How Unenlightened Self Interest Undermined Democracy and Corrupted Capitalism*. Business Insider, launched in 2009, has become a popular and, lately, profitable business and finance site that aggregates material from elsewhere and adds lively expert commentary and analysis, most notably by Joe Weisenthal. Founded by Henry Blodget, a former Wall Street analyst censured and barred by the Securities and Exchange Commission for his role in the tech crash, the site has been criticized for its aggregation methods and for its frequently misleading sensationalism, but it has also shown a flair for click-bait headlines and the digital medium generally. Dealbreaker, published by Breaking Media, has developed a large following with its cheeky blend of Wall Street gossip and jargon-free, conversational commentary on finance. Mainstream media added a few breakout stars to the blogosphere, Felix Salmon of Reuters, for instance, and Paul Krugman of the *New York Times* added blogging to his credentials. Meanwhile, the field of economic commentary has been greatly enhanced by influential blogs with credentialed economists, including Brad DeLong, Greg Mankiw, Mark Thoma, and Simon Johnson, and journalists, including Mike Konczal, Ezra Klein, and others. These writers are playing a significant role in shaping policy debates.

Special mention should be made of the digital-journalism pioneer *Huffington Post*. Founded by Arianna Huffington, the site has drawn heavy and well-deserved criticism for its reliance on unpaid bloggers and its editorial style of heavy-handed aggregation of material both sober and tawdry. However, the tabloid style and click-dependent model has allowed the site to develop a small staff that contributes important original, sometimes muckraking reporting on the financial system and the economy, particularly labor issues and unemployment, topics woefully undercovered in traditional media.

It should be said that all of the new entrants put together do not offset the losses of major metropolitan newspapers, like the *Washington Post* and the *Los Angeles Times*, which together have lost nearly 1,000 journalists and have severely cut back on business coverage. It is the difference between journalism on an artisanal scale and an industrial one.

But even granting the value of new entrants and the promise of journalism's digital future, if accountability reporting is to be the public's lodestar through the current journalism storm, and I believe it should be, it faces threats from two powerful forces now dominating the new ecosystem. One is old: corporatism, with its long-standing hostility to the difficulties, risks, and subversive nature of accountability reporting. The other is new; let's call it "digitism," which seeks to dispense with traditional journalism forms mainly because digital models cannot accommodate them. While they come from different intellectual traditions, they have meshed together with an uncanny exactness to undermine what is most valuable in the news.

Corporatism couches its opposition to accountability reporting as faux populism, deriding such vital tools as long-form stories as "boring," "self-indulgent" prize-mongering foisted on an unwilling public by journalists more interested in winning approval of their peers than in serving the public. This type of criticism has a long history. Indeed, there was no more severe critic of American journalism's alleged elitism, "arrogance," and "cynicism" than Al Neuharth, the defining executive of Gannett, a company that combined an anti-adversarial form of journalism with ruthless newsroom cost-cutting into a successful business strategy—and did more than perhaps any other newspaper company in history to strip the American landscape of quality local news. In his columns and his memoir, *Confessions of an S.O.B.*, the founder of *USA Today* relentlessly attacked journalism's supposed pretensions and the alleged arrogance of individual journalists. He blasted "cynicism" and "elitism" as the industry's greatest problems and routinely lambasted noxious elites "east of the Hudson and east of the Potomac" as their source.[8]

In the place of the cynicism he saw in professional journalism and its reporting on "bad and sad," Neuharth aimed to turn *USA Today*, founded in 1982, into a fount of something he called the "Journalism of Hope." An expression of market populism's encroachment into journalism, the Journalism of Hope was marked chiefly by a refusal to judge. Or as Neuharth put it: "It doesn't dictate. We don't force unwanted objects down unwilling throats." In Neuharth's view, as Thomas Frank acidly put it, "Elitism was a sin committed by authors, not by owners."[9]

Neuharth's 1989 memoir is filled with attacks on so-called elite papers, including, of course, the *New York Times* (which suffered from "intellectual snobbery") and, especially, the *Washington Post* (which exuded an "aura of arrogance"); both made the book's list of "10 most overrated newspapers," along with the *Miami Herald*, the *St. Petersburg Times*, the *Philadelphia Inquirer*, and others that we recognize today as having been the most aggressive, stiff-necked, and independent papers in the nation. Fatefully, Neuharth also listed the *Louisville Courier-Journal* and the *Des Moines Register*, two legendary statewide papers that Gannett had not long before acquired and was well on its way to gutting in the name of its famously high profit margins.

Sam Zell, who has resented serious journalistic scrutiny over his long career as a vulture investor, implemented his anti-intellectual and, frankly, juvenile ideas about journalism when he took over the Tribune Company in 2007 through a leveraged buyout that became by consensus the most disastrous deal in American newspaper history. Installing a former rock-and-roll radio executive and other nonjournalists in key posts, Zell and his team cast their efforts as a campaign against what he called stodgy thinking and "journalistic arrogance." Instead, they turned former bastions of serious reporting—with, of course, flaws, like everywhere else—into something resembling a frat house, complete with poker parties, juke boxes, and pervasive sex talk that frequently crossed into sexual harassment. A 2010 *New York Times* story on Tribune Company's travails quoted James Warren, the former managing editor and Washington bureau chief of the *Chicago Tribune*: "They wheeled around here doing what they wished, showing a clear contempt for most everyone that was here and used power just because they had it. They used the notion of reinventing the newspapers simply as a cover for cost-cutting." The Zell-led team drove the company into bankruptcy, from which it emerged far weaker but free, at least, of Zell.[10]

Most consequentially, Rupert Murdoch over the course of a long career has made clear his hostility to reporter-driven journalism in the public interest, calling it a self-indulgent, elitist pretension done to advance careers and impress peers. During and after News Corp.'s fateful 2007 bid for the *Wall Street Journal*'s parent, Dow Jones, Murdoch and his allies frequently cited long-form stories on Page One as a problem in need of a solution. "If I may be so bold as to say that in this country newspapers have become monopolized," Murdoch told a group of *Wall Street Journal* editors soon after taking over the paper. "They've become—some of them have become pretty pretentious and suffer from a sort of tyranny of journalism schools so often run by failed editors." The crowd laughed nervously. Speaking of the *New York Times*, he said: "One of the great frailties, I think, of that paper, is that is seems to me their journalists are pandering to powers in Manhattan. You know [pausing for dramatic effect] reporters are not writers in residence."[11] His biographer, Michael Wolff, reports Murdoch's views that journalism's main problem remains an inflated image of itself. "The entire rationale of modern, objective, arm's-length, editor-driven journalism—the quasi-religious nature of which had blossomed in no small way as a response to him—he regarded as artifice if not an outright sham."[12]

Murdoch's ideal newspaper was the *Mirror*, a bawdy and rambunctious British tabloid under the postwar editorship of Harry Guy Bartholomew, whom Murdoch called "a great editor," meaning, in Wolff's words, "not a great finder of facts but a great packager, showman, and drinker." In the Murdoch paradigm, tabloid-style journalism—commodity news repackaged under a cleverly written headline—is invariably described as vigorous, unpretentious, bawdy, fun, and, importantly, virile. This healthy, masculine form of journalism is juxtaposed against the kind that labors under unsexy names like "long form" or "public service" and is usually described as effete, elitist, and, invariably, feminine. Journalists who perform it are sissies. Or, as David Carr summarizes Sarah Ellison's findings: "Again and again, the new owners of The Journal see the newspaper's critics as left-leaning pantywaists and 'Columbia Journalism School' types."[13]

Thus, it is not surprising that Murdoch's chief target after taking over the *Journal* was long-form journalism. The Murdoch-installed managing editor, Robert Thomson, quickly moved to further dismantle Kilgore's Page One storytelling factory, which had already lost its autonomy under Paul Steiger in 2000. Thomson told a gathering of reporters that "a journalistic culture based solely on one story or two stories in the paper today is skewed in the wrong direction. Journalism is a lot more complicated and a lot more diverse than that. And I think people have to be doing several things, several types of stories at the same time. And that's a challenge, but that's a challenge every journalist around the world at every news organization is facing." At another gathering of reporters, he warned staffers to be more productive and said, in a phrase that would resonate, that some stories seemed to have "the gestation period of a llama," that is, nearly a year.[14]

Thomson's "Matter of Urgency" memo, quoted at the start of this chapter, was part of a larger reorganization at the world's leading financial daily that eroded the heart of Bernard Kilgore's legacy of literate, in-depth, polished daily reporting that appealed to readers' intelligence and offered them original stories unavailable elsewhere. Previously, *Journal* reporters, as distinguished from those of Dow Jones's wire service, had been judged on their ability to produce a range of stories, scoops, features, exposés, and so on. But the ability to produce long-form in-depth "leders"—considered an elite function—separated a *Journal* reporter from the wires. Now, incentives tilted decisively toward short-form scoops. As one journal reporter put it in 2010: "We give them three times as many things that are completely unimportant." Sure enough, the length of *Journal* stories plummeted after the Murdoch takeover. Page-One stories of more than 1,500 words fell from nearly 800 per year in 2007 to fewer than 300 in 2011. Stories of more than 2,500 words—often the greatest tales—dropped from nearly 175 a year to just a handful.[15]

As 2013 dawned, Murdoch appointed a new editor, Gerard Baker (and celebrated by pouring a bottle of champagne over Baker's head), and the turn toward access reporting became even more pronounced. In an internal memo to "All News Staff" under the subject line SCOOPS, a top editor drove the message home:

> Colleagues:
> Nothing we do as a news organization is more important than maintaining a steady flow of scoops. Exclusives are at the very heart of our journalism and of what readers expect of us. As Gerry [Baker] noted in his New Year's note, "Scoops are the only guarantee of survival" in a highly competitive news arena.
> And a week into the New Year, we want to underscore the need for a renewed, and ongoing, push for scoops. . . .
> With our ability to gain access, we should also be regularly conducting exclusive interviews around the world with news-makers from government, business and finance. . . . Success at obtaining scoops, and avoiding being scooped by competitors, will be central to how each of us is directly evaluated—just as it is central to how rightfully demanding readers evaluate us every day. As you dive into 2013, please keep this crucial need at the forefront of your thinking. . . .
> Thanks in advance for your accelerated efforts.

Later that spring, a veteran *Journal* investigative reporter, Ann Davis Vaughan, breaking the silence that financial vulnerability imposes on most reporters, published an essay described the debilitating effects on accountability reporting imposed by the new regime.

> Not long after Rupert Murdoch's News Corp. closed a staggering $5.6 billion takeover of our public company, Dow Jones, in 2007, he and his deputies began publicly disparaging the investigative reporting culture that had drawn me to the

Journal. They all but called our business coverage boring, and declared that the secret to arresting the decline in newspaper readership was to run more general interest news.

"Stop having people write articles to win Pulitzer Prizes," Murdoch said at a conference. "Give people what they want to read and make it interesting. . . ."

The first change I noticed was that editors I respected and had worked with for years—those still standing after a purge— came under heavy pressure to simplify stories that were pre- mised on nuanced points. Editors sent memos stating that stories needed to break news and carry a headline of just a few words to get prominent play. Nuance was suddenly our enemy, even if it was the truth.

Vaughan relays an experience in which she had returned from the second of two reporting trips to the United Kingdom and the Gulf Coast for a story on a collapse in the global oil-refining business. While not breaking news, it was a bread-and-butter *Journal* story that explained in a compelling way a complex problem with broad investment and economic implications. Instead, she was pulled off for a stint monitoring general news and wound up assigned to a story about Colorado parents who falsely claimed their six-year-old had been swept away in a helium balloon. Vaughan chased the story, known as "Balloon Boy," which was already overrun by dozens of other outlets and bloggers. A few days later, a disturbed army psychi- atrist massacred fellow soldiers at Fort Hood in Texas. And so it went. The refining story languished until two and half months later—when the *New York Times* ran a similar story. Davis was scooped. She left to start her own research firm.

Murdoch and Thomson love talking about how journalists at establishment papers feel entitled and presumptuous. I will concede this is sometimes true. But I would turn their point around: News Corp. feels entitled to ask highly skilled journal- ists to produce commodity journalism in return for a relatively low salary in a dying industry. If talented business journalists care at all about the long-term portability of their skills in a shrinking media world, succumbing to pack journalism in a crowded general news category is no way out. It makes senior, expensive reporters expendable. That was not the direction I wanted my career to be heading.

My career shift is not necessarily good for business journalism or Main Street investing. Increasingly, investors are paying investigative reporters like me to go digging exclusively on their behalf rather than publish our findings for a wider audience. But the exodus is inevitable as newspapers offer less space, time, and money for investigative reporting. At least the investment world, which is infamous for missing red flags and failing to ask painfully obvious questions, is now getting more of it.

Vaughan titled her essay "The Gestation Period of a Llama."[16]

It is not only ironic but entirely fitting that the most damaging blow ever delivered to Murdoch's News Corp. would come not from shareholders, regulators, or law enforcement but from forthright investigative journalism. Nick Davies and his colleagues at the *Guardian* explored for years allegations of phone hacking, bribery, and hush-money payments at the most notorious of News Corp.'s British tabloids, *News of the World*, which, along with other News Corp. media properties, entertained its audience with gossip while intimidating U.K. political and social elites who might have challenged Murdoch or his business interests. In July 2011, Davies and the *Guardian* revealed that among the thousands of the paper's hacking victims was a missing thirteen-year-old girl, Milly Dowler, who at the time was the subject of a nationwide police search. She later turned up murdered. The story gripped the public's imagination and, along with subsequent revelations in the *Guardian* and elsewhere, triggered a cascade of investigations, parliamentary hearings, and a public uproar over Murdoch's influence so loud that it became what commenters called "the British Spring."[17]

In researching this book, I had a chance to leaf through quite a bit of media criticism and theory from not so long ago, a body of literature that over the course of my working years I had never seen before. It was, so to speak, news to me. I was struck mostly by the well-meaning and thoughtful criticism from the 1980s and 1990s, before the main-streaming of the Internet, that worried about the perceived (and obviously real) imperiousness of corporate media and its concentration in a few not especially public-spirited hands. Ben Bagdikian, the venerable media critic, paved the way with his landmark survey of media consolidation, *The Media Monopoly*, in 1983 and updated it in 1989 in an article in the *Nation* that asserted the problem had only gotten worse: "As the world heads for the last decade of the twentieth century, five media corporations dominate the fight for hundreds of millions of minds in the global village."[18] Many thinkers called for a more responsive and open form of communication between press and public, a more permeable relationship, so to speak, more "horizontal," less top-down. Columbia's James W. Carey, a cultural critic and communications theorist, argued for what he called a "journalism of conversation," which he described as a sort of connective tissue of democracy:

> Republics require conversation, often cacophonous conversation, for they should be noisy places. That conversation has to be informed, of course, and the press has a role in supplying that information. But the kind of information required can only be generated by public conversation; there is simply no substitute for it. . . . A press that encourages conversation of its culture is the equivalent of an extended town meeting. However, if the press sees its role as limited to informing whoever happens to turn up at the end of the communication channel, it explicitly abandons its role as an agency of carrying on the conversation of the culture.
>
> Such a press treats readers as objects rather than subjects of democracy.[19]

When the Internet wrecked havoc on news-media business models, news professionals reacted with shock and dismay, but others saw rough justice. For a vanguard of technologically oriented news thinkers, the news organizations' financial problems were the market's verdict on imperious, bureaucratic, play-it-safe reporting. In the chaos, these digital-news advocates, intellectual heirs in a sense to Carey, saw an opportunity to sweep away corporatist journalism—all of it—and begin anew, based on a networked model that would allow a new flowering of citizen participation in the news.

This new wave of digital-journalism thinkers created a body of ideas that took hold around 2008 to 2010, a time of maximum panic in the news industry. I called it the "future of news" (FON) consensus.[20] According to this consensus, the future points toward a network-driven system of journalism in which news organizations will play a decreasingly important role. News won't be collected and delivered in the traditional sense. It would be assembled, shared, and, to an increasing degree, even gathered by a sophisticated readership. This model posits an interconnected world in which boundaries between storyteller and audience dissolve into a conversation between equal parties (the implication being that the conversation between reporter and reader was a hierarchical relationship).

At its heart, the networked-journalism consensus was anti-institutional. It believed that traditional news organizations were unsustainable in their current incarnation and that, in any case, a networked model, which it believes is more participatory and democratic, was preferable. Clay Shirky, a leading journalism academic, put it vividly in *Here Comes Everybody*, his 2008 popularization of so-called peer production, the participation of amateurs in professionalized activities: "The hallmark of revolution is that the goals of the revolutionaries cannot be contained by the institutional structure of the existing society. As a result, either the revolutionaries are put down, or some of those institutions are altered, replaced or destroyed."[21] Under this consensus, news is seen as an abundant and nearly valueless commodity. News organizations would become less producers of news than platforms of community engagement, and journalists would act as curators and moderators as much as they would reporters. Digital news, as originally conceived, was meant to be free—the better to interact with readers in a global "conversation." The thinking was that digital advertising would support the news operation as print ads have traditionally done. The higher the traffic to a news site, the more revenue that would flow. Elements of this consensus were adopted across the news industry, which, disoriented and unfamiliar with this new digital world, fatefully decided not to charge online for the same news its readers paid for in print. Meanwhile, news organizations frantically sought to adapt to the new tools, work habits, and idiom of the Internet.

Many of the ideas of the new journalism have been put in practice under the rubric of "digital first," the name of a company as well as a philosophy, which would radically revise what news organizations do. As Jeff Jarvis wrote:

> Digital first resets the journalistic relationship with the community, making the news organization less a producer and more an open platform for the public to share what it knows. *It is to that process that the journalist adds value.* She may do so in many forms—reporting, curating people and their information, providing applications and tools, gathering data, organizing effort, educating participants ... and writing articles.[22]

"Digital First" was adopted as the name of a company that manages the Journal Register Company and Media News Group, founded by William Dean Singleton, which publishes the *Denver Post* and fifty-two other newspapers, or "multiplatform products." Digital First implemented many innovations designed to more fully involve the public in the news and, according to the company's website, establish "a baseline of trust" between news organization and audience. For instance, it turned the newsroom of its *Register Citizen*, in Torrington, Conn., into a public café, open from 6 a.m. to 8 p.m., and invited readers to wander through the newsroom to "find the reporter that writes about their community or area of interest—or editors—and talk about concerns, ideas, questions." The *Register Citizen*'s story meetings were opened to the public, "at a conference room table at the edge of the cafe, and the community is invited to pull up a chair, listen in or participate," and simulcast on the paper's website. "Digital first reporting," meanwhile, "increasingly means, for us, that the audience knows what we're working on at the assignment stage or before (as in, the audience participating in the discussion that determines assignments)."[23]

But there are two problems with the model. First, the question of open newsrooms aside, the free-content system rewarded quantity—the more stories published, the more "inventory" against which to sell ads. And since no one can predict in advance what stories will generate traffic—an exposé of municipal corruption that took three months to produce or a video of a cat caught in a tree that took three minutes—incentives all run toward posts that can be done quickly. Free news, it turned out, created a downward spiral of quality. Long-form exposés could still be done under the new system, but under the logic of free news, from a business point of view, they made no sense.

The second problem was that Web ad rates—contrary to predictions—fell significantly as the Internet churned out a nearly limitless supply of ad space and Internet giants drove down prices with ruthless efficiency. Since no one knows in advance which post will generate traffic, the logic of the model calls for ever-increasing quantities of "content." Put simply, more posts equals more traffic equals more revenue. The free structure makes inevitable what I call the "Hamster Wheel." To achieve growth, the wheel must spin at ever-increasing velocity. What's more, even news organizations with successful websites, like the *New York Times*, which (depending who's measuring) reported 34 million unique visitors a month, or the *Guardian*, with even higher figures, must compete with the likes of Facebook, which has more than a billion active users.[24] The digital ad game became a model for ever-increasing effort to produce ever-diminishing returns. Such logic led AOL to issue a directive via PowerPoint, that reads like a time-motion consultant's fever dream: "The AOL Way: Content, Product, Media Engineering, and Revenue Management."[25] AOL floundered, amid much scorn, and finally acquired *Huffington Post* in 2011 for $315 million. Yet it, like all media organizations, still struggles with the logic of the free-content model.

The free model has been made to work financially, to varying degrees, at sites native to the Web, including *Huffington Post*, *Business Insider*, the gossip blog *Gawker*, and *Buzzfeed*, which mixes in hard news and an occasional long-form story with unapologetic clickbait designed to be shared on social media ("Breaking: Justin Bieber Might Finally Be Rejecting Harem Pants.")[26] They are even capable of producing, on occasion, great stories. A *Huffington Post* series on the lives of severely wounded veterans won a Pulitzer Prize in 2012. For that matter, *Deadspin*, a *Gawker* subsite, exposed as a hoax the heart-rending story of a star Notre Dame linebacker, who claimed that his girlfriend had died tragically in a car wreck. Much credit for exposing cyclist Lance Armstrong's now-admitted blood-doping goes to the cycling blog *NY Velocity*, which, among other things, published a 13,000-word interview that included damning findings from an Australian physiologist who helped develop doping tests.[27] But these stories are the exception that proves the click-bait rule. Laudable as they might be, they come not as a result of the free-ad model but in spite of it. Further, these operations are, after all, startups. They start small and, for the most part, they will stay small, with few if any ever exceeding the staffing levels of a single medium-sized regional daily in newspapers' heyday.

And what offers promise and opportunity for new, digitally native news organizations turns out to be wildly inappropriate for their already established "industrial-era" counterparts. Indeed, the free model took an enormous toll across the newspaper industry. A few resisted the trend, principally the *Wall Street Journal* and the *Financial Times*. After following evangelizing digital theorists and consultants for more than a decade, the newspaper industry, finally, almost universally realized its error and, led by the New York Times Company in 2011, reversed itself and began to put up paywalls that allow limited access for free and charge for unlimited access. The program was a resounding success for the *New York Times* and is on its way to becoming standard around the industry. Digital subscriptions, broadly speaking, have added a new revenue stream with small losses to traffic and minimal losses to digital advertising. Plus, it creates a far more intimate relationship with readers that can be valuable to boost ad rates. Among English-language papers, the *Guardian* is the most prominent to continue to resist digital subscriptions—and it is on an ominous track financially. As the media analyst Ken Doctor lamented in 2012, "Why didn't we think of this earlier, *before* the carnage of cuts overwhelmed the profession?"[28]

To be clear: no one should underestimate the digital revolution in the news. The shifts are tectonic, transformative, and permanent.

The relationship between readers and the news is forever altered. The shrinking of traditional news institutions has slowed but not stopped. With publishing no longer an industry but, as Clay Shirky has written, "a button," amateur-citizens increasingly find themselves in journalistic roles, particularly in breaking-news situations: the Fukushima Daiichi nuclear disaster of 2011, the Arab Spring, and even the assassination of Osama Bin Laden, first reported on Twitter by Sohaib Athar (Twitter name @reallyvirtual).[29] Crowds have proved immensely useful in sorting through large publicly posted data sets, as in the investigative site ProPublica's Dollars for Docs project, which enabled readers to sort through more than two million records documenting the flow of $2 billion from the pharmaceuticals industry to prescribing doctors. The limits of crowd-sourcing were reached during the Boston Marathon bombings of April 2013 when users of Reddit, a message board in which participants' votes determine an item's prominence, falsely identified innocent bystanders as suspects in a frenzy of anonymous speculation. Mangers of Reddit later apologized. Even so, as has been observed, the traditional self-conception of news organizations has been that of producer at one end of a pipeline, with the public at the other end.[30] Today that metaphor no longer holds, if it was ever accurate. News organizations will play the role of nodes on a network, a natural enough role.

But they are and will continue to be very, very big nodes. It's important to remember that the public, to an overwhelming degree, still gets news from traditional media. Certainly, readership of printed newspapers is declining rapidly, and the use of digital platforms is rising even more rapidly. Even so, seven in ten Americans said they got news the previous day from traditional media: watching TV, reading a print paper, or listening to the radio.[31] As for Twitter, a near-obsession among news professionals, a mere 3 percent of respondents said they got news on the social media site the day before, only 7 percent of young people 18–29, and only 11 percent of the public said they had *ever* seen news on Twitter. And while it is true that 39 percent reported getting news the day before from digital sources, and 19 percent from social networks, figures that rise to 45 and 32 percent among the young, those figures only speak to the platform on which the news is viewed, not who actually reported it.

For that, one turns to a 2010 Pew study of the Baltimore news eco-system, one of the few of its kind, which traced where "new informa-tion" actually originated for six important local stories across sub-ject areas (a police shootout, the governor announcing budget cuts, the closing of a local theater, etc.). The answer was the (hobbled) *Baltimore Sun*, other newspapers, local TV stations, and other "tradi-tional" sources, while new media pitched in a fraction of the report-ing. The findings are illustrated in figure 10.1.

The basic thrust of Pew's findings was reaffirmed by C. W. Ander-son in a study of Philadelphia's fragile news environment pub-lished in 2013. Anderson found that, despite the best hopes of peer-production advocates, the informal news networks that have emerged in recent years did not do so spontaneously but rather came into being only with the support of institutions, mostly charitable

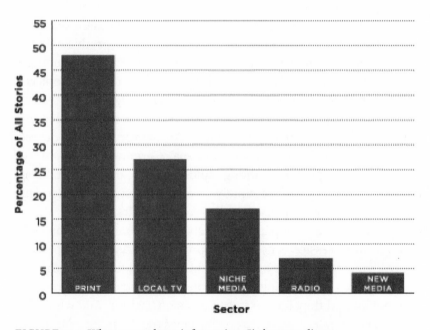

FIGURE 10.1 Who reported new information: Six key storylines
Source: Data from Pew Research Center's Project for Excellence in Journalism, "How News Happens: A Study of the News Ecosystem of One American City," January 11, 2010, http://www.journalism.org/analysis_report/how_news_happens.

foundations. The main fact gatherers, by a wide margin, remain the legacy news organizations, such as they are.[32]

This is only to say that what appears to be an increasingly lively and abundant news environment actually rests on—and masks—a shrinking fact-gathering infrastructure. And it is traditional media, ultimately, on which the vast majority of people rely. The issue is not whether experimentation with new technologies is good and necessary. All agree that it is. The problem is not trying to connect to, open dialogue with, or provide a platform for individual members of the public, which is valuable. The issue is not even the changes in attitude brought to news organizations, which sometimes seem to have placed news organizations in a prostrate posture in relation to the public and downgraded the reporters' status to the point of allowing visitors to interrupt them at their desks at random. The real issue is—whatever the medium and whoever performs the actual work, professional journalists or someone wandering in from the newsroom café—to what extent does this model produce original, agenda-setting stories that clarify public understanding of complex problems? And here we find the great weakness in the digital-first approach. It is, as it were, the hole in FON theory. It can't support the thing that matters most.

"The story is the thing," McClure would repeat often to his brilliant staff. It *is* the thing, the main thing that journalism does. Public-interest journalism is its core, around which the rest of journalism is organized. It's the rationale for all of it—the printing presses, the trucks, the ad departments, the journalism schools. It doesn't much matter that *McClure's* basically flamed out two years after Tarbell's Standard Oil series. What matters is that the kind of stories it pioneered are still being produced to this day.

In this book, I've spent plenty of time criticizing institutional media for their failure to do the basics—what journalism was able to do in 1903 it could not muster in 2003. And that's tragic. But institutions—flawed as they are—have proven over a century to be the best, most potent vehicle for accountability reporting. They deliver the support, expertise, infrastructure, symbolic capital, and, still, mass audience that makes for journalism at its most powerful. My concern is not with news institutions for their own sake, nor even with the well-being of professional journalism, as much as I value it. The point, in the end, is the need for agenda-setting stories that explain complex problems to a mass audience. These are the stories produced by Ida Tarbell, Lincoln Steffens, Ray Stannard Baker, Barney Kilgore, Robert W. Greene, Don Bolles, Susan Faludi, Seymour Hersh, Jane Mayer, Tony Horwitz, Alex Kotlowitz, James B. Stewart, Diana Henriques, Lowell Bergman, Donald Barlett, James B. Steele, Gretchen Morgenson, Mark Pittman, Michael Hudson, and countless others that belong to the same line of authority that made American journalism distinct and uniquely potent.

Institutionalized, professional journalism is certainly flawed, but then the question arises, compared to what?

As I write this in early 2013, some *new* new thinking is already underway. Journalism is experimenting with various ways of asking readers to pay a greater share of the cost of news. Further, a lot of free-floating anti-institutional talk has started to recede as the public for a while was faced with the actual prospect—not just idle chatter or, in Murdoch's case, malign jokes—of a world without the *New York Times.* Clay Shirky coauthored a significant report with Emily Bell and C. W. Anderson that, while certainly affirming journalism's entry into a "post-industrial" age and calling for a massive rethinking of the field, also *re*affirmed the importance of journalism institutions and, significantly, accountability reporting by a dedicated professional cadre. "What is of great moment is reporting on important and true stories that can change society," the authors say. Indeed. The trouble is that, as noted and as the authors themselves acknowledge, the very architecture of the Internet militates against such work.[33]

As we open a new era of digital journalism, it has been unnerving to witness how the Internet's strengths—precise quantity and popularity metrics, a limitless news hole, a 24/7 publishing schedule—have meshed with corporatist preferences with an uncanny exactness. Each, for similar reasons, views long-form investigative reporting not as an asset but a problem. Yet digital-first ideas continue to spread. In May 2012, media giant Advance Publications, closely held by the Newhouse family, announced sweeping changes to the venerable *New Orleans Times-Picayune*, a newspaper with one of the highest readership levels in the United States and one that had done its share of accountability reporting over years, including a five-part series in 2002 that tried to call attention to the flawed levees around the city that three years later did, indeed, fail.[34]

Advance, which also owns *Vanity Fair* publisher Condé Nast and other media properties, including Reddit (see http://www.advance .net/), said the paper and its website, NOLA.com, would be reconstituted into a new company, the NOLA Media Group, as a way of adapting to the new methods of news delivery and consumption in an increasingly digital age. In press releases and front-page editorials, the company and its executives cast the moves as bold and necessary, if painful, adaptations to new digital realities. Among the changes would be a reduction in the production of printed newspapers from seven days a week to three, but the company said it would also "significantly increase its online-news gathering efforts 24 hours a day." Incoming publisher Ricky Mathews said the changes were necessitated by revolutionary upheaval in the newspaper industry. "These changes made it essential for the news-gathering operation to evolve and become digitally focused, while continuing to maintain a strong team of professional journalists who have a command of the New Orleans metro area."[35]

Unmentioned in the story or in Mathews's subsequent 1,800 word column the next month was the fact that the "digital focus" would also entail laying off nearly half the *Times-Picayune*'s news staff, lowering headcount from 173 journalists to 89. The paper said 40 new people would be added back, presumably at lower wages and with less experience, leaving roughly 135 reporters, many of them covering entertainment and sports, who would be expected to produce more copy. There would also be a few "community-engagement specialists," a quasi-marketing position. The paper hired a "Staff Performance Measurement and Development Specialist" and issued story quotas, which were later, after protests, revised to "goals." As the paper itself said: "When the NOLA Media Group launches this fall, we plan to produce more content for our print readers and online users than ever before."[36]

Newhouse made similar, drastic moves at its Alabama properties, where it cut nearly 400 reporters, including 60 percent of the editorial staff at the *Birmingham News* and *Press-Register*, leaving 47 from a staff of 112, and 70 percent of the staff of the *Mobile Advertiser*, leaving 20 staffers were there once were 70. In place of edited and reported papers—none of them perfect but all with substantial public-service-reporting accomplishments to their credit—Advance substituted websites that would offer, it is fair to say, a degraded product that no amount of digital rhetoric could disguise.

Even on its own terms of profit-and-loss, the business case for the free-online plan was puzzling. Taking into account losses in circulation and print ad revenue that will attend the reduction in print distribution, media analyst Rick Edmonds wrote, "The disgruntled staff and readers of The Times-Picayune are getting it right. The move only makes financial sense as the occasion for dumping many well-paid veterans and drastically slashing news investment."[37] Ryan Chittum in the *Columbia Journalism Review* said a closer look at the numbers suggested the plan, rather than aiming toward growth, was a way to squeeze profits from the print operation while riding its decline toward an "orderly liquidation" of the entire enterprise. The profits from such an exercise, the analysis showed, would exceed proceeds from any sale. And while Advance is free to take this particular option, most of the rest of the industry is taking an alternative path, one in which they seek to sustain quality enough to justify a paywall while using paywall revenues to help sustain quality, all while the industry as a whole navigates a transition that is still in its early stages.

No one should be under the illusion that the Nola.com path is the only one available, at all inevitable, or, least of all, in any way desirable from the public's point of view. While community leaders and regular readers expressed outrage with the Advance plan, it received intellectual support from John Paton, CEO of Digital First, the New Haven, Connecticut–based newspaper chain owned by the hedge fund Alden Global Capital. Paton wrote a blog post that said Advance, albeit clumsily, was simply facing up to difficult realities that others were unwilling to acknowledge. Caustically, Paton wrote:

> Imagine the owners' surprise when they are lambasted for not continuing with the old line of business that is driving them out of business.

Imagine their surprise when community leaders—politicians, musicians, restaurant owners—demand the owners sell their business to them (for a song surely, it's a dying business after all) because they want to stick with the old dying business.

Imagine their surprise when their industry colleagues and critics lambaste them for changing when change is what is needed.

As for me, the owners are doing what they think right. . . .

Importantly, they remain committed to their core business and mission with what resources they have.

So I support them because their industry is my industry and it will not survive without dramatic, difficult and bloody change.

And like them I am willing to do what it takes to make our businesses survive.

On Twitter, Jeff Jarvis, the journalism academic and consultant, wrote: "I agree: (Disclosure: I have a relationship w/both)."[38] Thus, in a tweet, does the future-of-news intelligentsia unite behind corporate profit seeking to crush a long-standing news institution. Advance also owns, among other papers, the *Cleveland Plain-Dealer*, the *Portland Oregonian*, and the *Newark Star-Ledger*.

As we dig out from a collapsed financial system and the chronic political and social crises it caused, we are at the same time faced with the task of rebuilding a tradition of investigative reporting. This tradition, after all, is the way we, the nonexperts, understand complex social problems, such as the financial system. Understandably, everyone wants to know what the news will look like, how will it be gathered and presented, by whom, and who will pay for it. Will journalism ever manage to become, in the words of *CJR*'s founding editor, Jim Boylan, in 1961, "a match for the complications of our age"? Many people will offer solutions—business models, tools, and plans to rethink the gathering and distribution of the news. Some of the best minds in the media business, journalism, and the academy are hard at work on the problem. The time of uncertainty and financial free fall has also brought out the opportunists, but journalism has always had plenty of those hanging around.

One thing to watch out for, in my view, is the problem of "false realism"—no-can-do-ism, so to speak. That view will come from corporatists, who will assert that public-interest journalism is an affectation of self-important reporters and not economically feasible. And it will come from digital consultants who will disparage things—reporting, writing—that are not technologically determined. Both sides will seek to justify the "difficult" and "bloody" sacrifices—staff, investigations, long-form writing—that are necessary in this new reality.

It's time for the public to be let in on what reporters already know: accountability reporting is the thing. So keep your eye on the stories, particularly the public-interest investigations, like the kind McClure and Tarbell pioneered and that Bernard Kilgore laid the groundwork for. Those are the ones that are the hardest to do, the riskiest, most time-consuming, most expensive, and, as a result, most vulnerable. Those are the ones that journalism—as we've seen during the run-up to the financial crisis—sometimes goes to great lengths to avoid having to do.

Call it the Great Story theory of journalism. The Great Story is not going to save the world. Not every story—only the tiniest fraction, in fact—will be a Great Story. And not every Great Story will be all that great. But the Great Story—the one that holds power to account and explains complex problems to a mass audience, connects one segment of society to another—is, and has been for a century, the core around which the rest of American journalism culture is built. Other things are important, but this is more important.

The Great Story is also the one reliable, indispensable barometer for the health of the news, the great bullshit detector. Many people inside journalism would do and say anything—anything—to wriggle out from under the obligation to do the Great Story because of the risks, expense, and difficulty. It's too long. It's too boring. No one cares. It's elitist, it's patronizing, it's self-indulgent. It's something that might have been good once but isn't anymore. It's the past, not the future. Don't be fooled. If you want to know about something important—from police corruption to the financial crisis—chances are someone will probably have to go out and investigate it. If you want to explain complex subjects to a mass audience—not just to people already in the know—the best way is probably going to be in a story form, from the beginning. And if it's complicated, as many things are, you're probably going to need some space.

Was Mike Hudson the perfect reporter during the mortgage era? No. Was he the only reporter during the mortgage era? No. But he was a muckraking reporter during the mortgage era: a fact-intensive, anti-corruption storyteller who listened to outsiders, checked out what they had to say, and, in the face of vehement opposition from the subjects of his reporting, held power to account. And he got the story that an entire journalism subculture—business news—did not.

Could journalism have prevented the financial crisis? I report; you decide. It policed, to some degree, Fleet, FAMCO, Associates/Citigroup, and Household Finance, and it exposed Ameriquest. And as Christopher Peterson's 2007 *Cardozo Law Review* article observed, public exposure was kryptonite to powerful predatory lenders everywhere. A single story—the *New York Times*/ABC News exposé of Lehman Brothers's ties to predatory lending, had all of Wall Street running for cover.

If someone tells you this kind of reporting is not possible anymore, don't believe it. And if someone tells you that the Great Story isn't important, tell him that you read somewhere that that's not true, either.

The models that can produce the Great Story, along with the other wonderful things available to journalism today, are the models to keep. If that happens to be NOLA.com, more power to it. If digital advertising alone—with no paywalls—can pay for it, fabulous. But don't count on it. The models that can't support the Great Story—Digital First, for one—are to be deemed destructive if they are applied to existing news institutions, irrelevant if they aren't.

I say nothing here that reporters and editors don't already know.

What supports the Great Story is what we need. Everything follows from there.

NOTES

INTRODUCTION: ACCESS AND ACCOUNTABILITY

1. *Daily Show*, "Exclusive—Jim Cramer Extended Interview: Part 2," March 12, 2009.

2. Chris Roush, "Unheeded Warnings," *American Journalism Review*, February 15, 2009.

3. Kimberly L. Allers, "A New Banking Model," *Fortune* (March 2003); Mara Der Hovanesian, "Rewiring Chuck Prince," *Businessweek*, no. 3972 (2006); Neil Weinberg, "Sachs Appeal," *Forbes* 179, no. 2 (2007); Marcia Vickers and Doris Burke, "The Unlikely Revolutionary," *Fortune* 153, no. 4 (2006).

4. Bernard Condon, "Home Wrecker," *Forbes* 170, no. 4 (2002).

5. John Hechinger, "Best Interests: How Big Lenders Sell a Pricier Refinancing to Poor Homeowners," *Wall Street Journal*, December 7, 2001.

6. Michael Hudson, "Banking on Misery: Citigroup, Wall Street, and the Fleecing of the South," *Southern Exposure* 31, no. 2 (2003).

7. Later printed in Richard Lord, *American Nightmare: Predatory Lending and the Foreclosure of the American Dream* (Monroe, Maine: Common Courage, 2005), 34.

8. Theodore Roosevelt, "The Man with the Muck-Rake," *Outlook* (April 1906).

9. Michael Wolff, "Rupert Murdoch's Wall Street Journal Formula for News Corp Renaissance," *Guardian*, January 7, 2013.

10. Jeff Jarvis, @jeffjarvis, Twitter.com, July 8, 2011.

11. Lincoln Steffens, "The Shame of Minneapolis" (1903), in *The Muckrakers*, ed. Arthur Weinberg and Lila Weinberg (New York: Simon and Schuster, 1964); George Getschow, "Dirty Work: The Day Laborer's Toil Is Hard, Pay Minimal, Security Nonexistent; in Houston, the Jobless Fill Labor Pools That Retake Part of Each Day's Wage; the System at Crash Cabin," *Wall Street Journal*, June 22, 1983; Susan Faludi, "The Reckoning: The Safeway LBO Yielded Vast Profits but Exacted a Heavy Human Toll," *Wall Street Journal*, May 16, 1990; a 1978 *Philadelphia Inquirer* series on the police department of its home city; Gretchen Morgenson, "Behind Biggest Insurer's Crisis, a Blind Eye to a Web of Risk," *New York Times*, September 28, 2008; Nick Davies and Amelia Hill, "Missing Milly Dowler's Voicemail Was Hacked by News of the World," *Guardian*, July 4, 2011.

12. Walter Lippmann, *Liberty and the News* (Princeton, N.J.: Princeton University Press, 2008), 65.

1. IDA TARBELL, MUCKRAKING, AND THE RISE OF ACCOUNTABILITY REPORTING

1. Steve Weinberg, *Taking on the Trust: The Epic Battle of Ida Tarbell and John D. Rockefeller* (New York: Norton, 2008), 172; Ron Chernow, *Titan: The Life of John D. Rockefeller, Sr.* (New York: Random House, 1998), 437–38.

2. Arthur Weinberg and Lila Weinberg, *The Muckrakers* (New York: Capricorn, 1964), xix; "The Rise of Mcclure's," Allegheny College, http://tarbell.allegheny.edu/mc2.html.

3. Weinberg, *Taking on the Trust*, 171.

4. Peter Lyon, *Success Story: The Life and Times of S. S. Mcclure* (New York: Scribner, 1963), 199.

5. Ida M. Tarbell, *All in the Day's Work: An Autobiography* (Urbana: University of Illinois Press, 2003), 202.

6. Lyon, *Success Story*, 191.

7. Cecelia Tichi, *Exposés and Excess: Muckraking in America, 1900/2000* (State College: University of Pennsylvania Press, 2004), 2.

8. Weinberg and Weinberg, *The Muckrakers*, 73; attributed to David Graham Phillips as author of "Treason of the Senate," a portion of a chapter in the Weinbergs' book.

9. Lyon, *Success Story*, 11.

10. Harold S. Wilson, *Mcclure's Magazine and the Muckrakers* (Princeton, N.J.: Princeton University Press, 1970), 17.

11. Wilson, *Mcclure's Magazine and the Muckrakers*, 20.

12. Louis Filler, *The Muckrakers* (Stanford, Calif.: Stanford University Press, 1993), 32.

13. Wilson, *Mcclure's Magazine and the Muckrakers*, 285.

14. Tarbell, *All in the Day's Work*, 36.

15. Richard Hofstadter, *The Age of Reform: From Bryan to F.D.R* (New York: Knopf, 1965), 193.

16. Wilson, *Mcclure's Magazine and the Muckrakers*, 195, 196.

17. Hofstadter, *The Age of Reform*, 197.

18. Kathleen Brady, *Ida Tarbell: Portrait of a Muckraker* (New York: Seaview/Putnam, 1984), 122.

19. Wilson, *Mcclure's Magazine and the Muckrakers*, 132.

20. Chernow, *Titan*, 432.

21. Hofstadter, *The Age of Reform*, 214.

22. Hofstadter, *The Age of Reform*, 231.

23. Hofstadter, *The Age of Reform*, 235.

24. Chernow, *Titan*, 3.

25. Chernow, *Titan*, xiii.

26. Ibid.

27. Chernow, *Titan*, 439.

28. Tarbell, *All in the Day's Work*, 208.

29. Tarbell, *All in the Day's Work*, 209.

30. Ida M. Tarbell, *The History of the Standard Oil Company, Illustrated with Portraits, Pictures, and Diagrams* (New York: Macmillan, 1925), 1:65.

31. Tarbell, *All in the Day's Work*, 211–13.

32. Brady, *Ida Tarbell*, 132.

33. Theodore Roosevelt, "The Man with the Muck-Rake," *Outlook* (April 1906). Also see Weinberg and Weinberg, *The Muckrakers*, 58.

34. Tichi, *Exposés and Excess*, 3.

35. Lincoln Steffens, *Autobiography* (New York: The Literary Guild, 1931), 581; cited in Judson A. Grenier, "Muckraking and Muckrakers: An Historical Definition," *Journalism Quarterly* (Autumn 1960): 553.

36. Justin Kaplan, *Lincoln Steffens: A Biography* (New York: Simon and Schuster, 1974), 153, 150.

37. Tarbell, *All in the Day's Work*, 242.

38. Tarbell, *All in the Day's Work*, 226.

39. Tarbell, *All in the Day's Work*, 298.

40. S. S. McClure, "Concerning Three Articles in This Number of *McClure's*, and a Coincidence That May Set Us Thinking," *McClure's* (January 1903); quoted in Weinberg and Weinberg, *The Muckrakers*, 4–5

41. Tarbell, *The History of the Standard Oil Company*, 2:38.

42. Brady, *Ida Tarbell*, 137.

43. Hofstadter, *The Age of Reform*, 186.

44. Quoted in Chernow, *Titan*, 443–44.

45. Quoted in James Aucoin, *The Evolution of American Investigative Journalism* (Columbia: University of Missouri Press, 2005), 88.

46. Ida Tarbell, "John D. Rockefeller: A Character Study, Part II," *McClure's* (August 1905); 386; for a facsimile, see http://www.unz.org/Pub/McClures-1905aug-00386.

47. Tarbell, *The History of the Standard Oil Company*, 2:126.

48. Tarbell, *All in the Day's Work*, 230.

49. Chernow, *Titan*, 554.

50. Dr. Paul Giddens, quoted in Brady, *Ida Tarbell*, 160.

2. ACCESS AND MESSENGER BOYS: THE ROOTS OF BUSINESS NEWS AND THE BIRTH OF THE *WALL STREET JOURNAL*

1. Lloyd Wendt, *The* Wall Street Journal: *The Story of Dow Jones and the Nation's Business Newspaper* (Chicago: Rand McNally, 1982), 36.

2. Jerry M. Rosenberg, *Inside the* Wall Street Journal: *The History and the Power of Dow Jones & Company and America's Most Influential Newspaper* (New York: Macmillan, 1982), 8.

3. Stieg Larsson, *The Girl with the Dragon Tattoo*, trans. Reg Keeland (New York: Vintage Crime/Black Lizard, 2009), 70.

4. Wendt, *The* Wall Street Journal, 36.

5. Wayne Parsons, *The Power of the Financial Press: Journalism and Economic Opinion in Britain and America* (New Brunswick, N.J.: Rutgers University Press, 1990), 11.

6. Robert J. Shiller, *Irrational Exuberance*, 2nd ed. (Princeton, N.J.: Princeton University Press, 2005), 71.

7. Parsons, *The Power of the Financial Press*, 15.

8. Parsons, *The Power of the Financial Press*, 41.

9. Parsons, *The Power of the Financial Press*, 3.

10. Douglas W. Steeples, *Advocate for American Enterprise: William Buck Dana and the* Commercial and Financial Chronicle, *1865–1910* (Westport, Conn.: Greenwood, 2002), xxii.

11. Peter Thompson, "Journalists, Traders, and the Crisis," paper presented at Soothsayers of Doom: The Media and the Financial Crisis in Comparative and Historical Perspective, City University London, London, December 13, 2011.

12. Richard White, *Railroaded: The Transcontinentals and the Making of Modern America* (New York: Norton, 2011), 68.

13. White, *Railroaded*, 67.

14. Quoted in White, *Railroaded*, 71.

15. White, *Railroaded*, 97.

16. Quoted in Alfred D. Chandler, *Henry Varnum Poor, Business Editor, Analyst, and Reformer* (Cambridge, Mass.: Harvard University Press, 1956), 104.

17. Chandler, *Henry Varnum Poor*, 116.

18. Financial Crisis Inquiry Commission, *The Financial Crisis Inquiry Report: Final Report of the National Commission on the Causes of the Financial and Economic Crisis in the United States*, authorized ed. (New York: Public Affairs, 2011), xxv.

19. Thomas F. Woodlock, "Pioneer Financial News Trio Recalled by Sole Survivor of 1892 Local Staff," *Wall Street Journal*, June 27, 1932.

20. Wendt, *The* Wall Street Journal, 26.

21. Bonnie Kavoussi, "The Panic of 1907: A Human-Caused Crisis, or a Thunderstorm? A Comparision Between the *New York Times* and the *Wall Street Journal*'s Coverage of the United States' First Modern Panic," in *The 1907 Crisis in Historical Perspective*, Center for History and Economics, Harvard University, http://www.fas.harvard.edu/~histecon/crisis-next/1907/, 9.

22. Meyer Berger, *The Story of the* New York Times, *1851–1951* (New York: Simon and Schuster, 1951), 109.

23. Kavoussi, "The Panic of 1907," 9, quoting Berger, *The Story of the* New York Times, 109.

24. David Kynaston, *The* Financial Times: *A Centenary History* (New York: Viking, 1988).

25. Edward E. Scharff, *Worldly Power: The Making of the* Wall Street Journal (New York: Beaufort, 1986), 23.

26. Wendt, *The* Wall Street Journal, 31.

27. Francis X. Dealy, *The Power and the Money: Inside the* Wall Street Journal (Secaucus, N.J.: Birch Lane Press, 1993), 13.

28. Bruce J. Evensen, "Dow, Charles Henry," in *American National Biography Online*, October 2008, http://www.anb.org/articles/16/16-03537.html.

29. Wendt, *The* Wall Street Journal, 30–31.

30. Quoted in Wendt, *The* Wall Street Journal, 32.

31. Quoted in Wendt, *The* Wall Street Journal, 73.

32. Quoted in Wendt, *The* Wall Street Journal, 76.

33. Dealy, *The Power and the Money*, 15.

34. Dealy, *The Power and the Money*, 21–22.

35. Scharff, *Worldly Power*, 24.

36. Wendt, *The* Wall Street Journal, 76–77.

37. Wendt, *The* Wall Street Journal, 89.

38. "Will Not Let Him Alone," *Wall Street Journal*, March 4, 1904.

39. Quoted in Wendt, *The* Wall Street Journal, 90–91.

40. Kavoussi, "The Panic of 1907," 5.

41. "Clearing House Has Banking Situation Here Well in Hand," *Wall Street Journal*, October 22, 1907.

42. Kavoussi, "The Panic of 1907," 5, 15.

43. Kavoussi, "The Panic of 1907," 24.

44. Kavoussi, "The Panic of 1907," 17.

45. Thomas William Lawson, *Frenzied Finance* (New York: Ridgway-Thayer, 1905), vii.

46. Kevin J. Hayes, "Barron, Clarence Walker," in *American National Biography Online*, February 2000, http://www.anb.org/articles/10/10-00101.html.

47. Clarence W. Barron, *They Told Barron: Conversations and Revelations of an American Pepys in Wall Street: The Notes of the Late Clarence W. Barron*, ed. Arthur Pound and Samuel T. Moore (New York: Harper, 1930), ix.

48. Scharff, *Worldly Power*, 25, 11.

49. Barron, *They Told Barron*, xxiii.

50. Wendt, *The* Wall Street Journal, 108.

51. Dealy, *The Power and the Money*, 24.

52. Wendt, *The* Wall Street Journal, 112, 126.

53. Mitchell Zuckoff, *Ponzi's Scheme: The True Story of a Financial Legend* (New York: Random House, 2005), 208.

54. Quoted in Dealy, *The Power and the Money*, 26–27.

55. Dealy, *The Power and the Money*, 24–25.

56. Barron, *They Told Barron*, 21.

57. Wendt, *The* Wall Street Journal, 156.

58. Scharff, *Worldly Power*, 25.

59. Rosenberg, *Inside the* Wall Street Journal, 58; Wendt, *The* Wall Street Journal, 223.

60. Scharff, *Worldly Power*, 28.

61. Scharff, *Worldly Power*, 29.

62. Scharff, *Worldly Power*, 35.

63. Wendt, *The* Wall Street Journal, 154.

64. Wendt, *The* Wall Street Journal, 106.

3. KILGORE'S REVOLUTION AT THE *WALL STREET JOURNAL*: RISE OF THE GREAT STORY

1. Quoted in Francis X. Dealy, *The Power and the Money: Inside the* Wall Street Journal (Secaucus, N.J.: Birch Lane Press, 1993), 38.

2. "Atchison Net $2.93 on Preferred in '33," *Wall Street Journal*, February 7, 1934.

3. Victor Perlo, "People's Capitalism and Stock-Ownership," *The American Economic Review* 48, no. 3 (1958): 335.

4. Julia C. Ott, *When Wall Street Met Main Street: The Quest for an Investors' Democracy* (Cambridge, Mass.: Harvard University Press, 2011), 23.

5. Archibald MacLeish, "No One Has Starved," *Fortune* 6 (September 1932): 22–23; quoted in Michael Augspurger, *An Economy of Abundant Beauty:* Fortune *Magazine and Depression America* (Ithaca, N.Y.: Cornell University Press, 2004), 158.

6. Alan Brinkley, *The Publisher: Henry Luce and His American Century* (New York: Vintage, 2011), 149.

7. Quoted in Augspurger, *An Economy of Abundant Beauty*, 6, and Brinkley, *The Publisher*, 152–53.

8. Brinkley, *The Publisher*, 152.

9. Daniel Bell et al., *Writing for* Fortune: *Nineteen Authors Remember Life on the Staff of a Remarkable Magazine* (New York: Time, 1980), 30, 123.

10. Bell et al., *Writing for* Fortune, 46.

11. Hedley Donovan, *Right Places, Right Times: Forty Years in Journalism, Not Counting My Paper Route* (New York: Holt, 1989), 102.

12. Bell et al., *Writing for* Fortune, 40.

13. Brinkley, *The Publisher*, 155.

14. Quoted in Robert E. Hertzstein, *Henry R. Luce: A Political Portrait of the Man Who Created the American Century* (New York: Scribner's, 1994), 62.

15. Archibald MacLeish, *Archibald Macleish: Reflections*, ed. Bernard A. Drabeck and Helen E. Ellis (Amherst: University of Massachusetts Press, 1986), 151; Bell et al., *Writing for* Fortune, 41, 31; Eric Hodgins (unsigned), "Arms and the Men," *Fortune* (March 1934).

16. Augspurger, *An Economy of Abundant Beauty*, 114.

17. Jennifer Szalai, "Mac the Knife: On Dwight Macdonald," *The Nation*, Decmber 12, 2011.

18. Bell et al., *Writing for* Fortune, 155.

19. Bell et al., *Writing for* Fortune, 18.

20. Quoted in Augspurger, *An Economy of Abundant Beauty*, 137.

21. Chris Roush, "A Historical Perspective of BusinessWeek, Sold to Bloomberg," *Talking Biz News*, October 13, 2009, at http://www.talkingbiznews.com/1/a-historical-perspective-of-businessweek-sold-to-bloomberg/.

22. Christopher Winans, *Malcolm Forbes: The Man Who Had Everything* (New York: St. Martin's, 1990).

23. Quoted in Stewart Pinkerton, *The Fall of the House of Forbes: The Inside Story of the Collapse of a Media Empire* (New York: St. Martin's, 2011), 73.

24. Pinkerton, *The Fall of the House of Forbes*, 75, 101, 72.

25. Richard J. Tofel, *Restless Genius: Barney Kilgore, the* Wall Street Journal, *and the Invention of Modern Journalism* (New York: St. Martin's, 2009), 5, 215.

26. Tofel, *Restless Genius*, 101.

27. Quoted in Tofel, *Restless Genius*, 61.

28. Quoted in Tofel, *Restless Genius*, 63.

29. Quoted in Tofel, *Restless Genius*, 67.

30. Lloyd Wendt, *The* Wall Street Journal: *The Story of Dow Jones and the Nation's Business Newspaper* (Chicago: Rand McNally, 1982), 289.

31. Tofel, *Restless Genius*, 114.

32. Wendt, *The* Wall Street Journal, 274.

33. Wendt, *The* Wall Street Journal, 275.

34. Wendt, *The* Wall Street Journal, 289.

35. Wendt, *The* Wall Street Journal, 279.

36. Wendt, *The* Wall Street Journal, 301.

37. Tofel argues Kilgore's interest in changing the name has been overstated by historians. He says the memo was Kilgore's follow-up to an earlier discussion with his then-boss, Hogate, who had suggested the name "Financial America," and that Kilgore was offering alternatives as a "gentle rebuttal" to Hogate's idea. The name-change idea was dropped after Hogate's death not long afterwards (Tofel, *Restless Genius*, 236).

38. Dealy, *The Power and the Money*, 49.

39. Tofel, *Restless Genius*, 169.

40. Tofel, *Restless Genius*, 170; Andrew L. Yarrow, "The Big Postwar Story: Abundance and the Rise of Economic Journalism," *Journalism History* (Summer 2006): 10.

41. Michelangelo Signorile, "The Secret Gay Life of Malcolm Forbes," *Outweek*, March 18, 1990, 40; Winans, *Malcolm Forbes*.

42. Pinkerton, *The Fall of the House of Forbes*, 119.

43. Winans, *Malcolm Forbes*, 57, 197.

44. Pinkerton, *The Fall of the House of Forbes*, 47.

45. Pinkerton, *The Fall of the House of Forbes*, 122; R. L. Stern and R. Abelson, "The Imperial Agees," *Forbes* 149, no. 12 (1992).

46. Pinkerton, *The Fall of the House of Forbes*, 69.

47. Winans, *Malcolm Forbes*, 187.

48. Winans, *Malcolm Forbes*, 139.

49. Winans, *Malcolm Forbes*, 140.

50. Quoted in Stephen Shepard, *Deadlines and Disruption: My Turbulent Path from Print to Digital* (New York: McGraw-Hill, 2013), 91.

51. Shepard, *Deadlines and Disruption*, 102, 148.

52. Anthony Bianco, "Power on Wall Street: Drexel Is Reshaping Investment Banking—and U.S. Industry," *Businessweek*, July 7, 1986, 56.

53. Katherine Fink and Michael Schudson, "The Rise of Contextual Journalism, 1950s–2000s," *Journalism* (February 2013), reviews the literature, citing K. G. Barnhurst and D. Mutz, "American Journalism and the Decline in Event-Centered Reporting," *Journal of Communication* 47, no. 4 (1997): 27–53; C. S. Stepp "Then and Now," *American Journalism Review* 21 (September 1999): 60–75; S. E. Clayman, M. E. Elliott, J. Heritage, and M. K. Beckett, "A Watershed in White House Journalism: Explaining the post-1968 Rise of Aggressive Presidential News," *Political Communication* 27 (2010): 229–47.

54. Fink and Schudson, "The Rise of Contextual Journalism, 1950s–2000s."

55. William E. Blundell, *Story Telling Step by Step: A Guide to Better Feature Writing* (New York: Dow Jones, 1986).

56. Bryan Burrough, "Self-Made Man: Top Dealmaker Leaves Trail of Deception in Wall Street Rise," *Wall Street Journal*, January 22, 1990.

57. James Sterngold, "Too Far, Too Fast; Salomon Brothers' John Gutfreund," *New York Times Magazine*, January 10, 1988.

58. Carol J. Loomis, "My Fifty-One Years (and Counting) at *Fortune*," *Fortune*, September 19, 2005, http://money.cnn.com/magazines/fortune/fortune_archive/2005/09/19/8272904/.

59. Loomis, "My Fifty-One Years."

60. Joseph Nocera, "Heard on the Street: Disgruntled Heiress Leads Revolt at Dow Jones," *Fortune*, February 3, 1997; Nocera, "Attention, Dow Jones: Ms. Goth Wants Results Now!," *Fortune*, March 2, 1998.

61. Dealy, *The Power and the Money*, 303.

4. MUCKRAKING GOES MAINSTREAM: DEMOCRATIZING FINANCIAL AND TECHNICAL KNOWLEDGE

1. Michael Hudson, interview with author, May 29, 2011.

2. Michael Hudson, "Trail of the Tin Men," part of the series Borrowing Trouble, *Roanoke Times*, December 10, 1994.

3. Michael Hudson, "Loan Scams," Alicia Patterson Foundation, 1992, updated April 19, 2011, http://aliciapatterson.org/stories/loan-scams.

4. Mark Leibovich, "The Man the White House Wakes Up To," *New York Times Magazine*, April 21, 2010, http://www.nytimes.com/2010/04/25/magazine/25allen-t.html.

5. Michael Hudson, "Homes' Hurts Easy to Hide," first in the series Virginians at Risk: Neglect and Abuse in the State's Adult Homes, *Roanoke Times*, October 2, 1989.

6. Articles in the Borrowing Trouble series included "Trail of the Tin Men," December 10, 1994; "Bankers, Critics at Odds: Big Gap Remains in Black-White Loan Approval Rate," December 11, 1994; and "Little Relief for Consumers: A New Federal Law Will Help, but It Won't Wipe Out Fraud, Abuses," December 12, 1994.

7. "Company Overview of Landmark Media Enterprises, LLC," *Businessweek*, http:// investing.businessweek.com/research/stocks/private/snapshot.asp?privcapId =722183; Sarah Rabil, "NBC Universal, Bain, Blackstone Buy Weather Channel," Bloomberg News, July 6, 2008.

8. Edward S. Herman and Noam Chomsky, *Manufacturing Consent: The Political Economy of the Mass Media*, pbk. ed. (London: Bodley Head, 2008), xi, xii.

9. James Aucoin, *The Evolution of American Investigative Journalism* (Columbia: University of Missouri Press, 2005), 21–22, 27.

10. Aucoin, *The Evolution of American Investigative Journalism*, 28, 30.

11. Charles Francis Adams Jr. and Henry Adams, *Chapters of Erie and Other Essays* (1871; Ithaca, N.Y.: Cornell University Press, 1968), 5.

12. Kathleen Brady, *Ida Tarbell: Portrait of a Muckraker* (New York: Seaview/ Putnam, 1984), 132.

13. Aucoin, *The Evolution of American Investigative Journalism*, 33.

14. Roy J. Harris Jr., *Pulitzer's Gold: Behind the Prize for Public Service Journalism* (Columbia: University of Missouri Press, 2008), 138.

15. Aucoin, *The Evolution of American Investigative Journalism*, 36.

16. Aucoin, *The Evolution of American Investigative Journalism*, 38–39; Bruce Shapiro, ed., *Shaking the Foundations: 200 Years of Investigative Journalism in America* (New York: Thunder's Mouth/Nation, 2003), 361.

17. Katherine Fink and Michael Schudson, "The Rise of Contextual Journalism, 1950s–2000s," *Journalism* (February 2013).

18. Ryan Chittum, "Newspaper Industry Ad Revenue at 1965 Levels," *Columbia Journalism Review*, August 19, 2009, http://www.cjr.org/the_audit/newspaper _industry_ad_revenue.php.

19. Robert W. McChesney and John Nichols, *The Death and Life of American Journalism: The Media Revolution That Will Begin the World Again* (Philadelphia: Nation, 2010), 257, 71.

20. Michael Schudson, *The Power of News* (Cambridge, Mass.: Harvard University Press, 1995), 142.

21. Max Holland, *Leak: Why Mark Felt Became Deep Throat* (Lawrence: University Press of Kansas, 2012).

22. Aucoin, *The Evolution of American Investigative Journalism*, 119.

23. Aucoin, *The Evolution of American Investigative Journalism*, 143.

24. Aucoin, *The Evolution of American Investigative Journalism*, 128.

25. George Getschow, "Dirty Work: The Day Laborer's Toil Is Hard, Pay Minimal, Security Nonexistent," *Wall Street Journal*, June 22, 1983.

26. Aucoin, *The Evolution of American Investigative Journalism*, 85, 87.

27. Paul N. Williams, *Investigative Reporting and Editing* (Upper Saddle River, N.J.: Prentice-Hall, 1978), 12.

28. Protess et al., *The Journalism of Outrage*, 10, 92.

29. Peter Benjaminson and David Anderson, *Investigative Reporting* (Ames: Iowa State University Press, 1976, 1990), 17

30. Protess et al., *The Journalism of Outrage*, 6.

31. Cited in Protess et al., *The Journalism of Outrage*, 25n22.

32. Quoted in Aucoin, *The Evolution of American Investigative Journalism*, 88.

33. Donald Barlett and James B. Steele, "Speculators Make a Killing on FHA Program," *Philadelphia Inquirer*, August 22, 1971; Bartlett and Steele, "Wasted Billions: How Your Tax Dollars Were Lost on Synthetic Fuel," *Philadelphia Inquirer*, December 9, 1980; Bartlett and Steele, "The Great Tax Giveaway: How the Influential Win Billions in Special Tax Breaks, " *Philadelphia Inquirer*, April 10, 1988.

34. Donald Barlett and James B. Steele, "How the Game was Rigged Against the Middle Class," *Philadelphia Inquirer*, first of a nine day series, October 20, 1991.

35. Gallup Poll, "Investigative Reporting Has Broad Public Support" (1982), cited in Protess et al., *The Journalism of Outrage*, 14.

36. Editors, "In the Interpreter's House," *The American* (January 1907), cited in Judson A. Grenier, "Muckraking and Muckrakers: An Historical Definition," *Journalism Quarterly* (Autumn 1960): 556.

37. Pew Project for Excellence in Journalism, "The State of the News Media: News Investment," http://stateofthemedia.org/2010/newspapers-summary-essay/news-investment/.

38. Aucoin, *The Evolution of American Investigative Journalism*, 120.

39. "All Those Glittering Prizes—Your Favorite Writer Didn't Win a Pulitzer; Should You Care?," *Times Literary Supplement*, April 17, 1998.

40. Carol J. Loomis, "Have You Been Cold-Called?," *Fortune*, December 16, 1991.

41. Carol J. Loomis, "The Risk That Won't Go Away," *Fortune*, March 7, 1994.

42. "The Ugly Truth About IPOs," *Fortune*, July 5, 1999.

43. Stephen Shepard, *Deadlines and Disruption: My Turbulent Path from Print to Digital* (New York: McGraw-Hill, 2013), 147.

44. Michael Siconolfi, "The Spin Desk: Underwriters Set Aside IPO Stock for Officials of Potential Customers," *Wall Street Journal*, November 12, 1997.

45. Frank Partnoy, *Infectious Greed: How Deceit and Risk Corrupted the Financial Markets* (New York: PublicAffairs, 2009).

46. Timothy L. O'Brien and Raymond Bonner, "Activity at Bank Raises Suspicions of Russian Mob Tie," *New York Times*, August 19, 1999; Timothy L. O'Brien, "Follow the Money, If You Can," *New York Times*, September 5, 1999; and others.

47. Gretchen Morgenson, "Sleazy Doings on Wall Street," *Forbes*, February 24, 1997.

48. Gretchen Morgenson, "Heat from the Boiler Room," *Forbes*, March 9, 1998; Gary Weiss, "Did Bear Stearns Ignore a Stock Swindle?" *Businessweek*, November 23, 1998; "A Slap on Bear's Paw," *Businessweek*, July 12, 1999.

49. Susan C. Faludi, "The Reckoning: Safeway LBO Yields Vast Profits but Exacts a Heavy Human Toll," *Wall Street Journal*, May 16, 1990.

50. "Safeway's CEO Disputes Portrayal," *Wall Street Journal*, letter to the editor, 15 June 1990.

51. "Top Seventy-Five Retailers and Wholesalers, 2012," *Supermarket News*, http://supermarketnews.com/top-75-retailers-wholesalers-2012.

52. Ron Chernow, *Titan: The Life of John D. Rockefeller, Sr.* (New York: Random House, 1998), 554–55.

5. CNBCIZATION: INSIDERS, ACCESS, AND THE RETURN OF THE MESSENGER BOY

1. Herbert J. Gans, *Deciding What's News: A Study of* CBS Evening News, NBC Nightly News, Newsweek, *and* Time (1979; Evanston, Ill.: Northwestern University Press, 2004).

2. Pierre Bourdieu, "The Field of Cultural Production" (1993), in *The Book History Reader*, ed. David Finkelstein and Alistair McCleery (London: Routledge, 2002). Bourdieu's theory is nicely summed up in Rodney Benson and Erik Neveu, "Introduction: Field Theory as a Work in Progress," in *Bourdieu and the Journalistic Field*, ed. Rodney Benson and Erik Neveu (Cambridge: Polity Press, 2005), 1–12, esp. 1–4.

3. Edward E. Scharff, *Worldly Power: The Making of the Wall Street Journal* (New York: Beaufort, 1986), 191, 225, 195.

4. Scharff, *Worldly Power*, 277.

5. Anthony Lewis, "On the West Wing," *New York Review of Books*, February 13, 2003; Christopher Hitchens, "Bob Woodward: Stenographer to the Stars," *Salon*, July 1, 1996, http://www.salon.com/1996/07/01/woodward960701/.

6. Thomas I. Palley, "Financialization: What It Is and Why It Matters," Levy Economics Institute Working Paper no. 25, Social Science Research Network, http://ssrn.com/abstract=1077923.

7. Joseph Nocera, *A Piece of the Action: How the Middle Class Joined the Money Class* (New York: Simon & Schuster, 1994), 75, 180.

8. Nocera, *A Piece of the Action*, 11.

9. Quoted in Nocera, *A Piece of the Action*, 403.

10. Maggie Mahar, *Bull! A History of the Boom, 1982–1999: What Drove the Breakneck Market—and What Every Investor Needs to Know About Financial Cycles* (New York: HarperBusiness, 2003), 58–59; *2006 Investment Company Fact Book: A Review of Trends and Activity in the Investment Company Industry*, 46th ed. (N.p.: Investment Company Institute, 2006), http://www.ici.org/pdf/2006_factbook.pdf, 73.

11. Mahar, *Bull!*, 104.

12. *2006 Investment Company Fact Book*.

13. "The Soaring '90s: Behind the Investing Giants and Stocks That Marked a Decade," *Wall Street Journal*, December 13, 1999.

14. Howard Kurtz, *The Fortune Tellers: Inside Wall Street's Game of Money, Media, and Manipulation* (New York: Free, 2000), 26.

15. Kurtz, *The Fortune Tellers*, 43.

16. Kurtz, *The Fortune Tellers*, 210.

17. Kurtz, *The Fortune Tellers*, 31.

18. "Inside the Box: Squawk Box Has Brains, Beauty, Wit—and an Audience of Fanatics. This Is a Stock Market Show?," *Money*, July 1, 1998; David Teather, "Maria Bartiromo: Money Honey Who Stirred Ramone's Hormones: How the Pioneering Reporter Who Had the Pink Pages Panting Became an NYSE Icon and a Punk Muse," *The Guardian*, July 13, 2006.

19. Andy Serwer, "I Want My CNBC," *Fortune*, May 24, 1999; Charles Fishman, "The Revolution Will Be Televised (on CNBC)," *Fast Company*, no. 35 (May 31, 2000), http://www.fastcompany.com/39859/revolution-will-be-televised-cnbc.

20. Diane B. Henriques, "Business Reporting: Behind the Curve," *Columbia Journalism Review* 39, no. 4 (2000): 20.

21. These data are rough and don't take into account any increase in the number of publications or database changes, including any changes to the tagging system.

22. Dean Starkman, "A Narrowed Gaze," *Columbia Journalism Review* 50, no. 5 (2012).

23. Mahar, *Bull!*, 317, 154.

24. Dean Starkman, "In the Mad Money Swamp," *Columbia Journalism Review: The Audit*, March 24, 2008, http://www.cjr.org/the_audit/let_cramer_make_this _perfect_c.php?page=all.

25. Robert J. Shiller, *Irrational Exuberance*, 2nd ed. (Princeton, N.J.: Princeton University Press, 2005), 43.

26. Mahar, *Bull!*, 159.

27. Shiller, *Irrational Exuberance*, 120.

28. See Penelope Patsuris, "The Corporate Scandal Sheet," *Forbes.com*, updated September 2002, http://www.forbes.com/2002/07/25/accountingtracker.html.

29. Quoted in Howard Kurtz, "The Enron Story That Waited to Be Told," *Washington Post*, January 18, 2002.

30. "The 2003 Pulitzer Prize Winners: Explanatory Reporting," http://www .pulitzer.org/citation/2003-Explanatory-Reporting.

31. Mahar, *Bull!*, 431n15, cites the interviews with Lay.

32. Monica Langley, Clint Riley, and Robin Sidel, "In Citigroup Ouster, a Battle Over Expenses," *Wall Street Journal*, January 24, 2007.

33. Monica Langley, Clint Riley, and Robin Sidel, "In Citigroup Ouster, a Battle Over Expenses," *Wall Street Journal*, January 26, 2007.

34. Jeffrey A. Busse and T. Clifton Green, "Market Efficiency in Real Time," *Journal of Financial Economics* 65, no. 3 (2002): 13–14.

35. Allen Wastler, "Does Maria Really Move Stocks?," *CNNMoney*, http://money. cnn.com/2002/05/17/commentary/wastler/column_wastler/index.htm.

36. Gabriel Sherman, "The Information Broker," *New York*, November 16, 2009.

37. Andrew Ross Sorkin, "The New Dealbook," *NYTimes.com*, November 9, 2010, http://dealbook.nytimes.com/2010/11/09/editors-note-the-dealbook-re-launch/.

38. Andrew Ross Sorkin, *Too Big to Fail: The Inside Story of How Wall Street and Washington Fought to Save the Financial System from Crisis—and Themselves* (New York: Viking Penguin, 2009), 535.

39. Sorkin, *Too Big to Fail*, 533.

40. Sorkin, *Too Big to Fail*, 81.

41. Moe Tkacik, "Andrew Ross Sorkin's Book Party Was Filled with CEOs, Warts and All," *New York*, October 21, 2009.

6. SUBPRIME RISES IN THE 1990s: JOURNALISM AND REGULATION FIGHT BACK

1. Christopher L. Peterson, "Predatory Structured Finance," *Cardozo Law Review* 28, no. 5 (2007): 2193.

2. Peterson, "Predatory Structured Finance," 2200.

3. Peterson, "Predatory Structured Finance," 2204.

4. Securities Industry and Financial Markets Association, "Global CDO Issuance and Outstanding," updated April 8, 2013, http://www.sifma.org/research/statistics. aspx.

5. Joseph Nocera, *A Piece of the Action: How the Middle Class Joined the Money Class* (New York: Simon & Schuster, 1994).

6. Marquette National Bank v. First Omaha Service Corp., 439 U.S. 299 (1978).

7. Bethany McLean and Joseph Nocera, *All the Devils Are Here: The Hidden History of the Financial Crisis* (New York: Portfolio/Penguin, 2010), 29.

8. HUD, "U.S. Housing Market Condtions Historical Data, 1970–1996," table 16, http://www.huduser.org/periodicals/ushmc/spring97/histdat2.html.

9. HUD-Treasury Task Force on Predatory Lending, "Curbing Predatory Home Mortgage Lending," http://archives.hud.gov/reports/treasrpt.pdf; SIFMA, "Global CDO Issuance and Outstanding."

10. Michael Hudson, "Loan Scams," Alicia Patterson Foundation, 1992, updated April 19, 2011, http://aliciapatterson.org/stories/loan-scams.

11. Quoted in McLean and Nocera, *All the Devils Are Here*, 31. In fact, the market badly mispriced the risk of subprime lending, principally because, like the business press and others viewing the practice from a distance, it didn't understand the widespread fraud that lay at the heart of the subprime lending business or the perverse incentives among lenders, rating agencies, and Wall Street banks to perpetuate it. As a result, and as we'll see, the mainstreaming of subprime would push past all practical, ethical, and commonsense barriers.

12. Louis Hyman, "The House That George Romney Built," *New York Times*, February 1, 2012.

13. Paulette Thomas, "Race and Mortgage-Lending in America—Behind the Figures: Federal Data Detail Pervasive Racial Gap in Mortgage Lending," *Wall Street Journal*, March 31, 1992.

14. Elinore Longobardi, "How 'Subprime' Crushed 'Predatory,'" *Columbia Journalsim Review*, October 12, 2009, http://www.cjr.org/feature/how_subprime _crushed_predatory_1.php.

15. Cited in Longobardi, "How 'Subprime' Crushed 'Predatory.'"

16. Allen Fishbein and Harold Bunce, "Subprime Market Growth and Predatory Lending," in *Housing Policy in the New Meillenium*, ed. Susan M. Wachter and R. Leo Penne (Washington, D.C.: Department of Housing and Urban Development, 2000), 280; quoted in Longobardi, "How 'Subprime' Crushed 'Predatory.'"

17. Longobardi, "How 'Subprime' Crushed 'Predatory.'"

18. Senate Committee on Banking, Housing, and Urban Affairs, "Predatory Lending Practices: Staff Analysis of Regulators' Responses," report of the staff to Chairman Gramm, August 23, 2000, http://www.banking.senate.gov/docs/reports/ predlend/predlend.htm.

19. HUD-Treasury Task Force on Predatory Lending, "Curbing Predatory Home Mortgage Lending."

20. McLean and Nocera, *All the Devils Are Here*, 31.

21. Jay P. Pederson, *International Directory of Company Histories*, vol. 36 (Detroit: St. James Press, 2001).

22. Shawn Tully, "Can Brian Moynihan Fix America's Biggest Bank?," *Fortune*, July 7, 2011, http://finance.fortune.cnn.com/2011/07/07/can-brian-moynihan-fix -americas-biggest-bank/.

23. Peter S. Canellos, "Profitable Fleet Finance's Ethics Questioned," *Boston Globe*, June 9, 1991.

24. "A Matter of Interest," *60 Minutes*, November 15, 1992.

25. Michael Hudson, *The Monster: How a Gang of Predatory Lenders and Wall Street Bankers Fleeced America—and Spawned a Global Crisis* (New York: Times/Henry Holt and, 2010), 59.

26. Peter S. Canellos, "Bankers Under the Gun: Fleet Acts to Fend Off Suits, Protect Its Reputation," *Boston Globe*, October 9, 1992.

27. HUD-Treasury Task Force, "Curbing Predatory Home Mortgage Lending," 85.

28. HUD-Treasury Task Force, "Curbing Predatory Home Mortgage Lending," 29; Richard Lord, *American Nightmare: Predatory Lending and the Foreclosure of the American Dream* (Monroe, Maine: Common Courage, 2005), 20.

29. Hudson, *The Monster*, 186, 103.

30. Hudson, *The Monster*, 64; Michael Hudson, ed., *Merchants of Misery: How Corporate America Profits from Poverty* (Monroe, Maine: Common Courage, 1996), 43.

31. Hudson, *The Monster*, 149, 86.

32. Hudson, *The Monster*, 24, 187n54.

33. Hudson, ed., *Merchants of Misery*, 42–52.

34. Hudson, ed., *Merchants of Misery*, 47.

35. Jeff Bailey, "A Man and His Loan: Why Bennie Roberts Refinanced Ten Times," *Wall Street Journal*, April 23, 1997.

36. Hudson, ed., *Merchants of Misery*, 207; Richard W. Stevenson, "How Serial Refinancings Can Rob Equity," *New York Times*, March 22, 1998.

37. George A. Akerlof, "The Market for 'Lemons': Quality Uncertainty and the Market Mechanism," *The Quarterly Journal of Economics* 84, no. 3 (August 1970): 488–500.

38. William K. Black, "Wallison and the Three 'Des'—Deregulation, Desupervision, and De Facto Decriminalization," *The Big Picture*, http://www.ritholtz. com/blog/2011/02/wallison-and-the-three-%E2%80%9Cdes%E2%80%9D -%E2%80%93-deregulation-desupervision-and-de-facto-decriminalization/.

39. Michael Lewis, *The Big Short: Inside the Doomsday Machine* (New York: Norton, 2010), 3.

40. Lewis, *The Big Short*, 13–15.

7. MUCKRAKING THE BANKS, 2000–2003:
A LAST GASP FOR JOURNALISM AND REGULATION

1. Michael Gregory, "The Predatory Lending Fracas: Wall Street Comes Under Scrutiny in the Subprime Market as Liquidity Suffers and Regulation Looms," *Investment Dealers' Digest*, June 26, 2000.

2. "Greenspan Criticizes Predatory Lending," *Newsday*, March 22, 2000.

3. Kevin Guerrero, "Moving Against Preedators, OTS Takes Aim at Loophole," *American Banker*, April 5, 2000. The law was Alternative Mortgage Transaction Parity Act of 1982, Pub. L. No. 97-320, title VIII.

4. "More Jump on the Predatory Bandwagon," *CBA Reports* 80, no. 5 (2000): 1.

5. We selected a date range of January 1, 2000, through June 30, 2007, with the idea that the early date would capture the entire housing bubble and the later date marked the period after two Bear Stearns hedge funds publicly collapsed and all warnings became moot. We then came up with a commonsense list of the nine most influential business press outlets: the *Wall Street Journal*, the *New York Times*, the *Los Angeles Times*, the *Washington Post*, Bloomberg News, the *Financial Times*, *Fortune*, *Businessweek*, and *Forbes*. CNBC and other television outlets were excluded both for practical and substantive reasons. With the help of some colleagues, we searched the Factiva database for the names of important institutions—Bear Stearns, Countrywide, etc.—and matched them with search terms that seemed appropriate, such as "predatory lending," "mortgage lending," "securitization," "collateralized debt obligations," and the like. Of news outlets that volunteered their best work, some were more diligent than others, so, on that score, the *New York Times* might tend to be overrepresented, while the *Washington Post*, which declined to participate, might get shorted. Similarly, Bloomberg, the *Financial Times*, and the *Los Angeles Times* posed technical challenges. But while we didn't hesitate to differentiate among the performance levels of different outlets (and reporters, for that matter), the goal was to assess institutional performance, not who "won." The list was designed to capture *all* significant warning stories, not just some of them. The list also includes as guideposts bits of context that we felt would give readers some sense of what was happening on the finance beat at the time (e.g., "Fed Assesses Citigroup Unit $70 Million in Loan Abuse," *NYT*, May 28, 2004). Sprinkled throughout are some rah-rah stories ("Mortgage Slump? Bring It On: Countrywide Plans to Grab More of the Market as the Industry Consolidates," *Businessweek*, December 15, 2003) and a tiny fraction of the run-of-the-mill stories about important and guilty institutions that in retrospect were far from the salient point ("Power Banking: Morgan Stanley Trades Energy Old-Fashioned Way: In Barrels," *WSJ*, March 2, 2005). Our categorization is subjective, of course, but readers are invited to read the color-coded list themselves at www.cjr.org/the_audit/the_list.php and argue for and against stories that might be included in the "red," investigative category. We believe we were generous in our assignments. The list remains open, and readers are invited to submit samples of great stories we missed to editor@cjr.org.

6. *The 2008 Mortgage Market Statistical Annual*, 2 vols. (Washington, D.C.: Financial World Publications, 2008).

7. Tony Dokoupil, "How Often Does the Press Beat the SEC to Accounting Fraud Stories?," *Columbia Journalism Review*, May 21, 2007, http://www.cjr.org/the_audit/how_often_does_the_press_beat.php.

8. Richard Lord, *American Nightmare: Predatory Lending and the Foreclosure of the American Dream* (Monroe, Maine: Common Courage, 2005), 29, 30.

9. Kurt Eggert, "Held Up in Due Course: Predatory Lending, Securitization, and the Holder in Due Course Doctrine," *Creighton Law Review* 35 (April 2002): 588, 598.

10. Christopher L. Peterson, "Predatory Structured Finance," *Cardozo Law Review* 28, no. 5 (2007): 2214n176.

11. Peterson, "Predatory Structured Finance," 2216n184.

12. Robert Berner and Brian Grow, "They Warned Us About the Mortgage Crisis," *Businessweek*, October 8, 2008; Mortgage Bankers Association, press release, "Standard & Poor's to Disallow Georgia Fair Lending Act Loans," January 16, 2003, http://www.mortgagebankers.org/NewsandMedia/PressCenter/32153.htm, updated October 12, 2005; see also See Dean Starkman, "Spitzer's Ghost," *Columbia Journalism Review*, October 14, 2008, http://www.cjr.org/the_audit/spitzers_ghost.php.

13. Watters v. Wachovia Bank, 127 S. Ct. 1559 (2007); see Dean Starkman, "Spitzer's Ghost," *Columbia Journalism Review*, October 14, 2008, http://www.cjr.org/the_audit/spitzers_ghost.php.

14. Federal Trade Commission, "Citigroup Settles FTC Charges Against the Associates Record-Setting $215 Million for Subprime Lending Victims," press release, September 19, 2002, http://www.ftc.gov/opa/2002/09/associates.shtm.

15. John Hechinger, "How Big Lenders Sell a Pricier Refinancing to Poor Homeowners," *Wall Street Journal*, December 7, 2001.

16. Heidi Evans, "Mortgage Scam Targets Poor: Owners Lose Their Homes," *New York Daily News*, February 20, 2000.

17. Federal Trade Commission, "FTC, DOJ, and HUD Announce Action to Combat Abusive Lending Practices," press release, March 30, 2000, http://www.ftc.gov/opa/2000/03/deltafunding.shtm.

18. John Stark, "Tough Choices Produced HFC Deal; Documents Detail States' Efforts to Forge Settlement," *Bellingham Herald*, January 5, 2011.

19. Michael Lewis, *The Big Short: Inside the Doomsday Machine* (New York: Norton, 2010), 18.

8. THREE JOURNALISM OUTSIDERS UNEARTH THE LOOMING MORTGAGE CRISIS

1. Michael Hudson, "Banking on Misery: Citigroup, Wall Street, and the Fleecing of the South," *Southern Exposure* 31, no. 2 (2003): sidebar, "Special Child: For Mentally Retarded Borrower, Arbitration a Losing Proposition," 45.

2. California v. Countywide Financial Corp., et al., California Superior Court, NW dist., June 24, 2008, http://ag.ca.gov/cms_attachments/press/pdfs/n1582_draft_cwide_complaint2.pdf, 9; Dean Starkman, "Boiler Room," *Columbia Journalism Review* 47, no. 3 (2008).

3. Michael Hudson, interview with author, May 29, 2011, Brooklyn, N.Y.

4. Michael Hudson, "Banking on Misery: Citigroup, Wall Street, and the Fleecing of the South," *Southern Exposure* 31, no. 2 (2003): 25.

5. Michael Perino, *The Hellhound of Wall Street: How Ferdinand Pecora's Investigation of the Great Crash Forever Changed American Finance* (New York: Penguin, 2010), 6–8; Michael Perino, interview by Robert Siegel, *All Things Considered*, NPR, October 6, 2010, http://www.npr.org/templates/story/story.php?storyId=130384189.

6. Securities and Excange Commission, Citigroup Inc., "10-K405," 2001, see table Five-Year Summary of Selected Financial Data(1), http://www.sec.gov/Archives/edgar/data/831001/000091205701007605/a2040499z10-k405.txt, 5.

7. Thomas I. Palley, "Financialization: What It Is and Why It Matters," Levy Economics Institute Working Paper no. 25, Social Science Research Network, http://ssrn.com/abstract=1077923, 34–37.

8. Simon Johnson, "The Quiet Coup," *The Atlantic Monthly* (May 2009).

9. Gillian Tett, interview with author, May 3, 2013.

10. Gillian Tett, "Silence and Silos: The Problems of Fractured Thought in Finance," paper presented at the 109th meeting of the American Anthropological Association, November 19, 2010, New Orleans; see http://vimeo.com/17854712; Tett, interview with author.

11. Tett, "Silence and Silos" (paper); Tett, interview with author.

12. Gillian Tett, "Searching for Light in Murky Debt Pool," *Financial Times*, May 12, 2005; Tett, "Credit the US Banks for the Boom," *Financial Times*, July 28, 2005; Tett, "The Dream Machine," *Financial Times*, March 24, 2006.

13. Tett, "The Effect of Collateralised Debt Should Not Be Underplayed," *Financial Times*, May 18, 2007; Tett, "Financial Wizards Owe a Debt to Ratings Agencies' Magic," *Financial Times*, December 1, 2006.

14. Securities Industry and Financial Markets Association, "Global CDO Issuance and Outstanding," updated April 8, 2013, http://www.sifma.org/research/statistics.aspx; Tett, "Silence and Silos" (paper).

15. Gillian Tett, "Clouds Sighted Off CDO Asset Pool," *Financial Times*, April 18, 2005.

16. Gillian Tett, "Silence and Silos: Who So Few People Spotted the Problems in Complex Credit and What That Implies for the Future," *Financial Stability Review*, no. 14, Derivatives—Financial Innovation and Stability (July 2010): 121–29.

17. Gillian Tett, *Fool's Gold: The Inside Story of J.P. Morgan and How Wall Street Greed Corrupted Its Bold Dream and Created a Financial Catastrophe* (New York: Free, 2010), 252–53; Tett, "Silence and Silos" (paper).

18. Tett, "Silence and Silos" (paper).

19. Richard Lord, *American Nightmare: Predatory Lending and the Foreclosure of the American Dream* (Monroe, Maine: Common Courage, 2005), 5. For Lord's early subprime reporting in the *Pittsburgh City Paper*, see "Huffing and Puffing: When High-Interest Subprime Lenders Use Predatory Tactics, Borrowers Who Lose Their Homes Through Foreclosure Take It on the Chin," January 9, 2002; "The Wolf at the Door: National City Bank's Push Into the Subprime Lending Business Has Led to a Tripling of Foreclosures by its Affiliate, Altegra Credit," January 16, 2002; "The Hammer and the Nailed: Home Improvement Contractors and Mortgage Brokers Are Herding Pittsburghers Into the Subprime Lending Market," July 24, 2002.

20. Lord, *American Nightmare*, 20.

21. Lord, *American Nightmare*, 19; emphasis added.

22. Richard Lord, interview with author, April 24, 2013; Lord, *American Nightmare*, 33–34.

23. See, for example, David Brooks, "The Culture of Debt," *New York Times*, July 22, 2008; George Will, "The Horrors of a Crisis," *Washington Post*, April 13, 2008; Will, "Burning Down the House," *Washington Post*, July 11, 2011.

24. Financial Crisis Inquiry Commission, *The Financial Crisis Inquiry Report: Final Report of the National Commission on the Causes of the Financial and Economic Crisis in the United States*, authorized ed. (New York: Public Affairs, 2011), xxvi–xxvii.

25. Also see Bethany McLean and Joseph Nocera, *All the Devils Are Here: The Hidden History of the Financial Crisis* (New York: Portfolio/Penguin, 2010); David Fiderer, "The Big Lie Annotated: An AEI History of the Financial Crisis," Feb. 26, 2013, *The Big Picture*, http://www.ritholtz.com/blog/2013/03/the-big-lie-annotated-an-aei-history-of-the-financial-crisis; Ryan Chittum, "The Big Lie of the Crisis, Called Out by the Press," *Columbia Journalism Review*, November 11, 2011, http://www.cjr.org/the_audit/the_big_lie_of_the_crisis_call.php, Joseph Nocera, "An Inconvenient Truth," *New York Times*, December 19, 2011.

26. Quoted in Michael Hudson, *The Monster: How a Gang of Predatory Lenders and Wall Street Bankers Fleeced America—and Spawned a Global Crisis* (New York: Times/Henry Holt, 2010), 11.

27. Hudson, *The Monster*, 2, 257.

28. Hudson, *The Monster*, 143–44, 222, 229, 257, 228, 221.

29. Michael Hudson and E. Scott Reckard, "Workers Say Lender Ran 'Boiler Rooms,'" *Los Angeles Times*, February 4, 2005.

30. Hudson, *The Monster*, 36.

31. Dean Starkman, "Seidman Sued Over Its Auditing of A.R. Baron," *Wall Street Journal*, March 31, 1998.

32. Gary R Weiss, *Born to Steal: A Life Inside the Wall Street Mafia* (New York: Warner, 2003), 153.

33. Hudson, *The Monster*, 331n243.

34. Michael Hudson, "Ameriquest's Ties to Watchdog Group Are Tested: Greenlining Institute Returns a Donation as the Mortgage Giant Faces Lawsuits," *Los Angeles Times*, May 22, 2005.

35. Michael Hudson, e-mail to John Corrigan and Scott Reckard, July 8, 2005, provided to the author.

36. Hudson, *The Monster*, 221; Michael Hudson and E. Scott Reckard, "Workers Say Lender Ran 'Boiler Rooms,'" *Los Angeles Times*, February 4, 2005.

37. William K. Black, "Wallison and the Three 'Des'—Deregulation, Desupervision and De Facto Decriminalization," *The Big Picture*, http://www.ritholtz.com/blog/2011/02/wallison-and-the-three-%E2%80%9Cdes%E2%80%9D-%E2%80%93-deregulation-desupervision-and-de-facto-decriminalization/.

38. Hudson, *The Monster*, 212; McLean and Joseph Nocera, *All the Devils Are Here*, 138.

39. Ann Hardie, Alan Judd, and Carrie Teegardin, "Borrower Beware: Why Georgia Is a Bad Place to Borrow Money," *Atlanta Journal Constitution*, January 30–February 2, 2005.

40. Binyamin Appelbaum and Ted Mellnick, "The Hard Truth in Lending: Blacks Make Home Ownership Gains but Are Four Times More Likely Than Whites to Get High Interest Rates," *Charlotte Observer*, August 28, 2005; Binyamin Appelbaum, Rick Rothacker, and Ted Mellnick, "New Industry Fills Void in Minority Lending; Critics Say Borrowers Turn to High-Rate Lenders Because Bank Loans Too Often Not Available," *Charlotte Observer*, August 29, 2005; Binyamin Appelbaum "Mortgage Industry Outgrows Federal Regulations," *Charlotte Observer*, August 30, 2005.

41. Michael Hudson, memo to *WSJ* editors, February 20, 2006.

9. THE WATCHDOG THAT DIDN'T BARK: THE DISAPPEARANCE OF ACCOUNTABILITY REPORTING AND THE MORTGAGE FRENZY, 2004–2006

1. Ryan Chittum, "Newspaper Industry Ad Revenue at 1965 Levels," *Columbia Journalism Review*, August 19, 2009, http://www.cjr.org/the_audit/newspaper _industry_ad_revenue.php.

2. On the *LA Times* cuts, see John Koblin, "Los Angeles Times Cuts Staff for Third Time This Year; 10 Percent of Newsroom Let Go," *New York Observer*, October 27, 2008; on the 2007 declines, see Dean Starkman, "How Could 9,000 Business Reporters Blow It?," *Mother Jones* (January/February 2009): 24–30; on total job losses, see Robert W. McChesney and John Nichols, *The Death and Life of American Journalism: The Media Revolution That Will Begin the World Again* (Philadelphia: Nation, 2010), 18

3. Pew Project for Excellence in Journalism, "The State of the News Media: News Investment," http://stateofthemedia.org/2010/newspapers-summary-essay/news-investment/; Starkman, "How Could 9,000 Business Reporters Blow It?"

4. Ken Auletta, "Family Business," *The New Yorker*, November 3, 2003.

5. Dean Starkman, "The Tragedy of Peter Kann," *Columbia Journalism Review*, May 21, 2007, http://www.cjr.org/the_audit/the_tragedy_of_peter_kann.php.

6. News Corporation, "Annual Report 2010," http://www.newscorp.com/ Report2010/report/NewsCorp2010AR.pdf, 22.

7. Tom Lowry, "Bloomberg Wins Bidding for Businessweek," *Businessweek*, October 13, 2009, http://www.businessweek.com/innovate/FineOnMedia/archives/2009/ 10/bloomberg_wins.html.

8. Dean Starkman, "The Hamster Wheel," *Columbia Journalism Review* 49, no. 3 (September/October 2010): 24–28.

9. Steve Waldman et al., *The Information Needs of Communities: The Changing Media Landscape in a Broadband Age* (FCC, July 2011), http://www.fcc.gov/ info-needs-communities.

10. Dow Jones, 10-K filing with Securities Exchange Commission, February 28, 2007, http://www.sec.gov/Archives/edgar/data/29924/000002992407000056/ form10k20062284p.htm; Morgan Stanley, 10-K filing with Securities Exchange Commission, February 13, 2007; Rob Kelley, "Is John Mack Worth $40 Million?," *CNNMoney*, December 16, 2006, http://money.cnn.com/2006/12/15/news/ newsmakers/compensation/.

11. Financial Crisis Inquiry Commission, *The Financial Crisis Inquiry Report: Final Report of the National Commission on the Causes of the Financial and Economic Crisis in the United States*, authorized ed. (New York: Public Affairs, 2011), xviii.

12. Quoted in Starkman, "How Could 9,000 Business Reporters Blow It?"

13. Dean Starkman, "Power Problem," *Columbia Journalism Review* 48, no. 1 (2009): 24–34.

14. Leonard Downie Jr. and Michael Schudson, "The Reconstruction of American Journalism," report commissioned by Columbia University Graduate School of Journalism, *Columbia Journalism Review*, October 19, 2009, http://www.cjr.org/ reconstruction/the_reconstruction_of_american.php?page=all.

15. Peter Coy et al., "Is a Housing Bubble About to Burst?," *Businessweek*, July 18, 2004; Jim Carlton, "Home Investments (a Special Report); Boom vs. Bust: The Housing-Price Run-up Can't Last; the Housing-Price Run-up Will Go on; Two Experts Debate the Issue," *Wall Street Journal*, June 14, 2004.

16. Edmund L. Andrews, "The Ever More Graspable, and Risky, American Dream," *New York Times*, June 24 2004; Rich Miller and Christopher Palmeri, "Armed and Dangerous? Adjustable-Rate Mortgages Are Pulling in New Home Buyers—but the Risks Are High," *Businessweek*, April 12, 2004.

17. Greg Ip and Mark Whitehouse, "Stash Flow: Huge Flood of Capital to Invest Spurs World-Wide Risk Taking," *Wall Street Journal*, November 3, 2005; E. S. Browning, "Woodland Haven: U.S. Timberland Gets Pricey as Big Money Seeks Shelter," November 4, 2005; Patrick Barta and Mary Kissel, "Buying Bridges: From Australia, Money Chases Roads, Airports Around Globe," *Wall Street Journal*, December 6, 2005.

18. Michael Schroeder and Greg Ip, "Out of Reach: The Enron Debacle Spotlights Huge Void in Financial Regulation," *Wall Street Journal*, December 13, 2001; Jacob M. Schlesinger, "What's Wrong? The Deregulators: Did Washington Help Set Stage for Current Business Turmoil?," *Wall Street Journal*, October 17, 2002.

19. Alan Greenspan, "Risk Transfer and Financial Stabiity," remarks to the Federal Reserve Bank of Chicago's Forty-First Annual Conference on Bank Structure, Chicago, May 5, 2005, http://www.federalreserve.gov/boarddocs/speeches/2005/20050505/default.htm; Mara Der Hovanesian, Chester Dawson, and Kerry Capell, "Taking Risk to Extremes," *Businessweek*, May 22, 2005.

20. Mark Whitehouse and Gregory Zuckerman, "Housing Bears Bet on Shaky Credit," *Wall Street Journal*, December 12, 2005.

21. Emily Thornton, "Lehman's New Street Smarts," *Businessweek*, January 18, 2004.

22. Anton R. Valukas, examiner, *Lehman Brothers Holdings Inc Chapter 11 Proceedings Examiner Report* (Jenner and Block, March 13, 2010), vol. 1, sect. 2, 43–45 and 58–65.

23. Susanne Craig, "Trading Up: To Crack Wall Street's Top Tier, Lehman Gambles on Going Solo," *Wall Street Journal*, October 13, 2004.

24. Andy Serwer, "The Improbable Power Broker: How Dick Fuld Transformed Lehman from Wall Street Also-Ran to Super-Hot Machine," *Fortune*, April 13, 2006.

25. Roger Lowenstein, "Alone at the Top," *New York Times Magazine*, August 27, 2000; Carol J. Loomis, "Whatever It Takes," *Fortune*, November 25, 2002; Monica Langley, "Wall Street's Toughest Boss," *Wall Street Journal*, February 18, 2003.

26. Mitchell Pacelle, Monica Langley, and Sapsford Jathon, "People Power: Two Financiers' Careers Trace a Bank Strategy That's Now Hot," *Wall Street Journal*, January 16, 2004.

27. Mara Der Hovanesian, "Citigroup: Cleaned Up but Falling Behind," *Businessweek*, October 4, 2006; emphasis mine.

28. Marcia Vickers, "The Unlikely Revolutionary," *Fortune*, February 27, 2006.

29. Kimberly L. Allers, "A New Banking Model," *Fortune*, March 31, 2003.

30. Joseph T. Hallinan, "As Banks Elbow for Consumers, Washington Mutual Thrives," *Wall Street Journal*, November 6, 2003.

31. Shawn Tully, "What Went Wrong at WaMu," *Fortune*, August 9, 2004.

32. Joseph T. Hallinan, "Revolving Door at WaMu Thrift Is Hurting Stock," *Wall Street Journal*, March 8, 2005.

33. Stephen Mihm, "Dr. Doom," *New York Times Magazine*, August 17, 2008.

34. Michael Hudson, interview with author, May 29, 2011, Brooklyn, N.Y.

35. Michael Hudson, "Can Junk-Bond Funds' Streak Continue as Economy Slows, Default Rates Rise?," *Wall Street Journal*, August 11 2006; Hudson, "Market Puts Bet Behind Bernanke," *Wall Street Journal*, August 7 2006.

36. Gregory Zuckerman and Michael Hudson, "Moving the Market: Mortgage Industry Starts to Roil Bond Markets," *Wall Street Journal*, December 8, 2006.

37. Jon Hilsenrath, telephone interview with author, February 26, 2013.

38. Diana B. Henriques and Lowell Bergman, "Mortgaged Lives: Profiting from Fine Print with Wall Street's Help," *New York Times*, March 15, 2000.

39. Kate Kelly, "A 'Subprime' Fund Is on the Brink," *Wall Street Journal*, June 16, 2007. Jody Shenn of Bloomberg and Matthew Goldstein in *Businessweek* had explored the problematic nature of the funds' assets a month earlier: Shenn, "Bear Stearns Funds Own 67 Percent Stake in Everquest (Update3)," Bloomberg News, May 11, 2007; Goldstein, "Bear Stearns' Subprime IPO," *Businessweek*, May 11, 2007.

40. Serena Ng and Carrick Mollenkamp, "Merrill Takes $8.4 Billion Credit Hit," *Wall Street Journal*, October 25, 2007; Mollenkamp and Ng, "Wall Street Wizardry Amplified Credit Crisis," *Wall Street Journal*, December 27, 2007.

41. Mark Pittman, conversation with author, 2009; Pittman, "S&P, Moody's Mask $200 Billion of Subprime Bond Risk," Bloomberg News, June 29, 2007; Pittman, "Paulson's Focus on 'Excesses' Shows Goldman Gorged," Bloomberg News, November 5, 2007.

42. Gretchen Morgenson, "Behind Biggest Insurer's Crisis, a Blind Eye to a Web of Risk," *New York Times*, September 28, 2008.

43. Permanent Subcommittee on Investigations, *Wall Street and the Financial Crisis: Anatomy of a Financial Collapse*, April 13, 2011, http://www.hsgac.senate.gov//imo/media/doc/Financial_Crisis/FinancialCrisisReport.pdf, 48, 64, 4, 84.

44. Subcommittee on Investigations, *Wall Street and the Financial Crisis*, 96.

45. Subcommittee on Investigations, *Wall Street and the Financial Crisis*, 103.

46. Mara Der Hovanesian, "Nightmare Mortgages," *Businessweek*, September 20, 2006.

47. Subcommittee on Investigations, *Wall Street and the Financial Crisis*, 147; Sawall Chan, "Ex-Chief Claims WaMu Was Not Treated Fairly," *New York Times*, April 14, 2010.

48. Financial Crisis Inquiry Commission, *The Financial Crisis Inquiry Report*, 47.

49. Mara Der Hovanesian, "Sex, Lies, and Subprime," *Businessweek*, November 12, 2008; Michael Hudson, "Fraud and Folly: The Untold Story of General Electric's Subprime Debacle," Center for Public Integrity, January 6, 2012, http://www.publicintegrity.org/2012/01/06/7802/fraud-and-folly-untold-story-general-electric-s-subprime-debacle.

50. Subcommittee on Investigations, *Wall Street and the Financial Crisis*, 152.

51. Subcommittee on Investigations, *Wall Street and the Financial Crisis*, 153; Financial Crisis Inquiry Commission, 64, 63; Ben Walsh, "The Multimillionaire

Men of Lehman," Reuters Blogs, April 30, 2012, http://blogs.reuters.com/felix -salmon/2012/04/30/the-multimillionaire-men-of-lehman/. Hudson, "Fraud and Folly."

52. Alex Blumberg, "The Giant Pool of Money," *This American Life*, prod. Ira Glass, NPR (2008).

53. Jesse Eisinger and Jake Bernstein, "Magnetar Gets Started," *ProPublica*, April 9 2010, http://www.propublica.org/article/magnetar-gets-started; Eisinger and Bernstein, "The Magnetar Trade: How One Hedge Fund Helped Keep the Bubble Going," *ProPublica*, April 9, 2010, http://www.propublica.org/article/the-magnetar-trade-how-one-hedge-fund-helped-keep-the-housing-bubble-going.

10. DIGITISM, CORPORATISM, AND THE FUTURE OF JOURNALISM: AS THE HAMSTER WHEEL TURNS

1. Cramer later said he meant that depositors' funds were safe and was not discussing the firm's financial condition. See Dean Starkman, "In the Mad Money Swamp," *Columbia Journalism Review*, March 24, 2008, http://www.cjr.org/the _audit/let_cramer_make_this_perfect_c.php.

2. Produced in cooperation with NPR's *This American Life* and *Planet Money*.

3. Ryan Chittum, "Missing the Moment," in *Bad News: How America's Business Press Missed the Story of the Century*, ed. Anya Schiffrin (New York: New Press, 2011), 123.

4. Ryan Chittum, "A *BusinessWeek* Cover Crosses a Line," *Columbia Journalism Review*, February 28, 2013, http://www.cjr.org/the_audit/businessweeks_cover _crosses_th.php; Chittum, "More on That Businessweek Cover," *Columbia Journalism Review*, February 28, 2013, http://www.cjr.org/the_audit/more_on_that _businessweek_cove.php.

5. Ryan Chittum, "Reuters Gets a Scalp," *Columbia Journalism Review*, January 30, 2013, http://www.cjr.org/the_audit/reuters_gets_a_scalp_at_chesap.php.

6. Kocienewski's entire series, "Nobody Pays That," is catalogued by the *Times* at http://topics.nytimes.com/top/features/timestopics/series/but_nobody_pays _that/index.html. Barstow's entire series, "Wal-Mart Abroad: How a Retail Giant Fueled Growth with Bribes," is catalogued by the *Times* at http://www.nytimes.com/ interactive/business/walmart-bribery-abroad-series.html. See, specifically, David Kocieniewski, "At G.E. on Tax Day, Billions of Reasons to Smile," *New York Times*, March 25, 2011; "U.S. Has High Business Tax Rates, Technically," *New York Times*, May 3, 2011; "Companies Push for a Tax Break on Foreign Cash," *New York Times*, June 20 2011; "Rich Tax Breaks Bolster Makers of Video Games," *New York Times*, September 10, 2011; "A Family's Billions, Artfully Sheltered," *New York Times*, November 27, 2011; "Tax Benefits from Options as Windfall for Businesses," *New York Times*, December 29, 2011; Marjorie Connelly, "Americans Favor Budget Cuts Over Raising Corporate Tax," *New York Times*, May 3, 2011. David Barstow, "Vast Mexico Bribery Case Hushed Up by Wal-Mart After Top-Level Struggle," *New York Times*, April 22, 2012; David Barstow and Alejandra Xanic von Bertrab, "The Bribery Aisle: How Wal-Mart Used Payoffs to Get Its Way in Mexico," *New York Times*, December 18, 2012.

7. The entire series, "What They Know," spans three years and is catalogued by the *Wall Street Journal* at http://online.wsj.com/public/page/what-they-know -digital-privacy.html

8. Allen Neuharth, *Confessions of an S.O.B.* (New York: Doubleday, 1989), 257.

9. Neuharth, *Confessions of an S.O.B.*, 258; Thomas Frank, *One Market Under God: Extreme Capitalism, Market Populism, and the End of Economic Democracy* (New York: Doubleday, 2000), 331.

10. David Carr, "At Flagging Tribune, Tales of a Bankrupt Culture," *New York Times*, October 6, 2010.

11. Quoted in Sarah Ellison, *War at the* Wall Street Journal: *Inside the Struggle to Control an American Business Empire* (Boston: Houghton Mifflin Harcourt, 2010), 186–87.

12. Michael Wolff, *The Man Who Owns the News: Inside the Secret World of Rupert Murdoch* (New York: Broadway, 2008), 250.

13. Wolff, *The Man Who Owns the News*, 132; Ellison, *War at the* Wall Street Journal, 242; also see David Carr, "War@WSJ: New Book Pulls Back Blankets on Murdoch's Capture of The Journal," January 19, 2010, *New York Times*, http:// mediadecoder.blogs.nytimes.com/2010/01/19/warwsj-new-book-pulls-back -blankets-on-murdochs-capture-of-the-journal/.

14. Ellison, *War at the* Wall Street Journal, 219; Jessica E. Vascellaro, Merissa Marr, and Sam Schechner, "Editor out as Murdoch Speeds Change at WSJ," *Wall Street Journal*, April 23, 2008.

15. Dean Starkman, "The Hamster Wheel," *Columbia Journalism Review* 49, no. 3 (2010): 24–28; Ryan Chittum, "The Shorter-Form Journal," *Columbia Journalism Review*, October 10, 2011, http://www.cjr.org/the_audit/the_shorter-form_journal .php.

16. Ann Davis Vaughan, "The Gestation Period of a Llama (Or Why I Quit *The Wall Street Journal*)," in *Ink Stained: Essays by the Columbia University Graduate School of Journalism Class of 1992*, ed. J. J. Hornblass, Michele Turk, and Tom Vogel, unpublished draft manuscript, 25–30.

17. Nick Davies and Amelia Hill, "Missing Milly Dowler's Voicemail Was Hacked by *News of the World*," *Guardian*, July 4, 2011; Robert Shrimsley, "Murdoch Faces the British Spring," *Financial Times*, July 14, 2011.

18. Ben H. Bagdikian, "Lords of the Global Village," *The Nation*, June 12, 1989; reprint, in *The Journalist's Moral Compass: Basic Principles*, ed. Steven R. Knowlton and Patrick Parsons (Westport, Conn.: Praeger, 1994), 198.

19. James W. Carey, *A Critical Reader* (Minneapolis: University of Minnesota Press, 1997), 138.

20. Dean Starkman, "Confidence Game," *Columbia Journalism Review* (November/December 2011), 121–30.

21. Clay Shirky, *Here Comes Everybody: The Power of Organizing Without Organizations* (New York: Penguin, 2009), 107.

22. Jeff Jarvis, "Digital First: What It Means for Journalism," *Guardian*, June 26, 2011, emphasis added.

23. The Register Citizen Open Newsroom Project, "What the Newsroom Cafe Has Taught Us About Improving Local Journalism," September 13, 2011, http://

newsroomcafe.wordpress.com/2011/09/13/the-newsroom-cafes-first-six-months
-its-not-about-the-coffee/

24. "The New York Times Recent Web Traffic Numbers Neither Confirm nor Contradict the Paper's Paywall Strategy," *Talking New Media*, October 18, 2011, http://talkingnewmedia.blogspot.com/2011/10/new-york-times-recent-web-traffic .html; Drew Olanoff, "Facebook's Monthly Active Users Up 23% to 1.11B; Daily Users Up 26% To 665M; Mobile MAUs Up 54% To 751M," May 1, 2013, Techcrunch.com, http://techcrunch.com/2013/05/01/facebook-sees-26-year-over -year-growth-in-daus-23-in-maus-mobile-54/.

25. Nicholas Carlson, "Leaked: AOL's Master Plan," *Business Insider*, February 1, 2011, http://www.businessinsider.com/the-aol-way?op=1.

26. Amy Odell, "Breaking: Justin Bieber Might Finally Be Rejecting Harem Pants," *BuzzFeed*, March 1, 2013, http://www.buzzfeed.com/amyodell/breaking -justin-bieber-might-finally-be-rejecting-harem-pant.

27. David Wood, "Beyond the Battlefield: From a Decade of War, an Endless Struggle for the Severely Wounded," ten-part series, beginning, October 10, 2011, http://www.huffingtonpost.com/news/beyond-the-battlefield/; Timothy Burke and Jack Dickey, "Manti Te'o's Dead Girlfriend, the Most Heartbreaking and Inspirational Story of the College Football Season, Is a Hoax," *Deadspin*, January 17, 2013, http://deadspin.com/manti-teos-dead-girlfriend-the-most-heartbreaking- an-5976517; David Carr, "Chasing Armstrong with Truth," *New York Times*, October 28, 2012; and Michael Ashenden, interview by Andy Shen, *NY Velocity*, April 3, 2009, http://nyvelocity.com/content/interviews/2009/michael-ashenden.

28. Ken Doctor, "The Newsonomics of Pricing 201," Neiman Journalism Lab, September 2012, http://www.niemanlab.org/2012/09/the-newsonomics-of-pricing -201/.

29. C. W. Anderson, Emily Bell, and Clay Shirky, *Post-Industrial Journalism: Adapting to the Present* (Columbia Journalism School/Tow Center for Digital Journalism, 2013), http://towcenter.org/wp-content/uploads/2012/11/TOWCenter-Post _Industrial_Journalism.pdf, 22.

30. Jeremy B. Merrill, Charles Ornstein, Tracy Weber, Sisi Wei, and Dan Nguyen, "Dollars for Docs: How Industry Dollars Reach Your Doctors," ProPublica, http:// projects.propublica.org/docdollars/, updated March 11, 2013; "Reddit Apologizes for Speculating About Boston Marathon Suspects," *Huffington Post*, April 22, 2013, http://www.huffingtonpost.com/2013/04/22/reddit-boston-marathon-apology -suspects_n_3133472.html; Anderson, Bell, and Shirky, *Post-Industrial Journalism*, 22.

31. The Pew Research Center for the People & the Press, "In Changing News Landscape, Even Television Is Vulnerable," http://www.people-press.org/files/ legacy-pdf/2012%20News%20Consumption%20Report.pdf.

32. C. W. Anderson, *Rebuilding the News: Metropolitan Journalism in the Digital Age* (Philadelphia: Temple University Press 2013), 162–63.

33. Anderson, Bell, and Shirky, *Post-Industrial Journalism*, 3, 75.

34. The entire series of sixteen articles with graphs, charts, and pictures for "Washed Away" is catalogued by NOLA.com at http://www.nola.com/hurricane/ content.ssf?/washingaway/index.html.

35. "New Digitally Focused Company Launches This Fall with Beefed Up Online Coverage," *New Orleans Times-Picayune*, May 24, 2012, http://www.nola

.com/business/index.ssf/2012/05/nolamediagroup.html. Also see Ricky Mathews, "The Times-Picayune and NOLA.com Are Here to Stay," *New Orleans Times-Picayune*, June 17, 2012, http://www.nola.com/opinions/index.ssf/2012/06/the_times-picayune_and_nolacom.html.

36. Ryan Chittum, "The Battle of New Orleans: Is Advance Publications Securing the Future of Local News—or Needlessly Sacrificing It?," *Columbia Journalism Review*, March 1, 2013, http://www.cjr.org/feature/the_battle_of_new_orleans.php; "Will Nola.com Contain All the News That I Used to Get in the Times-Picayune?" June 11, 2012, http://blog.nola.com/updates/2012/06/will_nolacom_contain_all_the_n.html.

37. Rick Edmonds, "Cutting Print Is a Money-Loser for Times-Picayune, but Cutting Staff Makes Changes Slightly Profitable," Poynter.org, June 18, 2012 http://www.poynter.org/latest-news/business-news/the-biz-blog/177005/cutting-print-is-a-money-loser-for-times-picayune-but-cutting-staff-makes-changes-slightly-profitable/.

38. John Paton, "In Defense of the Times-Picayune," *Digital First*, July 11, 2012, http://jxpaton.wordpress.com/2012/07/11/in-defense-of-the-times-picayune/; Jeff Jarvis, @jeffjarvis, Twitter.com, July 11, 2012.

BIBLIOGRAPHY

Adams, Charles Francis, and Henry Adams. *Chapters of Erie*. Ithaca, N.Y.: Cornell University Press, 1956.

Akerlof, George A., and Robert J. Shiller. *Animal Spirits: How Human Psychology Drives the Economy, and Why It Matters for Global Capitalism*. Princeton, N.J.: Princeton University Press, 2009.

Anderson, C. W. *Rebuilding the News: Metropolitan Journalism in the Digital Age*. Philadelphia: Temple University Press 2013.

Applegate, Edd. *Journalistic Advocates and Muckrakers: Three Centuries of Crusading Writers*. Jefferson, N.C.: McFarland, 1997.

Aucoin, James. *The Evolution of American Investigative Journalism*. Columbia: University of Missouri Press, 2005.

Augspurger, Michael. *An Economy of Abundant Beauty: Fortune Magazine and Depression America*. Ithaca, N.Y.: Cornell University Press, 2004.

Barofsky, Neil M. *Bailout: An Inside Account of How Washington Abandoned Main Street While Rescuing Wall Street*. New York: Free Press, 2012.

Barron, Clarence W. *They Told Barron: Conversations and Revelations of an American Pepys in Wall Street: The Notes of the Late Clarence W. Barron*. Ed. Arthur Pound and Samuel T. Moore. New York: Harper, 1930.

Bell, Daniel, et al. *Writing for* Fortune: *Nineteen Authors Remember Life on the Staff of a Remarkable Magazine*. New York: Time, 1980.

Benjaminson, Peter, and David Anderson. *Investigative Reporting*. Ames: Iowa State University Press, 1990.

Bent, Silas. *Newspaper Crusaders: A Neglected Story,*. New York: Whittlesey House, 1939.

Berger, Meyer. *The Story of the* New York Times, *1851–1951*. New York: Simon and Schuster, 1951.

Blundell, William E. *Story Telling Step by Step: A Guide to Better Feature Writing*. New York: Dow Jones, 1986.

Brady, Kathleen. *Ida Tarbell: Portrait of a Muckraker*. New York: Seaview/Putnam, 1984.

Brinkley, Alan. *The Publisher: Henry Luce and His American Century*. New York: Vintage, 2011.

Bruck, Connie. *The Predators' Ball: The Inside Story of Drexel Burnham and the Rise of the Junk Bond Raiders*. New York: Penguin, 1989.

Burlingame, Roger. *Endless Frontiers: The Story of McGraw-Hill*. New York: McGraw-Hill Book, 1959.

Burrough, Bryan, and John Helyar. *Barbarians at the Gate: The Fall of RJR Nabisco*. New York: Harper & Row, 1990.

Byrne, Janet, and Robin Wells, eds. *The Occupy Handbook*. New York: Back Bay, 2012.

Cather, Willa. *The Autobiography of S. S. McClure*. 1914. Lincoln: University of Nebraska Press, 1997.

Chandler, Alfred D. *Henry Varnum Poor, Business Editor, Analyst, and Reformer*. Cambridge, Mass.: Harvard University Press, 1956.

Chernow, Ron. *Titan: The Life of John D. Rockefeller, Sr*. New York: Random House, 1998.

Cottrell, Robert C. *Izzy: A Biography of I. F. Stone*. New Brunswick, N.J.: Rutgers University Press, 1992.

Das, Satyajit. *Extreme Money: The Masters of the Universe and the Cult of Risk*. Harlow, U.K.: Pearson Financial Times/Prentice Hall, 2011.

Davies, Nick. *Flat Earth News: An Award-Winning Reporter Exposes Falsehood, Distortion, and Propaganda in the Global Media*. London: Vintage, 2009.

Dealy, Francis X. *The Power and the Money: Inside the* Wall Street Journal. Secaucus, N.J.: Birch Lane Press, 1993.

Derman, Emanuel. *Models Behaving Badly: Why Confusing Illusion with Reality Can Lead to Disaster, on Wall Street and in Life*. New York: Free, 2011.

Doctor, Ken. *Newsonomics: Twelve New Trends That Will Shape the News You Get*. New York: St. Martin's, 2010.

Donovan, Hedley. *Right Places, Right Times: Forty Years in Journalism, Not Counting My Paper Route*. New York: Holt, 1989.

Downie, Leonard. *The New Muckrakers*. Washington: New Republic Book, 1976.

Einhorn, David. *Fooling Some of the People All of the Time: A Long Short Story*. Hoboken, N.J.: Wiley, 2008.

Ellison, Sarah. *War at the* Wall Street Journal: *Inside the Struggle to Control an American Business Empire*. Boston: Houghton Mifflin Harcourt, 2010.

Ferguson, Charles H. *Predator Nation: Corporate Criminals, Political Corruption, and the Hijacking of America*. New York: Crown Business, 2012.

Filler, Louis. *The Muckrakers*. Stanford, Calif.: Stanford University Press, 1993.

Financial Crisis Inquiry Commission. *The Financial Crisis Inquiry Report: Final Report of the National Commission on the Causes of the Financial and Economic Crisis in the United States*. Authorized ed. New York: Public Affairs, 2011.

Forsyth, David P. *The Business Press in America, 1750–1865*. Philadelphia: Chilton, 1964.

Frank, Thomas. *One Market Under God: Extreme Capitalism, Market Populism, and the End of Economic Democracy*. New York: Doubleday, 2000.

Fraser, M. "Five Reasons for Crash Blindness." *British Journalism Review* 20, no. 4 (2009): 78–83.

Gans, Herbert J. *Deciding What's News: A Study of* CBS Evening News, NBC Nightly News, Newsweek, *and* Time. 1979. Evanston, Ill.: Northwestern University Press, 2004.

Gavin, Neil T. *The Economy, Media, and Public Knowledge*. London: Leicester University Press, 1998.

Gillmor, Dan. *We the Media: Grassroots Journalism by the People, for the People*. Beijing: O'Reilly, 2006.

Grant, James. *Mr. Market Miscalculates: The Bubble Years and Beyond*. Mount Jackson, Va.: Axios, 2008.

Grind, Kirsten. *The Lost Bank: The Story of Washington Mutual—the Biggest Bank Failure in American History*. New York: Simon and Schuster, 2012.

Hacker, Jacob S. *The Great Risk Shift: The Assault on American Jobs, Families, Health Care, and Retirement and How You Can Fight Back*. Oxford: Oxford University Press, 2006.

Harris, Roy J. *Pulitzer's Gold: Behind the Prize for Public Service Journalism*. Columbia: University of Missouri Press, 2007.

Herman, Edward S., and Noam Chomsky. *Manufacturing Consent: The Political Economy of the Mass Media*. Pbk. ed. London: Bodley Head, 2008.

Herzstein, Robert Edwin. *Henry R. Luce: A Political Portrait of the Man Who Created the American Century*. New York: Scribner's, 1994.

Hillstrom, Laurie Collier. *The Muckrakers and the Progressive Era*. Detroit, Mich.: Omnigraphics, 2010.

Hindman, Matthew Scott. *The Myth of Digital Democracy*. Princeton, N.J.: Princeton University Press, 2009.

Hofstadter, Richard. *The Age of Reform: From Bryan to F.D.R.* New York: Knopf, 1965.

Holland, Max. *Leak: Why Mark Felt Became Deep Throat*. Lawrence: University Press of Kansas, 2012.

Hudson, Michael. "Banking on Misery: Citigroup, Wall Street, and the Fleecing of the South." *Southern Exposure* 31, no. 2 (2003).

Hudson, Michael, ed. *Merchants of Misery: How Corporate America Profits from Poverty*. Monroe, Maine: Common Courage, 1996.

Hudson, Michael. *The Monster: How a Gang of Predatory Lenders and Wall Street Bankers Fleeced America—and Spawned a Global Crisis*. New York: Times/Henry Holt, 2010.

Hyman, Louis. *Borrow: The American Way of Debt*. New York: Vintage, 2012.

Jarvis, Jeff. *Public Parts: How Sharing in the Digital Age Improves the Way We Work and Live*. New York: Simon and Schuster, 2011.

Jarvis, Jeff. *What Would Google Do?* New York: Collins Business, 2009.

Jensen, Carl. *Stories That Changed America: Muckrakers of the Twentieth Century*. New York: Seven Stories, 2000.

Kaplan, Justin. *Lincoln Steffens: A Biography*. New York: Simon and Schuster, 1974.

Katz, Alyssa. *Our Lot: How Real Estate Came to Own Us*. New York: Bloomsbury, 2010.

Kavoussi, Bonnie. "The Panic of 1907: A Human-Caused Crisis, or a Thunderstorm? A Comparision Between the *New York Times* and the *Wall Street Journal*'s Coverage of the United States' First Modern Panic." In *The 1907 Crisis in Historical Perspective*, Center for History and Economics, Harvard University, http://www .fas.harvard.edu/~histecon/crisis-next/1907/.

Kerby, William F. *A Proud Profession: Memoirs of a Wall Street Journal Reporter, Editor, and Publisher*. Homewood, Ill.: Dow Jones–Irwin, 1981.

Knowlton, Steven R., and Patrick Parsons, eds. *The Journalist's Moral Compass: Basic Principles*. Westport, Conn.: Praeger, 1994.

Kynaston, David. *The Financial Times: A Centenary History*. New York: Viking, 1988.

Kurtz, Howard. *The Fortune Tellers: Inside Wall Street's Game of Money, Media, and Manipulation*. New York: Free, 2000.

Larsson, Stieg. *The Girl with the Dragon Tattoo*. Trans. Reg Keeland. New York: Vintage Crime/Black Lizard, 2009.

Latham, Earl. *John D. Rockefeller, Robber Baron or Industrial Statesman?* Boston: D.C. Heath, 1949; reprint, Whitefish, Mont.: Kessinger, 2008.

Lawson, Thomas William. *Frenzied Finance*. New York: Ridgway-Thayer, 1905.

Lears, T. J. Jackson. *Rebirth of a Nation: The Making of Modern America, 1877–1920*. New York: HarperCollins, 2009.

Leonard, Thomas C. *The Power of the Press: The Birth of American Political Reporting*. New York: Oxford University Press, 1986.

Lewis, Michael. *The Big Short: Inside the Doomsday Machine*. New York: Norton, 2010.

Lewis, Michael. *Panic: The Story of Modern Financial Insanity*. New York: Norton, 2009.

Lippmann, Walter. *Liberty and the News*. Princeton, N.J.: Princeton University Press, 2008.

Lloyd, Henry D., and Charles C. Baldwin. *Wealth Against Commonwealth,*. Washington, D.C.: National Home Library Foundation, 1936.

Lord, Richard. *American Nightmare: Predatory Lending and the Foreclosure of the American Dream*. Monroe, Maine: Common Courage, 2005.

Lowenstein, Roger. *The End of Wall Street*. New York: Penguin, 2011.

Lyon, Peter. *Success Story: The Life and times of S. S. McClure*. New York: Scribner, 1963.

Madrick, Jeffrey G. *Age of Greed: The Triumph of Finance and the Decline of America, 1970 to the Present*. New York: Knopf, 2011.

Mahar, Maggie. *Bull! A History of the Boom, 1982–1999: What Drove the Breakneck Market—and What Every Investor Needs to Know About Financial Cycles*. New York: HarperBusiness, 2003.

McChesney, Robert W., and John Nichols. *The Death and Life of American Journalism: The Media Revolution That Will Begin the World Again*. Philadelphia: Nation, 2010.

McChesney, Robert W., and Victor W. Pickard. *Will the Last Reporter Please Turn Out the Lights: The Collapse of Journalism and What Can Be Done to Fix It*. New York: New, 2011.

McClure, S. S., and Louis Filler. *My Autobiography*. New York: Frederick Ungar, 1963.

McCord, Richard. *The Chain Gang: One Newspaper Versus the Gannett Empire*. Columbia: University of Missouri Press, 1996.

McLean, Bethany, and Joseph Nocera. *All the Devils Are Here: The Hidden History of the Financial Crisis*. New York: Portfolio/Penguin, 2010.

Miraldi, Robert. *Muckraking and Objectivity: Journalism's Colliding Traditions*. New York: Greenwood, 1990.

Mollenhoff, Clark R. *Investigative Reporting: From Courthouse to White House*. New York: Macmillan, 1981.

Morgenson, Gretchen, and Joshua Rosner. *Reckless Endangerment: How Outsized Ambition, Greed, and Corruption Led to Economic Armageddon*. New York: Times/Henry Holt, 2011.

Mott, Frank Luther. *A History of American Magazines, 1885–1905*. 5 vols. Cambridge, Mass.: Harvard University Press, 1957.

Muolo, Paul, and Mathew Padilla. *Chain of Blame: How Wall Street Caused the Mortgage and Credit Crisis*. Hoboken, N.J.: Wiley, 2008.

Navasky, Victor S. *A Matter of Opinion*. New York: Picador, 2006.

Neuharth, Allen. *Confessions of an S.O.B.* New York: Doubleday, 1989.

Nevins, Allan. *John D. Rockefeller: The Heroic Age of American Enterprise*. 2 vols. New York: Scribner's, 1941.

Nguyen, Tomson H. *Fraud and the Subprime Mortgage Crisis*. El Paso, Tex.: LFB Scholarly, 2011.

Nocera, Joseph. *A Piece of the Action: How the Middle Class Joined the Money Class*. New York: Simon and Schuster, 1994.

Onaran, Yalman. *Zombie Banks: How Broken Banks and Debtor Nations Are Crippling the Global Economy*. Hoboken, N.J.: Wiley, 2012.

Ott, Julia C. *When Wall Street Met Main Street: The Quest for an Investors' Democracy*. Cambridge, Mass.: Harvard University Press, 2011.

Packer, Jeremy, and Craig Robertson, eds. *Thinking with James Carey: Essays on Communications, Transportation, History*. New York: Peter Lang, 2006.

Parsons, Wayne. *The Power of the Financial Press: Journalism and Economic Opinion in Britain and America*. New Brunswick, N.J.: Rutgers University Press, 1990.

Partnoy, Frank. *Infectious Greed: How Deceit and Risk Corrupted the Financial Markets*. New York: PublicAffairs, 2009.

Patner, Andrew. *I. F. Stone: A Portrait*. New York: Anchor, 1990.

Patterson, Scott. *The Quants: How a New Breed of Math Whizzes Conquered Wall Street and Nearly Destroyed It*. New York: Crown Business, 2010.

Pearl, Daniel, and Helene Cooper. *At Home in the World: Collected Writings from the Wall Street Journal*. New York: Wall Street Journal/Simon and Schuster, 2002.

Penn, Stanley. *Have I Got a Tip for You—and Other Tales of Dirty Secrets, Political Payoffs, and Corporate Scams: A Guide to Investigative Reporting*. New York: Dow Jones, 1994.

Perino, Michael. *The Hellhound of Wall Street: How Ferdinand Pecora's Investigation of the Great Crash Forever Changed American Finance*. London: Penguin, 2010.

Peterson, Christopher L. "Predatory Structured Finance," *Cardozo Law Review* 28, no. 5 (2007): 2185–2284.

Peterson, Christopher L. *Taming the Sharks: Towards a Cure for the High-Cost Credit Market*. Akron, Ohio: University of Akron Press, 2004.

Pinkerton, Stewart. *The Fall of the House of Forbes: The Inside Story of the Collapse of a Media Empire*. New York: St. Martin's, 2011.

Prins, Nomi. *Other People's Money: The Corporate Mugging of America*. New York: New, 2006.

Protess, David, et al. *The Journalism of Outrage: Investigative Reporting and Agenda Building in America*. New York: Guilford, 1991.

Reinhart, Carmen M., and Kenneth S. Rogoff. *This Time Is Different: Eight Centuries of Financial Folly*. Princeton, N.J.: Princeton University Press, 2009.

Richard, Christine S. *Confidence Game: How a Hedge Fund Manager Called Wall Street's Bluff*. Hoboken, N.J.: Wiley, 2010.

Rivlin, Gary. *Broke, USA: From Pawnshops to Poverty, Inc. : How the Working Poor Became Big Business*. New York: Harper Business, 2010.

Rosen, Jay. *Getting the Connections Right: Public Journalism and the Troubles in the Press*. New York: Twentieth Century Fund, 1996.

Rosen, Jay. *What Are Journalists For?* New Haven, Conn.: Yale University Press, 1999.

Rosenberg, Jerry M. *Inside the* Wall Street Journal: *The History and the Power of Dow Jones & Company and America's Most Influential Newspaper*. New York: Macmillan, 1982.

Saito-Chung, David. *Investor's Business Daily and the Making of Millionaires: How IBD Rewrote the Rules of Investing and Business News*. New York: McGraw-Hill, 2005.

Salisbury, Harrison E. *Without Fear or Favor: The* New York Times *and Its Times*. New York: Times, 1980.

Scharff, Edward E. *Worldly Power: The Making of the* Wall Street Journal. New York: Beaufort, 1986.

Schechter, Danny. "Credit Crisis: How Did We Miss It?" *British Journalism Review* 20, no. 1 (2009): 19–26.

Schechter, Danny. *Plunder: Investigating Our Economic Calamity and the Subprime Scandal*. New York: Cosimo, 2008.

Schiffrin, Anya, ed. *Bad News: How America's Business Press Missed the Story of the Century*. New York: New, 2012.

Schiffrin, Anya, and Eamon Kircher-Allen, eds. *From Cairo to Wall Street: Voices from the Global Spring*. New York: New, 2012.

Schlosser, Eric. *Fast Food Nation: The Dark Side of the All-American Meal*. New York: Perennial, 2002.

Schneirov, Matthew. *The Dream of a New Social Order: Popular Magazines in America, 1893–1914*. New York: Columbia University Press, 1994.

Schudson, Michael. *Discovering the News: A Social History of American Newspapers*. New York: Basic, 1978.

Schudson, Michael. *The Power of News*. Cambridge, Mass.: Harvard University Press, 1995.

Scurlock, James D. *Maxed Out: Hard Times, Easy Credit, and the Era of Predatory Lenders*. New York: Scribner, 2007.

Sennett, Richard. *The Corrosion of Character: The Personal Consequences of Work in the New Capitalism*. New York: Norton, 1998.

Shapiro, Bruce. *Shaking the Foundations: 200 Years of Investigative Journalism in America*. New York: Thunder's Mouth/Nation, 2003.

Shepard, Stephen. *Deadlines and Disruption: My Turbulent Path from Print to Digital.* New York: McGraw-Hill, 2013.

Shiller, Robert J. *Irrational Exuberance.* 2nd ed. Princeton, N.J.: Princeton University Press, 2005.

Shirky, Clay. *Cognitive Surplus: How Technology Makes Consumers into Collaborators.* New York: Penguin, 2011.

Shirky, Clay. *Here Comes Everybody: The Power of Organizing Without Organizations.* New York: Penguin, 2009.

Sinclair, Upton. *The Brass Check: A Study of American Journalism.* New York: Upton Sinclair, 1919; reprint, New York: Johnson Reprint, 1970.

Smith, Yves. *ECONned: How Unenlightened Self Interest Undermined Democracy and Corrupted Capitalism.* Basingstoke: Palgrave Macmillan, 2010.

Sobel, Robert. *The Manipulators: America in the Media Age.* Garden City, N.Y.: Anchor, 1976.

Sorkin, Andrew Ross. *Too Big to Fail: The Inside Story of How Wall Street and Washington Fought to Save the Financial System from Crisis—and Themselves.* New York: Viking Penguin, 2009.

Spitzer, Eliot. *Government's Place in the Market.* Cambridge, Mass.: MIT Press, 2011.

Steel, Ronald. *Walter Lippmann and the American Century.* Boston: Little, Brown, 1980.

Steeples, Douglas W. *Advocate for American Enterprise: William Buck Dana and the Commercial and Financial Chronicle, 1865–1910.* Westport, Conn.: Greenwood, 2002.

Steffens, Lincoln. *Autobiography.* New York: The Literary Guild, 1931.

Stewart, James B. *Den of Thieves.* New York: Touchstone/Simon and Schuster, 1992.

Strobel, Frederick R. *Upward Dreams, Downward Mobility: The Economic Decline of the American Middle Class.* Savage, Md.: Rowman and Littlefield, 1993.

Talese, Gay. *The Kingdom and the Power.* New York: Bantam, 1970.

Tarbell, Ida M. *All in the Day's Work: An Autobiography.* Urbana: University of Illinois Press, 2003.

Tarbell, Ida M. *The History of the Standard Oil Company, Illustrated with Portraits, Pictures, and Diagrams.* 2 vols. New York: Macmillan, 1925.

Tett, Gillian. *Fool's Gold: The Inside Story of J.P. Morgan and How Wall Street Greed Corrupted Its Bold Dream and Created a Financial Catastrophe.* New York: Free, 2010.

Tichi, Cecelia. *Exposés and Excess: Muckraking in America, 1900/2000.* State College: University of Pennsylvania Press, 2004.

Tofel, Richard J. *Restless Genius: Barney Kilgore, the* Wall Street Journal, *and the Invention of Modern Journalism.* New York: St. Martin's, 2009.

Warren, Elizabeth, and Amelia Warren Tyagi. *The Two-Income Trap: Why Middle-Class Mothers and Fathers Are Going Broke.* New York: Basic, 2003.

Weinberg, Arthur, and Lila Weinberg. *The Muckrakers.* New York: Capricorn, 1964.

Weinberg, Steve. *Taking on the Trust: The Epic Battle of Ida Tarbell and John D. Rockefeller.* New York: Norton, 2008.

Weiss, Gary. *Born to Steal: A Life Inside the Wall Street Mafia.* New York: Warner, 2003.

Weiss, Gary. *Wall Street Versus America: The Rampant Greed and Dishonesty That Imperil Your Investments.* New York: Portfolio, 2006.

Wells, Ken. *Floating off the Page: The Best Stories from the* Wall Street Journal's *"Middle Column."* New York: Wall Street Journal, 2002.

Wendt, Lloyd. *The* Wall Street Journal: *The Story of Dow Jones and the Nation's Business Newspaper.* Chicago: Rand McNally, 1982.

White, Richard. *Railroaded: The Transcontinentals and the Making of Modern America.* New York: Norton, 2011.

White, William Allen. *The Autobiography of William Allen White.* New York: Macmillan, 1946.

Williams, Paul N. *Investigative Reporting and Editing.* Upper Saddle River, N.J.: Prentice-Hall, 1978.

Wilson, Harold S. *McClure's Magazine and the Muckrakers.* Princeton, N.J.: Princeton University Press, 1970.

Winans, Christopher. *Malcolm Forbes: The Man Who Had Everything.* New York: St. Martin's, 1990.

Wolff, Michael. *The Man Who Owns the News: Inside the Secret World of Rupert Murdoch.* New York: Broadway, 2008.

Zuckoff, Mitchell. *Ponzi's Scheme: The True Story of a Financial Legend.* New York: Random House, 2005.

INDEX